Surplus Powerlessness

Surplus Powerlessness

Michael Lerner

The Psychodynamics of Everyday Life . . .
and the Psychology of Individual and
Social Transformation

The Institute for Labor & Mental Health

Oakland, CA

FOR AKIBA JEREMIAH LERNER

Published by
The Institute for Labor and Mental Health
5100 Leona
Oakland, CA 94619

Printed in the United States of America

Library of Congress Cataloging in Publication Data

Lerner, Michael
    Surplus Powerlessness

Library of Congress Catalogue Card Number 85-062314

ISBN 0-935933-01-8 (hard)   ISBN 0-935933-02-6 (soft)

Contents

Preface

IFIRST DEVELOPED THE IDEA OF SURPLUS POWERLESSNESS TO explain my own experiences in the social change movement of the 1960s. Although that movement was filled with a bravado about making revolutionary changes, I found that many of the people involved had a deep emotional commitment to losing, to being isolated, and to remaining powerless. Tactics and strategies often were shaped by an underlying assumption that no one would ever really listen or take them seriously. When the movement experienced surges of growth and public support, many of my fellow activists were suspicious and distrustful of new recruits, and certain that public support was only a ploy to ultimately co-opt them. They felt uncomfortable with any victories that they were winning—and felt a deep need to redefine the criteria of success in such a way that they could continue to see themselves as failing. Whatever the real powerlessness in the objective political reality, they were bringing to their experience a surplus of powerlessness that shaped how they perceived their possibilities and political options. And as I looked deeper, I found that this Surplus Powerlessness shaped their emotional lives in spheres far removed from politics.

The political movements of the '60s were excellent in their ability to teach about real powerlessness. Although at first I was very resistant to any theories that questioned the basic fairness of American society, my views changed as I began to study the details of the distribution of wealth and power. I came to understand that many people were relatively powerless, while a few had vast power to shape economic and political decisions. In my own experience in the anti-war movement I came to see how the media made it very difficult for anyone with an alternative vision to get an opportunity to be heard,

i

much less to be taken seriously. And I understood how powerfully persuasive large corporations could be in showing that if their interests were not accommodated to by the society, if they were going to be restricted in their ability to carry on their affairs as they saw fit, then everyone would suffer. This real power on the part of the few led to real powerlessness on the part of the many.

This was not, of course, absolute powerlessness—indeed, we were witnessing some real victories as Americans exercised political power to create poverty legislation and to limit the options of the war makers in Vietnam. The costs of winning these changes were high—they involved tens of millions of people becoming active in some form of protest, and many thousands risking their lives, their careers, and often facing jail sentences and beatings. Because it is impossible to continually mobilize this kind of energy, we can say that most people discovered real powerlessness by observing how much it took to accomplish some limited gains.

Yet there were real gains. What I was startled to discover was that the real accomplishments, the real victories, achieved by all that effort were continually being discounted by my colleagues in the movement. Instead of crediting what they had done, they described the reality in a way that made themselves seem even more powerless than they actually were. Moreover, they took this powerlessness as axiomatic, expected it, and then acted to ensure that it would remain the case. I call this phenomenon Surplus Powerlessness—the set of feelings and beliefs that make people think of themselves as even more powerless than the actual power situation requires, and then leads them to act in ways that actually confirm them in their powerlessness. While I originally discovered this in a political context, I have gone on to discover that Surplus Powerlessness pervades the lives of most people in our society, impacting on their personal happiness in a myriad of ways.

In my own life, Surplus Powerlessness has been an important dynamic. For reasons that I will explain in later chapters, almost everyone is affected to some degree by the dynamics of Surplus Powerlessness, and my family had its share. The poverty of the Depression and the insecurity and fear generated by the Holocaust left permanent marks in my parents' consciousness. They were always sure that the wolf was never too far from the door. But there was another side as well. They had participated as activists in a movement that won—they had been involved in the Zionist movement in the '30s and '40s when most Jews thought the establishment of the state of Israel about as likely as an imminent appearance of the Messiah. Having gone from being seen as crazy utopians to having their dreams realized through the success of a social movement they were part of, they came to believe th. . winning was possible. This optimism and political skill was turned to secular advantage when they became Democratic Party leaders. Thinking that they could win, they were able to see strategies and possibilities that others missed, thus helping their statewide party win victories that might otherwise have eluded it.

Like most other people, my parents were continually weighed down by the legacies of their own childhoods and by their experiences in the world of work—so that it was only in comparison with most of their contemporaries that they seemed to have a much greater sense of power and possibility. But compared with those whose wealth and inherited class positions prepared them to unselfconsciously run the society, my parents were constantly undermining themselves at key moments, and always contenting themselves with the impression of "having influence" on those whose power they never dreamed to challenge or acquire. After reading the rest of my analysis, it will come as no surprise why being part of a successful social movement would only go part of the way in undermining the powerful forces that generate Surplus Powerlessness.

Growing up in a household in which governors, congressmen, U.S. senators, and national liberal leaders were frequent visitors, I quickly began to see through the facade of American politics. My parents, too, saw the incredible corruption and the disjunction between what the political leaders said and what they actually believed and did. My parents were willing to endure the hypocrisy because, they told themselves, by having the ear of these powerful people they could protect the interests of the Jewish people and Zionism and prevent any future Holocaust. Not having personally experienced the growth of anti-Semitism and as a child being blissfully ignorant of how deeply ingrained in the dominant culture was the suspicion of Jews, I found my parents' attitude too self-serving and too much ignoring the universalistic calls of Jewish religion. Indeed, my first critique of my parents was framed entirely in terms of the Jewish religious tradition, and it was in the name of that religion that I began to grow angry at the repeated failures of liberal Democrats to live up to their stated ideals when they enacted legislation in Washington.

The short steps from Prophetic Judaism to radical politics were taken in the mid-'60s, when I became a leader in the Students for a Democratic Society (SDS) chapter at Berkeley. These were not easy steps—because, although my commitment to the ideals of a just society would lead me to take ever greater risks (eventually ending me up in a federal penitentiary as a defendant in the Seattle Eight Conspiracy Trial), I felt uneasy with what I took to be the dominant irrationality in the movement for social change. For the first time in my life, I was surrounded by people who shared my outrage at social injustice—but, quite surprisingly, I found them deeply committed to failing, to being isolated, to losing.

The theory of social change that the movement articulated seemed to make perfect sense on the surface. Understanding that many people had become socialized into powerlessness by the dominant institutions of the society, deeply impressed by Herbert Marcuse's analysis of the one dimensionality of the society and how powerfully it operated to keep people entrapped in a fundamentally irrational world, the movement proclaimed that people could be re-empowered through the slow but certain process of winning small victories. We also believed that we would grow from a small band of tens of thousands of protesters to a majority force of tens of millions by showing people that they could in fact have power and wield it effectively. These little victories, e.g., winning voter rights for Blacks in the South, winning "free speech" rights for students in the North, or winning majority opposition to a war that was at first of little concern to most Americans, would eventually lead people to feel that they could have real power, and hence encourage them to struggle for even larger transformations of the society.

This strategy was tried in practice and failed terribly. It failed because the activists in the movement continually managed to redefine the conditions of success in such a way that people could always feel "one-down" for not having accomplished enough. Of course, there was a rational element in all this—because as people became more involved in struggles to change things, they became more aware of how very large and powerful the dominant forces were. They had come to see that there was what I call real powerlessness—a real inequality between the power available to the elites that govern the American economic and political system, and the rest of us. But there was also an element of irrationality in their response—because people continually failed to credit their own real accomplishments or to realize how far they had moved the understanding of most Americans within a relatively short time. Instead, they redefined their victories as failures, vociferously pointed to how little they had accomplished, and convinced themselves that the powerful mass political forces they had energized were really insignificant and unimportant. I will tell this story in more detail in Chapter 14, but for the moment it is sufficient to note that the escalation from mass protests to acts of individual violence by the Weathermen as well as the mass defections into "counter-culture" and individual self-fulfillment and spiritual growth in the 1970s were outgrowths of a mass perception shared by tens of thousands of activists that their political movement had proved powerless and ineffective.

That this perception was being held at the very moment that every objective observer was barely catching their breath at the incredibly rapid growth of social change consciousness may be seen as symptomatic of a deep problem. There is no way to tell the story of the U.S. in that late '60s and early '70s without describing the incredible impact of the social change movement on every aspect of society: from education to art, from music to dress, from intellectual creativity to a climate within which feminism, minority consciousness, and incipient working class rebellions could begin to flourish.

Yet here I was surrounded by people who were either responding to Huey Newton's appeal for "Revolutionary Suicide" or responding to the various spiritual and psychological cults and "growth groups"—precisely in the name of the complete failure of their previous political activities! At first, I tried to respond to this by making counter-arguments and appealing to people's rationality. Having received a Ph.D. in philosophy, I was a strong believer in the importance of clear thinking. As a national leader in the anti-war movement (a status conferred on me by the U.S. government when I was indicted for organizing an anti-war demonstration in Seattle and was described by J. Edgar Hoover as "one of the most dangerous criminals in America"), I argued for the importance of building on the incredible political capital that the progressive forces had amassed. But I found myself drowning in a sea of people who were deeply convinced that all they had done had failed miserably.

Eventually I began to realize that no amount of argument was going to otherwise convince people who were committed to this self-perception of being failures and isolated. I had long been uncomfortable with the loser mentality that dominated the movement. All too often these New Leftists had projected a style that communicated a fundamental belief that nobody would listen to them. To outsiders it seemed that this was simply an elitism bred from the upper middle class origins of many movement leaders. But I always saw something else—a fundamental fear of winning, a fear rooted in a deeper belief that we didn't deserve to win, that we deserved to be isolated, that we were simply the kinds of people who would always be ignored or disparaged. Working from that assumption, the Left related to the rest of the population as though everyone else was the enemy, irredeemably lost in false consciousness and illusion. But this attitude of putting everyone else down, acting as though they were evil, was merely a public reflection of our own belief that we would necessarily be ignored, because that was the kind of people we were.

So I turned to psychological analysis to understand what was happening. I was deeply impressed by the questions and analyses of the early writings of Wilhelm Reich. Though I think that the details of his analysis were inadequate for understanding contemporary U.S. reality, he understood that the fundamental question of contemporary psychology must be, "What are the psychological forces that keep people from rebelling against a social order that is oppressive and prevents them from being all that they could be?" In abandoning my career as a philosophy professor at an elite college and my vocation as a political leader, I decided to dedicate my efforts to developing an approach to psychology that would assist people in coming to believe that they did have the right to win, and that their powerlessness was overcomeable. The research that I conducted for my Ph.D. in Psychology in the mid-'70s, and my subsequent work at a community mental health center in a working class area, provided me with initial clues.

First, I had to consider the more narrow hypothesis that perhaps the irrationality I experienced in the social change movements was rooted in dynamics specific to the kinds of people who are attracted to those movements. This hypothesis had extraordinary appeal to a variety of academic Marxists who used this analysis to justify their own current political inactivity. Their reasoning went this way: The social change movements of the '60s and early '70s had been essentially limited because they were based on students from upper middle class backgrounds who had no fundamental conflict with the system. Moreover, because they came from a class that did not have the real power of making the society run, like the venerable Working Class, these students would experience themselves as less powerful and ultimately give up. Only the Working Class could build a real movement for social change—and all attempts that started with people from the wrong class background would be doomed to failure. The happy consequence of this reasoning was that these academicians could pursue their own personal careers, passively waiting for this working class movement to come into being and castigating anyone without the right class background who had the temerity to try to change things.

There were many reasons why this reasoning was mistaken. The notion that only industrial workers were "real workers" was an outgrowth of a dogmatic Marxism that did not fit with the reality of the end of the 20th Century in America, in which scientists and engineers, health workers and teachers, therapists and specialists in electronics and computers, are increasingly becoming "proletarianized"—i.e., having to sell their labor power to large industries and government bureaucracies which increasingly restrict their freedom and creativity on the job. In this book, I see all of these people as part of America's working people, because my research confirmed to me that the dynamics faced by the new technological elite of workers are fundamentally similar to those faced by the more "traditional" working class groups.

A more fundamental reason for rejecting this analysis is that it makes no sense to think that movement activists have a special pathology that generates powerlessness. After all, these are the very people who were the most successful in overcoming their powerlessness. Literally tens of millions of Americans strongly opposed the Vietnam war in the late '60s and early '70s, but only a few million were able to translate their beliefs into action. Whatever the limits of how far they moved, they were certainly the sector of the society least paralyzed by an internalized powerlessness. Whatever limited them, I suspected, must be a reflection of something much larger, something that could account for why so many millions of others did not do anything at all even though they agreed with the thrust of the anti-war movement.

In short, powerlessness of the activists must be a special case of general powerlessness. Or, I reasoned, at least this is a plausible hypothesis from which to begin my investigations, now equipped with the tools of psychology.

Easier said than done. Psychology, I quickly discovered, had its own ideological framework, neatly coincident with the dominant ideas of American society. Just as the larger society claims that it is set up in a fundamentally fair way, in which people can make it if they really try, so psychology explains powerlessness as a product of the individual's personal failures. Something has gone wrong in the psyches of individuals, and the job of psychotherapists is to fix these individuals. The growing despair with the possibility of changing society was fueled by the ideological assault of pop psychology with its emphasis on individual transformation. The 1970s and '80s in the U.S. were dominated by this belief that the individual had only him/herself to blame if s/he faced a life that was unfulfilling. Whatever the particular remedy— long-term psychoanalytically-based therapies, or weekend transformations, or spiritual growth groups, or physical health obsessions—the general diagnosis was the same: the individual would have to make personal changes to deal with problems that were fundamentally individual and personal to them.

Yet there was a deep problem with all the frantic efforts at transformation: they only worked for that part of the population whose objective conditions allowed for real change. Corporate managers, upwardly mobile professionals, and a small percentage of working people found that there really was room for them to remake their lives once they had overcome their own personally imposed limitations. But most people found that even though they had had wonderful experiences in these therapies and growth processes, their work world remained oppressive, and though they could switch jobs, new jobs seemed to have other, but still fundamentally similar, limitations. Perhaps, many wondered, they hadn't really "gotten it" in their growth groups—perhaps they had once again failed to make their lives all they could be. This process actually intensified the self-blaming that I now believe to be a central element in Surplus Powerlessness.

Most working people never tried. They were fundamentally suspicious of all approaches to therapy—and wary of the class bias that therapists radiate. Yet, if any larger transformation of the society is possible, it must be based on a movement that attracts the majority of Americans. So if most Americans feel powerless and beaten down, pessimistic and suspicious of any social change movements, then a therapy practice must be developed to speak to their needs.

Following the lines developed by Reich, I realized that what might be needed was not a better form of individual therapy, but a larger approach to a "mass psychology" of empowerment. In fact, I quickly rejected various "radical therapy" approaches. I saw them as relying on simplistic formulas derived more from the current "correct lines" of progressive and feminist politics, then from an understanding of the specific case in front of them. I believe that it is often quite inappropriate to provide education about society to people who are coming to therapy to seek immediate help while they are in acute crisis and pain. Larger social change cannot be derived from clever manipulations, smart gimmicky therapy techniques or cultural hypes. We need a deeper social practice that sees the multi-layered nature of psychological reality, and presents a long-term strategy for social change. This book is a contribution to that effort, and a product of nine years of research and therapy practice that were aimed at this goal.

In 1977, having earned a Ph.D. in clinical psychology, I joined with a group of psychiatrists, psychologists, social workers, family therapists, union leaders and community activists to form The Institute for Labor and Mental Health. Our first goal was to understand and develop a response to the considerable distrust and resistance many working people have to "therapy" and to therapists.

We discovered that the hostility to therapy is partially the result of the fact that most therapy in working class communities has been available on a very short-term basis, primarily oriented towards people in acute crisis. The pattern of availability helps create a pattern of usage: only those who are in extreme crisis take advantage of therapy services. This, in turn, makes other working people feel that they have to identify themselves as being in acute crisis before seeking any support for dealing with their problems. But more important than this is the dynamic of self-blaming alluded to above. People are taught to feel ashamed of themselves for not having their lives "more together." To go to therapy is to make a more public declaration that one has made a mess of one's life.

Unfortunately, many therapists add to this problem. Unfamiliar with the real constraints in the lives of most working people, therapists encourage their clients to "take responsibility" for their own lives. They often assume that worker clients have the same opportunities to transform their lives that upper middle class clients have. This only intensifies the workers' self-blaming because it cannot help them distinguish between factors that are out of their control and about which they could be legitimately angry, and areas that could change if they were to change how they felt about themselves and how they lived their own lives. Not being able to change their lives the way upper middle class clients can, working people may feel that they have failed once again, and defensively end up denouncing all therapy as a waste of time.

Similarly, many of the Quality of Work Life (QWL) and Employee Assistance Programs (EAPs) that have been adopted at the "forward looking" corporations in the 1980s saw themselves as promoting a better "Person-Environment Fit." Workers often found, however, that the actual thrust of these programs was to change *them*—by making them fit better into an oppressive environment—rather than to help them change the environment. Once again, they are defined as the problem.

These sorts of experiences, when shared throughout a community, create a culture of distrust towards psychology. This distrust carries over into almost any activity in which working people are encouraged to explore their personal lives. Any approach to empowerment, any approach to mass psychology, must deal with this issue.

At the Institute for Labor and Mental Health we began by focusing on the problems of stress at work and stress in family life. The word "stress" has less of the self-blaming connotations, precisely because it has a structured ambiguity of meaning that refers both to the individual's reaction to a condition and to the fact that it is a reaction to something external and not just self-caused. We found people much more receptive to talking about stress in their lives. Nevertheless, the stigma connected to identifying oneself as "having a problem," persisted.

No one wanted to be publicly proclaiming "I am in trouble," or "I need help." Working with dozens of unions, we came to understand that what was needed was a larger campaign than could be done by any group of therapists on their own. We conceptualizerd that such a campaign must convince people that everyone faces stress at work and everyone faces problems in their personal lives. In contrast to the prevailing image that the work world is "just fine," and that only a few "troubled workers" need special help to "get themselves together," empowerment strategies must foster the understanding that most people face stress at work and in their family lives, and that these shared problems are not the fault of individually flawed people.

Our efforts in this direction led us to organize the following two events which became the focus of massive advertising and media outreach in which we articulated our message:

(1.) THE OCCUPATIONAL STRESS CONFERENCE. This event was publicized through all Northern California unions and at many non-union workplaces as well. Workers were encouraged to come to "tell your story" about the stresses that they faced at their workplace. In addition, unions sent representatives to describe stress conditions faced in their workplaces, and the problems they faced in negotiating better conditions for their members. Workers in the new high-tech industries in Silicon Valley came to discuss the new stress problems generated by the most modern and scientifically advanced work places. To hear this testimony, a host of government officials, public health officials, clergy and news media were invited to become members of panels "taking testimony."

Hundreds of working people attended, and many tens of thousands read about it in the newspapers or saw the detailed reports on tv news that evening. The event's drama derived from the moving testimony of workers, many of whom had never spoken to any public audience before in their lives, and who had certainly never been listened to with respect by people in supposed positions of authority and influence. The larger effect was in terms of the consciousness of the general public—who began to understand that stess at work is not merely a private or personal problem.

(2.) FAMILY DAY. The consequences of stress on the job frequently manifest themselves in personal and family life. But because most people think of their personal lives as an escape from the unpleasantness of the working day, they often accept the notion of a radical split between "personal life" and public reality. So when problems then appear in personal life, people blame themselves, rarely understanding how the stress brought home from work centrally shapes their personal experience. To undermine this spiral of self-blame, we created a large-scale public event in which people could speak about problems in family life.

Our public message that many of the problems people face in personal life are related to the experience they have all day at the world of work was widely disseminated through the media, and on billboards and posters that we rented throughtout Northern California. The message was not simplistic or reductionist. We did not claim that all problems derived from work, nor did we deny the importance of childhood experience in creating a legacy of pain (though here too we emphasized the significance of the class position and work situation of one's parents for understanding the specific ways that they related to their children). Our analysis, articulated in this book, emphasizes the dynamic interaction between stress at work, stress in family and personal life, and the legacy of childhood—and how this dynamic (some call it "dialectical") interaction makes people feel that their powerlessness is somehow "fitting" and appropriate. The thousands of people who attended this event, at a time when the newspapers were describing a "conservative" shift in the American working class, sufficed to convince us that the isolation of progressive forces in America was largely due to their failure to speak to the real emotional problems facing many Americans. Working people were tired of the clichés that Democrats had been using for the past forty years— but they were very open to a progressive politics that spoke to the daily pains inflicted on them in this social reality.

To continue this work, I developed a new educational/psychological tool: The Occupational Stress Groups. These groups, meeting once a week for two to three hours, were composed of ten to twelve people from unions and work places in California. Each group session had three parts: (1.) A structured presentation about the sources of stress (including topics that ranged from "the physiology of stress" to "anger and how to channel it constructively" to "strategies to make change at the workplace"); (2.) Discussion of how the issues presented in the first part apply in the work world and personal lives of the group participants; (3.) "Check-in" about personal life, in which group members discussed their personal lives and group leaders helped them understand how many of the "personal" problems could best be understood in social terms.

The transformative impact of these groups was immediately obvious to their participants and to those who led them. But to prove that this was not merely a subjective response, we did a more systematic study. With the help of a major NIMH research grant, we did a controlled experiment in which we tested the impact of the Occupational Stress Groups and compared it with a group of people from the same work places who had not gone through the groups. Our results, which we shall discuss in this book, provided dramatic "empirical" and "scientific" proof of the effectiveness of our approach.

Much of what I shall present in this book represents the other side of this research: not what the "objective scientific measures" taught us, but what we learned by listening to the thousands of workers who have gone through Occupational Stress Groups, participated in union trainings, attended our Family Day or Occupational Stress Conferences, wrote us, or came to individual or family therapy at the Institute for Labor and Mental Health. Yet it would be a mistake to describe this book simply as a report of their ideas.

One of the most clever ideological ruses of contemporary psychology is masked in the phrase "the clinical data shows . . . " Every clinician listening to patients tell their stories hears through his/her own personal ideological framework. What parts of the stories they attend to, and, for that matter, what stories their clients even bother to recount (based on their expectations of what their therapists want to hear about), as well as what they make of what they hear, is completely shaped by the clinician's world view. So also with this book. Although I have learned much from my clients and from the thousands of people who have participated in the activities of the Institute, many of the ideas articulated in this book were confirmed through that experience rather than generated whole cloth out of the experience.

Although I have strong problems with the traditions generated in their names, I have learned much from Freud and Marx. I do much of my own work in the psychoanalytic therapy tradition, and I benefited greatly from my own years in analysis and in therapy with psychodynamically-oriented therapists. I feel most comfortable today with the theorists of "object relations," though I also have deep criticisms of them. I have always been told by Marxists that I'm not one of them, particularly because of my positions on ethics and religion. Nevertheless, the democratic socialist tradition still is a source of inspiration for me. I am particularly indebted to Herbert Marcuse, whose close friendship and constant support I enjoyed for many years, and to Richard Lichtman, who was a constant source of intellectual challenge and a living proof that Marxism could be intellectually honest and deep. My debt to Reich is obvious, but I also learned about Reich through my deep experience in psychotherapy with Myron Sharaf. My ideas were refined through countless discussions with Peter Gabel, whose own deep understanding of the psychology of groups and whose own significant work in phenomenological Marxism helped me to transcend my own Surplus Powerlessness whenever it would rear its head in the past several years.

My most important teacher, however, was Abraham Joshua Heschel, and through him, Moshe Rabenyu. Heschel was my friend and teacher. He was the foremost interpreter of Jewish thought in the 20th Century, a theologian at the Jewish Theological Seminary who was both a poet and a mystic. It was from the depth of his Jewish commitment that he became the foremost Jewish critic of the war in Vietnam. Through him I first understood the importance of the prophets' rage for justice, and also through him I learned of the centrality of compassion as the guiding value in Jewish tradition. I believe that it would be best to understand this book as a Midrash on Torah spoken in the language of our age.

It was standing on the shoulders of these giants that I learned how to frame the questions from which I then derived the insights that would guide the approach of the Institute for Labor and Mental Health. That approach, in turn, produced some very powerful results—so strong that I now think it worthwhile to ask you to read this book and consider its insights. But I should also report on the limitations of what we have so far accomplished. The Occupational Stress Groups produced tremendous transformations in many people. But these people then looked around at the society and wondered what they could do next, how they could become part of a larger social change movement that would actually win. The Institute is not a political organization, so we could not provide that leadership and organizational framework. Nor could we point to an existing social movement composed of working people who would provide a good setting for people who have newly become interested in changing their world. Nor could we find hints of an emerging movement for compassion such as I describe in the last section of this book.

In the absence of any larger social movement, the people who had gone through these groups eventually grew despairing that what they learned about themselves and their world would have much practical use for them. While there were many dramatic changes in their immediate personal lives (some became union activists, others became active in local Democratic Party politics), the absence of any larger sense of "a movement" made it hard for them to sustain their vision that the world could be changed.

Similarly, within the Institute itself we experienced schisms and splits, disillusionments and periodic bouts of despair, as we all internalized the effects of living in a historical period in which the forces of conservatism seemed so much on the ascendancy. Again, no surprise—for what institution or organization has not reflected the inevitable human inadequacies of those who constitute it, and has not been molded by the larger societal perceptions, even when they were organizations or institutions committed to changing that larger social reality and to healing the persons who constitute it?

What our experience suggested was simple: In order for our work to proceed, we need to have tens of thousands of other people who take these ideas and strategic directions, the psychological and ideological analysis of powerlessness and the mass psychology of compassion, and attempt to apply them in their own realities. It is only when that happens on a mass scale that the truth of our ideas will receive serious empirical testing. It is my contention that a fundamental transformation of American society is possible—but it is only possible if it is generated by people who understand the dynamics of Surplus Powerlessness and who can generate a movement for compassion similar in fundamental respects to that described in the last section of this book. This book provides a strategy for social change that could be adopted by the Democratic Party, by progressive forces, by feminists, by the labor movement—indeed, by anyone who was committed to creating a more demo-cratic society.

Surplus Powerlessness is also a new kind of self-help book, useful not just to those who want to change society, but to individuals trying to understand how to make sense of their experience and to become more effective in their lives. It is "new" because it insists that the self that needs help is intrinsically social, and that the help we can get will be most effective to the extent that it leads us to create a "We" rather than an isolated but stronger "I." This kind of thinking will seem foreign to those who are convinced that the very reason that they need self-help is because they have learned that they are really alone and can count on no one else. But it is that very thinking which is being challenged here, in part through an analysis of what kinds of things happen to us to make us give up on others, in part through a strategic focus on how we could overcome this isolaton and despair and build a community of trust.

The research on this book was supported, in part, through the National Institute of Mental Health, Grant No. MH-36768. I wish particularly to acknowledge the insight and vision of Dr. Elliot Liebow for helping make possible the work of the Institute for Labor and Mental Health, as well as the important role played in the Institute by Lee Schore, Aaron Back, Abby Ginzberg, Paul Lowinger, Richard Epstein, Gail Weiner, Peggy McClure, Karen Trocki, and Wilson Riles, Jr. More gratitude than can be expressed is owed to the thousands of working people who have come to the Institute to tell their stories and to work with us in developing a deep understanding of the psychodynamics of workers' lives in the United States. Very often it was they who provided an insight into the meaning of each others' stories that would have not been easily accessible to me. I am deeply grateful to Nan Fink, whose insights, editorial skills, and thoughtful comments are re-flected throughout this book. Without her commitment to this project, it might have never been completed. Finally, my deepest thanks to my son Akiba, from whom I have learned the most about psychology. He has some-times suffered from my Surplus Powerlessness, but he also helped me over-come it. It is to him that this book is dedicated, in recognition of his insights, his gentleness, his humor, and his irrepressible loving being.

• Part I •

The Psychodynamics
of Everyday Life

Chapter 1

Powerlessness Corrupts

W HEN WE FEEL POWERLESS FOR ANY EXTENDED LENGTH OF
time, we tend to become more willing to accept parts of the world we would
otherwise reject. We act in ways that go counter to our best visions of who
we are and who we can and want to be.

Powerlessness corrupts.

Powerlessness corrupts in a very direct way: It changes, transforms, and
distorts us. It makes us different from how we would otherwise want to be.
We look at our world and our own behavior, and we tell ourselves that
although we really aren't living the lives we want to live, there is nothing we
can do about it. We are powerless.

We've all gone through this experience as we grew up. Try to recapture
the set of feelings and fantasies you had as a child about what you wanted
to do with your life. Then trace the experiences that molded you into your
adult reality. Remember all the ways in which you had to give up parts of
your earlier visions. It's somewhat painful to think about.

To some extent, this was simply a process of coming to grips with adult
reality, with the way the real world actually functions. Everyone has to grow
up—so of course you had to leave behind some aspects of your childhood
fantasies. But precisely how much did you really have to abandon? How
much of the accommodations you made was based on a realistic assessment
of how the world must be, and how much was based on accepting aspects
of the world that could be different if we changed it?

The sad part of "growing up" is not the process of learning about reality. It is the process of accommodating to deformities in the world, and then allowing oneself to be shaped by a desire to fit in and be part of the world as it is currently constituted, regardless of how corrupted that world is. But isn't "real" maturity just coming to accept our own limitations and learning to work within the context of reality as given? The short answer is "No."

The reason why our lives are not all they can be is that we have come to believe that nothing can be changed. But things can be changed, in the most fundamental ways. The greatest obstacle is our own internalized sense that everything has to remain the same, that the way people treat each other and live together and work together is part of some fundamental and unchangeable reality.

If we want to change things, we first need to understand why people have come to believe that nothing can or will be different. This belief is one of the most cherished ideas of daily life. People hold onto it with a deeper conviction and certainty than almost anything else. It is an idea that has been established and re-confirmed in our own daily life experience. People have many stories to tell about the times that they thought things could be different—and how "they learned better."

There is an element of truth in their experience. There really is a structure of power in the world—and it is not easy to change. But apart from this real powerlessness, our encounters with real powerlessness are often misinterpreted in ways that make us think of ourselves as even more powerless than we really are. This is what I mean by Surplus Powerlessness—the ways that we see ourselves as lacking the real power, limited though it is, that we really do have. It is our Surplus Powerlessness that keeps us from making the changes that we actually could make.

Surplus Powerlessness is not just a belief—it's a whole way of approaching reality, a "way of life." It embodies our feelings, our thoughts, our perceptions of who we are and who we could be. Once we are stuck in Surplus Powerlessness, most of the evil and destructive things in our world seem to us to just be "reality." If people treat each other in hurtful ways, we say, "That's just human nature." If people betray each other, we say, "Look out for yourself—it's all you've got." If people are unable to find a loving relationship or are stuck in a marriage or family where they feel little love, we say, "Life isn't a bowl of cherries—so don't expect foolish romantic ideas to work in adult life." If families are full of pain, we say, "Learn new expectations, make the best of this reality." If work is frustrating, we say, "Who ever expected work to be meaningful—at least it gets the rent paid." The list could go on. Every unsatisfying part of life is justified in this same kind of way.

The world could be changed. But one of the major reasons it stays the way it is is because of our deep belief and conviction that nothing can or will change. This is really a new development in history. In past historical periods, the main reason things stayed the way they were had little to do with people's beliefs and convictions and feelings about themselves. Think of the life of a slave in the Roman Empire (most people were slaves) or of a serf during the Middle Ages. True, there were elaborate religious systems that told them that God willed them to be good slaves or good serfs, and that they would be rewarded for "staying in their place and obeying the duly constituted authorities." But the ruling classes did not rely on these ideas—they relied on brute physical force. Slaves failed to rebel, and serfs failed to run away, primarily because of the fear of physical pain or death that would be inflicted upon them by the armies, knights, or other enforcers of the established order.

The primary change in the modern epoch is that the ruling classes rule by consent—they have managed to get the active participation of the people they rule in the process of policing the established order. We become our own jailkeepers.

In the early part of the modern epoch, the way that this happened was rather straightforward: the champions of the new ruling classes could tell the rest of us that this was truly a wonderful world that was being created. And compared to the oppression of feudalism, most people could quickly get the point. The modern world looked rosy indeed. No longer would one be born into one life position as serf, and stuck there forever. The "free market" seemed to promise that everyone could go out and work their way into anything that they wanted for themselves. It was a world of seemingly endless opportunities. Societies which forced people by law into one way of living their lives were replaced by a society in which people were free to make their own choices.

Or so it seemed. But there were some major problems. The economic system required that people compete with each other for scarce jobs, companies compete with each other for scarce markets, and countries compete with each other for scarce natural resources. This led to a war of all against all: everyone using every opportunity to advance themselves, even if that meant hurting other people along the way. On the international scale, tens of millions of people died in murderous wars fought to advance the power of one nation or another as they scrambled to dominate the world's shrinking resources. And on a smaller scale, the freedom to choose one's job was often offset by the reality that the choice was between one oppressive work situation and another equally oppressive setting. This kind of freedom seemed less desirable than the cheerleaders of the established order had promised.

Gradually over the course of the past hundred years the tone of praise has changed. Instead of focus on how wonderful the current reality is, increasingly the focus has been on how awful the alternatives are, or why the current reality is the only possible one, or why it is childish to hope for a less alienated existence. This has involved not just ideas but a whole new way of feeling about oneself. Increasingly we have the society producing people who don't believe that they deserve to have a better world, or people who believe that they are fundamentally incapable of getting anything that they really want. We have a society populated by people who accept the way things are because they don't believe that they could possibly make things different—not because they think things are so wonderful the way they are.

This is the special power of Surplus Powerlessness. It is the new form by which people are kept enslaved. It is inside our own heads, and it is recreated by us in every thought that assumes that how things are is the equivalent of "reality." It grows stronger every time we blame ourselves for having failed in some important way—and have no compassion for ourselves in light of all the ways that the structures of reality push us to be less than we want to be. And it is nourished by our endless betrayals of our loved ones, of our friends, of our own highest visions of who we should be.

Nothing in our life is exempt. Surplus Powerlessnss might sound like a political idea—but it has just as much application to how we treat someone on a date, or how we feel about our parents, or why there is so dramatic a rise in cancer and heart disease in the past fifty years. They are all connected.

We will start by talking about how we come to feel powerless, and then shift to how we have come to think about ourselves as powerless. But feelings and thoughts aren't separate. The reality is that although we talk in this book about things as though they were separate, everything is interconnected with everything else. Everything that ever happened to us, at work, in our families, in our childhoods, all comes together and shapes how we feel and how we think at any particular moment.

All these things work together to create Surplus Powerlessness.

But, in turn, once we act from Surplus Powerlessness, we tend to make things even more the way we don't want them to be. So, treating other people badly is often a result of our previous Surplus Powerlessness, particularly our belief that everyone always will be hurting each other so we'd better do it first before it is done to us. But then when we do it first, and other people get hurt, that becomes a reason for them to be less trusting, and to act in ways that make our initial distrust seem to be justified. In computer language they call this a feedback loop. We can say that it is an interactional perspective: we are all of us continually recreating the very chains that we then use as our excuse for acting in ways that we wish we didn't have to act. But we don't do this out of a conscious self-deception, or because this is the easiest path. On the contrary, as we shall see in a short while, Surplus Powerlessness leads us to accept a world in which there is much pain and unhappiness. We who build our own chains are also deeply hurt by them, and truly wish things could be different even as we desperately strengthen those chains.

All Against All

The world would be much easier to understand and to change if there were some easily identifiable enemy that did all the evil to to us, and the rest of us were merely the passive victims of the powerful few who ran things. But it is not just the big guys who screw the small in this society. We are constantly experiencing ways in which the people around us are letting us down, not coming through for us when we need them. For example:

• It is a painful process when you tell a friend or neighbor about something that makes you feel particularly vulnerable, hoping that they can give you comfort or advice, and they don't pay attention. They ignore your pain and focus on their own needs. Possibly they even use what you confided in them against you, or make you feel bad about yourself.

• You are attracted by someone you meet. At first the other person seems to understand you. They seem just as excited by you as you are by them. You open up sexually and emotionally and begin to develop fantasies about how this person could become a lifetime partner. Then, through no fault of your own, your new found friend becomes distant and hostile. Perhaps he or she runs away from the relationship. You are left with your shame and humiliation. You have made the "mistake" of allowing yourself to believe in another person and in the possibility of love. Often in these circumstances you feel bad not only about your loss, but also about yourself. Secretly you believe it was your inadequacies that caused the failure of the relationship. You will be more cautious the next time.

• You grow up in a neighborhood, go to school with children of diverse economic and racial backgrounds. You make friends with people who are different from you in many respects. You seem to be overcoming the rigid boundaries of class and sex and race that the adult world places so much emphasis upon. You hang out with each other, play basketball, go to movies or shopping. You tell each other that all those adult abstractions about racial and class differences have no meaning—that all you care about is people— not labels. And then, slowly, the unity you felt begins to break down. Some of the kids don't go to college because their parents can't afford to send them. They go directly into the job market, or into the pool of the un- employed. Others go to community colleges where they will be tracked into clerical or blue collar jobs. Others go to four-year colleges where they are encouraged to compete for grades that lead them into better paying jobs or professional schools yielding fancy and higher paying careers. And at each stage of growing up, you leave some others behind, or are left behind. Childhood solidarity dissolves quite frequently along predictable class, race and sexual lines. Either you feel embarrassed at leaving others behind (which you then justify by developing elaborate justifications about your own merit which must not be thwarted) or betrayed because your former friends seem to care more about their own personal advancement than about the good feelings you had developed as you grew up together.

• You work in a factory or office with a number of other people. You hang out together for lunch and share common complaints about how things are being run. You talk together about your kids and how they are doing in school, what is happening to your lovers, what you plan to buy with the money you have saved. Then one of you is given the opportunity to become a supervisor. At first, you are jealous. You ask, why her and not me? Was she chosen because she is a woman? Third world? Did you fail to notice how she was playing up to the boss? But you suppress these feelings, because after all, the new supervisor is a person who is a "friend." You should be happy that one of you is going to be a supervisor, perhaps you will get some better understanding. But you are unpleasantly surprised. After six months on the job, your former friend is acting just as bad as the last supervisor— maybe even a little worse because she knows how to get at you even more, knows the ways that you have been cutting corners or slacking off a bit.

As a result, you feel betrayed and become distrustful of the others. Which of them is going to be promoted next and use information that you gave them against you? Better to keep the lunchtime conversation superficial and light, to talk about one's personal life in a more superficial way, to hide one's vulnerabilities, to protect yourself.

● You have just gone through a long training to become a professional. Now you are in a firm with many other bright young people like yourself, lawyers, architects, industrial artists, media people, residents in a hospital, or psychologists in a social service setting. You have a bright idea about how to change things, make things better, get services made available in a more humane or decent way. So you share the idea with some colleagues, or an immediate supervisor, and they like the idea, promise to help you advance it, make it a reality. Then a few weeks later you see that same idea being advanced, or implemented. All the credit goes to your colleague or supervisor. You begin to shrink from the people around you, realizing that you have been too open and trusting, that others will advance themselves without any regard for your personal welfare.

Is it any wonder that people who have been scarred by these experiences will produce a basically inhumane, paranoid, rapacious society whose dominant idea is "Look out for Number One"?

Suspect Your Neighbor As Yourself

The Jewish theologian Abraham Joshua Heschel once described this society as one based on the principle of "Suspect Your Neighbor as Yourself." It is the common sense of people who have been socialized in the advanced dog-eat-dog industrial world which teaches that you are naive if you trust other people to be fair in their dealings with you. Learning to "win through intimidation" may not be the only style of winning that is advocated, but there is a clear suggestion in the culture that unless you are concerned about winning, you will lose.

Given that this is the conventional wisdom of our own world, perhaps it is not so hard to understand the many betrayals of daily life. At first, we might be tempted to judge those who let us down as evil people, people who are fundamentally corrupt and have no moral sense. But once we become acquainted with the betrayers, we find that they are like everyone else, with reasons, justifications and excuses.

Consider neighbors or friends who ignore our pain. When they tell their story it turns out they were simply acting out the dominant ethos of the society. They thought that it would be inappropriate to stay focused on your pain because they didn't trust that you would really want them to be there for you. They believed that if they opened up their own deep desires for meaningful contact by really nurturing you, they would make themselves vulnerable to you. The host of feelings that they had about wanting a close and loving relationship would emerge once again and they would be reminded of all that they had failed to achieve. It is so much easier not to trust. To refuse to acknowledge your desire for closeness and caring.

A lover has abandoned you. At first it seems that he has simply rejected you. But then you learn that he was acting out of strong fear that no one will ever be there for him, fear that he himself will be abandoned. He tells you stories of others who betrayed him, and how he got so used to expecting betrayal that the only way he could defend himself from pain was to split first before someone could leave him. He had no real desire to cause you pain. On the contrary, he had deserted you simply to protect himself from another set of bad feelings and disappointed hopes.

In fact, once we begin to look at this deeper level, many of us recognize that in many of our interactions with other people we create the same kinds of betrayals. We treat others with the same kind of distancing, the same kind of certainty that they don't really want emotional honesty and closeness. We treat the waiter as a waiter, the telephone operator as an operator, the secretary or receptionist as a receptionist, the politician as a politician, the news reporter as a reporter, the teenager as a teenager, the teacher as a teacher. We relate to roles rather than people, precisely because we want to keep an emotional distance and believe that they want the same.

It is no harder to understand the behavior of our childhood friends, co-workers who become supervisors, competitors in professional work. Each one of them will tell you that they expected that you would have done the same thing to them. Everyone will tell quite reasonable stories about their own childhoods, about growing up, about their work experiences, which showed them that if they wanted to take care of themselves and their own families they had to protect themselves by taking every possible opportunity for self-advancement. They had no desire to hurt you, and if they now look down on you for not having managed to advance yourself the way they did, it is only because they believe that they are living their lives "realistically" according to the norms that everyone else shares. If there is a war of all against all, that's not because anyone of these people wanted it that way. They have simply learned how to be "realistic" and thus to "survive."

These aren't just excuses people will give you—they are the real reasons they give themselves about why they act as they do. The shared belief that nothing can change and that the dog-eat-dog nature of contemporary society is "fixed" provides the basis for everyone to continue to act in these same ways. We thereby reproduce a world that causes us all a large amount of emotional pain, isolation and despair—a world in which it then actually does become "rational" to be distrustful, distant, competitive, and self-interested. Our sense of powerlessness creates a world in which the war of all against all predominates. Yet this very world which we are continually in the process of re-creating in every action of mutual betrayal and every act of manipulation and exploitation is a world that makes people profoundly unhappy.

Powerlessness is Bad for Your Health

If it is true that there is so much unhappiness, why don't people talk about it more? The answer is that they do talk about it when they feel safe to do so. But most of the time, people don't feel safe. They are particularly unwilling to let others know how they have "messed up their own lives." People have come to believe, for reasons we shall explore in the coming chapters, that it's their own fault, that they have no one to blame but themselves for their lack of fulfillment, and that almost everyone else is doing a better job than they are of keeping things together.

The anger that might be reasonably directed against a social order which generates personal unhappiness is instead directed inwards. So the unhappiness, instead of being talked about in the public arena, manifests itself as cancer, heart disease, headaches, ulcers, and a variety of other physical health problems that are increasingly linked to life-situational factors in a growing body of contemporary research.

For many people, it is easier to handle the unhappiness this way. Disease has an important advantage over unhappiness—it seems to be external, happening to everyone, and hence not a reflection of some personal problem or failure.

The popularity of the disease model is rooted in this externality: diseases are something that merely happen to us, and therefore somthing over which we have no control. Whereas unhappiness seems to be our "personal" problem, disease is seen as more in the realm of "fate." In fact, it is precisely this aspect of the disease model that made it seem like a relief to people who had, in past centuries, used a "sin" model to explain why their personal health wasn't doing well.

The problem with the disease model is that it doesn't accurately account for the two most important contemporary killers—heart disease and cancer. Both of these physical health problems are directly linked to the levels of stress that we face in our lives, and to the support systems and styles of coping that are available. For that reason, we find that different societies have lower incidences of these diseases than those of the "advanced industrial nations,"—and this leads us to suspect that physical health is reflective of other, non-physical factors.

The emergence of a "holistic health" approach to medicine reflects this understanding. The holistic health movement has encouraged people to take an active role in maintaining their health, through participation in planning their own diet and exercise, and through adopting "healthy lifestyles." This has positive effects, to the extent that it encourages people to take power into their own hands and not believe that they can only be passive in relationship to their own health. But, on the other hand, there is the danger that many people hear these messages and interpret them to mean that they have no one but themselves to blame for sickness. As such, it may play into the self-blaming that is a central force in keeping people powerless.

Health may indeed be a product of our choices and the way we live, a bodily reflection of the corruption of our lives. But the corruption of our lives is not our own individual fault—but a product of a social organization that prevents us from living a whole and integrated and humanly fulfilling life. Because we experience ourselves as powerless, we simply accept the stress as inevitable, internalize the anger and self-blame, and then face physical health problems. Our powerlessness can't be dismissed as "merely political." When we get sick, we may be showing in a public and bodily way that we cannot escape from the negative effects of powerlessness by pretending that "it really doesn't matter."

So if we accept this society as unchangeable and make ourselves more powerless than we need be, we may also be thereby playing a role in making ourselves sick. Taking responsibility for our health should mean overcoming our despair and cynicism about social change.

Ironically, it seems as if a society may get the kind of disease that best mirrors its own inner essence. The scourge of cancer is all the more insidious because it directly reflects the way that social problems get lived out as individual and personal dilemmas. It may very well be that the stress of living in a society where we must be constantly mobilizing our resources to defend ourselves against attack from the competitiveness of not only enemies but also friends and co-workers produces a set of bodily responses that weaken the immune system and allow us to be more susceptible to cancer. And the daily ingestion of poisons in our food and in our air may have a cumulative impact that allows bodily systems that would otherwise be strong let down their defenses and begin to degenerate or become open to cancer cells. Yet when all this happens, people experience it as a purely personal problem—an event in one's personal life rather than an episode in a socially generated epidemic—and act as though the disease had nothing to do with the way things are structured in the society. Having come to accept so much else that is overwhelming, people feel ready to accept this new disease that has become an epidemic as though it were built into the nature of reality.

Again, my point here is not to condemn individual victims of cancer. It is not that it strikes this person rather than another because of some specific thing that they did wrong. On the contrary, the manifestations of accepting powerlessness may just as likely show up in heart disease or other forms of sickness that medical research now link definitively with stress. Rather, what I am pointing to is that there is no escape from the consequences of living in a society shaped by powerlessness—that even when it doesn't show up in the more obvious ways, it shows up in the ways that we die. That health has been seen to be an individual problem must thus be understood to be just one more manifestation of the devastating consequences of living in a society in which powerlessness leads to accommodation with that which is destructive and hurtful.

War and Nuclear Madness

In November of 1983 over 100 million viewers watched a television show called "The Day After," which purported to show the effects of nuclear war on a Middle-Western American city. While the devastation was underestimated (most technically informed experts believe that there would be virtually no survivors and that the chaos would be much more extreme), the show did give people a full view of the incredible insanity of nuclear war. Most viewers understood how pointless it would be to ask, "Who started it and why?" once the bombs were falling—because no set of reasons could ever come close to justifying the massive destruction of life on this planet and the probable end to the human race that would follow.

Yet, there was no large outcry of anger after the show had been seen. The Reagan Administration proceeded to place its medium-range weapons into Europe, and the arms race continued apace. The very public who had viewed the television show now sat passively as the Pentagon created conditions that might bring us all much closer to destruction. A few months later when some candidates made their opposition to the nuclear madness their central theme, they found little response from the electorate.

In my own investigations of this phenomena doing a selective sampling of the population in the Bay Area, I found that most people did not need to be convinced that nuclear exchanges were unlikely to be limited, but would soon escalate to total conflagration. Most believed that further developments of weapons systems would only make such war more likely and would add little to the deterrence power that already exists. And yet most people had no intention of doing anything about the nuclear arms race.

Their reasons were simple: they were convinced that nothing could be done, that the experts would make the decisions as they always had, and that they either didn't know enough to suggest specific alternatives, or that they didn't believe anyone would pay attention to what they wanted anyway. The same argument was made for why they didn't bother to get involved in supporting an anti-nuclear candidacy: since it wasn't going to win anyway, why bother?

It is instructive to see how the campaign of Senator Hart in 1984 manifested this same kind of reality. Until he came in second in the Iowa primaries, his candidacy received little support nationwide. But once the press had anointed him the "likely alternative" to Mondale, his campaign caught on, suddenly receiving waves of support and enthusiasm. He became the repository of anti-establishment feelings that pervaded the American public, quite independent of whether or not he himself actually articulated the concerns that were being vested in him. Yet it was only after he had been seen as a possible winner that people responded to him. Molded by the press—to be sure. But the media cannot be given full blame here; it is the ongoing internalization of powerlessness that produces this sheep-like behavior. When the candidate is then elected who doesn't really do what people want, they will be full of frustration, and tell themselves that they should never have allowed themselves to hope. And yet, it was their own inaction at critical moments that shaped this reality.

Similarly, it is the inaction of the anti-nuclear forces that must share some of the credit for why 1984 did not become a watershed of political opposition to nuclear war. The anti-nuclear movement was not even able to create a unified structure for itself, to choose recognized leaders who would be charged with developing and announcing new tactics, or even to create a democratic structure that would allow those who wanted to be involved to participate in shaping a national strategy for all anti-nuclear forces. Rather, the movement was so suffused with its own sense of powerlessness that it could not formulate a clear and coherent way for it to be effective. At some critical moments the disarmament movement wins victories despite itself, because the frenzy towards survival moves so many people that even their own sense of powerlessness is temporarily transcended. But as an ongoing political force, the disarmament movement continually undermines itself. No wonder, then, that so many other people end up making immoral trade-offs, supporting a candidate who will push for a decrease in one system of armaments only if they can simultaneously increase another, or supporting very partial proposals for reducing weapons when deep down they know that nothing but a worldwide mutual disarmanent can ever bring them the kind of world peace that they so deeply desire.

The Social Unconscious

Much of what I have been describing as Surplus Powerlessness involves conscious, though misguided, assessments of how much one can accomplish in any particular moment. The set of beliefs and feelings about ourselves leads us to feel that we will lose, that we will be isolated, that other people won't listen, and that in turn leads us to act in ways in which these very fears turn out to be true. We are so convinced others will betray us that we betray them first, and we are so sure that no one will take care of us that we act in ways that make it impossible for anybody to come close. We act passively when we could act decisively; or we give out signals that make others believe that we don't really want them to listen to us, and then when they don't listen to us, we tell ourselves that this proves that nothing could be different.

There is another way that Surplus Powerlessness functions—through what I call the Social Unconscious. Whenever we have a perception of some aspect of reality, that perception does not stand in isolation. Unlike the great empirical philosophers like Locke, Berkeley and Hume who thought that we received perceptions directly from the universe as basic building blocks from which we built up more complex ideas about reality, I believe that every perception we have is shaped by our understanding of the totality of all things. The meaning of any physical object or event is shaped by our understanding of its relationship to all other objects and events, and this meaning shapes how we perceive it. This is particularly true when we are perceiving human reality. The events of daily life do not "speak for themselves" nor are human meanings simply "self-evident." In every specific human interaction the meaning of what is happening is shaped by our understanding of the world that we live in, and what is to be expected in it.

Sometimes we are aware of the meanings that we bring to our perceptions, but often we are not. I use the term "The Social Unconscious" to refer to those shared meanings that most people assume in their daily interactions with others of which they are not aware and which they would resist knowing should they be pointed out.

Surplus Powerlessness is most powerful when it manifests through our Social Unconscious. In these cases, we are not even aware of making any judgment or drawing any conclusions. We are just directly perceiving reality. The totality of our beliefs and understandings about how the world is and how it can't be changed, then, enter into every specific assessment we make, every specific way that we experience any given moment in our life. Each perception takes into account the totality, including our set of deeply held feelings of powerlessness and the inevitability of isolation and defeat, and shapes how we experience everything from a first date to tv news shows to standing in line at the movies.

Real Powerlessness

While the bulk of this book is aimed at showing the ways that we come to overestimate and recreate our own powerlessness, we must start our discussion of Surplus Powerlessness by acknowledging the actuality of an unequal distribution of power in this society. In the short run, if a small number of us try to change things, we will run up against a brick wall. In fact, even if millions of people were engaged in activity to change things, in the short run we would find our society very difficult to change. The brick wall is not just a subjective illusion. We did not create the wall, and none of us is free to wish it away by an act of will or hope.

The basic fact is this: American society is a class-dominated society. What that amounts to is:

(1.) A small number of people have vast economic power while the overwhelming majority has almost no power in the economic realm. The few million who own the vast resources of our society get to shape the basic decisions of production, employment, and how resources will be used.

(2.) Economic power gives that small group a huge amount of political power. While the rest of us have some political power, it takes vast expenditures of energy and time to win small victories, while the basic framework is set by those with economic power. For example, millions of people could spend years of time and energy fighting to change U.S. foreign policy so that it would support democracies and oppose dictatorships—as they did in the anti-war movements of the 1960s—only to find that having won a single victory of getting U.S. troops out of Vietnam, the U.S. would then get involved in supporting military repression in El Salvador and armed intervention against a popular revolution in Nicaragua, while continuing to allow trade and investments in a racist South Africa. As long as these various policies are in the interest of American corporations, no matter how wildly they violate American "principles" as stated in our democratic ideology, they will be pursued. Yes, people can spend a huge amount of energy and time to win a single victory in one place—and perhaps by the time you read this American resources will have switched sides and now be supporting the struggle for democracy in South Africa while actively opposing military dictatorships in the Philippines, South Korea, and throughout Latin America. But the chances are that in the course of winning one such battle hundreds of thousands of Americans will have had to make huge personal sacrifices, while those whose economic interests benefit from these policies will find new areas within which they can get financial arrangements that benefit them at the expense of the larger population. So my claim is not that these people have unlimited power, or that nothing can be won if enough people engage in struggle, but only that there is a fundamental inequality of power in the political sphere which tends to discourage most people from even bothering to get too deeply involved.

(3.) Most institutions of our society accept this framework as given, and then try to serve the interests of those with power. Whether they be the universities or public schools, the hospitals or the city government, the television networks or the churches—there is a general willingness to shape established practices and services and goals and visions to meet the demands and needs of those who have the greatest power. Only rarely do these institutions allow democratic decision making to have much influence on what they are going to do, what goals they are going to serve, and how they are going to deliver their services.

Nor is all this the product of irrational catering to the wealthy. Within the confines of the current system of power, it really is in the best interest of everybody if the needs and desires of the ruling class are satisfied. The reason is that the people with disproportionate power can make things much worse for a lot of people if they don't feel well treated in this society. "A poor business climate," a state of affairs in which those who own capital feel unsafe and under attack, usually leads to a strike on the part of the wealthy: they simply refuse to invest, or they take their investments overseas to countries where locally established dictatorships will grant our corporate leaders all the cheap labor and low taxation rates they desire. When capital strikes, everyone else suffers. We have high unemployment and inability to pay for social services from tax revenues. So, unless people would stand up to challenge the right of capital to have this mobility—a fight that would take millions of people through some decades of struggle—it is not unreasonable to see many people and institutions act like they do best by serving the interests of the wealthy.

All of this is what I mean by "real powerlessness"—that there is a class-dominated society and that it won't go away just because people wish that we would have a more democratic society. Those with power have extraordinary resources at their disposal to keep things from changing very much. A great deal of the reforms we have "won" in the past can also be understood as "defeats" the rulers were willing to sustain precisely because they simultaneously would function as a means of strengthening the system as a whole and relegitimating existing inequalities.

But to say that the elites of wealth and power have overwhelming power is not to say that they have absolute power. Things could be quite different if people were to engage in the struggle to change things. It would be a real struggle—and there would be many difficult defeats.

My concern in this book is to understand why people don't engage in that struggle, the heavy costs that we pay on a physical and emotional level for not being in that struggle, and what could make that change. Absent that struggle, our lives begin to look so hopeless and bleak that many people end up in a cycle of self-blame and self-destruction that is as bad and often worse than any price they would have to pay by being engaged in the difficult struggle to change that larger picture.

It is critical to see that the Surplus always is conditioned by the Real. When we get too far away from understanding the Real Powerlessness in any situation, we end up blaming the victim. The victim, we think, should simply have overcome false ideologies or bad emotional conditioning and become more effective. Ironically, this then leads to a self-blaming of the victim, which in turn makes people more powerless. So it is always important to understand the real constraints in any situation that make it more intelligible why people don't simply overthrow Surplus Powerlessness through an act of will.

Much of this book is about this dynamic interaction. When I talk about the world of work, unions, family life, and childhood, what I am attempting to do is to show you how people have come to understand their reality in ways that make them more powerless than they need to be. But my reference point is the real powerlessness in the situation which shapes the way that we then overestimate our powerlessness. So, while I want to insist on the possibility of change, I also want us to understand how powerful are the forces that any given person is up against.

I do so not to counsel despair. Rather, it is my view that precisely by recognizing how the Surplus is rooted in the real that we can get beyond the Surplus. I shall argue that it is precisely self-blaming that plays a central role in Surplus Powerlessness—and that self-blaming becomes less powerful to the extent that we can come to forgive ourselves and each other for the multifold ways that we have failed to be all that we should be. The central element is compassion, and the strategy for overcoming Surplus Powerlessness is a strategy to develop compassion on a mass scale in our society. Yet precisely the key to developing that compassion is to understand the real constraints that people have faced, and the real powerlessness that has limited their options and alternatives, shaped their realities, and made their lives far less than they would have wanted. When we can really understand this about ourselves and each other, we are a long way down the road towards compassion and empowerment. Yet the key here is to not fall into a new victimology in which people are merely passive victims of some externally constructed oppression. Rather, and this is the subtle point which requires the kind of phenomenological sophistication I hope you will find in this book, we must understand precisely how people have participated in and constructed a social reality which, in the short run, functions as an objective constraint and reinforces their powerlessness.

Grounds for Hope

It is possible to get the wrong idea in the first part of this book. Because I try to describe the multifold ways that we are ensnared into a process of Surplus Powerlessness, you may become overwhelmed by how powerful the forces are that work towards disempowerment. Yet my conclusions actually lead me to be very hopeful.

My reason for hope is this: both Surplus and Real Powerlessness require a repression of our fundamental human essence. But this is impossible, at least for any length of time. Our desires for fullness and joy and community may get repressed, but they can never be fully extinguished. If the society can manage to make people feel that they should participate in work that is humanly destructive, it's not as if the basic needs that have been thwarted simply disappear. There are some Marxists who think that human needs themselves get fully constituted by the nature of the society, so that what they actually come to is radically plastic. I have no such view. Human beings have needs which, when they are not met, cause problems that cannot be ignored. It is true that sometimes the problems will not lead to a revolutionary movement—and the contradiction in basic human needs may show up in the form of a societal wide epidemic of cancer. But people can't live with cancer, and eventually they will begin to ask whether this sickness is not itself related to a sick society. Intuitively they understand what later research may yet prove in greater detail, that the diseases dominating modern society have a lot to do with how we live, and cannot be reduced to the pre-eminence of some new bacteria or virus. Or the contradiction may show up in crime waves, or in mass hysteria, or in wars. My general point is that we may succeed in mystifying ourselves about the cause of our pains, but as long as we are engaged in repressing our fundamental human needs, the pains will show up in some form that cannot be ignored, and will eventually force us back to dealing with the central issues.

In our historical moment, the unhappiness and tension and alienation created by living in a repressed society shows up in family life, in our personal relationships, in our crime figures, in the way that we treat each other at work and in our neighborhoods, at sports events, at the movies, in our PTAs, and in our churches. The alienation in this society is overwhelming—and it cannot be ignored. Precisely because denial of our fundamental human needs hurts so much, there is continual hope that we will break through our isolation and connect with each other in a deeper way and find ways to change the larger situation.

This is not merely a prophetic hope. Every day we can read about people who have broken through passivity and mutual distrust. Be it in a church organization suddenly championing the poor or opposing the military budget, or in a union in which people have moved beyond "bread and butter issues" and have gone on strike around the quality of work life, or in the untold acts of human kindness and generosity that often go unnoticed in the media, people are acting. Our basic humanity is continually reasserting itself and demanding to be taken seriously. While individual acts are not sufficient by themselves to change things, we should remember that each act of human kindness and compassion is also a statement of the deeply shared need that this society can neither obliterate nor fulfill: the need for a loving community.

Our need for that loving community pushes us all towards overcoming our powerlessness. And when we immerse ourselves in understanding the ways that powerlessness has become internalized, we become more powerfully equipped to combat it. We discover that things can be changed, and that the cynicism that surrounds us can be defeated. I don't want to oversimplify or be Pollyannish—the forces arrayed against us are formidable, and it is critical to understand them in detail. But read on past the analytic sections of this book and you will find my reasons for optimism and hope and my sense that we can right now begin to adopt a strategy that could, within our lifetimes, actually produce a social transformation.

Two Tips on Reading the Next Several Sections

Tip 1. In order to analyze how we come to feel powerless, I have divided the discussion into chapters about seemingly separate issues like work, family life, childhood, ideas that generate passivity, etc. But the phenomenon we are discussing doesn't operate like that. In real life, all these dimensions constantly go together, mutually interact and shape each other. For example, how we feel about ourselves as children is constantly present in shaping our experience of the world of work, and how we feel about ourselves at work is constantly shaping what theories about the world seem plausible to us. The interconnections are rich—but to see them, I must first tell the story by focusing on each part as a discrete unit. If you keep this issue in mind, then the discussion of each separate part should not be too disturbing.

Tip 2. In choosing to focus on some of the more difficult and unrewarding aspects of work and personal life, I don't want you to think that I am denying that many people have more fulfilling experiences than those described here. Although my descriptions are based on research with thousands of working people in every kind of job from teamster to college professor, from laboratory technician to lawyer, from school teacher to computer scientist, from engineer to secretary, from assembly line worker to machinist, from research scientist to plumber, from construction worker to expert in the new technologies of the future, I am still aware that you may find that your experience is different in some important respects. But allow yourself to ask, "What part of this account does capture something of my reality, and how much of it might capture the reality, or at least the way they perceive their reality, of the people who live in my neighborhood, ride the subway or bus or are in the next lane on the freeway, the people who voted differently than I would have wanted them to, the people who surround me and who I often see as an anonymous 'they.' " Allow yourself to see the world as if this account were mostly true about them, and somewhat true about you, and then see how differently you might want to act in the world.

Chapter 2

Stress at Work

POWERLESSNESS IS SO PERVASIVE IN OUR EXPERIENCE THAT it is rarely noticed as such. Rather, it manifests in our experience through what is popularly called "stress." Stress is a uniquely social problem—the result of the way that we organize society to ensure that most people are powerless to control their lives. Like powerlessness, stress itself is increasingly accepted as an inevitable fact about our society. But the specific way that we experience stress is very much a product of the way things are organized. I learned about this from many of my working class patients.

Jan was a 43-year-old secretary with a pharmaceutical corporation. When she entered an Occupational Stress Group she said that her primary reason for coming was to learn about the stress that others faced—she herself had really adjusted well to her workplace, and her only problems came from a boyfriend whose wandering eyes made her feel insecure. Jan weighed 200 pounds, and mentioned that she felt terrible about her weight.

In the first few weeks of the group Jan refused to discuss her job. She wanted her time to be spent talking about how bad her boyfriend really was to her. I wondered what it was in her life that made her feel the need to stick with this particular boyfriend—he did indeed sound like a rather unsavory fellow. But I didn't want to push her beyond what she was willing to explore on her own. The opening came, however, in the fifth session of our group when she mentioned that ten years before she had weighed only 115 pounds, and that, "I guess working at the company hasn't been all good for me." Group members jumped in to ask her to tell the story, and soon Jan was describing a deeply but subtly stressful work situation.

18

I want to emphasize subtle, because Jan was paid better than most secretaries, and had been able to purchase a small house and even had her own hot tub in which she proudly relaxed after work. But she had also been subjected to a daily degradation of her own capacities and intelligence. At first, her work had given her some limited opportunity to use her creativity— she had sometimes been consulted by her boss, and had felt sure that her advice, which she saw was being taken very seriously, would lead to promotions and perhaps even to an opportunity to join with management. But instead the office had been re-organized during her second year of work, and from then on she had been given rather narrow job assignments. She was detailed to a typing-pool, and, after complaining about that, had been promoted a year later to a filing job in which she had some limited control over the categories in which information was filed. When computers were introduced a few years later, Jan was asked to sit in front of a video display terminal and to type information into the system. She was renamed an "Information Technician," but she found a narrowing rather than expanding of her actual job tasks.

It was about this time that Jan began to eat excessively. She took an evening course in "gourmet cooking" and another in "natural foods"—and boasted that here was a place in which she was really tops. Her friends agreed, and soon people were pushing for an opportunity to be invited over. Jan felt popular, though she suspected that people really liked her for the food she was serving, rather than for who she was as a person. And as her worries increased, so did her eating of the wonderful foods that she cooked. While the eating helped her forget about these insecurities, they generated new insecurities—because Jan was growing unattractive. It was in this context that she began to relate to her present boyfriend, someone who seemed to like her even though she was fat. But his liking her was mixed with abuse, and Jan was terrified that he might leave her and that she would then have no one at all.

Some group members wanted to focus all their attention on the destructive relationship. They hoped Jan would break out of it, thereby taking a step towards a renewed sense of esteem. But Jan was very articulate in showing them that she had no place to go—that she was very unattractive by conventional standards, and would never find another man. She had read several books on how "fat" was a feminist issue, a category that was used to oppress women and to force them into a mold that they need not be in. But while Jan was impressed by these books, and understood that her fatness was in some way a response to her situation as a woman, she found it all rather "abstract." What did all these ideas have to do with her?

What she had never thought about before, however, were the connections of her eating to her work world. She had once gone to a discussion group about weight and feminism, but had never even talked about her job situation there. She was somewhat embarrassed to do so—because she was the only person in the group who wasn't a professional, training to be a professional, married to a professional or someone with lots of money.

In the stress group she made the first specific connections between her eating and her work world. She had just never thought about it that way before, she told us. A few group members were quite annoyed with Jan for "letting work get to you." Why should work be so important?

The answer was demonstrated graphically when group members drew charts of their waking hours and how they were spent. Everyone discovered that most of their waking hours were involved with work and in getting ready for and transit to and from work. Work fills a massive amount of our waking energy—so it's no wonder that the emotional dynamics that emerge at work should have a massive impact on the rest of our lives.

Not just that, other group members pointed out—you really can't escape work. One young woman pointed out how often she has been in social situations where the first thing she is asked is "What do you do?" All too often she sees the other people quickly lost interest when she tells them she works for the phone company. Another man reported how he often covers up his job—a clerk in the post office—by trying to take charge of conversations the moment he enters them by directing them towards things far away from the world of work. Yet another group member mentioned how hard it was for her to have her children watch tv shows in which working people are often portrayed as stupid.

For weeks the Occupational Stress Group had skirted around the issue of work—everyone thinking that it was embarrassing to admit that their work was dreadfully boring and stultifying. But once the ice had been broken, one story after another poured out about the conditions of stress at work. Over the years I have heard hundreds of these stories, and my research into the causes of stress at work has led me to believe that occupational stress is a major health hazard. But what I learned showed me something else as well—that the way people understand and interpret the stressful conditions generates a deep and abiding self-blaming process that often spills over into "personal life." Because people blame themselves for the stress thay are facing, they often feel terrible about themselves, and that feeling shapes the psychodynamics of family and personal life as well. But before exploring those connections, we need to understand more deeply how stress at work functions, and how it generates self-blaming.

The Concept of Stress

Because the concept of stress has been used to refer to a wide variety of different phenomena, it is important to pause for a second and consider what is useful about the concept. To do so, let's look at how this concept functions in ordinary discourse.

Stress is often thought of as a bodily response to an external stimulus. And the response is sometimes referred to as "flight or fight response." Human beings have been endowed with a natural physical response to extraordinary circumstances. Our bodies are prepared to gear up for dangerous situations—and they respond by secreting a set of chemicals that have very specific functions to enable us to perform physical feats that we would not otherwise be able to do. As the adrenalin and other stress-related chemicals are secreted from our endocrine system, we become fully mobilized for the situation. The blood rushes to our brain and to our heart, and away from our extremities (which is why people sometimes experience "cold feet" or "cold hands" in stressful situations). Our muscles are given some extra energy, and we find that we actually are stronger than usual. This bodily response, it is often thought, was developed by people in earlier human history. Imagine that you are walking in the primeval forest and you meet a tiger, or some other threatening animal, person or situation. Your body becomes mobilized and you are able to either fight or flee to cope with the situation. This same bodily response remains with us today, so that when we face emergency situations our bodies are ready to cope, our minds are alert, and we can handle the situation. Afterwards, the body demobilizes and other chemicals are secreted that create what has been called "the relaxation response." Our body settles into a heightened sense of well-being and relaxation, and we are able to experience the pleasure of a deeper sense of calm.

This is what I call "normal stress." Sometimes you hear people say, "There's nothing wrong with stress—it's good for you." They are right, when they are referring to normal stress. Our bodies are well equipped to handle these special circumstances, and to return to a state of deep relaxation. Normal stress may be faced when you have to take a college entrance examination, or when you face a difficult first date, or when you are going to a job interview, or dealing with your first week at work, or when you are engaged in sports, or when you face a civil emergency (like an electric blackout or a fire or a sudden encounter with a violent criminal or policeman). It typically has the following characteristics:

(a) The source of the stress is easily identifiable.

(b) It is of relatively short duration.

(c) It is followed by a relaxation response.

In contrast to this, we have "toxic stress"—stress that is not normal and which cannot be easily accommodated to by your body. The key characteristics of toxic stress are:

(a) The source of stress is hard to identify; in some way it seems to be diffused throughout the environment in a way that makes it mysterious or hidden.

(b) The stress persists; it doesn't seem to have a clear beginning or a clear end, it is just there as part of what is happening in one's life.

(c) Because it persists there is no clear moment in which the relaxation response happens.

Toxic stress is a central feature of contemporary advanced industrial societies, and it is the reason that those societies face specific kinds of physical health problems. Though all the physical mechanisms have not been discovered yet, many researchers believe that it is the continuing emission of stress-related chemicals into our system in an ongoing way that causes bodily changes that lead to heart disease and that causes the breakdown of aspects of the immune system that makes the body susceptible to cancer. The amount of chemicals being released, of course, is much less than in an emergency when we give our normal stress response. But because it is persistent, and because it is never followed by a full relaxation response, the actual damage is much greater in the long-run. I want to emphasize that the whole physical/ chemical picture of how this works has not yet been fully discovered, but we do know that it is this prolonged and continuous stress, hard to identify in source, pervasive through the environment, and not followed by a relaxation response, that plays a causative role in a wide variety of physical illnesses.

Perhaps it will be clearer now why I argued that stress is the way that people experience their powerlessness. It turns out that chronic stress is a direct product of the way society is organized. Of course, at this point many people will rush in with assurances that there is no other way society could possibly be organized, and that hence stress is inevitable if we want advanced industrial societies. We shall discuss this question in more detail when we show how chronic stress is partly a product of the way work is organized, and we will show that work might be organized quite differently and generate less stress. For the moment, it is sufficient that we understand that stress is a social phenomenon, and that its negative or destructive manifestation, chronic stress, is a product of a form of social organization.

An important objection can be raised at this point. I have talked as if stress were purely a mechanical and almost automatic response to an external stimulus. But Richard Lazarus and Susan Folkman, in their research at the Stress and Coping Project at the University of California, have shown that it is often useful to think of stress as a relationship between the person and the environment that is appraised by the person as taxing or exceeding his or her resources and endangering his or her well-being.* It is important to emphasize this internal or subjective feature to stress—because stress is a peculiarly human problem and is based in part on human appraisals of the situation. The appraisals in question are multi-layered. For example, different people may experience a situation as more or less stressful, and this may depend on their own personal histories and on the resources at their disposal. The same stimulus can appear to be more threatening to one person than another based on differences in cognitive knowledge of the threatening stimulus. Or the same stimulus may be appraised as threatening by different people, but cause less stress in some because of their sense of themselves as having adequate tools to deal with the potential threat. These differences are important, and they make it possible for us to believe that people can learn techniques or approaches to coping with stress that may reduce the stressfulness of some stimuli.

The danger in this subjectivist approach is that it leads to one variant of self-blaming: If you are experiencing stress, the problem is thought to be that you haven't learned the appropriate techniques of coping. "Come to my stress reduction program," many of the new "stress reduction experts" seem to be arguing, "and I will teach you how to cope. If you are still facing stress, it is only because you are doing something wrong—not coping cor-

---

* These ideas are discussed in detail in Richard S. Lazarus and Susan Folkman, *Stress, Appraisal, and Coping* (New York: Springer Publishing Co., 1984).

rectly." Another variant of this approach often emanates from those who emphasize "Person/Environment Fit" in dealing with stress at work. All too often, when we examine how this concept is applied, we see that it is the person who is required to change while the environment is felt to be a fixed feature of "Reality" that one needs to learn to cope with. The subjectivist approach seems to suggest that people can cope with anything if they have at their disposal the correct techniques. But this is decidedly not the case.

Human beings are creatures with a particular set of needs, and if those needs are not met, people will experience stress. While it would be impossible here to try to define all of those needs, a central part of the need structure of human beings is what I call the Human Essence, or what Marx called species being. Human beings have a need to actualize their capacities for loving, creativity, freedom, solidarity, and understanding. When these needs are not being met, human beings have physical and emotional health problems. If we keep this reality in mind, we can understand what I mean when I talk about powerlessness. People are powerless to the extent that they are prevented, either on an individual or social basis, from actualizing their human capacities. Real powerlessness refers to the fact that economic, political, and social arrangements prevent this actualization from occuring. Surplus Powerlessness refers to the fact that human beings contribute to this powerlessness to the extent that their own emotional, intellectual and sprirtual makeup prevents them from actualizing possibilities that do exist within the context of real powerlessness in ways that might potentially yield more possibilities for them to actualize their Human Essence.

Chronic stress is often, though not always, an experiential manifestation of precisely this kind of powerlessness. Chronic stress is stressful not because it threatens immediate physical devastation or even immediate social isolation of one's conscious goals, but because it prevents us, in an ongoing way, from being the kind of human beings we need to be. We can see this most immediately in the work situation, because it is here that people most typically experience chronic stress. And it is precisely because the work situation is one that prevents us from actualizing our Human Essence that it is stressful.

In talking about a Human Essence, I am moving away from a subjectivist position about stress. Our imagined protagonist might now respond by saying, "Sure, I know that many people experience work as stressful, but that is because they have incorrect or distorted expectations. If they could see the larger picture, they would understand why things are organized as they are, and could then learn techniques to accommodate themselves to the situation."

It is this move that I am resisting by insisting that there is a Human Essence. My contention is that social realities that are destructive to our fundamental human needs will always have disruptive and hurtful consequences, no matter how we teach ourselves to "appraise" them. If the consequences do not manifest overtly in the form of alienation, they will manifest more subtly in terms of physical health or mental health disruptions that are usually wrongfully interpreted as having nothing to do with the social world in which we live. I know full well that there are millions of people who have learned to "accommodate," who are experts in "coping," and who will tell themselves and others that they are perfectly happy in jobs in which they have neither power nor control. Yet these people still are powerless in the relevant respect that they can't actualize their human potential. Not surprisingly, these people are still subject to stress-related diseases, quite independent of their conscious assessment or appraisal of the situations they face. It is my contention, based on my clinical experience and based also on data I will cite in the next few paragraphs, that chronic stress can take its toll quite independently of appraisal, because it conflicts with fundamental human needs that can be suppressed from consciousness but cannot be eliminated from the essential nature of human beings.

It is no news to us in the health professions to learn that people who suffer from stress-related illnesses often have suppressed any awareness of stress in their lives. It is quite frequent to hear the story from families of our coronary patients that the patient "never let anything get to them," and "they seemed to be able to cope with anything." The stress seems to have worked on the patient quite independent of their knowing about it.

This fact was further confirmed by research done by Robert Karasek* at Columbia University and by recent research which I have completed. Karasek evaluated a wide variety of professions and occupations according to two criteria: whether the work provided a high degree of demand on the worker and whether it provided a high degree of control. Control was assessed in terms of how much opportunity the worker had in his/her job to determine what s/he was doing and the pace at which s/he would be doing it. Demand was assessed in terms of how many tasks were asked of the worker within a given period of time, and how much attention to the tasks was required. Karasek used a variety of independent observers and then pooled their assessments to arrive at a consensus about which occupations were to fit into which categories.

Karasek placed each of the occupations into one of the categories, according to the assessments of his independent observers and then studied the results of research on coronary heart disease for each occupation. He discovered the following: people in jobs that were high demand but low control had a much greater risk of coronary heart disease than people in high demand but high control occupations. Another way of putting this: having control in your work place can serve as an important buffer to your risk for coronary heart disease.

These results are startling for two reasons. First, they belie the often repeated apologia for management that they are suffering such heavy stress precisely because they have such heavy responsibility generated by the control they have over the workplace. On the contrary, it turns out that people who have less control than these managers have a greater risk of heart disease!! This is not to deny that many managers do face considerable stress—but it is to assert that this stress comes not from the aspects of the situation in

---

* Robert Karasek *et al*, "Job Decision Latitude, Job Demands and Cardiovascular Disease, "*American Journal of Public Health,* July 1981, Vol. 71, No. 7, pp. 694-705.

which they have control, but from the aspects of the situation
are working without real control. This is particularly and obvi
for middle management, whose appearance of control may be
powerlessness. But it may even be true of top management ~~ ~~ ~~
that their choices are externally imposed by economic constraints of an irrationally operating marketplace over whose primary operations they have
little influence.

Also, the results of Karasek's research show that stress operates independent of conscious appraisals. The data for coronary heart disease seems to
suggest that regardless of whether a given individual is appraising his or her
situation as stressful or not, the very fact of lack of control operates to put
the worker in a position of risk. The workers may be telling themselves,
their families, and their co-workers that they are doing just fine, that the
stress isn't "getting to them" in any way. But to the extent that their life
situations violate fundamental human needs to actualize their human capacities, they will suffer physical consequences.

Similarly strong results were obtained in my own research on occupational
stress. Respondents were asked to answer a series of questions in which they
described various aspects of the demand and control they faced in their jobs.
From these answers, we assigned different people to the appropriate square
in the demand/control chart above. We then looked at their scores on a
variety of standard psychological tests for psychic distress (the tests included
the Profile of Mood States [POMS] and the Hopkins Symptom Check List
[SCL-90]). We discovered that people in low control but high demand jobs
were at greater risk for psychic distress than people in high control but high
demand jobs. Psychic distress here included measures for depression, anxiety,
and general affect. In short, what we were finding in our 1985 research was
that control at work is a buffer to psychic distress, or that people would be

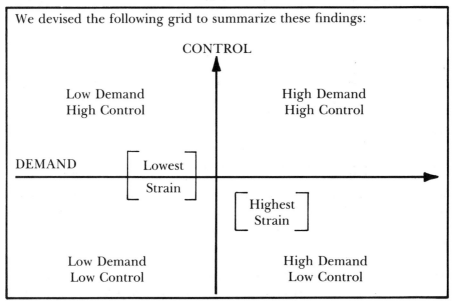

We devised the following grid to summarize these findings:

CONTROL

Low Demand   High Demand
High Control   High Control

DEMAND   Lowest
                Strain   Highest
                         Strain

Low Demand   High Demand
Low Control   Low Control

ιore healthy emotionally if they had control in their work situations.

Various studies of stress factors at work have identified a wide variety of factors that may lead to chronic stress. The literature identifies factors that include: (1) lack of control over your work situation, (2) lack of opportunity to use your own creativity and intelligence in your work, (3) lack of say over what you are producing and how, (4) lack of control over what hours you work and for how long, (5) lack of job security and the fear of unemployment, (6) inadequate recognition for the work that you do, (7) insensitivity or lack of respect from supervisors, managers, work superiors, (8) isolation from fellow workers, either physically or psychologically, (9) sexual harassment, (10) racism and sexism, (11) fear of accident or even death on the job, (12) conflicting job demands, and (13) underload of work.

I believe that all of these, when studied carefully, can be understood in terms of the ways that they prevent human beings from using their natural capacities, and/or in terms of making us blame ourselves for our inability to use those capacities. The deep need for control is a need to have the opportunity to use our human capacities to the fullest. People need to have a work situation in which they can make the decisions about what is produced, how it is produced, and what will happen to the finished product and to the profit from this work. It is a need the frustration of which leads to the wide variety of physical and mental health problems that are today called "stress-related."

All this suggests that a democratization of the workplace is not simply a "good idea" or an ethical necessity. It is also and most urgently a health necessity. This is why I argued in the last chapter that powerlessness was bad for our health—to the extent that it makes us feel that we can't change aspects of our social world that we need to change for the sake of physical and emotional health.

I do not mean to be suggesting that most working people perceive their work situations this way and wish to make changes in their situations. On the contrary, many workers systematically shut out of their awareness any features of their jobs that they experience as frustrating their human capacities. Their ability to do so is an important defense mechanism that enables them to survive in jobs which they must, in any event, keep in order to have enough money to pay for food and rent. Given their perception that nothing can be changed, a perception that they imbibed with their childhood nurturance and which has been reinforced by most of their adult life experiences, it makes absolutely no sense to them to keep themselves "open" and "sensitive to their experiences." They know all too well that the people who remain sensitive and open in this way simply cannot function in what is "the real world" for most working people. Sure, they may end up with heart diseases or cancer, ulcers or emotional problems, at some later date. But in the short run they know that they and their families have no one else to rely on but themselves, so they see no point in paying attention to aspects of their work that are conflictual with their basic needs as human beings. To survive, it seems to be better to narrow one's focus and learn denial and repression of awareness of parts of oneself that have, in any event, never been validated or given much opportunity to develop. For all these reasons, many workers in stressful jobs will boast of how they don't let anything get to them, and insist that it is enough that they earn good money and "what else could there be from a job, anyway?"

Furthermore, many working people will tell you that the last thing they want is to have more decisions to make. They will assure you that they are quite happy to let decisions be made by someone else—and that they would find making decisions more stressful than just doing their jobs as currently defined. Many of these workers deeply resent any specific set of decisions that their workplace forces them to make. They know they don't have power over the larger picture. They don't want decisions being offered them that are "unreal" or "phony." After a lifetime full of opportunities for choice that, in retrospect, seem to be no choice at all, they eventually become so cynical that they are doubtful of any democratic process. Having learned that nothing really changes through the kinds of decisions that they were offered in their past, they give up on the possibility that anything much is going to change in the future. And if nothing much is going to change, why should they be involved in work decision-making now? They suspect, sometimes rightly, that new schemes of progressive management to offer them limited decision-making may have more to do with forcing them to take more responsibility for the future of their workplace than they want, without corresponding power to actually shape the fundamental nature of what is being produced and how and what will be done with the profits. So the cynicism that gets expressed by this resistance is based on an often correct assessment of the real limits on any proposals for democratization.

This kind of resistance is no more a proof that there is no fundamental need for control (in the sense of actualization of one's capacities to create) than is people saying they no longer want to be loved a proof that there is no fundamental need to love and be loved. Therapists often find clients who tell us that they have given up on loving or being loved, or that they don't want any contact with other human beings. We can believe that they are telling us the truth of their perceived experience, but we do not thereby conclude that this is a different kind of human being who doesn't have the same needs as others. Rather, in both the case of those who deny a need to love and those who deny a need to have some control over their lives, we must try to understand the social conditions and psychological traumas that produced this kind of consciousness.

Once we understand the social nature of stress, we can also understand why stress is so much a unique product of contemporary civilization. Precisely because working people have had less control over their workplaces, and because they have come to blame themselves for that lack of control, the stress increases. And with that increase in stress comes an increase in stress-related physical and emotional problems. Our powerlessness may be hidden and mystified, but it nevertheless shows up in very hurtful and destructive ways. Because stress is a problem that has potentially explosive social consequences, a tremendous effort is made by the dominant society to mystify us about its causes and to lead us to blame ourselves for the stress.

Mystifications of Stress

One reason that people don't recognize stress more at the workplace is that stress manifests itself in different ways for different people. It may be expressed as a drinking problem for one person, a heart problem for another, headaches for a third, and frustrations with spouse or children for a fourth. There are a wide variety of physical health problems that are stress related, including back and neck pains, liver and kidney problems, muscle tensions, insomnia, dizziness, skin rashes, and susceptibility to colds and flus. All of these problems seem to be a personal problem of the person suffering from them, so people rarely make the connections. They may work in a place where everyone is suffering from some behavioral problem or health problem, yet never see that these problems may all be different responses to a common stressful work place. They may not realize that the person who got into an accident coming to or from work may have been affected by workplace stress just as surely as another co-worker who has been drinking too much and yet another who had a cancer diagnosis last week. Imagine the discussion over lunch with everyone sympathetically discussing everyone else's problems, but nobody seeing it as a common problem. Each person perceives the problem as his or her own personal problem. The common sources of these problems are usually obscured.

But even when people do make the connection between their own health and the situation at work, they often feel bad about themselves for not being "tougher" or "better at coping." "After all," many people reason, "I should be able to handle it." The ideology of male chauvinism has particularly reinforced this way of thinking: if a man is really a man, he should be able to handle hard situations. So workers will sometimes hide from each other their perceptions of the connection between "personal problems" they are facing and the roots of these problems in the work world. After all, why admit one's own failures to others around—particularly in the more competitive work situation where one's own weaknesses are often used against you by others trying to get an advantage?

More recently, this same dynamic has begun to affect women in traditional job roles. As women become aware of the negative impact of the job on their health, they begin to blame themselves for not being tougher. "After all," they reason, "men were able to do this job and take the stress—so I should too." To complain about the stress on the job might make oneself vulnerable to the charge that this has now been proven to really be a job that a man should handle. "For the sake of the advances made by women to date," some women confess in Occupational Stress Groups, "I should not make a fuss about the stress on this job." So these women often eschew discussing with co-workers the stress they are facing on the job. And they often don't realize that the men were equally stressed—only their social conditioning kept them from talking about it or letting it show.

The mystification of stress is even more complex than this. Even when many individuals become aware that it is not their own personal failure to be "more together" that causes the workplace stress, even when they can see that in fact their jobs are truly stressful and would be for anyone who had them, many workers are embarrassed nevertheless that they have stress on their jobs. They feel ashamed that they have ended up with jobs that are stressful. They believe that if they were more competent (or smarter, or "more together") they would have "better" and less stressful jobs. Being aware of the stress of their jobs is a reminder to them of what they perceive to be their own personal failure. So they repress the awareness of the stress, because they don't want to be in touch with the pain that they experience when they think about how stressful their jobs are, and what they personally did or didn't do that got them these kinds of jobs. To understand this more fully, we need to understand the ways that we have come to blame ourselves unfairly.

Work and Self-Blaming

The negative impact of chronic stress is often accompanied and worsened by the presence of self-blaming. Self-blaming is a central way that Surplus Powerlessness gets affixed to Real Powerlessness—it is one of the most important psychological dynamics that tie us to a world of oppression. Yet, self-blaming as a phenomenon of mass psychology is a relatively recent development which has only become a dominant factor in the past two hundred years.

It made little sense in a society governed by fixed allocations of resources and rewards to blame oneself for one's situation. In most "traditional" or "feudal" or "peasant" societies it is hard to find much evidence of self-blaming. One's fate in this world was understood to be virtually sealed at the moment of one's birth. If you were born to be a serf or a peasant with a small piece of land, that is where you would remain. The hardships you suffered seemed to have very little to do with how hard you worked or how smart you were.

The capitalist revolution of the late 18th Century seemed to promise a very different world. No longer would there be an authoritative allocation of rewards. Each person was in principle free to make whatever they could of themselves. Where one ended up would be a reflection of one's own efforts and capacities.

What was left out of this account was the effect of the actual distribution of wealth and power in this society. Although there were no longer any legal constraints, you still had to find some way to feed your family. As enclosure laws threw literally millions of peasants off the lands that they had held for centuries, they were forced into the emerging industrial cities, where the only way they could make a living was to sell their labor power to those who owned the large factories and work places. Though no law required you to sell your labor power to any particular capitalist, there was real economic coercion to sell your labor power to someone—and at whatever price that the owners of these factories were willing to offer. It was only through a costly and perilous struggle that workers were able to force higher prices for their labor—and that struggle has been going on ever since.

Part of the reason those struggles could be won was that the economic pie as a whole was expanding greatly. Partly as a result of the ability of the

industrialized countries to exploit the resources of what came to be called
"the third world" and partly because of the greater productivity generated
by modern technology, the general wealth of the society as a whole expanded
dramatically. Even if the relative distribution of wealth remained much the
same, on a personal level you could see how your own absolute level of
material well-being was expanding. Union struggles could be fought and
won, and the workers could have the sense that things were really getting
better. And within this context of general expansion, a few individuals could
figure out ways to change their class positions. Somebody would start a
business and "make it" (though most who tried were likely to fail). Or they
could send their child to high school (or later college) and they would then
get a better job with slightly better pay or better working conditions. While
most people in the past hundred years were actually experiencing the economic difficulties of such routes, and as small farmers were increasingly forced
out of existence by the pressure of the economy, we went from a society in
which self-employment decreased from fifty percent in the 1860s to less than
ten percent in 1980—the newspapers and the media played up the mythology
of endless opportunities for advancement on the part of those who were
industrious and smart. Since some people really did have this experience of
"making it," and since almost everyone had the experience of some part of
their life growing better, the general celebration of "Endless Possibilities"
became enshrined in the unconscious of most Americans.

The ideology of the society, taught in schools and churches and reinforced
by the theories of almost all the political parties and the daily focus of
newspapers and media, focused on the reality of mobility. Since most people
had personal experiences of improving their own situations materially in
some way during the course of their lives, and saw that the situation improved
even more for their children, they began to accept as the basic truth of the
society the fact that real change in one's position was possible.

From this it was only a short step to accepting the dominant justification
for capitalism: that people can make whatever they want of their lives, and
that where you end up is a function of how much effort you expend, and
how much talent you have. We can call this the Theory of the Meritocracy:
Where you end up in the class hierarchy is a function of your own individual merit!!!

The idea of the Meritocracy has usually been rejected by the more active
union people. Workers who organized the unions realized that how far they
"advanced" had little to do with individual merit and much more to do with
collective solidarity and struggle. But in the past fifty years, the constant barrage
of propaganda from the larger society has helped create "historical amnesia."
As union struggles became less frequent, and models of individual advancement were seductively presented to workers through mass media images of
material well-being, the meaning of the militancy of the past became less
clear. Those who talked in terms of "class struggle" were increasingly marginalized and portrayed as "traitors" by virtue of their alleged commitment
to communism and to a foreign power. As a result, many working people
came to interpret their experiences increasingly in terms of the Meritocracy
and to attribute the expansion of their material fortunes to their own indi-

vidual efforts. As younger workers who had never participated in the militant struggles of earlier eras and who had never been exposed to the pro-worker explanations of reality entered the work force, unions themselves became less effective as vehicles for transmitting a countervailing set of values and worldviews to the dominant individualism.

The post-WWII years have seen a dramatic increase in the degree to which people have come to accept the ideological framework of the Meritocracy. And with this belief comes a very important corollary: if you are in a stressful job, you have none but yourself to blame. After all, reason many workers, "If I were smarter, or more energetic or had tried harder when I was younger, or was more personable, or had used my resources better, or hadn't made so many dumb mistakes, or hadn't wasted so much time, or had done something different or had been in some way a better person, I wouldn't be in this mess in the first place." Different people fill in their stories in different ways, each with subtle nuances that relate to their specific histories, but the common theme remains: "If I were different or had done something better, I wouldn't be facing the life situation I now face. I've made a mess of my life, and it's my own fault that I now experience this stress as a result."

Ironically, the self-blaming process has become most intense at precisely the moment in American history when the ideology of the Meritocracy is most obviously mistaken. The re-emergence of Europe and Japan as rivals to American capitalism has changed the picture of an expanding American economy that can endlessly raise the standard of living of American workers. While there is still some mobility, it is available to less than ten percent of the American population. And those who are able to advance usually can do so only at the expense of others. The more dominant reality is this: jobs are being exported to other countries, and the American worker is increasingly forced to bargain away benefits so as to make his/her labor more "competitive" with other work forces where American corporations threaten to move.

Nor is the contradiction between mythology and reality only manifest in the lives of traditional workers. In the early 1980s, Silicon Valley in California was being used as the model for the economic growth of the future: high-tech corporations would provide a new way for working people to survive in America. Hundreds of thousands of young Americans began to learn the skills of the new technologies that would dominate in the future. While many have found jobs, many more have found that these new industries quickly reach a peak and then decline. Competition from abroad and the development of yet newer technologies quickly dislocate tens of thousands of skilled workers. Many who are not forced into unemployment are nevertheless forced into endless shifts in their own skills so that they can find some way to hold onto jobs in the ever-larger and ever-more-impersonal corporations. Many of those who fantasized that the new "small corporations" that new technologies made possible would provide them with more humane work places have found that small doesn't necessarily equal humane, and that the large corporations are, within a short time span of five to ten years, able to catch up and swallow up the smaller enterprises. Yet while all of this is happening in front of their very eyes, with their own fates being determined by market forces over which they obviously have no control, many of the new young professionals and scientists and engineers and computer specialists and new technologists enthusiastically buy into the very ideology of Meritocracy that has increasingly less applicability to the realities of their lives.

Partly this happens because most of us know so little about macro-economics. Economics is talked about in language that few of us understand, as if it were a realm of "science" which operated independently of the will of any of us. The upshot is that many people are not aware of the tremendous changes that have taken place, and particularly not aware of the degree to which the notions of mobility and Meritocracy are increasingly irrelevant to the realities of our time.

What this ideology then leads to is this most bizarre and yet pervasive reality: workers blame themselves for the stressful work they face—not because they think that they created the stress, but because they think its their own fault that they have the jobs that they have.

Most working people find this self-blaming to be very painful, and do much to hide it from themselves. There is a theory popular in contemporary social psychology that argues that in blaming themselves people are really regaining a new kind of control over the situation. By a twisted logic, the very epitome of powerlessness is thus transformed into an expression of power. Perhaps self-blaming is a step above depression and suicide, and in that sense represents some power on the part of the oppressed. But it is a power which simultaneously reinforces powerlessness, because it deflects attention from the real problems and hence from any real solutions. Moreover, self-blaming is experienced at a terrible psychic cost. Most people find it so difficult to deal with their own self-blaming that they repress the awareness of the stress they are facing. They are reluctant to look at the degree to which their work thwarts and maims them, because in so doing they would have to face their own negative self-judgments that it was their own fault they were experiencing the stress. The self-blaming is in many ways harder to deal with than the stress itself, and so the stress is allowed to continue and is consciously ignored so that one doesn't have to acknowledge what people think they "know" about themselves: that they are really, at the deepest level, the real problem.

Self-blaming thus becomes central to Surplus Powerlessness. To the extent that individual workers are unwilling to acknowledge the ways that their work world is repressing their basic human needs, they disempower themselves in the struggle to change their work conditions. Those who do try to act often find themselves isolated and alone. As a therapist, I have seen this process time and again as working people refuse to consider the possibility that they could win any significant change in their work conditions. When talking about the situation with their guard down, many of these working people confess to a deep conviction that they don't really deserve to win substantial changes. Repeatedly the themes are the same: "I can't change anything in the larger picture of job or society—after all, I haven't even been able to get my own life together. Look at the job I have; look at what a mess it makes of me; and look at what a mess I've made of my life so that I ended up in this job in the first place." Locked into that framework, workers abandon each other and their own best ideals and compromise with realities that are ultimately self-destructive. Powerlessness corrupts.

The psychodynamic dimensions of this process are striking: the justified anger that one might feel at a situation in which one's capacities are being thwarted gets repressed, and is directed inward at oneself. This process of internalization of anger is extremely destructive. Because the stress they face is systemic and chronic, working people are often engaged in a process of internalization of anger that is ongoing and subtle, leading to a build-up of anger that can reach dangerous proportions.

Decreasing Militancy

Once crippled by self-blaming and internalized anger, most workers don't feel that they have the right to demand substantial structural changes in the work world. If the anger were properly directed at the source of the stress, working people would achieve a considerable reduction of tension. But failing that, they become their own worst enemies.

People begin to feel that at some deep level they really deserve their jobs, and they don't have the right to fight for something different. Of course, workers do not passively accept every outrage that is put down on them. The more obvious abuses of power, the more extreme and evident moments of exploitation, are struggled against; but to the extent that the stress has accelerated and the self-blaming has become more central to the consciousness of working people in the past forty years, there has been a decrease in challenges to the fundamental structures of the workplace itself. And while workers have often struggled to defend what they perceived as their rights in the situation, the self-blaming contributed to a decrease in worker militancy over the past sixty years.

Needless to say, worker militance has not decreased solely as a result of Surplus Powerlessness. The failure of militant forces within the labor movement itself and the emergence of a labor bureaucracy that hoped to win all struggles through rational accommodation with management was a factor. But this is a consequence of Surplus Powerlessness. Why, after all, were working people willing to go along with this kind of leadership? A militant labor movement could potentially have forced legislation to limit the ability of capital to move out of the country, or limit the ability of plants to shut down without regard to the well-being of their communities. The power of capital to get away with all this is not a "fact of nature," but a reflection of its relative political power, given the absence of a coherent labor movement that can stand up to it. Nor is it sufficient to talk about this being "a period in which capital is strong and labor weak" as though that were somehow a fact of nature, like a period in which we have lots of earthquakes. The reality is that if labor is weak, it is weak in part because of choices that working people have made not to exercise many of the potential powers that they could have if they stood together and developed common long-term strategies. In short, it is not possible to describe "objective" or Real Powerlessness independent of talking about Surplus Powerlessness. There is a complex and ongoing interaction between the two. This is why both psychological and socio-economic reductionists are missing the boat.

I don't want to attribute worker passivity entirely to psychological realities. The struggle to change the workplace would require much energy, solidarity, and long-term struggle. People would have to be prepared to make real sacrifices in the short run, and could not be certain of victory in the long run. If everyone were to engage in this struggle, of course, it would be no problem. But building struggles to limit the power of capital to move requires that some people start first, get out in front, and take especially high risks. So I don't want to make it seem as if there is nothing but psychological problems standing in the way of social transformation. It is precisely people's assessment of their real powerlessness in many of these struggles that plays an important role in keeping them from getting involved in the first place.

Nevertheless, it is also my contention that major gains could be won if people were to engage in that struggle, and it would be in most people's long-term rational self-interest. In my interviews with thousands of working people from a wide variety of different occupations and unions, the explanations for political passivity were most typically phrased in personal terms— not in terms of the difficulties of developing a correct political strategy or the difficulties in gathering allies. Their responses centered around their perception that they could never win, that they didn't have a chance of ever changing anything, and as their proof, they continually turned back to their own failures in their personal lives, and their own failures in their work worlds. It was their interpretation of themselves as failures that over and over again was central to their vision of themselves as unable to become part of a larger successful political movement. Their self-blaming became central to generating a level of Surplus Powerlessness that, coupled with correct perceptions of relative real powerlessness, was sufficient to convince them that they could do nothing but accommodate to a reality that they found stressful and oppressive.

Empirical Proof

The relationships between stress, self-blaming and powerlessness that I discovered in the course of reflecting on what I was hearing from working people made intuitive sense to me. But not everything that sounds plausible is also true. To prove the connections that I had uncovered, I developed a research project that would test my hypotheses.

I had developed Occupational Stress Groups as a way of providing a safe context for people to learn about the ways that stress was rooted in their environment, and as a place in which people could discuss the relationship between what was happening to them at work and what was happening in their family lives. The Occupational Stress Groups (henceforth referred to as OSGs) were designed to decrease self-blaming and legitimate working people's anger at oppressive work conditions. If these groups worked to decrease self-blaming, I reasoned, then we should also see some important changes in other areas in people's lives. The evidence, which I present below, bore out my hypotheses.

Let me describe our research design first. Participants were recruited on the basis of publicity circulated through their unions and at their workplaces. Research subjects were drawn from the members of the Communication Workers of America; the American Federation of State, County and Municipal Employees; the Office and Professional Workers; the American Postal Workers; and the United Auto Workers. The workers included mail sorters, telephone operators and installers, electronics specialists, secretaries, construction workers for a local utility, hospital lab technicians, workers in a payroll division of a large corporation, clerical workers, security guards, sales clerks at retail department stores, machinists at an auto plant, and assembly-line workers at an auto plant.

The recruitment information emphasized that the OSGs were not for people "in crisis," but rather for those wishing to learn how to deal with the day-to-day stresses everyone faces. In addition, applicants were screened, and people requiring immediate therapeutic treatment were referred elsewhere. The applicants were then randomly assigned into the "Experimental" or "Control" groups. Both groups were to go through the Occupational Stress Groups. But the "Control" groups would do so only after waiting seven months. In the meantime, they underwent the same battery of research interviews and questionnaires as the "Experimentals": before the groups began, immediately after the groups finished, and a third time four months later. Because the Controls were drawn from the same exact population, received the same tests, and differed only in not being exposed to the intervention (the OSGs), the research was a true experiment meeting the best scientific demands of rigor and objectivity.

Because we relied on self-report materials, we made independent reliability checks. Interviewers called family members, union co-workers, and workplace supervisors to ask them to evelute the research participants' progress. They were asked many of the same questions that we put to the participants— e.g., about absenteeism, degrees of social support, trust, participation in various activities, etc. Overall, we found that our outside observers gave the same description of the research participants' behavior as the research participants gave of themselves 80% of the time, with some questions revealing higher reliability (absenteeism rates were 84% confirmed) and some lower (down on some questions to 72%).

The first result, shown in Chart 1, shows that the OSGs reduce the self-blaming of people who participated in them. This should be no surprise, because this is precisely the result that we sought to achieve directly by discussing self-blaming and legitimating blaming social and economic conditions for generating stress at work and stress in family life. Nevertheless, it is useful to compare this with our control group, because we see in these results that the decrease in self-blaming was not merely random, but rather was a significant decline when compared with a comparable group drawn from the same population.

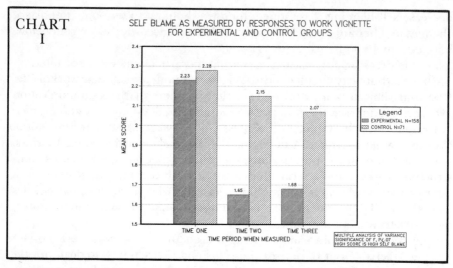

CHART I

SELF BLAME AS MEASURED BY RESPONSES TO WORK VIGNETTE FOR EXPERIMENTAL AND CONTROL GROUPS

Legend
EXPERIMENTAL N=158
CONTROL N=71

MULTIPLE ANALYSIS OF VARIANCE
SIGNIFICANCE OF F, P<.07
HIGH SCORE IS HIGH SELF BLAME

But it is interesting to see what else happens to people going through this process. With the reduction in self-blaming comes a reduction in health problems. Our questionnaire asked about heart problems, high blood pressure, migraine headaches, ulcers, colitis, lower back pains—the sorts of physical health difficulties found to have a strong relationship to stressful conditions in previous research. Our findings indicate that the OSG participants improve on these measures, while those in the control group deteriorate slightly.

When we look at mental health issues, the same important results occur. We used the Profile of Mood States (POMS) and the Brief Symptom Inventory (a variant of Hopkins SCL-90). We found that on all of the subscales of each of these measures there was an improvement for participants in the OSGs that was greater than any improvement in the control groups. I present here one of the important measures to demonstrate this point.

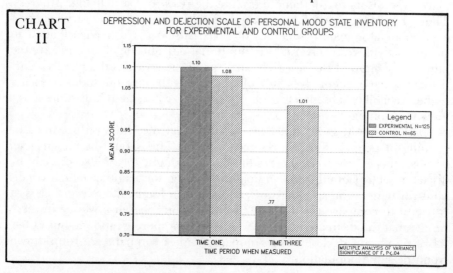

CHART II

DEPRESSION AND DEJECTION SCALE OF PERSONAL MOOD STATE INVENTORY FOR EXPERIMENTAL AND CONTROL GROUPS

Legend
EXPERIMENTAL N=125
CONTROL N=65

MULTIPLE ANALYSIS OF VARIANCE
SIGNIFICANCE OF F, P<.04

The importance of these results for the whole area of mental health cannot be ignored. They suggest very strongly that if our society wishes to improve the mental health of the population, an important place to start would be to undermine the process of self-blaming that is generated by the mythology of the Meritocracy, the internalization of anger, and the concomitant process of "going along" with oppressive work conditions. Various social change advocates have suggested this relationship in the past—but these results do more than merely suggest the relationship, they demonstrate precisely how powerfully that relationship functions.

OSGs also reduce the amount of alcohol consumption. This is no real surprise to me. In line with an important body of scientific research, OSG participants reported that they often used alcohol to deaden the negative emotions generated at work. However, their alcohol usage was not simply aimed at dulling the pain of the actual stress; more important was the effort to suppress the hurt generated by self-blaming. This explains why other researchers have found that among "highly self-conscious subjects" (people who are aware of how they appear to others) there is a decrease in self-blaming when there is an increase in levels of alcohol consumption. Obviously, the consumption of alcohol plays a functional role in helping people avoid the negative feelings that they would have about themselves if they were to simply reflect on their work. What other researchers had not noticed is *how* this relationship works, because they had not understood how the belief in the Meritocracy leads people to feel terrrible about themselves and their work. So, once we understood this, we had a sure-fire way to reduce alcohol consumption. The OSGs, by reducing the level of self-blaming, decrease the need for alcohol. The improvements that we found did not appear immediately, however; while some people in the group reported an immediate drop in alcohol consumption, the decline did not become statistically significant for our sample as a whole until the follow-up interview four months after the end of the group.

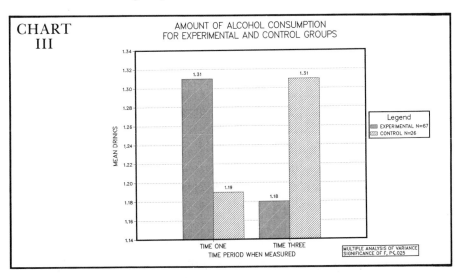

CHART III

AMOUNT OF ALCOHOL CONSUMPTION FOR EXPERIMENTAL AND CONTROL GROUPS

MEAN DRINKS

Legend
EXPERIMENTAL N=67
CONTROL N=26

1.31 1.31
1.19
1.18

TIME ONE   TIME THREE
TIME PERIOD WHEN MEASURED

MULTIPLE ANALYSIS OF VARIANCE
SIGNIFICANCE OF F, P<.025

This result should be taken seriously by government and industry sources committed to reducing alcohol problems. My guess is that the same results would be obtained for cocaine usage, and other hard drug problems. Many people in our groups reported a decrease in the usage of drugs as well as alcohol, but we had not designed our research to trace this result carefully. Drug and alcohol prevention programs have basically missed the boat because they never take into account what function the drugs and alcohol play in people's lives. If they understood that the function of drugs and alcohol was to help people avoid the self-blaming, they might then understand how central it should be to create programs that provide psychological training in reducing the self-blaming generated by the ideology of the Meritocracy.

One of the more startling results was that OSGs increased productivity by decreasing absenteeism. What we discovered in listening to the workers in their OSGs was that oppressive and stressful work situations generate intense ambivalence towards work. The repressed anger and rage at a lifetime in which creative capacities are rarely tapped is often expressed in physical or psychological symptomatology. In that sense, the stress at work is reflected directly in physical and emotional health problems which then interfere with the workers working. But we also discovered that this dynamic shows up in a rarely understood symptom: workers "can't get it together to get to work today." Many times workers experiencing this problem don't have any conscious awareness of why—they just experience a lack of energy and focus. But the OSGs change all this. As workers get the opportunity to express their anger and to feel that their complaints are really legitimate, they begin to reconnect with long-suppressed feelings of anger about their situation. A new sense of efficiency replaces the diffuse discontent characteristic of previous emotions toward work. This sense of efficacy leads them to feel optimistic about tackling problems. As a result, they have new energy to come to work, and productivity increases. These results hold up not only between Experimental and Control groups, but within the Experimental group as

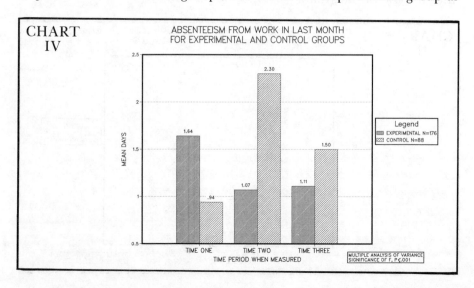

CHART IV

ABSENTEEISM FROM WORK IN LAST MONTH FOR EXPERIMENTAL AND CONTROL GROUPS

Legend
EXPERIMENTAL N=176
CONTROL N=88

MEAN DAYS

2.5
2.30
2
1.64
1.5
1.50
1.07
1.11
1
.94
0.5

TIME ONE   TIME TWO   TIME THREE
TIME PERIOD WHEN MEASURED

MULTIPLE ANALYSIS OF VARIANCE
SIGNIFICANCE OF F, P<.001

well. When we look within the Experimental group, we find that those who decreased self-blaming decreased on absenteeism, while those group members who did not change by reducing self-blaming also had no significant improvement on absenteeism.

The sense of efficacy mentioned above showed up in some other important ways as well. With a decrease in self-blaming comes an increase in ability to cope with stress at home and at work. This is partly explained by the increased sense of personal power that comes from being able to focus anger at oppressive work conditions. But it is also explained by the fact that once people are no longer totally disempowered by self-blaming, they are in a better position to formulate plans for how to engage in concrete struggles to change their environments. Even when the victories are not immediately won, stress group participants feel more optimistic about their long-term possibilities of changing their work environments, and as a result they appraise the stress as less overwhelming. Again, these results hold up if we just look at the Experimentals: those who increased their problem-focused coping were precisely those people who decreased on self-blaming.

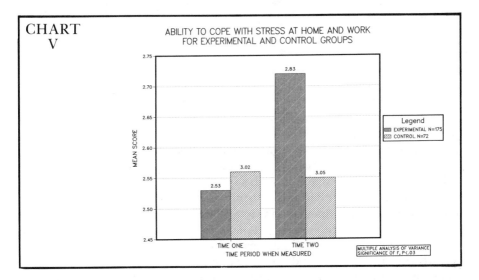

CHART V

ABILITY TO COPE WITH STRESS AT HOME AND WORK FOR EXPERIMENTAL AND CONTROL GROUPS

Legend
EXPERIMENTAL N=175
CONTROL N=72

MEAN SCORE

2.53   3.02   2.83   3.05

TIME ONE   TIME TWO
TIME PERIOD WHEN MEASURED

MULTIPLE ANALYSIS OF VARIANCE
SIGNIFICANCE OF F, P<.03

It would be unrealistic to expect that OSGs could change the power relationships in the participants' world in the course of a twelve-week period. But what does change is this: there is a marked decrease in Surplus Powerlessness. Participants come to see the ways that they have been holding themselves back, interpreting their situations as more hopeless than they actually are, and accepting as "given" various aspects of their world that could be changed if people worked together for change.

The change in sense of power is only partly rooted in the participants' rethinking their basic assumptions about how society works. Equally important are their actual experiences in the group. The most fundamental assumptions of powerlessness are connected to people's beliefs that they are all alone and that others cannot be trusted to share their perceptions or common interests. As the OSGs push deeply into the participants' personal experiences, probing self-blaming and exploring the sensitive spots in which people feel badly about themselves, group members begin to see how much they share with others. In this process, a new sense of trust and a corresponding belief in "possibility" emerges. The result is that participants increase their sense of power over the larger society, over their job situations, and over their unions.

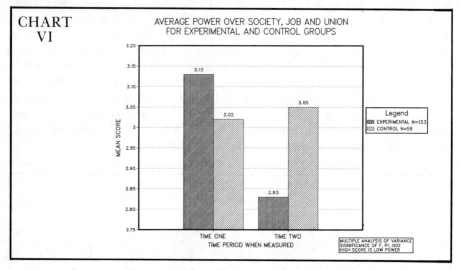

CHART VI
AVERAGE POWER OVER SOCIETY, JOB AND UNION FOR EXPERIMENTAL AND CONTROL GROUPS

Stress researchers have noticed for many years that one way to buffer the worst effects of stress is to increase social support. However, they have not fully understood how this dynamic actually works. My research provides an answer to several of the issues related to social support.

First, it was noticed that although support buffers stress, it turns out that people tend to use their naturally existing social support systems (e.g., friends, family members, and co-workers) less when they are facing severe stress. Just when they need them most, people tend to make the least usage of these potential supporters. Why? Considering the previous discussion in this chapter, we can easily understand the problem: people tend to feel that they are to blame for the stress that they are facing. Even though many workers are cognizant of the fact that the stress is rooted in their jobs, and that anyone having their jobs would find such conditions stressful, they are still reluctant to talk about that stress to other people. The reason is that they blame themselves for *having* these jobs in the first place. They think they will merely be exposing their failure in life if they turn to others to talk about the stress they are experiencing. Stress is experienced as humiliation—because they believe they have no one but themselves to blame for being in the situation in the first place. They thus are unable to avail themselves of potential support—because to do so would be to expose to others about whom one cares, one's own deepest shame. Once charged with this meaning, stress at work takes on overtones that makes it too hard to talk about, particularly to those whose opinions count to you.

Second, it has recently been noticed that if we look at social support in terms of numbers of times people have contact with friends, co-workers, or family members, and use that as our criterion of how much social support a person has, then it turns out that not all social support is supportive. Sometimes, it has been argued, one might do better with less support. This result, however, is based on an external definition of support. Support must be experienced as supportive. But what makes some interaction supportive? Many researchers have attempted to answer this question, but few have realized the critical importance of undermining self-blaming. Interactions are supportive to the extent that they undermine self-blaming. This happens most effectively and most explicitly when individuals come to see that they are not alone, and that the situations they face are shared situations, based not on the individual's personal inadequacies but on problems that are external, problems that are faced by others, and problems that require connection and help from other people by whom one is also needed. Of course, not every instance of supportive support makes all this articulate and conscious. Nevertheless, when support is supportive, it manages to convey, sometimes in ways that neither party could consciously articulate, precisely this set of understandings. And when people have these understandings, they are more able to connect with other people, to act in trustworthy ways, and to establish real connections with them.

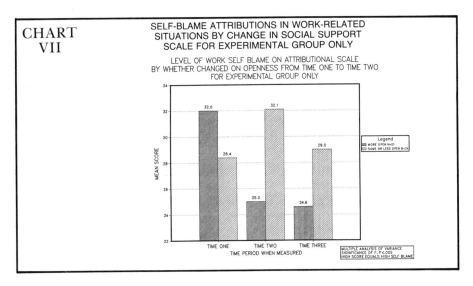

CHART VII

SELF-BLAME ATTRIBUTIONS IN WORK-RELATED SITUATIONS BY CHANGE IN SOCIAL SUPPORT SCALE FOR EXPERIMENTAL GROUP ONLY

LEVEL OF WORK SELF BLAME ON ATTRIBUTIONAL SCALE BY WHETHER CHANGED ON OPENNESS FROM TIME ONE TO TIME TWO FOR EXPERIMENTAL GROUP ONLY

We might wonder here whether it is the decrease in self-blaming that causes a decrease in stress and stress-related problems, or whether it is the increase in social support. My answer is: Both. Self-blaming operates as a major cause of Surplus Powerlessness, and it is this Surplus Powerlessness which joins with real powerlessness to make people unhealthy. But when we decrease self-blaming and increase social support, we get another effect as well. One of the main factors that makes stress stressful is the degree to which it prevents our basic human needs from being met. One of those needs is our need for connection, communication and trust with other human beings (what I called earlier "solidarity"). This set of needs is precisely what is addressed when we get real social support. To the extent that we get this real need met, social support is directly undermining stress. So we find the undermining of self-blaming to be valuable to the extent that it makes social support possible, and also to the extent that it makes us feel potentially powerful to change our real situation. And one of the steps in changing that real situation is to increase our social support.

Cautionary Note on the Research

I have reported here only those results which were found to be "significant" using social scientific research criteria of significance. The results were obtained from a MANOVA (multiple analysis of variance) on data analyzed through the University of California computer system. My caution is this: in presenting this information through graphs and using the "strict canons of scientific objectivity," I may be reinforcing a set of prejudices that makes you, the reader, feel that this kind of information is what is really "Real," and that everything else is "mere speculation." The truth is that we didn't need to learn any of these results from a computer analysis of "objective data"—we saw all this happening in front of our eyes. And, had we been less successful with some of our questions, or had we not been able to achieve the appropriate level of statistic significance, the results would still have occurred. The "data," while confirming our hypotheses, should not be given an importance which they don't really deserve.

The fact is that we saw a much deeper and truer level of change happening in these groups than any questionnaire could capture. As we watched the participants develop, we observed how their self-conceptions and sense of possibilities changed. We listened to their stories, and they told us the many ways that their lives were changing: the way some group members were finally able to tell spouses what they needed, articulate to supervisors their need to be listened to, find outside classes to develop skills they had always suspected they'd had, make themselves heard in their unions, talk more deeply to their children, stop drinking, give up cocaine, get over annoying migraine headaches or stomach cramps or insomnia. We listened to group members tell stories of reaching out to fellow workers at their workplaces, often to people whom they had previously distrusted, and how they had worked together on common problems. We heard stories of workers achieving specific changes in workplaces, or organizing struggles that had not yet been concluded by the time the groups were over, or getting their unions to become sensitive to workplace issues when contract negotiations began, or beginning to create informal stress groups with co-workers and friends. Equally important, as experienced therapists, we could recognize the signs of growth and development quite apart from any specific stories we were told—in the way that group members changed how they would talk about themselves, their willingness to look at issues that just a few weeks earlier they had strongly avoided, their manners of self-presentation, and the degree to which they felt comfortable dealing with their own and each other's emotions.

These changes were precipitated by our conscious attempts to undermine self-blaming, to confront the emotions and ideas that generate Surplus Powerlessness, and to encourage people to see the stress they were facing at work not as a justified punishment for inner failures, but rather as a specific result of the ways that the world of work is organized—ways that could be changed.

I have brought all this empirical proof into our discussion at this point to show a very important point: decrease in self-blaming will reduce some of the problems that I have attributed to self-blaming. But why aren't the results even more dramatic? The answer is, of course, that the fundamental problem is not just self-blaming, but the stress itself. Or, to put it another way, we need to reduce self-blaming as a cause of Surplus Powerlessness, but this does not eliminate the need to deal with Real Powerlessness, as manifested in the lack of control that working people have at the work place. The way that Surplus Powerlessness functions intensifies the negative effort of Real Powerlessness and, conversely, a decrease in Surplus Powerlessness will make us both more healthy and more able to deal with Real Powerlessness. Nevertheless, both exist in a dynamic interaction with each other, and it is this dynamic interaction that I have been concerned to explore in this chapter.

Stated simply, the relationship is this: Stress at work is the "objective manifestation" in the physical and emotional lives of working people of the fact of their real powerlessness. But stress is made worse by the way that we understand stress—through the process of self-blaming. The self-blaming interferes with our ability to mobilize our resources to struggle to change the stressful conditions. But even if we were to engage in those struggles, we would be up against very real and powerful odds, and it would require a long struggle to win. In such circumstances, it is not surprising that many people have given up, and believe that such struggles are utopian and impossible. But then, facing life as individuals, they begin to accept the dominant ideology of the society that tells them they have "made their own beds"—and with that, they become deeply engaged in self-blaming. The self-blaming intensifies the negative effects of the stress, and makes it even harder for people to feel that they have any common basis for unity.

To understand these dynamics at work more fully, we need to explore two other aspects of the work world that help reinforce the ideology of self-blaming. In the next chapter we shall consider how the way work is organized intensifies self-blaming. In the chapter after that, we shall consider how people's experiences in unions further confirms this destructive dynamic.

Chapter 3

The Organization of Work

STRESS IS DETRIMENTAL TO THE PHYSICAL AND EMOTIONAL health of workers. So why doesn't management do more to change the workplace to make it less stressful? After all, a healthier work force would be a more productive one. Seemingly, management should be in the forefront of innovation in creating more humanly satisfying workplaces.

But this does not turn out to be the case. Stress may be detrimental to production, but worker self-blame that typically accompanies this stress actually has beneficial results for management. Even though workers may have higher rates of absenteeism and lower levels of productivity—it may still be more efficient for management to have workers feel bad about themselves. The very consequences that we mentioned in the past chapter—that workers may then feel powerless to change the stressful work conditions and powerless to change the way things are organized in the larger society—may actually be valuable resultants from the standpoint of management efficiency.

To see how this can be true, we need to understand the concept of "efficiency." Efficiency means: the best and least costly way to achieve one's ends. But the problem with this statement is that the concept of efficiency seems to leave open the question of whose ends, and which ends are appropriate. When we look at the issue of efficiency in the workplace, we find that it is management which has the power to define what the goals and ends should be for which they can then seek efficient means. If we look carefully, we will find that for most management, the goals or ends include:

(1.) To produce goods and services that make maximum profits for the owners of the corporations;

(2.) To keep significant decisions in the hands of the fewest number of people possible, and to ensure that the right to make these decisions is in the hands of the owners of capital and those whom they hire who are loyal to their interests;

(3.) To ensure that their own importance as managers who are indispensable as mediators between the needs of those who own the firm and those who work for it is recognized by everyone.

As it is currently organized, efficiency at work does not include the following goals:

(1.) To produce only goods that are necessary and thus save scarce natural resources;

(2.) To maximize the health and well being of workers;

(3.) To provide for meaningful and fulfilling jobs for workers;

(4.) To teach workers skills in decision making and cooperative work styles;

(5.) To provide for the development and use of new skills by workers;

(6.) To use the expertise of workers in the shaping of products or services to be produced or delivered.

The goals of production are not democratically chosen nor are they oriented to the best needs of the society; but they are in the best interests of the owners, who have disproportionate power in this society. The rest of us go along because we have been taught to think that the main area of importance to us is the arena of private life and personal consumption of material goods. We are encouraged to think that if we go along with the way things are, we will get our rewards, our salaries or paychecks, which will enable us to buy the goods and services that we need in our personal lives. We are encouraged to focus away from the human costs of this process, and to think that it is simply "unrealistic" to expect that anyone would consult us about ultimate goals.

Management in the public sector, while not aimed at creating profits for absentee owners, often follows this same model. The need of management to limit the power of workers may even be intensified by the fact that they are now managing a group of workers whose intelligence and competence is often a criterion for getting the job in the first place (e.g., through civil service tests). For management to keep control, to show that they are really needed, they may have an even higher stake in defusing any ideas that workers might have that they could run things by themselves, or that they could make fundamental decisions without the help of the management bureaucrats. Moreover, the more intelligent public sector bureaucrat has already recognized that the people who have disproportionate economic and political power in the private sector also have great influence in shaping public sector policy. So these bureaucrats often try to shape their own institutions so that they can appear to be efficient in ways that those with private sector power would appreciate and commend. Those commendations may come through reappointment to continue in top management positions, or through being offered better paying jobs in the private sector once one has shown how well one can do in the public sector. However they come, most public sector bureaucrats model themselves on the criteria and ways of thinking about management that have been developed for the large competitive capitalist firms.

But perhaps we should give credit where it is due. After all, one might think, even if things aren't organized for the benefit of our well-being, nevertheless those in power in corporations and public sector enterprises sure are good at getting the greatest productivity out of the workers. If we thought this, we would be wrong. Studies show that productivity may be increased when workers have greater ability to participate in the decision making in production. When workers feel invested in their work they often produce more quality goods, and they often put more energy into the whole enterprise of production. This is as true in office and service sector work as it is in factories. People come to work with a new excitement and dedication when they feel that they have work that is more fulfilling and personally rewarding to them—work that allows them to satisfy more of their fundamental human needs. Moreover, as I showed in the last chapter, if they face less self-blaming they will actually be absent from work less.

The problem for the owners of capital, and the managers of public sector enterprises in which management holds its position by virtue of proving how indispensable it is, is that these very processes of giving workers more power in production would tend to create working people who had a stronger sense of themselves and their rights, and these workers would soon challenge the right of owners to profit from their work. If we are doing *all* the work why should we let the owners keep all the profits and then use them to get the political power to dominate us? Why should we be producing goods that really are not needed or which are destined to quickly fall apart, when we know that as consumers we would be better off with products that were well made? Or why should we let them run hospitals, schools, and government offices that actually do little to serve the real needs of the people, when it is we ourselves who will need those services?

These questions are not new ones. At the beginning of the 20th Century there was a growing socialist movement which proposed that workers should own and control production and benefit from the products of their own labor. This was a chilling thought for most capitalists, and much of what they have done since has aimed to prevent this and to ensure their continued control over production. The organization of work today reflects not the absolute necessities of productivity, but the necessities of capitalist productivity.

A strong and self-assured working force, a group of workers that felt confident in their own intelligence and creativity, would be directly counter to the interest of the owners, even if that work force produced more goods in the same amount of time, and hence increased profits. The only kind of increase in production that is desirable from the standpoint of capitalist efficiency is one that does not increase the relative power and self-confidence of the workers. So, owners have resisted any forms of organization of work that might lead to the challenge of their authority and power. This has required severely limiting the ways that workers might exercise their own power, creativity and intelligence.

The desire for control by owners is ultimately rooted in the desire to ensure long-term access to profits. But in the short run, control becomes an independent need, and decisions on how to organize things are made with this need clearly and strongly in mind. The primary job of managers is to organize production in such a way that workers produce according to the criteria of capitalist efficiency. Just as managers who failed to get their workers to produce goods would be dismissed as very inefficient, so managers who had their factories or workplaces seized by militant workers demanding workers' control would be dismissed, no matter how high a level of profit they had turned in the previous year.

Control has become so central to the psychology of management that we almost begin to think of "control" as an independent psychological dynamic. But here we are not talking of control as the ability to exercise creativity and self-determination in one's work. Managerial control is power over other people, imposing managerial goals and actions in place of those that workers might choose. In this society, people have power when they have this kind of control. People begin to talk of "the need for control" and "controlling personalities" as if these were manifestations of some underlying basic human need to control other people. In fact, the need to control is partly generated by the necessities of a class-dominated society, and makes perfect sense within it. To the extent that people's jobs require that they control other people, it becomes rational for them to develop these kinds of personality structures. It helps them to get better jobs and higher salaries. The need for control is constantly reinforced and recreated by a social system that rewards those who most effectively control others. People who develop this kind of personality structure find themselves succeeding in the economic marketplace— though they may also find themselves having deep problems establishing loving relationships and enduring friendships in their personal lives.

De-skilling

In light of management's overriding need to keep control and to reinforce passivity, we can understand that major themes in the organization of the workplace in the past several decades. In almost every sphere of work the tendency of management has been to organize things so that people have less opportunities to use their intelligence and creativity and job tasks become increasingly narrowed. All work that requires independent thinking is increasingly channeled to "mind workers" and the mind workers are then physically separated from the workers doing rote tasks. Within the group of mind workers, the various intellectual tasks are carefully broken down, and specific tasks given to different workers, so that fewer and fewer workers have any overview or comprehensive understanding of the totality of the production. The overview is restricted to ever narrowing groups of managers, and they are paid much higher incomes than everyone else so that they begin to feel that they have great stakes in the success of their enterprises and can identify more with the interests of the owners who run things than with the workers whom they supervise.

The process we have been describing has been called "de-skilling" in the recent literature on management. As production becomes increasingly complex, working people actually become less and less skilled. Many of the skills that people needed in the past are no longer needed and workers are given no opportunity to develop or utilize them. Talents and skills that are not used tend to atrophy.

The process of de-skilling in the workplace originated in the early part of the 1900's with the rise of a new theory of management called "scientific management" or "Taylorism" (after Frederick Taylor, the industrial engineer who first popularized it). Before Taylorism became popular, many workers had all the necessary skills and knowledge to design, plan and manufacture a product. It often took years to develop the skills required for many of the skilled trades and crafts, and people took great pride in their work. With the adoption of Taylorism by a management increasingly concerned to control a potentially rebellious workforce, engineers with stopwatches and tape measures were brought into workplaces where they simplified, fragmented and compartmentalized work tasks and placed workers under continuous supervision. And, as Taylorism grew more effective in controlling production in the factories, its techniques spread to offices, to clerical and white collar and service workers as well.

One benefit to management of de-skilling: by making work more machine-like, managers created the possibility of having more work functions replaced by machines. For example, by taking away the wide range of functions that secretaries used to perform, and instead dividing them into different job categories (e.g., the typist, the stenographer, the receptionist, the filer), management created the possibility that it could then get new technology that would make many of these functions irrelevant. If new typewriters or word processors could eliminate the need for much of the secretarial force, so much better for management costs. If dictaphones could eliminate the stenographer, or if sophisticated computer devices could eliminate needs for filing, so much the better for management costs. De-skilling becomes an important step towards the elimination of many jobs. The new technologies that are being introduced accelerate this process.

You might think that the new technologies, because of their sophistication, would require that people develop more complex skills. This is sometimes true for a small population in the workforce in the first years of the development of new technology. But the tendency of management is to develop new refinements in the technology that will allow further division of skills among those using it. This happened, for example, in the history of computer technology. At first, more sophisticated holistic understanding of the equipment was required, but over the course of twenty years the tasks were refined and broken down so that most of them could be defined more narrowly, and the level of training necessary to run them could be reduced.

The introduction of computers has tended to accelerate the restructuring of large organizations into departments organized by function, rather than into departments that handle a wide variety of tasks for a geographical area (cf. Stephen Hill, *Competition and Control at Work,* p. 37). Departments emerge with specialized functions like data preparation, billing, advertising, and this results in specialization of job tasks. In computerized offices the level of skill and individual initiative or creativity is reduced, while higher level jobs become more complex and interesting. Lower level work becomes increasingly that of feeding information into computers and then doing tasks as prescribed by the computers. The collection of data itself becomes more routinized because the kind of data and its form are increasingly dictated by the computers themselves. Senior managers get more information, and increasing scope of decision making, and the job for them becomes more interesting and challenging. This experience itself helps to make them oblivious to any humanly destructive aspects of the de-skilling process—after all, if the workers had wanted interesting jobs, they would have gotten their lives together more effectively and then taken the interesting jobs that these senior managers now find available.

Another obvious consequence of de-skilling is that it becomes increasingly easy to replace workers who leave for any reason. Sometimes it may take a few months to retrain a worker, but that is quite different from jobs that used to require skills that had been built up over years of training and experience. If more easily replaced, workers have less power in bargaining for wages and improved work conditions. If a worker strongly objects to how things are organized, s/he can be fired. In a strike situation, the management can hire scabs who can learn to do the jobs in question. And it doesn't have to come to the actual strike. Workers typically understand that they have lost power and tend to be more docile and less prone to confrontation because they understand the decrease in power that de-skilling has generated. The fact of de-skilling plays a role in shaping the Social Unconscious: our apprehension of the totality which molds how we perceive our possibilities at any given moment.

One of the most important consequences of de-skilling is what it does to the self-esteem and sense of power that workers have. Work that requires only certain specialized skills does not provide workers with the chance to develop a sense of their ability. Many workers come away from work believing that they are not capable or intelligent, because their work gives them no opportunity to use and develop their abilities to think and be creative. They come to believe that they are the kinds of people who have only the talents and skills appropriate to do what they actually do and nothing more. Gradually they become so unused to using their intelligence that they become scared to try.

This process is often helped along considerably by foremen, supervisors, and other management personnel. Workers are often treated like children and told to keep their ideas to themselves. They are given the message that their ideas are unimportant.

Supervisors will often turn workers against one another by making a put-down remark about one worker to another. Or they will suggest that they want to make an alliance with one worker against the other. Sometimes workers will fall into this, playing up to the managers or supervisors so that they can get better work assignments, chances for transfers and promotions.

But sometimes workers play along because, by identifying with management, they can prove to themselves they really are "better" than co-workers, and thus can avoid the nagging feeling that they are really failures. By dividing workers, management helps to create a climate of mutual distrust that undermines the possibility of collective struggle. The more workers can be divided, the less likelihood of any permanent anti-management alliances emerging or sustaining themselves.

Most working people want to work, but they want work that is meaningful and for which they are respected. As they become socialized to the world of work they come to understand that their actual jobs are going to give them neither opportunity for being creative nor opportunity for respect. Eventually, they develop various ways to resist, to reclaim dignity by not giving all that is wanted by management. If they cannot have their real needs met, they will assert their autonomy and a measure of power for themselves by refusing to go along with the programs set by others. They will work more slowly, or make mistakes on purpose, or find ways to increase lunch or coffee breaks or show up late to work (in the few jobs where this behavior doesn't get them fired), or spend excessive time at nonessential tasks. Often these strategies are not entirely conscious—but their function is to provide ways of resisting the total domination sought by management. They are often learned from co-workers who have already developed them. New workers, however, or workers from other cultures (e.g., Filipinos in the S.F. Post Office) don't always understand these moves, and sometimes think that their fellow workers are just "screw-offs." And sometimes even the very workers who engage in this behavior don't understand the deeper meaning of their own actions as real, though often inept, attempts to reclaim their power and dignity. They will put themselves and their fellow workers down for engaging in this kind of behavior. "No wonder we get treated so badly—we really deserve it" is a theme not infrequently heard amongst some workers.

From the standpoint of the bosses or supervisors, these strategies of resistance on the part of workers are precisely what justifies them in trying to find new techniques of manipulation and control. They will tell themselves, "Look, these workers don't work unless I can find some way to pressure them to do so. Sure I might talk rough to them, put them down, make them feel bad—but that's the only language they understand. Give them an inch and they'll take a mile."

Many supervisors and foremen came up from working class backgrounds themselves. They had to leave jobs in which they worked with the kinds of people they must now control. This is a psychologically difficult transition. After all, they are now working for the very bosses that they previously identified as a common oppressor. While people rarely formulate it this way, most of these managers who have made it up through the ranks feel badly about themselves for leaving their fellow workers behind—and know that they are now betraying the very comradeship that they previously enjoyed.

To make this transition palatable, many of these managers adopt "put down" attitudes towards their former comrades. "I have this management job because I was smarter than the other people, and my smarts have been rewarded," they explain to themselves. "And I know how people shirk off responsibilties and don't work hard on this job. I did it myself, and I've seen lots of others do it. But now that this company is recognizing me and my talents, I may have a future and not be stuck in a dead end job forever. Who knows how far I can go if they recognize my value to them? So I've got to stop these workers from being so lazy and unproductive." Of course, this very change in the attitudes of the managers makes workers more fearful of co-workers. Who knows who will be the next to betray them? Indeed, in some workplaces it is the policy of management to find the most effective union representatives and offer them well-paying management jobs—and when some of these people accept, often because they have been disappointed that the union isn't really doing enough for the workers anyway so why not be out for themselves, then the rest of the workers become even more suspicious and distrustful of their co-workers, and even less willing to seek social support for stress amongst the people with whom they work.

The distrust among workers is often consciously fostered by management personnel. Divide and conquer is not a new strategy—but it is one that has been developed to a point of fine tuning by many managers. This is not because these managers are born evil or have evil inclinations. It is rather because their jobs are to control, and one of the most effective strategies for exercising that control is to generate feelings of lack of worth, inadequacy and mutual distrust amongst the people whom they supervise.

While I have been discussing capitalist versions of control, permit me to digress for a moment to mention that I believe that ruling elites in the "communist" countries and in many totalitarian third world countries have similar stakes in controlling workers. In future years they will increasingly use similar strategies to those described here as they learn from "Western know-how" techniques for replacing the more overt uses of force that many of them rely on today. The so-called liberalizations of these countries will likely be merely the adaptation of these more subtle forms of manipulation and control that are already so sophisticatedly functioning in the Western world.

Given these realities, management views the stress-related health problems as an unfortunate but necessary cost that is still more rational for them than any plan to reorganize the workplace and make it less stressful. No matter how much it worries about loss of productivity caused by absenteeism, alcoholism, or other stress-related problems, it has a real and rational stake in maintaining the conditions that generate that stress. For that reason, when they talk about "stress management," they must restrict their interest to teaching their workers how to better accommodate themselves to the stress, rather than to considering ways to transform the conditions that cause the stress.

The lived experience of all this for most working people is a tremendous feeling that they have failed. To the extent that they believe that their fellow workers are equally undeserving (otherwise why would they be in these stressful and unrewarding jobs?), they feel that they have no one to turn to, no one whom they can respect and trust, with whom they can share their feelings. I have heard hundreds of workers say, almost unconsciously, about fellow workers, some dismissive remark of the following form: "What kind of person would take this kind of job who wasn't a dud or a failure?"—and use this to explain why they wouldn't think of going beyond superficial comradery with fellow workers. The psychological upshot of all this is that many workers feel anger and rage at themselves—an anger or rage which sometimes explodes at fellow workers or at supervisors. When the rage is kept inside, it is often managed through drugs or alcohol. But when it explodes irrationally at work, the explosions are themselves very costly, because they isolate the individual from fellow workers, and may put one's job in jeopardy. The very outbursts of anger make the worker even more self-doubting and distrusting: "Why have I acted in such an uncontrolled way?" The experience of having all this anger inside is often misinterpreted by the very people who are victims of this oppressive situation as a further confirmation that they actually deserve to be in the situation—because if they were "more together" they'd probably not be stuck in this job, with so many "irrational" people around them. So the process tends to confirm self-blame and Surplus Powerlessness.

Strategies of Control

The conditions we have been describing put the objective interests of workers in conflict with those of the managers and owners. At the same time, the process of de-skilling helps to disarm workers, to the extent that it decreases their ability to feel the right to struggle against the conditions they are facing. While this may be the most sophisticated way that workers are controlled, it is not the only method.

It may be useful to distinguish between three major forms of control over the work force.* First there is direct control—exercised in an immediate way by the boss. Direct control is associated with small firms in which the bosses can directly oversee the workers, fire those who are not doing it the way they want, and generally ensure directly that their will is done. The problems with this emerge as the firms become larger and the bosses must hire intermediaries: foremen or supervisors. But the foremen do not have the same ultimate power as the bosses nor do they directly benefit from production (i.e., they don't get the profits that workers make for their bosses). Also, foremen or supervisors are often only a few steps removed from being workers themselves, and may have much greater fears of being returned to the ranks of the workers than the bosses, because they don't own the factories or have access to their own independent sources of capital. In these circumstances, foremen or supervisors often develop an interest in the power of their positions, and develop ideas to justify their right to that power. They fear that the workers may get out of control (and if they did, that would

---

* There is an excellent exposition of these ideas by Rick Edwards in his book *Disputed Terrain.*

endanger the foremen's or supervisors' jobs). So they develop ideas that tend to put workers down, see them as unintelligent and unable to use creativity, and hence justify the creation of work conditions that do not require or even allow the use of those capacities. In seeing workers as somehow inferior and always potentially incompetent and untrustworthy, managers are able to justify to themselves their right to have more power and to exercise control. This fits perfectly with the system that benefits greatly from the creation of sentiments of self-blame in working people.

But there is a corresponding problem with direct control; it sometimes generates unnecessary opposition from the workers. Foremen or supervisors often use their power arbitrarily and in ways that generate resentment, resistance, and ultimately strike activity. The insecurity of the foreman or supervisory position can lead to the development of personality traits that are so obnoxious or insensitive that the workers strongly react. Higher level managers have tried to deal with this problem by providing special courses on communication for their lower level managers, to deal with their stress, and to train them more effectively to control workers. But the model of direct control relies too heavily on the personalities of those in these lower level positions and, for that reason, cannot be fully trusted from the standpoint of management efficiency.

A second form of control is based on the technical organization of the workplace itself. The worker appears to be controlled by the needs of the work itself, rather than by the management. The perfect example of this is the assembly line conveyor belt. Instead of the supervisor having to speed up the worker, the speedup seems to be a product of something external to the managers or supervisors: this is just a function of the technology itself. Instead of the worker having to challenge the arbitrary power or authority of the supervisor's orders, the worker now is faced with an order mediated through the technology itself. The orders seem to be coming from the production equipment itself, almost an order from science and technology rather than from the bosses. How can the worker refuse to work in accord with the needs of modern technology? "Obviously," managers suggest, "the only reason that they would do so is because they are too stupid to understand the needs of efficiency." And their resistance can only be understood as standing in the way of "progress."

The owners of capital are able to enlist science on their side since they have the money to employ the engineers. scientists, and inventors, as well as the political power to set the priorities within which "pure" scientific research is done. But much more directly, they control the directions for applied scientific research and development. Nor is this any hidden conspiracy: the government and the universities, as well as private research institutions, make quite clear that their priorities are to help the general welfare, which as they understand it, means increasing the productivity and efficiency of American corporations. The current organization of work, described in the section above, is seen as the given, and scientists are asked to create new technologies that will serve the interest of efficiency in this context. Built into this is a bias towards de-skilling and specialization at the

expense of human health. But the scientists or engineers or inventors proclaim that they are not interested in discussing the social implications of their
work: they are not interested in political issues of this sort. They will earnestly
tell you that they are just trying to design products that will meet an "existing
need" (as defined by those who have the the power to have their needs
count—namely those with the capital to pay for others to develop products
for them.) So what happens is that technology gets introduced that can serve
the interest of dividing the work force, narrowing job tasks, de-skilling, and
providing repetitive and unfulfilling job tasks, and these are presented under
the banner of "scientific progress."

The advantage to management is that the control being exercised is more
mystified to the workers. Lower level managers and supervisors do not appear
to be exercising arbitrary authority—they are only doing what the machines
require. And workers are encouraged to feel that they are reactionary because
they are standing in the way of what science and progress demand if they
don't do their work at the pace that the machines demand. In the face of
this, workers have sometimes managed to limit the introduction of new
technology on the grounds that it was costing jobs—but almost never on the
grounds that it was humanly destructive. At least you can count the number
of jobs that would be lost—it seems to have this "hard" quantitative aspect
that puts it in the same universe of discourse with those who are talking
about progress. But it is almost impossible to talk about human costs that
are not seen as quantifiable in this way—so typically workers have been
forced to silence their doubts as new forms of control were introduced in
the forms of new technologies. This process has accelerated in the past few
years, because now the owners can argue that unless the new technologies
are introduced, foreign competitors will introduce them and beat out the
American workers' productivity, thereby causing them to lose their jobs. In
the face of this threat, most remaining constraints on the introduction of
new technologies have been severely weakened, with a concomitant acceler-
ation in the ability of management to accelerate this form of control.

The disadvantage to management of technological control is that these
machines and technologies have sometimes increased the potential power
of workers through strikes and "job actions" that cause slowdowns or disruptions of production. If the assembly line, for example, requires each person
to do his/her part before the next stage of the line can do its, then a small
group of dissidents could slow or disrupt the line. And valuable technology
could potentially be put in danger by militants willing to seize or destroy it.
The seizure of factories by workers in France in 1968 reminded many owners
of a lesson they had learned during the sit-down strikes of the UAW in 1937:
their technology was vulnerable to worker militancy, should that militancy
develop. This kind of problem leads owners to seek a more internalized
form of control.

The third form of control, bureaucratic control, is the most sophisticated
part of management strategy. The defining feature is that the rule of law
and regulations replaces rule by supervisors' commands. Work activity is
governed by a set of work rules that seem to stand independent of the wills

of individual supervisors. Each job has a prescribed set of rules, and these rules also tell workers the criteria by which work will be judged, the rewards for doing the job correctly, and the penalties for inadequate work. The supervisors are no longer the bosses, but are merely there to monitor the ways that the workers work, according to criteria not set by the supervisors. The supervisors, in turn, will be judged by a set of rules that are over them. In this case, the supervisors can reasonably say to workers, "All I'm doing is following orders, doing my job, by making you do the job the way I say. This is what your job is—and you should have known that by reading the basic contract. And if I don't report what you are doing or institute appropriate discipline, I myself will be in trouble, because I must follow the rules governing my job or else risk termination myself."

Bureaucratic control is wonderful for mystifying the basic power relationships at work. There seems to be an outside force, "The Rules," that governs everything. Indeed, even when you get to the very top of the corportation, those with power will tell you that they are merely following rules of procedure forced upon them by the laws of the economy. Everyone is merely doing what they have to do, following forces that are out of their control, and everyone must do it if they are to keep whatever rewards are gotten by being employed in the enterprise (primarily, jobs that can pay mortgage or rent and food). How can one be angry at bosses who are just following the rules?

Moreover, since each job has its own set of rules governing it, workers tend to see their jobs more individualistically, less as part of a common work situation with other workers. Hundreds, sometimes thousands, of different job titles and descriptions help separate the workers from each other. The individual worker begins to see her/himself as alone in the huge bureaucracy, without a common basis of unity with fellow workers. What advances one worker will not necessarily advance the other. Each particular job situation has different rules.

Bureaucratic control is firmly established in many corporations and public sector workplaces where there are no unions representing workers. But even where there have been unions, they have tended to accept the organization of work as defined in the rules and to put their energies into issues like wages, benefits, pensions, hiring and firing. The basic right of the management to set the rules has remained relatively unchallenged. In fact, sometimes the unions take as their goal the task of making the rules more explicit, demanding that management define the expectations more clearly, so that workers will no longer feel under the thumb of particularly oppressive supervisors. Thus, instead of challenging the right of management to make the rules, the workers may actually be perceiving a victory simply from having the rules clarified.

In this situation we get the picture of supposed militancy: a grievance is being vigorously pursued against a supervisor for violating the rules. Sometimes the grievance will be won, though more often the workers' energies are tied up in a bureaucratic morass for months, sometimes years, as the particular grievance goes through the torturous process of administrative procedures. Instead of workers acting together to affect change through some kind of militant collective action, workers are encouraged to define their own private problems, and then to pursue individual solutions through the grievance process. Whatever potential anger might otherwise have erupted has now been neatly contained within the pre-established channel, a channel neatly governed by the very people who run the workplace itself. And the appearance of rules seems to provide an aroma of "fairness" to the whole process. What it in fact does, and quite effectively, is legitimate domination as it mystifies the actual distribution of power.

The impact on the workers is to reinforce their tendency towards self-blaming. Workers come to feel that the problems they face are their own failures to adjust to the given reality. They end up blaming themselves for aspects of their situations that are built into the structure of the economic world in which they function. The organization of work that leads to de-skilling is experienced as "the facts," specified in the contract, which even their union with all its militants has accepted. So if they don't fit in and operate according to the rules it's because they have some personal problems. The creation of Employee Assistance Programs and Stress Management Programs are designed to help individual workers get these allegedly personal problems under control, so that they will not interfere with the smooth functioning of their enterprises as a whole. The problems, of course, are always the workers'.

Counselors may sympathize with the reactions their worker clients are having at their workplaces, but their underlying assumption is that the problems are poor "worker-environment fits" and that, in such cases, the workers must either change themselves or leave their jobs—never that the workplaces must be made more humanly satisfying and fulfilling. So this "generous" support through Employee Assistance helps to reinforce the basic message that the fault lies within the worker.

Bureaucratic control is the most effective way of reinforcing self-blaming; though we have seen that direct control, with its explicit use of supervisor putdowns of workers' intelligence and competence, and technical control, with its implicit accusation that workers must be standing in the way of scientific progress if they object to the way things are organized, are also powerful reinforcements of the self-blaming process.

The three often co-exist in the same work situation, mutually reinforcing the feelings of failure and incompetence and sometimes even "craziness" that many workers experience. Together they provide a daily dose of direct experience for the worker about why s/he is not really together enough to run things, doesn't really deserve to have power, and really should just leave the big questions to those who know better.

There are some important qualifications on what we have said thus far. The tendency to self-blame is not absolute: it is just a tendency, and often the dominant one, but it can co-exist with powerful counter tendencies. Workers often see through the various forms of control, and often understand that they are not really at fault for the problems they face in the work world. Each new form of management control, each further elaboration and sophistication of the process, has become necessary precisely because workers have often been able to see through what is happening, and have moved collectively to change the situation or at least to struggle against it.

Despite awareness of management techniques, the tendency among workers is still to hold onto the self-blaming ideas and feelings. The self-blaming approach is rooted deep in the unconscious, and is hard to dislodge. Workers in the same interview can say that they hate what is being done to them at work, and also claim that they are doing it to themselves and that it is their own fault, that they are the kind of person who deserves what is happening to them. No matter how politically conscious they are at other levels, the constant reinforcement of the idea that they live in a Meritocracy has taken hold inside themselves. The experiences in the world of work play an important role in continually reinforcing this way of viewing reality—but the idea is so massively asserted in every institution in American life that it is simply the "common sense" which is assumed and never challenged by individuals as they try to explain to themselves what has happened to them. While we are focusing on the ways that this happens in the world of work, the self-blaming consciousness is at each moment reenforced by how people understand their own childhoods and how they interpret their own personal lives at the moment. It is because these work together to form a seamless whole of integrated self-blaming that this consciousness appears opaque—not as a problem, but just as "how it is."

One of the consequences of this tendency is that workers have often fought in ways that undermined their own potential power, accepted much less than they really wanted, and often accepted less than they had to accept, had they pressed on the struggle even further. All too often, the reasons why they didn't continue that struggle were their deep-seated beliefs that they couldn't win, didn't deserve to win, and ought to be happy with whatever they already had won, because at some level it was more than they deserved. While this has not been the major dynamic thoughout the history of the working class, it has become increasingly common in the past several decades.

Workers cooperate with management not just because they accept management ideologies of control, or out of beliefs that justify the right of the owners to run the system, but also because they sometimes believe that "teamwork" is in their own interests. Even when workers may see through everything and reject any form of self-blaming, they may wish to increase the general competitive strength of the firm in which they work, simply on the ground that the firm provides employment which is badly needed. They may have lots of anger at how the profits are being divided up, and lots of anger at how work is organized, even an awareness of the destructiveness of the work process to their physical and emotional health, and still quite reasonably want to keep their firm producing successfully enough so that it doesn't have to shut the gates and force them into the army of the unemployed. Of course, management can play on this, forcing cutbacks in wages and further deterioration of work conditions with the threat that all these are necessary in order to improve the competitive advantage of the firm in relationship to some foreign competitor. But while they may be

exaggerating dangers in order to force concessions, the danger is certainly
real, and so workers can be seen to cooperate not just out of Surplus Powerlessness but also out of a realistic concern with their own jobs and futures.

For the workers, facing the situation of possible unemployment in the
short run, it is certainly reasonable to be worrying about their own employment situations. And, to the extent that this worry is legitimate in the short
run, it is perfectly rational in the short run to give at least some energy to
making the firm "work" within the confines of its present repressive existence.
So the point here is not to jump too quickly at pointing the finger at irrationality or blame workers for cooperating in the process of self-blaming, but to
see the complexity and recognize the many different levels on which the
struggle against Surplus Powerlessness must be waged.

Job Enrichment

It will not be surprising if more intelligent managers attempt to develop
new strategies of control or attempt to eliminate some of the bad consequences of existing strategies. The bottom line is to maintain control and
profits, and everything else is negotiable. Two such moves have been tried
in recent years, and we may expect to hear more about them in the years
ahead: First, "Quality of Work" (QWC) groups. These are groups set up by
management which attempt to involve line workers and management in discussions about the production process, and to heighten workers' commitment to the
productive process. The groups attempt to enhance communication between
workers and supervisors, and also to allow workers an opportunity to express
their dissatisfactions, suggestions for how things should be changed, and
other ideas. These groups are one attempt to overcome the loss of motivation
and commitment to productivity that has been a concomitant to the de-skilling
process.

But the scope of their mandate is severely limited by management from
the start. Management wants workers to talk about the details of their own
immediate operations—but they do not want workers to talk about the larger
issues of the firm: how it is organized, what its products or services really
are and how they might be altered and improved, what happens to the
profits, investment decisions, rates of production, or what the productive
process is doing to the health of those who work there. Expressions of anger
are seen as "problems" of the individual workers who can be therapized in
the groups or sent to Employee Assistance Programs for straightening out.
A Quality of Work Circle or group must accept the basic framework set by
management, and thereby it actually functions to provide a more effective
vehicle for management to get its message of needed cooperation into the
minds of line workers. The appearance of concern and interest in the ideas
of workers, combined with the reality that the really basic issues remain
mystified and out of the control of workers, often creates confusion and
tension among the workers who are eager to believe that finally the firm is
taking them seriously. The workers who get "hooked" by this process sometimes wonder to themselves: "Why am I not feeling more committed to this

workplace? I should feel differently, more enthusiastic. Look at all these people are doing for me—they are showing me that I'm really respected by giving me this opportunity to have feedback and input." In short, the QWC can intensify self-blaming and delegitimate workers' anger at oppressive and unfulfilling job situations. What they rarely do is change the real power relations at work.

A class-conscious work force could use these circles in a different way than intended by management. Unions could prepare their activists to use the QWCs as ways to organize and politically educate fellow workers. To do so, they would need to take the leadership of these circles away from the thera- pists and management consultants who run them. QWCs could be effective vehicles for unions if they trained people on how to use them—but no doubt if unions employed this strategy these circles would fall out of favor by a management seeking to enhance systems of control. Whatever new names management comes up with for other "humanizing" enterprises in the future, whether they be called "self-development" groups or "communications skills" or whatever, the same problems will persist.

Job enlargement (adding new tasks without increasing skills levels) and job enrichment (increasing autonomy, skills and responsibility) are being tried in some firms. These changes, while often to the good, are almost always severely restricted in scope. As Stephen Hill points out,

"The overall design of production process and the design of individual jobs within these processes are still managerial functions which workers do not control, and the technical function of coordination resides with management. The labor control function is still exercised by managers, no longer perhaps by direct supervision and overseeing, but just as effec- tively by monitoring worker activity and intervening when necessary."*

So, while a limited autonomy may be created in certain job categories, the basic decisions and power remain in the hands of management. This creates the same psychological dynamic as QWC: workers are told they should feel grateful for their enhanced prestige and power, when in fact they are ex- periencing only very limited changes in their basic positions. The result: workers feel bad about themselves, and don't understand why they are not responding in the ways that they are supposed to.

There is another reaction, often on the part of workers who have a higher degree of class consciousness: they will resist participation in these schemes. Aware of the manipulations involved, worn out by a lifetime of phony choices in the electoral arena and in other areas of their lives, many workers will tell you that they don't want any more responsibility or any more decision making of the kind they are likely to be given by management. This refusal is a plausible way of responding to the psychological manipulations inherent in new management schemes of control. Ironically, outsiders then use this fact as evidence that workers are really satisfied with the way things are and

---

* See Stephen Hill, *Competition and Control at Work,* Cambridge, MA: Massachusetts Institute of Technology, p. 50.

don't want any enhanced control or power at work. What they miss is what some of these workers see: that job enrichment or QWCs provide the appearance of power without its actuality and may in fact actually increase the ways in which workers can be effectively dominated. Not all workers have the language to articulate this point, but many have gut feelings that lead them to resist these new mechanisms of control that parade under the banner of "work humanization."

While QWCs and job enrichment must be carefully scrutinized, I believe that they may potentially be useful to a class-conscious movement. To the extent that they project the notion that workers have a right to be respected, they can be used as vehicles for raising consciousness and demanding that the restrictions placed on them by management be transcended. Here, as in any other area in which potential reforms are introduced, the critical issue is: To what extent does the reform allow for the possibility of enhancing the sense of power and dignity and self-respect of those who are its beneficiaries? In the case of these "work humanizations" the potential exists in both directions either to increase self-blaming and mystification, or to enhance self-esteem. If workers, with the backing of their unions, can see how management is trying to use these techniques as instruments of control and, at the same time, be shown how the very same techniques can be used to enhance solidarity and prepare for larger demands for substantive control at work, they can have a positive influence. Without this, work humanization becomes only another variant of bureaucratic control, replacing technical control by an enhanced internalization of the norms and rules of management and an enhanced ability to induce self-discipline and self-blame.

The impulse on the part of many workers to approach these management "innovations" with high hopes, openness, and eagerness to make them work is another manifestation of a deeper dynamic: most working people want their work lives to become meaningful expressions of who they really are. Even those who express verbal cynicism are often ready to drop their doubts and try their hardest if there is a chance that something will be different at their workplaces. I have found that most workers want their work to be a real contribution to others, want to make a real contribution to society, and want to use their creative talents. This need to be creative and to make real contributions stands in sharp contrast to the picture of workers as self-indulgent and lazy.

Over and over again working people will attempt to express their fundamental humanity and intelligence even in conditions that systematically undermine any possibility for more fulfilling work. People will take pride in their tasks, no matter how narrowly defined they are, and will give their best to make their tasks work. They will fight for their "turf" at work, even if that turf seems trivial to others, because in that little arena they can get fulfillment. (In fact, many of the people who appear to be merely "bitchy" or "small-minded" in the ways that they engage in office politics or in rigid behaviors at worksites are merely acting out in the only way that they have available to them the desire for some degree of control in their lives, even if this means stepping on other people around them with whom they might, under other circumstances, have friendly relationships.) They will also find small ways to put their own individual stamps of creativity on their work, take pride in their products, and find the best ways to accomplish their tasks even if the tasks themselves are not very pleasing. Many workers realize how much more they understand than their supervisors about how to run their workplaces, and how much better they could do so if management didn't get in the way. But while this understanding should enhance their self-respect, it simultaneously intensifies their self-blaming, because they often think themselves at fault for being in subordinate positions.

We must not think of workers as victims—but as people who in fact are doing extraordinary jobs of survival within conditions that are humanly destructive. The anger that they sometimes turn on each other at work, the pettiness and the seeming selfishness, are often the only available forms they have for expressing their frustrations at the life-denying reality. The enjoyment of the little ceremonies honoring the person who has worked in the unfulfilling workplace for twenty years—perhaps a little banquet or a gold chain or a watch—give testimony to frustrated desires for a work world in which there would be a real community and not just something that is manifested in unusual moments. It is this indomitable urge on their parts to assert their fundamental humanity and to fight for it with whatever emotional and intellectual tools available that created the labor movement as a vehicle for the right to dignity and respect.

In the next chapter we shall explore the unions as one strategy for overcoming powerlessness. Here it is useful to conclude by noting that the struggle against powerlessness at work is often subtle and usually not understood explicitly even by those most fiercely engaged in the battles. The organization of the work world presents itself as a "natural" reality to which workers are supposed to adjust, and the various indirect ways in which workers, sensing their humanity threatened, either fight back or end up feeling terrible about themselves are often not identified by the participants. The impact of this system as a whole is to increase the process of self-blaming and to strengthen Surplus Powerlessness. The constant eruptions and bumpy and irregular aspects of "how workers are," while not often the most effective way to protest, testify to the continuing difficulties management has in totally homogenizing and pacifying the society. While the world of work generates and sustains Surplus Powerlessness, when we look deeper we see that people have not been totally smoothed out, and that the underlying and fundamental need of human beings for a deeper respect, for a loving commmunity, and for the opportunity to actualize their deepest human capacities continues to assert itself and will not be silenced.

Despite the powerful tools of psychology, management, and "communication experts," the task of completely subduing and internally defeating these basic human needs by accommodating people to a world in which they have no opportunity for expression is ultimately a task that will never succeed. But in the process, most of us pay a very heavy price and, in the short run, end up feeling bad about ourselves, despairing about co-workers, and cynical about the possibility that anything real can really change.

Chapter 4

Union Blues

ONE OF THE GREATEST DISAPPOINTMENTS OF MANY WORK-
ing people has been the failure of their unions to promote real power for
workers. Many working people feel that their unions are largely unresponsive
to their needs, out of their control, and run by "others" who don't really
understand or care about their real problems.

In spite of these feelings most working people do not want to give up
their unions, no matter how distant they feel from them. The unions are
correctly perceived as having won for workers important financial gains and
important benefits, but this is largely because of the pressure created by the
existence of the union movement. Non-union enterprises are often willing
to make concessions on wages and benefits as a way of heading off union
representatives, because unions still have the potential of empowering workers in ways that management would prefer to avoid. But if the union movement were to suffer a severe or crushing blow, all working people would
soon experience a decrease in their bargaining strength when facing
management.

Many working people deeply appreciate the ability of their unions to put
some minimal curbs on the most arbitrary actions of management. The
grievance procedures, often won through extensive bargaining and sometimes with strike actions, are seen as an important protection for workers.
While they can see how the rules may play a role for increasing management
control, most working people feel that the benefits of placing constraints on

arbitrary discipline and firings by foremen or supervisors are an important victory that unions sometimes deliver. Without those safeguards, many people think they would be out on the streets looking for new jobs.

Yet, despite these important qualifications, most working people are very disillusioned with their unions. Top union leadership is not democratically selected and does not represent the membership. "Nobody elected Kirkland, and yet he speaks for me," is a sentiment voiced over and over again. The unexpected showing for Senator Gary Hart in the 1984 elections was a sharp reminder of this fact. Many union rank and filers may have known little about the actual politics of Hart, but they knew that their leaders had endorsed Mondale without any real process of consulting their memberships: and they voiced their resentment of being ignored by voting for Hart. "I've got a mind of my own," said many union members—and all too often they have the feeling that their leaders don't take that fact very seriously. It is rare indeed for union members to feel that they are being consulted before a decision is made—though often they are expected to be the troops who will carry out that decision later on.

The Executive Committee of the AFL-CIO has completely isolated itself from democratic control by its membership—yet it continues to be supported by union dues. Most union members don't even know who the AFL-CIO Executive Committee is, much less how they got there or what they'd have to do to get them replaced. Similarly, within many of the biggest national unions there are no direct votes on national leadership. Instead, union locals select representatives to attend national conventions, at which they get to vote for the national leadership. But since the issues and personalities are rarely made known to the membership before these conventions, only rarely does the selection processs of delegates rest on the issues of who the local members want as their national leadership.

Democracy is often absent not only from selection of leadership, but from the whole process of the unions' functioning. National contracts are often negotiated without very much opportuntiy for the membership to discuss the options and alternative perspectives.

All too often memberships are faced with tentative contract settlements that do not reflect their own priorities or interests. They are then asked to ratify or reject them (often after they have already gone back to work with the dynamic of struggle largely undermined). In these situations, they have the democratic power to reject what their leadership has negotiated, but they don't have the opportunity to formulate their own alternative sets of demands or priorities. This is a very weak kind of democratic control. And it is made even weaker by the absence of a free press within the union movement that would represent all sides fairly. Instead, opposition groups and ideas rarely get mentioned in any official union publications, except when they are being caricatured. In these situations, it becomes exceedingly difficult for the average working person to imagine any plan that could potentially change the unions and make them more representative of rank-and-file concerns. Moreover, democratic forms are used in fundamentally anti-democratic ways. Local union meetings are rarely open for serious discussion of basic issues confronting the leadership. The use of Robert's Rules of Order, originally meant as a safeguard against tyranny, becomes a club by which the membership is confused and made to feel that it really doesn't understand what is happening and so should just be quiet and go along.

The unions are often perceived as uninterested in the most important problems facing working people. Unions make little or no attempt to think out in a systematic way what a real program of stress support would be like. If anything, many unions tend to see stress as a personal problem of workers—something that they will negotiate as a "mental health benefit" rather than as a core problem facing all working people, directly shaping their sense of powerlessness.

Moreover, the unions seem to be impersonal bureaucracies, more interested in the dues that they automatically receive than in what is happening in the lives of their members. Many union members begin to think of the unions as small-scale insurance companies: there to provide benefits and to prevent excesses of management behavior, but operating essentially as businesses rather than as something that relates to their personal needs.

The upshot of all this is that unions sometimes make working people feel even more despairing and powerless about their lives. After all, they reason, if the very institutions that they set up have become corrupt or off-the-track in this kind of way, then what hopes are there for anything changing at all? If they can't control their own organizations, how can they hope to control the larger society? And with these questions there develops a conviction there is no basis for changing anything. Workers begin to see themselves as people who can't get anything together and as needing someone else to run things for them. These feelings play into the already existing patterns of self-blaming described above, and reconfirm people in Surplus Powerlessness.

There is often a very intense splitting mechanism that operates when this judgment is made. Many working people will talk about "workers" or "unions" as something other than themselves—and then pour abuse on this other thing. Yet meanwhile, while not acknowledging directly what this does to their own self-images, they feel increasingly bad about themselves for being in this category, the "other" members of which are "all screwed up" or "not together." As much as working people will bitch about their unions and union leaders, I have found much less anger than deep and pervasive shame in workers that their very own institutions have turned out so badly for them.

Where Did All the Passion Go?

Unions did not start off being conservative or bureaucratic. There was an intense battle fought inside unions over which directions to pursue. In that battle government and the owners of capital squarely sided with the more conservative tendencies. At the height of their potential power, unions were subjected to an intense "Red Scare" in which anyone advocating more militant policies, or policies that widened the scope of the unions beyond narrow economic reforms to address the issues of power and control at work, was called a communist, thrown out of the union and blacklisted from other jobs. If unions would not agree to police themselves against "red" infiltration, they were thrown out of the AFL-CIO as a whole, isolating them so that they could become more easy prey to government witch-hunts. The more conservative union leaders posed the following choice to the membership: either follow this "red" leadership and struggle for larger demands that are unwinnable, or settle for our leadership, in which case we will bring you concrete material gains in the form of higher wages and benefits. This choice was put most starkly in the post-WW II years.

We should be aware that there were several reasons that people leaned away from the larger struggle to keep their unions involved as instruments of social change in the way they started to be during the Depression. First, in the wake of the powerful impact of World War II, with the sense of national purpose transcending what were termed more parochial interests—there was a feeling of exhaustion and tiredness on the part of a working class that had put so much of its effort for years into the "larger" causes. Second, with millions of people newly demobilized from the army, there was a resurgence of unemployment and a decrease in the relative power of workers to negotiate their demands. Third, there was a widespread belief that the benefits of the New Deal could be spread through the continued dominance of the Democratic Party, and that political change could be accomplished in that arena—so the unions should not try to advance themselves as the agents of change, but rather as supporters of elected Democrats who would do it for them. Of course, in each of these conservatizing factors·there was an element of Surplus Powerlessness operating; people simply accepted "realities" that could have been changed. But given their perceptions, the move to follow more conservative leadership in the short run was understandable.

The conservatizing of the unions was accelerated by the media attack on the Communist Party (CP). The important contribution that the CP made in the 1930's to the organization of the CIO put it in a position to play a leadership role in many unions. The American corporate elite understood the potential threat in this development, and began to mobilize anti-communist sentiments into a full scale campaign, including the outlawing of the CP through the Smith Act (1942). Fearful that they might be sent to jail if their true affiliations were known, CP members often kept their relationship to the Party quite secret, even as they continued to provide leadership in the unions. When the anti-communist campaign became a full-scale crusade in the post-war decade, union members began to discover that many of their trusted leaders and union militants were or had been secret Party members. These revelations, manipulated by the dominant media, helped generate a feeling on the part of many workers that they had been manipulated or lied to by activists whom they had previously trusted.

The feeling of distrust was intensified by a serious error in the strategy of the CP. The CP, mistakenly believing that the Soviet Union was on the way to building socialism, tended to place the needs of the Soviet Union as its highest priority. When the Soviet Union made a pact with Hitler, the American CP defended it. When the U.S. allied with the Soviet Union to

fight Hitler, the CP put the goal of fighting the anti-fascist crusade above
all other goals, even agreeing to a "no-strike" pact that effectively disenfran-
chised workers from participating in the same war-generated economic pros-
perity that their bosses were beginning to enjoy. When workers discovered
that those co-workers who had been advocating these policies were secretly
members of the Communist Party, and seemed to be more concerned about
the Soviet Union than about the immediate needs of the workers, they had
a personal experience that seemed to give credibility to the media-orches-
trated campaign of fear about "fifth column" elements who could not be
trusted.

So when the big guns of corporate America took aim at the unions, and
demanded a purge of communists and communist-dominated unions, it
wasn't totally surprising that many workers felt unsure of how to respond.
The in-fighting in the unions seemed both too ugly and, in light of the
perceived deceptions, too confusing to get directly involved in. To stand
against the purging of communists involved risking one's own position—perhaps you too would be identified as a communist, or a "fellow traveller" or
a "dupe." And could you really be sure that everything being said against
them was really not true? Especially when the charges were being made not
just by bosses, but by opportunistic union leaders as well? And could you
fully dismiss the shocking stories of ex-communists as they proceeded to tell
how they had become progressively disillusioned, how they had been coerced
and lied to by CP comrades, and how the horrors of Stalinism were still
being covered up by the post–WW II American communists?*

The result was not so much a willing participation of rank and file members
in the anti-communist crusade as it was a withdrawal from politics on their
part. If the risks were high and the confusion great, why not withdraw from
this arena altogether? Let those who liked political life stay involved—after
a decade and a half of depression and war, many unionists would turn their
attention to private life and personal fulfillment. As this move progressed,
even non-CP militants in the unions were increasingly vulnerable to the
conservative attacks, easily labelled as "Communists" and then isolated. Without being able to plead their cases to their memberships, themselves increasingly unwilling to come to unpleasant meetings dominated by in-fighting
and confusion, these militants could only get their sides heard through the
media. But the union media was increasingly in the hands of the conservative
leadership, and the larger societal media was already engaged in a major
campaign to discredit activism and put unions on the defensive. So those
who stayed and fought were often badly burned, and came away bitter and
disillusioned about politics and about their own labor movement.

The result of all this was the emergence of a union movement in the 1950's

---

* Even now I find it shocking that these CP activists supported the Hitler-Stalin Pact
from 1939–1941, and apologized for Stalin's atrocities. How sad for American workers that their legitimate radicalism became so strongly identified with the Communist
Party that the underlying moral vision could be obscured and then, in despair,
repudiated.

whose primary leadership had been molded in the fights against communists and union militants, and whose frame of reference was directed at keeping control of the union away from all those who wanted to "politicize" every issue. The model that was built of a unionism for the 50's and 60's had a "professional" feel to it: they, the union leaders, would be the experts who would, if left alone, deliver the goods to the membership. The conservative leaders could confine their attention to monetary demands, and push hard for economic concessions from the companies. Union members would occasionally be asked to strike, but rarely would they be involved in the thinking and planning of strategies or even in the details of bargaining demands. A good member could simply pay the dues and receive appropriate instructions on what to do and when to do it. Increasingly, the union was seen not as a democratic forum in which the working class shaped its own programs and strategies for achieving its ends, but rather as a detached organization that would represent the workers' material needs and interests. Union business agents or paid officials would make decisions, and members could, if they wished, attend union meetings to ratify those decisions.

That this strategy could work at all was dependent on the ability of these leaders to "deliver the goods." And that, in turn, was dependent on the ability of American corporations to make monetary settlements with unionized workers that increased the workers' pay and hence the workers' material well-being. This was possible—not because the corporate elite had suddenly become generous, but because of two other factors.

First, there was the immense and growing power of American corporations throughout the world in the 1950's and 60's, a power that depended on America's economic penetration of world markets that had previously been dominated by the countries whose economies had been left in tatters by the Second World War. This allowed them to bring home to the U.S. enough wealth that some part of it could be distributed to American workers without dampening high profits for the owners. Also, there was a growing recognition that labor peace, bought by helping the more conservative leaders, would have long-term benefits for the economic well-being of the owners.

It would be a mistake to over-emphasize the degree of labor-management harmony. Even in the periods of greatest collaboration between unions and management, there were still important struggles and strikes that continued to be waged. Management did not "give" its concessions willingly and without coercion. So even in the 50's and 60's many of the labor leaders found themselves leading strikes, and perceived of themselves as quite militant in fighting for the needs of working people. Though the militancy was often expressed in tough bargaining sessions, union leaders saw themselves as doing the best they could for their members. While they were being denounced by an increasingly small opposition for being "sell-outs," they and their memberships often saw themselves as doing the best that could be done. Moreover, their strategy of narrowing the issues seemed to be working as the larger social demands, the political concerns, were in fact being handled by their elected representatives. Even Republicans failed to repeal the benefits of the New Deal, and Democratic Party majorities could sometimes force extensions of these benefits and programs. Under Nixon, the labor movement won the Occupational Safety and Health Administration, and even President Reagan was forced to keep his attacks on social benefits during his first term to those who were most poorly organized politically (e.g., welfare mothers, children's health programs, etc.).

Working within the Democratic Party, labor leaders won legislative protections for gains achieved in collective bargaining. They were less successful in getting the Democrats to provide the basic social welfare benefits available to most Western European workers: e.g., adequate health care or family support programs. But to many labor leaders, the disappointments with Democrats did not vitiate what seemed obvious— that they were winning some important social reforms through electoral politics, and that they would continue to do so as long as they could count on mobilizing the troops at election time.

We Do It All For You

But there has been an unintended and disastrous effect: the unions began to be instruments of disempowerment for working people. The basic message given out by the mainstream unions was: "Don't worry about anything, just leave it to us to handle your problems. The problems we can't handle aren't real ones, so stop bellyaching and get back to work." Even today, this message comes through from many business agents and union leaders. It is not uncommon for union members who have specific ideas about political strategies or social change to be told, "Well, let's refer that to our lobbyist at the state capital or in Washington, D.C." It is not uncommon for workers facing a grievance at a worksite to be strongly urged not to take collective action, but instead to use grievance procedures that often run for months and sometimes years. It is not unusual for workers who are pursuing grievances to find out that the union's message to them is: "Leave it to your shop steward or business agent, or our lawyer, to figure out the best strategy. We'll call you when we need you."

The message is one that implicitly suggests that workers can't handle their own problems and that they need experts who really understand how to do the work. The unions thereby create a culture of passivity, in which union members are encouraged to see themselves as unneeded and unwanted by their unions. In spite of appeals to membership participation, unions often communicate to their members a strong sense that they are not welcome, that their ideas are not important and that perhaps the members really aren't too bright anyway.

Nothing reinforces this message more dramatically than the union meeting. Most union meetings are dominated by a format that is at once boring and virtually impossible to understand by any except those who have attended them for years. Reports from committees, financial matters, and old business always seem to dominate the discussions—and they are often presented in ways that obscure whatever policy issues are at stake. Debates are covered up and disagreements amongst leaders are rarely presented. Information about directions in the union Internationals, analyses of the country's overall economic and political directions or questions about one's own particular industry are almost never discussed. Raising political discussions "from the floor" is almost always seen as a disruptive activity, and members who persist in attempting this are soon treated as "kooks" or "provocateurs." The elaborate process of parliamentary procedure serves to mystify most members, and to make it easy for leadership to keep control of their previously planned business. Members who wish to have new issues discussed rarely get a chance to shape the agenda, and only those who have already mastered a high degree of personal aggressiveness are able to get union executive boards to put their concerns on the agenda. I have interviewed many members who tried to go to meetings. The most common response was frustration, coupled with a persistent anger directed at themselves for not being "more together" so that they could handle the situation more effectively.

Even the moments of real solidarity are less effective than they could be. The exhilaration of a strike or the development of contract demands can create a moment in which the separateness and divisions of the workplace are momentarily overcome. People are suddenly confronted with the potential of their own real power, and the common realities in which they jointly live. The strike situation often brings out the very best in the union members—and many will tell you that even though they had less materially, they were more spiritually whole and uplifted in the heights of their strike experience.

All the more disastrous, then, that the solidarity is so often dissipated by the way the strikers are treated in their own unions. All too often the union leaders make no efforts to maintain a sense of unity and togetherness. Picketers are kept isolated from each other, and mass rallies at which people could be reminded of their collective strength are few. The fears and financial worries that come up are treated as the individual problems of union members—with little opportunity for people to get together and share their problems with each other or to use their collective wisdom to problem-solve together. Union leaders, worried that the militancy will "get out of hand" and lead to an unwillingness to settle for "realistic compromises," often do their best to keep union members from discussing the issues of the strike or the details of a proposed settlement at union meetings. So, even here, the individual member begins to experience himself/herself as alone, as unable to really reach out and "be with" the others. And once again a phony group process emerges in which everyone behaves as they are supposed to, both "being a worker on strike" and simultaneously feeling an emptiness and failure to connect with others that is all the more disillusioning because it is so close to being a meaningful experience.

It is partly out of this disillusionment that people feel reluctant to sing their own union songs—because the spirit and the words remind them of the solidarity that they so yearn for and which they feel it is foolish to believe in anymore. So the experience of the strike often leaves people even more despairing about the possibility of real unity, and more convinced than ever that everyone is only out for themselves and that nothing will ever change that.

The feelings of powerlessness that get engendered in this process are carried with workers into their work situations and into the rest of their lives. Their inability to feel powerful or needed or intelligent or competent in their own unions is just one further confirmation of the feelings of self-blame that have already been festering through their experiences at work. Surplus Powerlessness, then, gets reinforced rather than undermined when workers have these kinds of experiences in their unions.

Nor are these feelings confined to the rank and file membership. I have witnessed union locals in which the leadership itself felt totally unable to affect anything that was happening in their International. They were often confused as to the larger policies, and frustrated that they did not have even basic information that they could themselves use to understand union policies.

One classic example occurred in one of the largest locals of the Communication Workers of America. A nationwide strike had been called, then cancelled, then called again. The local president received a call in the middle of the night ordering him to bring out the troops to picket. But he was not informed, nor could he determine through a series of subsequent phone calls, on what issues the negotiations had broken down. He was completely unable to formulate a leaflet explaining the demands of the strike for his membership, and couldn't even answer the most rudimentary questions about what was at stake. So for the first twenty hours of the strike he made himself inaccessible to the membership, embarassed at the way he was being treated and sorry that he couldn't give information to his members. The International then called off the strike, and reached a settlement. But the information was not communicated directly to the union locals. Instead, management people learned about the settlement and its terms first, and then approached union pickets telling them that the strike was over. When the pickets çalled the union office, the leadership called Washington for instructions and was finally told that the settlement had been reached, but not told the terms of the settlement. For several days thereafter it was only management that knew and communicated the terms of the settlement. The frustration the members felt towards their local leaders was mirrored by the anger that the local leaders felt towards the International. This anger had to be skillfully hidden lest the International leadership become estranged from the local and the leader of this local suffer a loss of influence.

Union Leaders

Unfortunately, if we are to understand the dynamics in unions, we must acknowledge how the process of disempowering members sometimes seems to serve the interests of union leaders. There are many union leaders who are quite content to run their union locals or regions as if they were businesses, and to see their members as passive recipients of "benefits" delivered by the leadership and union staffs. Anything that might potentially disrupt the equilibrium established between labor and management, anything that might "politicize" the internal life of the union, is seen as a threat and "disruptive." People who wish to debate politics or to help chart the future directions of their unions are considered "trouble makers," and some of these union leaders are quick to move against them.

The reason for this position on the part of union leaders is not hard to understand. Most of these leaders came off of the shop floors and understand how oppressive the daily work situation really is. The last thing that they want is to create conditions of instability inside the union that might lead to alternative leadership emerging that might challenge them, win an election, and have the current leadership sent back into the jobs they used to hold. It is quite rational from the standpoint of their short-term self-interest to squash this potential opposition before it can become a threat. And what better way than to have institutional forms like boring meetings, a leadership-controlled press, and an ineffective shop steward structure that discourages participation without appearing to be a union policy against participation.

At the same time, many union leaders feel unsupported by the rank and file. Without understanding the consequences of their own behavior, some leaders blame their members for their passivity. It is a fact that in most unions it is a difficult task to just get a quorum at normal monthly meetings, and unions that get 20% of their membership at union meetings are thought to be extraordinarily successful. Without any awareness of the cause, union leaders describe in very discouraged tones how the members don't seem to care about their unions, can never be counted on to participate in anything, and don't even bother to read their own union contracts. The daily experience of "being out there in the trenches by yourself," as one union leader described it to me, created a feeling that the leaders are the only ones who really care, and that the membership is too stupid to really understand all that is being done for them. Many leaders start out as dedicated and idealistic activists who become socialized to the prevailing cynicism in the cadre of professional unionists after years of feeling deserted and uncared for by the rank and file. Few members have ever thanked them for tireless efforts—but only criticized them when something didn't work out. Feeling no solidarity from below, they begin to feel very alone.

It is this sense of isolation and lack of support from the membership that leads leadership to feel justified in many of its moves that might be seen as "conservative" or "manipulative" from the outside. For example, if the membership can't be counted on to even come to meetings, the leadership reasons, it certainly can't be counted on to take the risks involved in a long and militant strike. So, unless the management forces a strike by absolute intransigency on key issues, it makes more sense to make accommodations with management. This is even more the case with issues that seem to affect only a part of the union membership, or with "quality of life" or "social" issues that might in any event be dealt with through the legislative process. So the leadership feels that it has a mandate, stemming from membership passivity, to "play ball" with management in negotiations. This same attitude is reflected in the pursuit of union grievances through the appeals process negotiated in previous contracts: Whatever the injustice facing a specific worker, all the co-workers are encouraged to "calm down" and let the grievance process take its course. The initial anger dwindles, and after months of delays few people care. The union itself has so many of these, and such a small staff that it rarely can become too militant about any given specific. But the individual member, having lost the possibility of real solidarity and joint action from co-workers, now faces his/her issue alone, often disappointed in the union's powerlessness, and so eventually feels distant from the union and sees no reason to attend its meetings—reconfirming the fear of the leadership that no one would be interested should they choose a more militant path.

Both rank and file members and leadership interpret each other's behaviors through the frame of the dominant ideology that tells them that everyone is out for themselves, that idealism is dead, and that the only rational thing to do is to look out for yourself. Each gives up on the other, and proceeds to act accordingly.

The upshot is a tremendous reinforcement of Surplus Powerlessness. The frustrations and feelings of impotence that are generated at work are re-experienced at the union meeting or in one's attempts to get the union to involve itself in changing oppressive work conditions. Unions are the one vehicle that workers created for themselves to deal with changing the larger picture—and yet even here workers feel impotent and useless. Not just because the corporations are stronger and might win in a potential struggle—but because one can't even get co-workers to come to union meetings; one can't even understand what is going on at union meetings; the union seems to be dominated by people who are more interested in their own egos and power than in changing things; and there seems to be no way to control this institution. No wonder so many union members withdraw, give up, and thereby accept the inevitability of their own powerlessness. It is this cynicism about their own unions that plays a critical role in convincing workers that there is nothing that they can do about the world of work, that their best bet is to try to forget about it as quickly as possible, and try to find some compensation for a life being wasted by finding fulfillment in "personal life."

Chapter 5

The Frustration in Family Life

ONE REASON WHY PEOPLE DON'T GET MORE UPSET ABOUT the pain of work is because they tend to accept the myth that Personal Life will make up for it all. Personal Life will be their compensation for the frustration of work, for the powerlessness they experience in their unions and in the political arena, and for the absence of any larger sense of purpose and meaning in life. "Don't worry about this area of Public Life," we are told, "because you can't expect anything in that sphere. But there will be a magical reward, a terrific Relationship that will make up for all your other deprivations."

The locus of the fantasy that someone will come along and make everything OK changes with age. In the teen years, it tends to be identified with movie stars, sports heroes, rock musicians, or "Miss Wonderful" or "Mr. Right." In the years of early adulthood it tends to be identified with a partner or series of partners. In the thirties and sometimes early forties it can be identified with actual or possible children. The content of the fantasy, however, remains constant. We are going to have a very deep and meaningful relationship with some person who will make the pain go away, who will make up for all the crap we have had to suffer through in the rest of our lives. There are wide varieties in the forms of relationships that different people seek to fulfill the fantasy. Some people seek one permanent commitment, others have a series of monogamous relationships, others build gay or lesbian relationships, others are involved in single parenting, and others are involved in some forms of communal child-rearing. But whatever the form through which the relationship is sought, there is little difference between all these very different lifestyles in terms of the role the relationship plays in the conscious and unconscious fantasy life of people in this society. People deeply believe that Personal Life will make up for everything else that is so frustrating and unfulfilling, that it will be a "safe space," a "haven in a heartless world," a "shelter from the storm," a place unaffected by the cruelty and insensitivity that surrounds us all day in the world of work.

In the years 1977–85 researchers at the Institute for Labor and Mental Health interviewed several thousand working people from a wide variety of work situations, representing a cross-section of workers in manufacturing, transportation, service, government, high technology, and educational enterprises. These were people whose lives were not "in crisis." They were workers who were facing the normal stresses of the work world, and they came to us only after we had engaged in extensive work to assure them that this was not a service for "people in trouble," but for people facing the normal stresses at work. What we discovered was that there is a very widespread pain in Personal Life, a pain that pervades thousands of families whose outward appearance is often very much that of a family which has no problems and is working very well. Beneath the surface, we found that in these "normal families" the level of pain was quite intense.

The fantasy of finding a haven in Personal Life is rarely fulfilled. Most people end up with relationships which do not meet these expectations. For a variety of reasons which we shall explore in this chapter, most people in this society fail to find the magical relationship that will compensate for the alienation of the world of work and the frustrations of the public world. But instead of understanding the way that the original fantasy could not be fulfilled, they then turn on themselves. Most frequently they see themselves as having failed, and feel terrible about themselves. The self-blaming that had been taking place all day in the world of work is now massively reinforced by self-blaming about their failures to create for themselves the kind of compensation that they fantasize is available to people who deserve to have a good life. Here again they typically see themselves as the kind of people who don't deserve to succeed or "win." They perceive their powerlessness as fitting and an inevitable result of who they are as persons. In their frustration, they become angry at their spouses, lovers, children, parents—but ultimately these are most typically manifestations of a deeper level of anger at themselves. Without any social perspective on their individual experience, they come to see themselves as the source of their own continuing failures and unhappiness—and conclude that they have neither the right to complain nor the right to expect that anything will be different for them in their lives. And this set of feelings eventually leads to a sense of resignation and a personal politic of powerlessness and passivity.

Bringing Stress Home

Most people spend most of their waking hours at work and in transit to and from work. It should be no surprise, then, that the ways people come to feel about themselves at work, the sense of powerlessness, frustration, and self-blame that we described in earlier chapters, has a deep and profound impact on how they feel about themselves in their remaining waking hours when they are not at work. The stress that they experience in the work world and the self-blaming that typically accompanies it, cannot be taken off like so many dirty clothes and thrown into the washing machine, while the real self suddenly emerges untainted and undisturbed.

People typically return home from work feeling tense, often upset, sometimes depressed, almost always with a deep sense of frustration at what they perceive as their own failure to create a fulfilling life for themselves. They blame themselves for the frustrations at work. They are often filled with rage that has had to be suppressed all day and they are often afraid that this rage might get out of hand. They suspect that their anger is itself proof that they deserve the pain of their lives. Typically, these feelings are layered over by a surface level of calm and relief at getting home. Most workers attempt to present themselves as not "letting it get to them." They try to pretend that they are unaffected by stupid bosses, arrogant supervisors, new techniques or processes that they aren't quite sure they can master and feel they must, sales that didn't go through, people whom they aren't sure they have impressed enough, co-workers with whom they must compete for praise or promotions, changes in the economy that may make their product less desirable, or people whom they work with who aren't doing their part of the work competently and who thereby make it harder for everyone else. "Oh no—nothing is going to get to us—we can just leave it all at work." Most frequently I found that people don't want to know about the psychic costs of work, or even begin to think about them. They tell themselves that all this can be quickly forgotten in some form of "relaxation" at home.

Some people are so successful in building a set of psychic defenses around themselves that they're literally unaware of the tensions that they bring home. They seem completely unbothered by their own powerlessness. As we mentioned above, these people often end up in their late forties and early fifties suffering from chronic stress-related illnesses. Other people show nothing more than a slight feeling of being tired or without energy. But these are the exceptions. Most workers do have more obvious ways that the stress shows up in their lives. Their fierce though often unconscious struggle to repress the pain and anger and self-blaming that they have experienced all day is not quite working. They try a wide variety of strategies to bury these feelings and keep themselves unaware of the huge burden they are bringing home into their Personal Life. Among these strategies are the following activities:

• People try to bury their pain through watching tv. Nothing seems to do it quite as well as tv. People are able to sit and watch program after program, sometimes allowing themselves to experience some limited set of feelings evoked by the programs, but mostly numbing themselves to all feelings. The rapid succession of programs does not allow for time to reflect or get too deeply attached to the meanings and feelings of any one program. The rapid pace in each particular show forces them to pay so much attention to what is happening that there is no chance to distance, to think, to deeply feel. The beauty, the vivid colors, the quick movements, the rapid succession of images—all help to recreate a world of fantasy within which non-work hours can be lived. The narcotizing effect is powerful. People can escape the self-paralyzing feelings they have brought home from work by living through this new fantasy world.*

• People also use alcohol or drugs—the "royal road" to forgetting the frustrations at work. Alcohol and drugs deaden the pain, suppress the memories, and create a new emotional reality based on artificial stimulations. The importance of these narcotics lies precisely in their ability to contain the anger that we feel at our world and at ourselves. The narcotic allows us to let the feelings pass, and inclines us to pretend that the pain and anger are gone.

Sometimes the narcotics or alcohol are not strong enough to repress the feelings of anger and pain. They come out anyway. But in this situation, we can blame the outbursts of anger on the drug or alcohol. "It wasn't me who said all those things—I was drunk, I was stoned, and it was the substance that took me over." This is a frequently used strategy by people who are terrified of their own real feelings, and who think that their anger is further confirmation of "how bad" they really are. They can release the anger but blame the drug or alcohol. Similarly, there may be secondary gains of this sort when a person moves from light or social drinking to overt alcohol abuse. The sense of failure that many people have about their work life and

---

* When we understand the role television plays in helping us avoid painful and oppressive reality, we can get a deeper understanding of the tastes of consumers. TV producers often justify the mindlessness and superficiality of their shows by claiming that they are merely responding to the desires of the audience. "People," they tell us, "simply won't watch shows that are too deep and serious. So we give them what they want." The tv apologists are partially correct—because people do want a tv reality that provides an escape from their oppressive reality. When faced with the choice of being re-presented with the same realities and understandings that they have been dealing with all day, or escaping into fantasy, people often will choose fantasy. But the reason for that is partially the fault of the tv programming itself. TV could present the world not as fixed and given, but as open and possibly changeable. In doing so, it could enter a different kind of fantasy—a fantasy about how the world could look if people were to act powerfully and with a full sense of their own right to control their destiny. This fantasy would present reality as it actually is—but then emphasize the potentialities for how things could be different, and how people have succeeded in the past in actually changing things. TV could tell true stories about how people have actually succeeded in changing reality. When it has tried to do so, as e.g., in the show *Roots* about slavery in the U.S., it has usually managed to attract massive audiences. But if the choice is between retelling the story of daily life with all the despair and cynicism that people normally experience there and a choice of escaping into some kind of mindless fantasy, people often and not surprisingly choose the world of fantasy, because they already have enough of a picture of how hard life is, and if tv is not going to provide new hope, then at least it can provide narcotizing escapes. While the elitists like to conclude that people's choice of tv shows how stupid the public is, the truth is that such choices only show how beaten down most people are and how desperate to forget.

their family life may now be attributed to the alcohol or drug—"My life is a failure because I became an alcoholic." This attribution, difficult as it is, sometimes feels safer to some people who would otherwise attribute their failure to their own personal failings as a person (given their persistent belief that the world is a Meritocracy and that they should have done better).

Ironically, those who try to combat alcoholism or drug abuse often engage in therapies that are aimed at reinforcing the very dynamics that led to the abuse in the first place. Patients are taught to "take responsibility" for their addictions, and take charge of their lives. While this may sometimes work to cure the abuser of drugs or alcohol, it actually tends to reinforce the underlying dynamics that led to the alcohol or drugs in the first place. Denying the social roots of our personal problems thus leads to an ongoing drama in which one attempt to bury the pain may fail, and will then be replaced by some other denial mechanism. Of course, getting people away from addiction is a valuable thing to do—but to the extent that the method reinforces the underlying dynamic, we have little reason to be hopeful that other self-destructive behaviors will not recur at later points.

● People sometimes engage in frenetic activity in sports, religion, politics. Too often these activities serve a destructive function for working people because they are used as ways of escape from the feelings of pain of the world of work. This is particularly true of people who throw themselves into these activities, allowing their entire emotional lives to be consumed and leaving no space for reflection, self-introspection, or time to calm themselves down from the stresses of the work world. Many people feel that their athletic programs are forms of stress reduction. They will report that their jogging, bowling, baseball, political meetings, PTA, scouts, or church activities actually serve to calm them down. For some this may be true, but for many more all they do is divert attention from the pains of the work world. The pains don't go away; they persist and function on an unconscious level. They will sometimes re-emerge in the form of aggressive competitiveness with other people. The anger that they have felt all day at work gets directed at the "opponent" on the sports field, the "politically misdirected foe," or the "Russians who are about to invade us," or some religious grouping that doesn't share our approach and is therefore "keeping us all from salvation." In this way these frenetic activities allow some people to remain completely out of touch with their underlying feelings of anger and upset, and still let some of them out through a symbolic acting out of aggression. While this displacement of aggressive feelings may sometimes seem safe (e.g., when we are cheering on a particular sports team), they are not so safe when they begin to shape what candidates we back for office, what foreign policy we support, or what religious groups we revile. Nor are they safe when they get played out in the form of angry hostilities in our churches or schools or community organizations, when one group pushes for its policy with a level of insensitivity that tramples on all others around them. Yet because we are expecting people to have magically transcended the anger and frustration at work, we act surprised when it shows up in church or politics or social life, and then see this as somehow confirming our worst fears that everyone around us is just naturally bad or aggressive.

• They try sexual "acting out" or "profligacy." The decline of rigid standards of sexual behavior has had mixed results. On the one hand, sexual experimentation has permitted many people to try "living together." Sexual contact before marriage gives them a much better idea of their potential compatibility. The rejection of notions that implied sex was "dirty" or was solely for procreation has created a potential for new levels of pleasure and freedom. On the other hand, sexuality itself has become a new form of escape from feelings generated in the world of work. At work itself people spend a huge amount of time fantasizing about sex so that they can avoid thinking about how unfulfilling their work feels. Then they return into Personal Life with the hope that a myriad of sexual experiences will drown out the pain and frustration of their working lives.

Through an endless and all-consuming quest for new social alliances and sexual conquests, the emotionally battered worker seeks to forget about the daily assaults on his/her dignity and worth at work. Whether it be through illicit affairs, or through an endless sequence of new sexual connections, or through nightly partying in the search of Mr. or Ms. Right, the worker experiences a pseudo liberation that would be more real if a deep emotional contact with other human beings could be made. That contact is precluded by a desperation generated in part by the feelings that one is wasting one's life at work, so one must find some peak satisfaction immediately and constantly in "Personal Life." Yet ironically the very pain that one seeks to escape guarantees failure by making sex incomplete and unfulfilling.

It follows that those who are most interested in creating a deeper level of sexual morality than is available in contemporary society would do better by spending their energies on trying to reshape the social world in such a way that people had real satisfactions available to them in the world of work than by crusading against the moral profligacy of individuals. While the sexual crusaders are right, I believe, in arguing that divorcing sexuality from love and commitment and a sense of the sanctity of other people is a destructive path, they could actually change things if they joined with forces that seek to democratize and humanize the world of work. Similarly, it follows that those who believe that sexuality is not fully experienced on deep levels in this society would be more effective in promoting satisfying sex if they were to devote their attention to changing aspects of the society that lead people to the need to repress their own feelings and to be out of touch with their bodies—of which stress at work is certainly primary.

My main point, however, is this: tv, alcohol, drugs, sports, frenetic activity in politics and religion, and frenetic sex have in common the function of providing ways for people to stay out of touch with pain and anger and self-blaming that they have experienced all day at work. But, precisely because these activities work in keeping us out of touch with these painful feelings, they also work to ensure that our personal lives will be unfulfilling and fail to provide us with compensation. If what we hope for are fulfilling relationships, they can only be built through deep connection and communication. But what all these "Personal Life" activities do is to keep us further out of touch with our feelings, and thus to perpetuate the suppression of our emotional realities that we were engaged in all day at work. The huge emotional energy that gets put into repressing the alienation, self-blaming and anger that we experienced at work leaves us too little energy to develop emotional connectedness. Equally important, when we have shaped ourselves into the kinds of people who are regularly out of touch with our feelings, we simply don't have the skills to suddenly jump into a whole different kind of consciousness and be loving and open and honest partners in relationships.

The narcotizing activities may succeed in temporarily cutting us off from the seething feeling of anger and upset, but most people discover that these feelings cannot be permanently repressed. The anger and frustration eventually builds up and explodes into personal life in destructive ways.

Frequently this happens when one is engaged in an argument with a spouse, lover or a child. Suddenly, what might otherwise have been a little issue is blown out of proportion. There is a sudden eruption of anger, sometimes in the form of unnecessarily yelling, sometimes in the form of a swift slap to their child, sometimes in the form of a sudden withdrawal and turning away from a loved one. It is important to emphasize that these behaviors may occur in contexts in which people have legitimate gripes. Perhaps their partner wasn't adequately sensitive to their needs, or disappointed their expectations. Perhaps their child didn't do the chores or left a mess, or didn't heed instructions, or acted disrespectfully. But the response is all out of proportion to the actual offense—and a small thing is blown up to a large incident.

The first few times this happens there is usually no serious damage. But as instances of inappropriate levels of anger begin to accumulate, the other parties involved begin to back off, to be less trusting, more fearful, and less open. Spouses begin to wonder if they need to be on emotional guard, ready to ward off assault. Children begin to keep some distance, fearful of overreaction to any misdeed they might commit. Gradually, patterns of defensive interaction begin to dominate relationships—partners become wary that something will go wrong, that they need to be on their guard. The emotional armoring that has been built up at work becomes necessary protection for domestic war.

People whose anger tends to explode inappropriately are as much unsettled by the experience as their family. Typically, neither they nor their family have any social perspective on their anger. They view it as an individual problem, a failure to adjust to reality. Workers who have been fearful of their anger become even more scared of themselves. They don't want their personal lives to fall apart. They will make even more frantic attempts to narcotize themselves to hold things in check. Or they will make greater efforts to "work on themselves" through psychotherapy, religious discipline, meditation or Eastern body disciplines. Their goal, supposedly, is to suppress or dissolve the anger, which is seen as an irrational and destructive element in one's personality. Rarely is there any recognition that the anger is merely the deflection of feelings that have been generated in the world of work, feelings that may have been perfectly appropriate in their original context, though too dangerous to be expressed without loss of job.

People who are trying to hold their feelings in check are apt to be blocked when it comes to making deep emotional contact with their spouses. Their spouses are seeking to have them be "open" and available—and yet this is the last thing that stressed-out workers want to do, because they fear that the only emotions that would pour out were they to be open would be these feelings of anger that they are doing their best to keep under control.

There is another source of being "cut off" from feelings that has become increasingly important in the last third of the 20th Century. We have a growing sector of workers whose primary task in the world of work is to sell themselves and their products. To make themselves into attractive commodities, they must carefully study the latest trends and fads in their fields, and then look and act in the "appropriate" way. There are scores of self-help books selling millions of copies, each aimed at telling people how to become the kind of person whom others will like and hence reward. The person on his/her way up in the corporate world is continually in competition with others who might sell themselves better. But this same dynamic increasingly dominates the lives of lawyers, doctors, mental health professionals, real estate and insurance agents, managerial personnel, clergy, teachers, college professors, people in the field of publishing, media, and government as well. As people come to look at themselves from this external perspective, to tailor their attitudes and lifestyles to fit their needs for success, they become increasingly alienated from themselves and their own feelings. Their daily reality of trying to "make it" forces them into a competitive and distrustful mode with everyone around them. But at an even deeper level, they are alienated from themselves, their own real needs. They have become so externally attached to becoming pleasing and satisfying the needs of others that they are at a loss to find their own inner selves.

Ironically, these people turn out to be very fixated in their private lives on finding personal satisfaction. Many run from one relationship to another, or from one fantasy escape to another. One year it is organic gardening and the next it is jogging, then onto aerobics and from there to gourmet cooking, then onto some new therapy or self-help transformation or new spiritual discipline. They have been described as narcissistic personalities by those familiar with some of the characteristics of clinical narcissism, but most only partially fit into this characterization. What they mostly share is a deep and abiding trouble with intimacy. They are afraid of getting close to others and afraid that they will be swallowed up by others should they do so. But this fear, while in some cases rooted in childhood experiences, is most often a product of their acute sensitivity to the reality of the economic world in which they live. Their fear of intimacy is not just paranoia—it is the correct perception that in the world in which they live a lot of other people actually would take advantage of them, use any opportunity in which they showed themselves as weak as a potential weapon in the ongoing struggle for "success" and "making it" in the world of work. So when people buy books like *Winning Through Intimidation,* and *Looking Out For No. 1* they are not doing so out of some childhood narcissistic fixation, but out of a correct understanding of the world that they must live in.

But people who come out of this kind of a work situation are very poor candidates for intimacy. How can they suddenly be expected to drop all the defensive moves and the paranoid postures that serve them so well in the world of work? How can we expect someone who looks at him/herself as a commodity to suddenly be in touch with the real self and share it with others? It is not so much that this kind of person resists intimacy as that he or she doesn't know what it is, does not know how to get in touch with him/herself, and hence can only act sincerely puzzled when their partner demands a truer and closer level of connection. Therapists have often acted astonished at the difficulty in breaking through to these people, and the label "narcissism" is used as often as a justification for the therapists' inability to make deep contact. But there would be no astonishment if we understood how the very behavior which is destructive to closeness and undermines the possibility of deep and committed relationships is the very behavior which gets strongly rewarded in the corporate, governmental and professional sectors of the world of work.

Difficulty in being close to family members—whether it be through destructive outbursts of anger, through withdrawal, or by not knowing how to be intimate—creates a legacy of pain and frustration in family life. Over time many relationships become deeply troubled as emotional contact becomes more shallow.

Of course there are people who are able to make the huge leaps that take them from the consciousness of the world of work into the reality of an emotionally deep personal life. This is not logically impossible. But the amount of energy required for this is usually not available, and the people who are best able to do this are those whose work world and class position drain them the least. For most of the rest of us, the degree of emotional realness and deep contact in relationships is far less than either partner really desires or needs.

It would be inaccurate to characterize all family relationships as unhappy. There is a vast spectrum of relationships in this society, and it varies from those that are extremely happy to those that are literally falling apart. But the vast majority are on the part of the spectrum in which there are some joys but also a very large amount of pain, disappointment and frustration. I know these words seem to overplay the reality. But that is because most people have come to expect that they will feel high levels of pain in their lives, because that's the kind of people they are. They feel that it is foolish or self-indulgent to complain. But when they tell their stories, over and over one hears the unmistakable cries of despair of a population that feels lonely and isolated and without hope even in its most intimate relationships.

In this society there are millions of families who appear to be functioning in a perfectly happy way, but who in fact are suffering from loneliness and isolation. This is one of society's most closely guarded secrets—but it can be discovered by talking to large numbers of people in an atmosphere in which they feel safe. In every sector of this society people feel desperately alone, unhappy, and despairing about their family lives—and also terrible about themselves for feeling this way, convinced that their own failure here is much greater than that of others, and hence committed to portraying themselves as having a perfectly wonderful family life to all the other people around them.

The phoniness and need to portray everything as "just fine" is not confined to the people outside the family either. The cover up of pain in family life would never work if it were simply a conscious form of deceit. The rifts and isolation in families do not appear dramatically one day—they are the products of a gradual and ongoing process that also has moments of real connectedness and transcendence. For that very reason, the moments of real connection can be used to hide from oneself the larger pattern of despair and isolation. And even as this forces itself on one's consciousness, the self-blaming involved leads to new forms of denial. "It isn't really happening—it's just me," is one of the most typical methods of coping. This in turn may lead some people to doubt their own sanity—"I must be crazy to feel so isolated here, when everyone else seems to be acting like things are fine." Or it may lead to people thinking "I'd better not ruin things for everyone else by acting as though I'm not really satisfied." Or to a feeling of deep despair, "No matter what is really going on, I'm just the kind of person who is never going to be satisfied, so I might as well pretend that everything is fine and just go along with things as they are." What typically results from this and other strategies of denial is the creation of a set of phony and self-denying reactions, in which each person in a relationship tries to act in the ways that s/he thinks the other people in the family are expecting him/her to act. Through denying their own needs and their own perceptions, they manage to "keep things together." And because each person experiences everyone else as holding up their side of the bargain, it feels far too dangerous to admit into their consciousness feelings and thoughts that might upset the apple cart. When such feelings crop up, they are quickly dismissed as some form of disloyalty to the collective falseness.

This commitment to a false unity based on each person's fear of discovering his or her own needs to be unmet in the family is nevertheless not sufficient to keep everything running smoothly. It is the rare family that does not face some way in which the phoniness is broken through, even though usually in ways that allow people to ignore the larger problems. Families fight—and the fights are rarely about the underlying sets of disappointments. Or families have children who suddenly do some remarkably irrational acts—like shoplifting, setting fires, or getting into drugs or promiscuous sex. The child is doing his/her best to express the feeling that "not everything is OK," and perhaps even to force a more intense level of emotional honesty by modeling what real problems look like. Or a teenager gets pregnant, or does poorly in school, or picks on a younger sibling—all as inarticulate ways to say to the family: "Things aren't really OK here, so why must everyone keep on pretending?" Or the perfect family is hiding a parent who has become addicted to drugs, tranquilizers, or alcohol, or a parent who is acting out violence towards spouse or children, either overtly, or through sexual abuse of children. No matter how perfect the family next door seems to appear, my research convinces me that there's a very good chance that precisely the families that appear most together are very troubled.

It would be foolish to argue that all families share all these dynamics to the same extent. There is a wide variability in family life. And there are ways that some families have managed to escape these dynamics. Not every workplace is equally stressful. Not every person has equally bought into the idea of the Meritocracy. Some people have had the benefit of political activism, the women's movement, or other experiences that help them understand that personal problems are often a reflection of social realities and not their own faults. Some people have learned better than others how to deal with their anger—and not to fear it. Some couples have learned to recognize that the tensions they generate are often a reflection of external realities—so they can have a good fight, and then use that as a springboard to deeper levels of intimacy. Some families are rooted in ethnic minority cultures in which they have learned to recognize the phoniness of the dominant culture, and are able to use that sense of the difference between appearance and reality as a frame through which they can understand their own tendencies towards falseness in family life. Some families have learned how to consciously process their own developments—so that when there is a tendency towards withdrawal and hiddenness, it can be recognized and named without causing fear and emotional hiding. These are all important qualifications on all that has been said, and they pull for the need to recognize the richness and diversity in family life.

But while there is great variety in family life, and while the dynamics I have described apply differently and to different extents in different families, there is nevertheless a very widely shared reality of pain in family life that is usually underplayed or acknowledged in the same passing way that I have acknowledged the mitigating factors in the previous paragraph. The central dynamic facing American families is the wide range of pain they face, and the fact that underlying much of this pain is a set of emotional dynamics that has been generated in the world of work and then brought home. The way that people have been shaped all day in the world of work has a profound impact on how they will be in their family life. It is unrealistic to expect that these dynamics can be overcome through individual or family therapy—they require, instead, a massive restructuring of the world of work. And a first step in that is for us to recognize how the pain, rather than being a badge of individual shame and failure, is a reflection of a social reality we did not construct and which we as individuals cannot change without the creation of a very large movement for social change.

The Isolation of Families

Most people deeply believe that it is only their own personal family life that has not been working and that most other people around them are really doing much better. A major source of this misconception is the social isolation of families.

People usually have very little idea of what is happening in the emotional lives of families around them. The emergence of isolated families is a rela-

nt phenomenon—200 years ago most people lived in rural commu-
ch were small enough so that family secrets were the exception.
ler communities, however, existed in a social order whose moral
standa.. s were dictated, often rigidly, by a ruling class operating through
a powerful church organization. Many people experienced the tight-knit
existence of these small communities as oppressive, and sought liberation in
the anonymity of the larger towns and cities that developed with industrialization. In comparison with a lifestyle based on restrictive morality that imposed a "right way" for almost every situation, the solitude and being-left-
alone quality of the cities seemed welcome relief.

But that freedom was deceptive. A new kind of coercion was created, the
coercion of the marketplace. Individuals were still forced to sell their labor
power to those with wealth and power, only there was a deceptive veil of
"individual choice." Similarly, in matters of consumption, there was the false
illusion of the power of the individual consumer. The alternatives were still
limited, and, in the modern period, sophisticated advertising strategies have
helped shape consumers who would want whatever products the powerful
corporations could dream up.

This illusion of freedom is particularly important for understanding why
working people continued to put up with oppression in the world of work.
As people increasingly buy into the notion that freedom can be obtained in
personal life, they are willing to put up with alienation and pain at work, so
long as it generates an income that can be used to buy compensation in
private life. It is here, supposedly, in one's role as a consumer, that one will
experience "real power." So work isn't so important—it should be seen merely
as enabling you to get to what is really important, the sphere of personal
consumption.

If real freedom is to be found in consumption, then, according to this
logic, the more goods, the freer one becomes. So individual households begin
to accumulate more and more, and to depend less and less on friends and
neighbors for services. The market gears its products to create independent
households that will be totally self-sufficient and workers begin to see themselves as more powerful the less they have to depend on others. Families
have less and less common time with other families. Increasingly, they use
products that make their own family allegedly self-sufficient. It seems like
freedom. It is a welcome relief from the long hours of work in which there
is no opportunity to be anything but the way others want them to be.

Television, home computers and videos continue to augment the illusion
of freedom. They do away with the need for contact with others for entertainment and fun. There is no need to depend on others or to subject oneself
to others' expectations or needs. This is welcome relief for many who have
come to believe that they have very little to offer. They are reluctant to make
themselves available to others who might "discover" them to be the failures
they already "know" themselves to be. Given the psycho-dynamics of self-
blaming, interaction with others is filled with tensions. We must always be
on our guard that we don't let show who we "really" are, lest they find us
as unattractive as we find ourselves. No wonder, then, that we feel "more at

home" by ourselves or with our families than we do with friends or neighbors with whom we are constantly having to pretend to be other than we feel ourselves to be. Television lets us have contact with the rest of the world without letting it have contact with us. And a mere switch on the channel gives us a new sense of power and ability to determine what our lives will be like. It is precisely this feeling of pseudo-power that plays along with the narcotizing effects of tv, making tv an effective counter to the pain of the world of work.

There is a heavy price to be paid, however. Television gives us a false picture of the emotional realities facing other people's lives. The primary models for family problems are presented in a format which enables them to be resolved within a 27½ minute time frame. Even the more "serious" programs typically have endings in which things have been neatly worked out and resolved—completely unlike life itself, where the problems are on-going. Moreover, the content of programs rarely emphasizes the relationship between pain in family life and pain at work—so even when individuals are beginning to make those associations about their own lives they will tend to feel isolated and alone on this issue—because work doesn't seem such an issue for others.

When people compare their own lives to those of families on tv, the most typical conclusion is that their own problems are worse than "average." Most people realize, of course, that the families they see aren't quite real. But they nevertheless come away feeling badly about themselves. Even when people on tv are portrayed as having real problems, the problems are usually defined one-dimensionally. Yet most people watching see their own anger, their own frustrations, their own complicated sets of self-perceived failures as much deeper and much less likely to be solved than those they see portrayed on tv. They may recognize that other people have problems too, and even serious problems (like those portrayed in dramas about drugs or alcohol). But they see their own lives as even more messed up, more entangled, and solutions less accessible than those that get presented within the short television time frame.

Yet this is increasingly the primary way that people learn about what is happening in other families—through tv. And as we become convinced that our own problems are deeper and harder to deal with than others, we are more reluctant to talk honestly about what is really going on—even to our friends and neighbors. The circle of self-blame and isolation is easy to understand: (1.) We feel that we are really the cause of our own problems. So if we tell our neighbors or friends about our pain, we are really telling them about our failures. And what, exactly, are they supposed to do—except to feel pity for us for being such failures? So, we reason, what good is their pity—it only makes us feel worse about ourselves. Better not to even start telling them about our experiences, because all that can do is lead us to feel all the worse about ourselves. (2.) We don't want to be a burden to others. It's bad enough that we haven't gotten our own lives together—at least we can deal with the mess ourselves. Why should we expect others to take care of us just because our lives aren't working? We think we have no right to impose on them. (3.) And they won't even want to hear about our problems—

they will be polite, but they will feel burdened by hearing our story. After all, they, like us, have bought into the model of freedom as isolation and non-dependence on others, so anything that we do that might be suggestive of our need for their help may itself cause them to flee even further from us, because our neediness could be a new form of enslavement of them. We know that we wouldn't want others to become dependent on us, so we protect them from our neediness by presenting ourselves as "just fine." (4.) But since each other family thinks the same set of things, each family tries to present to the world its best appearance. The result is a society filled with families that are in deep pain, each one presenting itself to all others as though things were going great. Each time people speak of their personal lives with friends and neighbors and keep it at a relatively "safe" level of distance and emotional unreality, the other people in the conversation are reconfirmed in their belief that nothing is really seriously wrong in anyone's life but their own, or that talking about these issues would be unwelcome and threatening to the people that they care about.

In an earlier chapter I argued that real social support depends on the ability to undermine self-blaming. Yet the isolation of families is both a result of pervasive self-blaming and simultaneously contributes to strengthening that self-blaming. The upshot is that we have a society that is rich in the fabric of social life, with endless groups that get together to provide social contacts, in the context of churches, schools, sports, aerobics and exercises, politics, charities, civic organizations, unions, social change organizations, camping and vacationing. But with all this social mixing, there is amazingly little deep emotional contact, amazingly little sharing of the real stories about daily life and daily pains that break through the shared falseness, and hence amazingly little social support. I believe that the impulse that people have to participate so much in these myriad forms of social and community life stems from a deep desire to have contact, and is a manifestation of reaching out to others. But the ideological hold of self-blaming is so powerful that people are often unable to take the decisive step to transform the context of being with other people into a context in which they can talk honestly about the things that are really happening—including the pain that they bring with them.

The upshot is that each family, no matter how deeply enmeshed in social networks, is forced to deal with its problems by itself, and in the process each family comes to believe that its problems are potentially worse than those of most other people who are even vaguely comparable (sure, there are other people who are worse off, but not people who in other respects are like them). The result is an intensification of self-blaming.

Nor should we expect that these dynamics are significantly different in non-traditional families. Gay families, single-parent families, even communes manage to recreate the same set of expectations: that in these alternative forms there will be the kind of humane relating that isn't available elsewhere in the society. By abstracting what happens in family life from the context in which the family members live most of their days, the competitive and alienating and oppressive realities of the world of work, this expectation can then fuel the same disappointments as face any traditional family. The idea that people can simply rearrange their family forms and thereby escape the massive impact of the rest of the society is naive. We should expect just as many shattered families, just as much unhappiness, just as much a sense of alienation in any of these non-traditional arrangements—as long as the people who are in them are subjected to the crippling dynamics of the world of work each day and as long as they have no clear sense of how their intimate lives are likely to be misshaped and undermined by the inevitable legacy of daily life in a world of oppression.

The isolation of families from each other could be overcome. It is possible to create a movement within which families begin to meet with each other, to share with each other the real stories about the problems and upsets, the pains and joys, that each has been experiencing. Just as the women's movement in the 1960s created a safe atmosphere within which women who had felt isolated and competitive with each other began to break down their barriers and talk deeply about shared problems and frustrations and pain, it is possible to create a societal context within which people could begin to talk honestly with each other about the pains in their family lives. We shall discuss how this might work in the section on strategies towards the end of this book, but for now we must only note that as long as this isolation persists, the fundamental process of self-blaming will continue to have a powerful hold and, with it, the dynamics of Surplus Powerlessness will remain intact.

Breakdown of Communities of Meaning

The fantasy that Personal Life could compensate for the alienation and oppression that people experience in their work is historically recent. The creation of a "personal sphere" apart from work could only have relevance to working people who have time off from work. When people worked from dawn to dusk on the farms of landlords or small family farms, or when they spent every waking moment in mines or factories, there was little sense in the idea that life at home was going to make everything OK. But as working people began to organize themselves and win struggles to limit the power of landowners and bosses, the sphere of non-work time gradually increased, and the powerful could try to convince the powerless not to struggle in the sphere of work but to save their energy so that they could enjoy themselves in the private sphere where their true humanity could flourish.

The locus of this fantasy—the Family—becomes the center of attention and concern. It should be no surprise to us that the Family assumes this special importance as a vehicle for true fulfillment not to be found in the world of work. This expectation is built on the reality that families have been around for thousands of years, and they have traditionally been the place within which non-market values have predominated. Whatever the failings of any specific family, the Family is the only institution whose fundamental mission has been to provide nurturance and support. So if people were now going to seek someplace where they might find a counter-weight to the exploitative and dog-eat-dog values of the marketplace, wouldn't the Family be a logical place to look? Given this reasoning, it was only a short step to the growing emphasis on Family as the place where we will be able to provide a sense of purpose and goal that we cannot find in the world of work. Hasn't the Family always served this function?

Not exactly. To understand the qualifications on our answer, we must think about the family historically. It is true that families have been an important part of providing emotional nurturance and support. But it is also important to understand that families were almost always quite different from the contemporary nuclear family. Families were typically multigenerational, and the burden of child rearing and the domestic work, the responsibilities of caring for the sick and the elderly, were all distributed amongst this much larger family unit. Nurturance was usually defined in behavioral terms, not in the expectation that one could satisfy all the emotional needs and desires that arose. Moreover, the sets of emotional needs and needs for intimacy were themselves socially shaped, so that expectations of what was possible or desirable in these spheres were often quite less developed than we see in the contemporary family.

Equally important, the family was embedded in larger communities, and many of the experiences of daily life, from childbirth to death, family quarrels and family choices, were themselves shared and shaped by these larger communities. Nor were these larger communities simply aggregations of people "living nearby," as one might expect in a city neighborhood today. They were part of a shared "community of meaning," a community of people who shared common values and goals, hopes and fears, symbols and rituals.

It was these communities of meaning that gave purpose and shape to the individual family. Whether the community was defined primarily in terms of religion, or politics, or social change goals, or defense of workers' rights, they shared important elements: a sense of what was right and wrong; a moral ordering of the universe within which any particular choice or situation could be evaluated; a set of rituals and symbols that could express the common understandings about the nature of the universe and one's place within it; a shared vocabulary for making sense of things; and a common agreement that people would support each other in creating a world that corresponded to these shared visions.*

Individual families were not seen as the purpose of life, nor did anyone suppose that an individual relationship made sense by itself. Rather, families and relationships were consecrated and given meaning precisely to the extent

---

* I do not mean to idealize these pre-capitalist societies as "good old days." The specific content of these communities was shaped by the current levels of knowledge and superstition, the ways that people had learned to treat each other in a feudal society, and the continuing problems of material scarcity. In this frame, village life sometimes involved persecution of witches, smoldering family feuds, backbiting gossip, envy and jealousy of one's neighbors, fear of the unconventional and lack of knowledge about the outside world. Just as the call for full employment is consistent with the call for meaningful work, so the call for communities of meaning is consistent with the creation of new kinds of communities other than the oppressive ones that existed in the Middle Ages.

that they were seen as vital parts of a larger and non-family-based vision. A family got its purpose by virtue of its relationship to this larger community of meaning. The family would raise children who could then enter into this larger community, and the community would support that venture because the children were seen as part of the ongoing life of the community. Life's hardships and defeats were absorbed and interpreted in terms of the community's goals, and the defeats and disappointments in each family were shared by the community as its own problems and not just "personal problems."

The breakdown of these larger communities of meaning is a process that has developed over the course of the past six hundred years, gradually accelerating to a point where it has been an avalanche in the 20th Century. An important reason for this breakdown has been the emergence of a new view about what is important in life, a view which has stressed individual freedom and liberty. This view, in turn, has been largely the product of the bourgeoisie: the small shopkeepers, traders and money lenders of the late Middle Ages who gradually rose to power, became consolidated as a new class, and eventually succeeded in overthrowing the power of more traditional societies. This development helped create a new way of looking at things, in which community supports began to be experienced by people more as constraints than as assistance.

Of course, it would be an exaggeration to say that these communities of meaning have been totally eliminated. People couldn't give them up because they supplied too many good things. But there has been a steady erosion of their power and influence, and increasingly they become merely adjuncts to personal life rather than the defining feature of life.

The breakdown of these communities of meaning has not occurred simply because people decided that they wanted more freedom to define life for themselves. If that were all that was at stake, we might have expected older community forms to fall apart, only to be replaced by less coercive and more voluntary communities created by newly liberated groups of people. To some extent this has happened. The wide variety of voluntary associations in modern America testify to the fact that the communitarian urge has not been totally suppressed or forgotten.

. People do need each other, want contact with each other, and seek ways to achieve it. But a major force pushing towards the dissolution of these connections between people has been the logic of the economic marketplace. People were encouraged to see themselves as independent entrepreneurs in the economic marketplace, each one selling his wares to the highest bidder Such a view tended to make much more sense for the emerging capitalists, who actually had something to sell, and much less sense to the workers who only had their labor power to sell. But as the capitalist class gained power and was able to define the world of work for everyone, their paradigm about how to think about things became increasingly authoritative. And in this process, people were encouraged to think of themselves alone, responsible only for themselves, and not as part of some larger community of support.

If you begin to think of yourself as "out for yourself" then you have less ties to the larger community. You want the right to enjoy the fruits of your own labor—and that means that you don't want others who may not have worked as hard as you, or been as clever, or been as lucky, pushing their way into your life and claiming some part of what you have earned.

Families become much more privatized, much less likely to share what they have with the larger community. Correspondingly, they feel much less right to make claims on the community, to count on it for support, either emotionally or financially. The goal of work life increasingly becomes to make it for your family. However, the ethics of self-interest soon begin to infect the family itself. Even within the same family, the more successful people begin to feel resentful at any potential obligation to the less success-ful—so instead of brothers taking care of each other, or children feeling an ongoing responsibility for elderly parents, we increasingly get the model of everyone out for themselves and neither counting on nor trusting other family members to take care of them at points of adversity.

The breakdown of communities of meaning, then, is part of the same process that creates the incredible isolation of families and the pain and loneliness within families. Once the values that those communities of meaning used to teach begin to disappear we find the dominance of another set of values that place the emphasis on the individual—but the individual concep-tualized as separate and apart. We are then taught to think of individual satisfaction as counterposed to community, and self-realization as possible only in isolation from others.

While it would be foolish to think that anyone consciously intended this result, it is nevertheless important to understand that the isolation from communities of meaning and the breakdown of public space actually fits quite neatly into other aspects of a capitalist system. If people in an extended family can share a large house together, then they may need only one tele-vision and one kitchen. And they may need much fewer appliances if they live in a neighborhood where people regularly share what they have with each other. On the other hand, if people feel that they aren't free and independent until each person has their own household, then not only do they need endless construction of condominiums and houses, but also the production of endless consumer goods that in previous epochs might have been shared. The breakdown of family life and the creation of a "singles" culture, far from challenging the basic needs of the system, actually helps to develop an even greater marketplace for these goods, as more people feel compelled to set up their own households to feel independent and free.

The imperative to buy goods is not only generated by the physical isolation that attends the breakdown in communities of meaning, but also by the deep psychological loss entailed. In a quite literal sense, people feel the need to fill themselves up for what they experience as lost—and through clever media manipulation and the creation of cultural norms related to consump-tion, the society helps to shape people who attempt to compensate for this loss through the consumption of goods. It is a futile pursuit—because what people are seeking in the way of lost community and purpose can never be compensated for by better cars, fancier houses, or more impressive electronic and computer technologies. But all too often when these things fail to satisfy, people believe it is only because they don't have enough money to buy the better quality items, or more items, and feel badly that they haven't been successful enough to get all that they really need. We should add that no matter how much people have, these goods never satisfy, and yet even those with loads of money to spend on these goods fantasize that if they had more money to buy more goods they would get that satisfaction that so far has eluded them.

However functional this way may be for the large corporate interests who benefit from our obsessive spending, this way of living stands in dramatic contrast to the values taught by many of the previously existing communities of meaning. This is particularly true in thinking about the religious communities that have often sought to criticize the materialistic focus on acquired goods, and have counterposed to that focus the values of salvation and love. Many religious communities support values which, if taken seriously, would require some constraints on the power and freedom of the capitalist marketplace. This was most clear in the Middle Ages, when the Catholic Church had a doctrine of "fair price" and "fair profits" that severely limited the ability of the growing capitalist class to get whatever they could manage to get for their products. Today, a sector of the Catholic Church challenges the rights of American corporations to support Latin American dictators, and insists that social justice requires redistribution of land in such a way that extremes of poverty are eliminated. In the name of its gospel of love, Protestant churches often criticize practices of the American corporate elite that have generated its profits, e.g., its willingness to shut down plants and leave thousands of people unemployed without taking responsibility for the effects on those communities.

These criticisms do more than sting—they generate another way of thinking about political reality that could potentially lead to serious constraints on corporate power. It is no surprise, then, that in the name of "progress" or in the name of "individual freedom" the dominant forces in our society have made a frontal assault on most of the established communities of meaning. Religion may be given verbal acknowledgement, but the underlying subversive values are dismissed. People are encouraged to let go of traditional ways, to see everything from the past as "old fashioned" and to see allegiances with others as only temporary and governed by short-term self-interest. Any sense of commitment to larger institutions and purposes is portrayed as either silly, self-defeating or fanatical. We are taught that common sense should lead us to look out only for ourselves, not to trust others, and not to expect anything from anybody else. Dominant approaches in psychology, political science and sociology suggest that the only logical bedrock for action is individual interests, and the only rational systems are those that appeal to individuals in isolation from each other.

Of course, this tendency towards the breakdown of communities of meaning is an ongoing process, and different people find themselves in different stages of that process. There are still millions of Americans who belong to churches or other larger communities. But one of the striking things that has happened in these communities is the way that they have increasingly lost their inner core and oppositional flavor. There is a strong tendency to make all these communities "modern" by emphasizing the absolute priority of the individual within them, and to drop as coercive and old-fashioned the values that reflect a sense of community. The forms may persist, but the underlying content is dismissed. So, for example, labor unions continue to have millions of members, but the value of solidarity and the desire to remake the world on principles of justice and fairness are no longer the central rallying cries and guiding visions. Indeed, in almost every sphere where the communities of meaning persist, they have tended to narrow their visions and become supplements to personal life rather than the deep core meaning of life itself. While I believe that the subversive content of these communities still exists, I am also aware that the struggle to individualize human lives and to isolate them from communities can often be most effective by de-legitimating the value of community within the remnants of previously strong community foci. I shall argue in the chapter on religion that it can play a very important role in countering this process, but only where religion is taken seriously and not seen as an adjunct to personal fulfillment.

The process that I have been describing eliminates for most working people the last vestiges of an alternative frame through which they could understand their experiences in the economy and the world of work. Lacking an alternative frame of meaning, they are most susceptible to the dominant ideology and its frame—the frame that tells us that everyone is fundamentally alone in this world, and that anyone can make it if they really try, but only by looking out for their own interests at the expense of everyone else. The one relief from this total aloneness is supposed to be one's nuclear family.

But one's family is increasingly unable to provide for compensation. Family life in the past was always enmeshed in a series of larger communities—and it was in terms of these communities that family life was seen as having meaning and purpose. Birth and death, marriage and celebration—all were celebrated in one's family but through the frame of a larger community of meaning that interpreted and made sense of one's own individual family experience. Whether one was giving one's energies or one's life for the nation, the socialist transformation, or the salvation of humanity, individual events got meaning from their relationship to a larger history and a sense of embeddedness in a shared communal drama. Without that context of meaning, each individual episode in family life takes on a whole new meaning.

The upshot of this absence of the larger frames of meaning is that each relationship and, increasingly, each episode within a relationship, must be self-justifying. Everything must feel good in its own terms, and in the short-run. Moreover, the people entering these relationships are increasingly facing a world of work that is alienating and oppressive and stressful in the ways we described above. They are encouraged by the dominant culture to expect that each individual relationship will provide a compensation for the world of work. Any given relationship must become the meaning and purpose of life—for people who have not been able to find meaning and purpose at work and who find their larger communities of meaning appearing increasingly problematic and abandoned. This is a burden that few relationships can bear. Without this larger frame of meaning, relationships that were perfectly functional and satisfying a hundred years ago suddenly feel totally useless or unfulfilling.

Add to this another reality factor: as families become increasingly nuclearized they actually have to take on a greater set of support functions than in the past. Without the extended family networks which used to engage in child-rearing, taking care of elderly parents, and coping with demands for entertainment and recreation, the very same burdens that once were distributed amongst a large clan are suddenly heaped on the shoulders of every two-person nuclear family. The nuclearization of families has actually made them much less functional and placed much heavier burdens on them—and this at precisely the moment when these same units carry heavier metaphysical burdens from the breakdown of community, and heavier emotional burdens from the load of self-blaming generated by the ideology of the Meritocracy.

No wonder so many couples find their relationships not quite living up to their very intense levels of expectation! Yet, without a social framework within which people can see that the pains and disappointments that they are experiencing in family life are a shared problem and a problem that is massively reinforced by the way our society is organized, they often end up blaming themselves for their personal failures. After all, while all this is going on they are simultaneously being exposed to a daily dose of music, movies, television shows, and superficial conversation at work that seems to suggest that wonderful personal life relationships are available to everyone else, and that if things aren't quite working for them they merely need to try a little harder, perhaps change something about themselves that isn't pleasing ("Can we sell you some perfume, or better clothes, or a better car, or a more effective therapy, perhaps, to make your personal life work better?"). And then, if they are basically OK people, things will work out just fine for them. When it doesn't, they turn on themselves with anger and, when that is too painful, they turn in anger on those around them.

This last dynamic deserves some greater highlight. In my research I discovered a fascinating relationship: when the Occupational Stress Groups had succeeded in decreasing self-blaming, an unexpected consequence was that other-blaming, particularly blaming of friends and co-workers and family members, also decreased significantly. And in my in-depth interviews with workers, as well as in my therapy practice, I saw this same relationship: People blame others as a way to escape the too-intense feelings of self-blame that they cannot handle. Given the massive indoctrination of self-blaming, many people feel so terrible about themselves that they can only continue to function by massive repression of these feelings. This can be achieved through alcohol, drugs or tv, or through the development of an insensitive and phony exterior, or it can sometimes be achieved by letting out hostility randomly on those around one. This random hostility decreases when people direct their anger at the appropriate source: the social roots of their frustration. But, when the anger is just let out randomly, it does not dissipate but merely covers a deeper level of self-blaming. It is the failure to understand this relationship that leads some people to think that the most healthful thing is to teach people to stop blaming anyone, and to simply learn to focus on taking responsibility. Their perception is that other blaming is just as harmful as self-blaming. But this is only true if the other-blaming is inappropriate. And in most people's lives, the focus of that other-blaming really is inappropriate, and, at some deeper level, the very people who are emotionally beating up on their lovers, spouses, or children really know that it is inappropriate. They may consciously tell themselves how all their problems are caused by their "bad" spouses or "bad" children, but at a deeper level they feel bad about themselves, either because they know that they are involved and implicated in what is going wrong in the family, or because they blame themselves for having failed to have better spouses or children. Inappropriate other blame merely covers self-blame.

Though most people relentlessly blame themselves and their partners and their children when personal life fails to compensate for the alienation of the rest of their lives, and this blaming only makes things worse and sometimes makes home life as painful as work, an increasing number of people are searching for alternatives to the purely personal solutions to alienation. Many turn to seek new communities of meaning, and many affiliate with false communities that end up oppressing them. People are desperately seeking some new "We," to overcome the isolation and despair of the "I." They reach out to the promise of a community in the ever-larger corporations, desperately trying to hide from themselves their knowledge of the fundamental oppressiveness of their lives in that corporation. Or they reach for a religious or spiritual or political community, even when that requires swallowing leaders and dogma that make no sense to them. Too often we enter these communities with such a sense of our own inadequacy and such a fear of deeply connecting with other people (lest they discover our own supposed inadequacies) that we participate with only parts of ourselves, splitting off and repressing our deeper doubts and misgivings about the whole enterprise. The people around us in these corporations and in these religious communities often have the same fears of rejection or exposure, and so they project back to us the same partial selves we present to them. As a result, the experience of these communities becomes less rich and more contrived. And at this point we get two very typical responses: (a.) Those who suppress their intuitions about what is really going on, and become all the more desperately attached to their needs for these substitute communities to work—furiously suppressing their own doubts and showing anger at any outsiders who would question their pretenses. I have seen this militant crushing of doubts in some of the "Born-again" Christian evangelicals and Right-wing fundamentalists, but I have also seen it in Left-oriented supporters of third world liberation movements, and I have seen it among humanistic psychologists as I have seen it in the fanatics of the political middle (the moderates and political pragmatists of both major parties whose very anti-ideological stance becomes the new dogma that defines a community of true believers who will save the country from everybody else who they see as irredeemably "lost" by virtue of believing in ideals). (b.) Those who become disillusioned with all these communities, feel that they have suddenly "discovered" the truth in the wisdom of the marketplace that you have nobody you can trust but yourself, and who then return to their isolated lives with a higher level of cynicism and despair, ready to once again hope that "the right relationship" will ultimately turn up or be forged, or else ready to live a life without hope. They will tell you with great passion how they tried some new community in their youth, be it political, spiritual or religious, and assure you how "they know" that all things must fail. What they have never done is to understand the social realities that shaped the psychological dynamics that kept people from being emotionally real, kept people from talking about the deepest levels of their fears, pains and needs, and hence kept people locked in to a level of phoniness that then became the shared ethic of these unsuccessful experiments in community.

Singles: The Escape That Doesn't Work

Partly as the result of the frustrations many people have experienced in families and because of the increasing difficulties people face in meeting suitable partners, an increasing number of people have opted to increase the time that they remain single before marrying. A variety of support institutions have been created to assist the single, from singles programs in churches and community centers to alternative newspapers, bars and counseling centers.

The creation of a social space in which it is "OK" to not be married is an important and valuable contribution to a healthier society. The social and economic pressures that operated in the past to force people into marriages were destructive to the emotional health and well-being of those people, and limited the levels of intimacy and caring that such marriages would produce. The resentments stemming from such pressure were often taken out on spouses or children—and even when that did not lead to divorce, it led to crippling emotional pain within families. We are better off without such pain, so it is important to validate the right of people to remain single.

The strengthening of the singles options for women can be an important contribution to the fight against sexism, by providing a way for women to leave oppressive relationships and still find that they have viable and non-degrading options for life outside of bad marriages. Indeed, the very existence of these options strengthens the bargaining power of women in relationships and encourages women to demand the respect and equality of power that is rightfully theirs—and which, in the long run, will make relationships more healthy and stable.

It is equally important to validate the single-parent family. Support for family life must include single parents. There should be no enshrining of the nuclear family as the only appropriate or legitimate form of family life. Children in non-traditional families often do better emotionally than children in families in which there is no remaining love, but in which the parents are staying together out of economic necessity or out of fear of being alone. Similarly, the refusal to sanctify one form of family life as legitimate creates the space for gay and lesbian families to create new forms of connectedness and child-rearing, and removes from them the distorting pressure to be in traditional heterosexual couples that could only be emotional disasters for everyone concerned.

The insistence on the right to remain single, then, is a positive achievement that must be maintained. On the other hand, it is important to avoid the tendency to suggest that the current development of singles "lifestyles" and single-parent families represents a higher form than two adults who have succeeded in building a long-term committed stable relationship. It is my belief that a long-term loving relationship between adults constitutes the most fulfilling way for human beings to live. Part of fostering the possibility of these relationships is to make it OK for people to *not* be in them, so that when they are built, they are built on the basis of real love—and not on the basis of subtle social or economic pressure.

The pressures on single people are immense. There is a constant implication, generated by the mythology of "the relationship as compensation" for the alienation of work, that singles are people who have failed to get their compensation, and who probably don't deserve decent relationships. Moreover, there is a fear of singles by people in couples—either that the single person will seduce their partner, or that the single will make it appear that the freedom of singles living is more attractive than married or coupled life. The single often experiences the world as primarily coupled and finds it hard to travel in the same social circles with those who are coupled—mainly because they aren't invited to do so. In these circumstances, there is much artificial pressure for the single to get into a couple and to settle for relationships that may not work in the long-run but provide a short-run escape from isolation.

For many people, being single is not a real choice—it is just all that is available to them, given the current organization and fragmentation of this society. Consider those who remain single in their late twenties and thirties. I have spoken to literally thousands of those singles. The vast majority tell me that they don't want to remain single, but that they have great difficulty in finding partners. Certainly the expectation of finding a person who will compensate for all the frustration and lack of fulfillment in the rest of one's life must play a distorting role in this judgment. But there are realistic factors as well. The legacy of sexism creates men who have been armored against their feelings, and the psychodynamics of the world of work creates women and men who bring a great deal of pain and self-blaming into their social encounters. When these people meet, they recognize in the other's pain some of the very feelings that they were trying to escape in themselves, so they are "turned off" by being reminded of this pain when it shows through in others. This, in turn, encourages them to be less emotionally real in their self-presentations, for fear that they will reveal the pains that they carry with them. The result is that partners begin to appear more hollow, less deep, more out of touch with feelings. So it may even be the more sensitive and emotionally "real" people who choose to remain single for longer periods— given the problems of finding lasting partners amidst the vast numbers of casualties of this numbing psychological reality.

Additionally, there are few social forms that provide a safe place for people to meet each other when the goal is more than casual sexual encounters. In the closer knit communities of the past the responsibility for helping singles connect was a community task. Parents, friends and neighbors all involved themselves in helping to arrange for singles to meet, and to think collectively about who would fit with whom. While this had its oppressive side, it also flowed from an understanding that the individual was not alone in the world, and that her/his choices would affect the whole community. Today, typically only the individual involved takes any real responsibility for finding a partner.

The result for many singles has been a dramatic escalation in self-blaming. The model of the Meritocracy prevails in our evaluation of social life: if you are alone, it is probably because you don't deserve to have a fulfilling relationship. The pain and self-doubt that this generates is often debilitating. While many singles muster the energy to put on a good public appearance, they become increasingly upset with themselves as they grow older. What seemed to be a cornucopia of fun and experiences in one's early twenties often turns to pain and self-blame in one's mid-thirties.

Nor can one typically count on others to help out. Even the best-meaning of friends will often back away from introducing you to other people, explaining that: (a.) They don't want to impose; or (b.) They don't know if it will really work (as if they were supposed to produce a guarantee); or (c.) They think these things should happen more spontaneously (scant compensation for the person for whom it isn't happening spontaneously); or (d.) They don't want to embarrass you by suggesting that you might want to meet someone (thereby implicitly reinforcing the notion that singles are justifiably embarrassed, because their being single and not wanting to be is an inadequacy which is "showing in public".) All this boils down to the simple reality that singles have to work it out without much communal help. This is an experience that is very deeply reinforcing of the individualism of the economic marketplace. People are learning that at some very deep level they are really alone, can count on no one, and that even friends are unwilling to empathically relate to their situation. It is this kind of situation, watching how little others are doing to help, that makes so many people doubt that they could trust others around them. This has a profoundly conservatizing effect. People who have this experience are not likely to take risks in political movements that depend on people trusting each other.

Most of the problems facing single people apply even more strongly to single parents (the vast majority of whom are women). Because of the decreased mobility faced by a single parent with children, the problems of meeting other single adults is intensified. The decreased options make it all the more likely that when they do meet someone they will be all the more interested in making it work—and this typically leaves many single mothers particularly vulnerable to sexual and emotional exploitation by men. After a number of these kinds of affairs, many single mothers become more discouraged about the possibility of trusting any man, and withdraw their energy into a primary attachment to their children. The children become the locus of their hopes, and often the main source of emotional intimacy (and this special role may create emotional burdens for the children who have to "take care" of their mothers in ways more suited for adult partners).

The singles experience is just another part of the failure of personal life to be a compensation for the lack of meaning in the world of work. The pains and frustrations experienced here are not fundamentally different in kind from the pains that are the common reality in other parts of family life. It is as much an illusion for people to believe that they can escape the pain in single life through finding a perfect relationship as it is for people in relationships to fantasize that the freedom and seeming autonomy of singles life would provide real fulfillment. Every way that we organize our personal lives, whether we be single or married, "straight" or "gay," alternative or traditional, will still face the same overwhelmingly powerful forces that create pain and unhappiness: the alienation at work that is brought home into personal life, the self-blaming and anger that this generates, the increase in individualism and the breakdown of larger communities of meaning, the unrealistic expectations that we are encouraged to place on personal life as a compensation, and the intensification of self-blame that results when our personal lives don't seem to measure up to our fantasies of what others have managed to achieve for themselves.

The Pleasure in Loving Relationships

It would be foolish to ignore the very real pleasures that people find in their relationships. I have emphasized the incredible pain in people's lives, because this is the secret that keeps so many people enslaved and powerless. But I should stop for a moment to acknowledge the other side of the reality: the many real joys that we all experience in our personal lives.

Human beings are wondrous and preciously unique. When we encounter other human beings we have an opportunity to experience once again the incredible complexity and beauty of the human spirit. And people are end- lessly inventive and fun. To be close to another human being is almost always rewarding and exciting.

No matter how contorted our society becomes, these aspects of human life cannot be fully repressed. The flowering of human beauty pushes through some of the roughest and toughest concrete. In the midst of all the distortions, we find countless pleasures and joys in being with each other.

It is precisely these joys that give us hope. When a human being is funny, loving, spontaneous, bubbling with happiness, we remember why we are so deeply attached to life. No amount of societal distortions can ultimately stamp out that reality.

All the more reason why we want to understand the many ways that people end up being much less happy and joyous than they could be. Yes, most people have many real moments of pleasure and satisfaction in their relationships with others. But most people also have a tremendous amount of pain and upset.

We live in a society which is committed to looking on the cheery side, being optimistic, even when that means denying reality. Public norms encourage us to talk about the happy-making experiences—but to remain all too quiet about the pain. Yet that very quiet becomes a cause for why the pains get worse. People have an incredible amount of frustration and upset in their personal lives. Yet they experience these frustrations and pains as personal problems—and usually as something that makes them "worse" than other people around them. They feel ashamed that their lives aren't working as well as everyone else's—and that in turn seems to fit perfectly with the feelings that they had at the workplace that made them feel that they deserved to have unfulfilling work.

People burdened down with this kind of pain, and this interpretation of the source of their pain, feel that they do not deserve a life of real fulfillment. They lower their expectations, accept that things are not going to be what they want, and try to tailor their needs to what they think they can get.

It is this very process that makes them feel unworthy of having power, and foolish to even think about it. Powerlessness seems appropriate and inevitable. As many people have told me during the interviews I conducted with them, "How can I possibly worry about changing things in the larger picture—I can't even get my own life together . . ." This sentiment underlies their inability to conceive of themselves as potential agents of social change in anything but the smallest possible spheres.

The deep irony here is that it is this very perception that sustains them in their powerlessness. Of course people won't be able to get their lives together as long as they feel this powerless—because their personal lives are massively shaped by larger social realities that can only be changed by people who feel that they have the right and the inner strength to demand a different kind of world. Of course, there are real constraints on how powerful we could be even if we began to struggle to change the larger social context within which we live our individual lives. But what could be accomplished is never even attempted—because we make ourselves more powerless than we need to be by blaming on ourselves the supposed failures to achieve a deeply satisfying personal life. Debilitated by the self-doubt that our pains and disappointments engender, we feel unable to take seriously any larger struggle for social transformation that would involve commitment, trust in others, and hope. And our very failure to engage in such struggles confirms us in a world in which we will both expect satisfactions that we never achieve and interpret those failures as badges of personal shame.

The Politics of Personal Life

One of the ironies of late 20th Century American life has been the growth of a conservative movement that puts itself forward as the champion of "the Family." It is ironic, because so much of what has weakened family life is caused by the competitive nature of the economy, the breakdown of larger communities of meaning, and the psychodynamics of work that are brought home, all of which are caused by the very capitalist system these conservatives are so deeply committed to. But the conservatives had clear sailing in taking this issue—because so many liberals and progressives have dismissed the

concern about family as inherently a "Right-wing" issue. Rightly concerned
to defend the various freedoms that individuals have won in the past decades,
many liberals and progressives have wrongly eschewed the whole issue of
family and thought they could do politics by just addressing the issues of
economic and foreign policies, with a smattering of equal rights thrown in.

This has been a tragic mistake. We may well see a shift again to liberal
and progressive forces in the 1990s—but how much they can accomplish in
office will always be limited by the enduring political power of the Right,
power that is based not just on its access to money, but on its popular support
amongst many sectors of the population whose economic interests the Right
doesn't serve. The popularity of this Right is based directly on its ability to
speak to the emotional pain that people feel, to the fears that they experience
in their own lives about not having achieved the kind of happiness that they
so badly desire.

The Right's approach is to re-legitimize the desires for a strong and fulfilling family life. While some people may be attracted by a covert appeal to
sexist values, many others hear the Right calling for a return to conditions
of the past when family loyalties were taken more seriously and people could
escape to family for emotional stability and caring. Whatever the element
of fanciful reconstruction of an idealized past in ths approach, it nevertheless
appeals to people's deep sense that there is something really wrong with the
current period, and that family life is not providing for them all that it
should. The Right's analysis is profoundly mistaken, but it has hit on an area
that is of legitimate mass concern. In fact, by talking about the problem as
a social issue caused by wrong social policies, the Right helps to decrease
self-blaming and make people feel better about themselves. For that result,
many people are willing to buy into programs and analyses that could easily
be shown to misconstrue the real foundations of the problem. They are led
into scapegoating gays or into denigrating feminism, or into struggles to
limit individual freedoms, thinking that thereby they will recreate a better
social context for strong families.

Liberals and progressives have consistently misunderstood the appeal of
the Right—always failing to understand the rational kernel within the irrational shell. Instead of acknowledging that the Right speaks to real pains in
daily life, but provides solutions that only divert attention from the real
sources of family pain, the liberals and the Left have often dismissed the
entire Right-wing constituency as either stupid or reactionary. While this is
certainly true for some percentage of its supporters, it is decidedly not true
of many tens of millions of people who get attracted to the Right because
they hear the Right talking about their own real fears and real pains. Even
if the Right doesn't provide solutions that work, at least it appears to understand the problems and care about them, and thus to provide a community
within which one's own problems in family life appear to be part of a more
general and shared problem.

It is in this light that we can also understand the great popularity President
Reagan enjoyed in the first years of his Presidency, and his landslide re-elec-
tion. When people are in great pain, they need one of two things: (a) either

a way to understand and overcome that pain, or (b) a temporary pain killer. The Democrats provided neither—they did not understand the pain, and insisted on talking about "the deficit" and other political abstractions. Reagan provided a pain killer: he talked about how wonderful things had been and how wonderful they could be; he provided cheerleading for all that was good; he helped people temporarily focus away from their pain. In acknowledging that family life has been less than it should be, then arguing that it could be happily restored to an arena of true fulfillment, Reagan spoke to the fantasies that were the very source of the pain—both reinforcing the fantasies and increasing the trap of individual self-blame, and simultaneously projecting the possibility of transformation and transcendence through participation in the mythical community of harmonious America. Such a deal! But it was the only game in town—because the other side, instead of taking this up as its central issue and acknowledging the real pain that people experience and pinning the blame on the social system that has played such a central role in generating that pain, has again and again thought that it could do politics without dealing with the emotional needs of the American people.

However, there may be a deeper reason why the Democrats have ignored the issues raised here. To really address the pain of daily life would require fundamental transformations in the political and economic system of the society. Instead of basing their politics on giving everyone an equally fair chance to compete, the Democrats would have to challenge the very nature of the competitive system itself. Instead of talking about ridding the workplace of this or that poisonous chemical or accident-prone product, they would have to talk about occupational stress and its roots in the lack of power that workers have to control production. Instead of talking about economic redistribution, it would have to talk about basing a society on love and mutual caring. These are profound political changes, and though they may provide the soundest basis for building an alternative to conservative politics, they also require a very different political alignment than that based on the two major parties, both of whom are deeply committed to the current distribution of economic and political power and to the continued well-being of the multi-national corporations.

In the mid-1980s I met with national leaders of the American labor movement and talked to them about the importance of family life as a progressive issue. Most of them were extremely resistant—and told me that dealing with family life would open a can of worms that they couldn't handle. This response only makes sense if you don't understand how central the dynamics of family life are to the generation of Surplus Powerlessness. Working people feel demoralized and despairing about their family lives, and feel that they personally have made a mess of things. Given this perception, they are very reluctant to think about handling any "bigger" societal issues. Their alienation from politics, particularly progressive politics that ignores family issues, is largely based on their feelings that they don't have the right to have a society that deeply fulfills their needs. This feeling of disentitlement is based on the interplay of work and family life and the set of emotions that they generate.

No empowerment of working people is possible as long as people feel so badly about their supposed failures in their personal lives. In this very important sense, the personal is the political. Not in the trivialized and mistaken sense that every change in one's personal life is a political change and therefore all one need worry about is one's own personal life, but rather in the sense that the way we have constructed the social world makes personal life inevitably frustrating and usually deeply unfulfilling for tens of millions of Americans—and that until people come to understand the social and political roots to private unhappiness they will remain immobilized in self-blaming, cynicism and despair.

Chapter 6

Unequal Power

THE HIDDEN INJURIES THAT WE BRING HOME FROM WORK make family life very difficult. And the isolation of families from each other hides from everyone the fact that their own personal pains are widely shared. "But at least we are in this together," a loving couple often whispers to each other in the early blush of romantic optimism. "It's you and me against the world."

The odds wouldn't be very good even if this were true. But it usually isn't true, because right in the middle of this alliance there is a reality that continually makes a couple distrust each other. It is the reality of unequal power, or what some people call sexism.

"Oh no, not sexism again." That's a standard reaction whenever the topic gets brought up in the 1980s. "We all know about sexism—we have done that number already, it's stale news. We've gotten beyond that kind of concern now."

It is true that sexism has gotten lots of exposure, and that the grossest examples of inequality are now either illegal or are so widely resisted that they no longer really work. But it's also true that inequalities of power, particularly in personal relationships between men and women, have found more subtle forms of expression and have proved much more lasting than anyone would have thought possible a decade ago.

103

This was brought home to me most forcefully when I saw a husband and wife, each in separate stress groups. Both were activists in their union local and both were widely respected by fellow members. But she was ready to quit the union. Her husband, who mouthed total commitment to equality in his public work, was furious with her if she did not have the energy or inclination to serve him when they got home. He was happy to have her be an activist in the union—but only as long as it didn't interfere with her ability to give him the nurturing energy that would take care of him. "What about me?" she complained. And his response was "I need you to have more energy for me." It is a response I found to be very common among men who verbally support every public demand of the women's movement.

Sexism obstructs the development of healthy families. Sexist practices cripple both men and women, making them feel frustrated and unable to get what they need in personal life. And yet, people continually miss the importance of this social reality, and blame themselves for not having single-handedly made a perfect relationship for themselves. And this self-blaming helps strengthen the very dynamics of Surplus Powerlessness that make us believe we can never change these inequalities—that we are stuck with them and had just better make the best of them.

The fantasy of a compensation for the world of work was historically based on the role of the woman as "homemaker" whose job was to make things wonderful when the man got back from work. What this fantasy always left out was the reality of experience for the wife. Housework is real work—and it is often every bit as exhausting as the work done by the male breadwinner. Where was the wife supposed to derive the energy to be a therapist, lover, child-rearer, etc., when she too had been subjected to a hard day's work?

More importantly, the mythology never takes into account the psychological costs for women of being constrained in increasingly isolated households. Not only do women who work at home have jobs that are often rote and unrewarding (as many household tasks are), but they are not paid for the work. Housework is trivialized—so that the real contribution the women make to the continued ability of the male to go back to work each day is discounted. Of course, as women are made to feel that their contribution is unimportant, they begin to develop feelings of inadequacy and self-blame about themselves—they are not really valuable, their real worth is their ability to hold a man, etc. The contradiction, of course, is that women who feel bad about themselves will not have the energy to nurture others. The result is that men come home to a household in which the wife/homemaker is doing her best to be all things to the man, but because she feels badly about herself she may be unable to provide the expected nurturance. Given the ideology of sexism which many women still buy, women feel inadequate when they cannot serve their husband's needs, and this makes them feel worse about themselves.

We have seen what happens to relationships when one partner comes home feeling badly. Now imagine when the partner at home is, for similar reasons, feeling badly about her life and denigrating her value because the home life that she has been taught it is her function to make wonderful is actually not feeling good at all. Women react in a wide variety of ways, depending on the previous psychological history, class position, and intellectual development of the people involved. Sometimes the woman will do her best to please her husband, but gradually grows more and more resentful of him, leading eventually to explosions and possible dissolution of the marriage. Or she will do her best to contain her anger, but it will come out in "bitchiness" towards her husband, or sexual unresponsiveness, or constant arguments about seemingly trivial matters. Sometimes the woman will begin to drink, bury herself in front of the tv, or take drugs as a way of containing her anger and frustration. Some women invest their energies in their children, hoping to live through their anticipated futures, simultaneously pushing them to be more successful than they are and resentful of their independent achievements that only remind them of their own dependency. Likewise, some women invest their energies in endless new plans to please their husbands, hoping to be "the total woman," and succeed in cutting off all awareness of the frustration they are experiencing, pushing the pain down to the unconscious level where it often becomes somatized and emerges as stress-related physical health problems.

The picture has changed somewhat now that over fifty percent of families have both adult partners working outside the home. Even with lower paying jobs, the possibility of having an independent economic base has made it possible for many women to consider leaving oppressive marriages. This has given them much more freedom within marriages to demand more satisfying relationships. But we should not overestimate this development. Even though experience in the world of work gives the sense of what financial independence would be like, for many it only reconfirms the necessity to stay in a marriage regardless of the emotional costs. Oppressive, low-paying jobs, and high costs of childcare play a significant role in keeping many women hooked into family situations they find oppressive, knowing how very difficult it would be to survive in the kinds of working-class jobs that would most likely be available to most of them.

The woman who has entered the job market with the impression that she will find true liberation there is often in for a big disappointment. The same dynamics of repressed anger and self-blaming attacking both psyche and body operate for women just as they do for men. Women's return home is complicated by the ideology and practice of sexism. At home a Second Job typically awaits them, keeping home and family together. Most women are expected to do the shopping, cooking, cleaning, and housework—just because they are women. They are expected to have the children taken care of, prepared for school, their homework done, and their daily lives planned. And as if this were not enough, they are expected to be both therapists and nursemaids and sexual goddesses for their husbands, fulfilling male fantasies about being taken care of and receiving compensation from the world of work.

Is it any surprise that many of these women with two jobs find the tasks progressively more discouraging, and don't always have the energy or will to live up to the expectations of their husbands? And is it any surprise that men often fight hard for the fantasy to come true—seeing this fantasy as their last hope for making any sense out of a life that has otherwise seemed to be meaningless and oppressive? We have here a recipe for misunderstanding and conflict. All too often the women themselves accept the expectations of the dual job situation, and then feel bad about themselves for not living up to them. The outbursts of anger or resentment that push their way up to the surface are not understood even by many women themselves. It is not atypical to find those women who really think they ought to keep their family more together and ought not to feel anger engaging in a variety of "coping techniques" to keep their anger from getting "out of hand." These often include alcohol, prescription tranquilizers, or various types of therapy in which their "problem" can be analyzed and behavioral techniques can be learned to keep things under control. Nor is it unusual to find that many of the women who report middle-age depression or depression related to their children leaving home are actually sitting on a pile of stored-up anger that is threatening to get out of control now that previous coping devices are no longer functioning.

Many working women face a double whammy. They have all of the frustration of not having lived up to their husbands' socially-sanctioned expectations of what a good wife would be, plus they have the whole set of frustrations from the world of work—the stress and self-blaming that we have described in previous chapters, which would be sufficient in themselves to generate considerable pain and upset. At work they feel terribly about themselves for not having generated respect and decent treatment and meaningful labor, and then come home and feel terrible for failing to have created the kind of home life that they have learned women are supposed to create. Even several decades of women's liberation movement activity cannot dislodge this nuturing expectation, because the desire to provide this nurturing is typically learned by little girl children in the first few years of their lives, and is sustained by years of conditioning into the culture of being women. Nor is there something fundamentally wrong about this desire—the value of nurturance is reasonable and is only misused when it is the exclusive province of one sex to provide for the other, rather than equally a responsibility of both sexes.

But given the impossible expectations on women to make everything work, where are they supposed to get their own nurturing? Certainly they won't get this nurturing from their men, who come home from work with little nurturing energy left. Nor is there much to encourage men to develop this nurturing capacity—given the realities of the world of work that they must deal with. It is sometimes noted that men seem to be more oriented towards power, ego and control, while women seem to be more attuned to caring and to relationship needs. In recent years there has even been an attempt to ontologize these differences by suggesting that there is a difference in developmental patterns—as though these patterns were not themselves a direct product of the sexual division of labor in the society in which children are growing. In "enlightened" circles where people have attempted to take seriously the feminist critique of sexism there sometimes develops an anti-male bias, in which men are seen as having bad "male" traits, while women are seen as having these more humane "feminine" traits. The reality is that to the extent that men have developed an orientation towards power, control and mastery while underdeveloping relational and nurturing energies, it has been a direct product of their correct assessment of what will be required of them in the world of work if they are to succeed. There are many men who would be very happy to give up the need to make it in the economic sphere and would be quite happy to let someone else support them—but as long as they are going to have to make a living, they are going to need to have "male" traits. That this is not just some rationalization developed as an afterthought is testified to by the fact that an increasing number of women are developing "male" traits as they start to compete in the economic marketplace. The truth is that the "female" traits like nurturing and relational skills are among the few privileges that women get out of the otherwise largely degrading sexist arrangements—and it is quite unfair to berate men for not having this privilege and then acting as though this was a reflection of some innate problem with the male of the species.

The demand that an increasingly feminist-conscious subculture is pushing onto men is: be a success in the world of work and also be a competent nurturer at home. The reality is that just as this double whammy can only increase self-blame on the part of most women, so it will make men feel bad but rarely change their reality. Nor will this be eased by new courses or therapies aimed at developing these nurturing capacities, any more than the problem is eased for women by creating courses on how to succeed in the world of business (read: "act like a man"). Of course, for some small percentage of men whose work world is less stressful and allows greater flexibility in hours and greater opportunities to use their own intelligence and creativity, these new appeals to develop nurturing capacities will actually improve things somewhat—and they can then become the new "feminist males" whose example can be used as a club against all the other men who are in turn written off as insensitive lugs. But for the majority of men, the emotional exhaustion, stress and self-blaming at work is so massive that little can be done to suddenly rejuvenate them. And little boys in working-class cultures who are preparing themselves to grow up and manage to make a living in the world as constituted should not be blamed if they begin early to brace themselves for the shock by developing sets of character structures that allow them to function in an oppressive reality.

On the other hand, while we can have compassion for the men who are socialized into this reality, we must see how unfair the arrangement then becomes for women. It is one thing for the men to be caught in a difficult situation—but it is quite another for them to project and sustain a set of beliefs that women also buy that require women to have a super-human capacity for nurturing. It would be a fundamental step towards empowerment of both sexes, and a huge advance in relationships, if each sex could see and articulate how the other has been faced with a set of life situations that will probably make them less fully available and less fully wonderful than they might otherwise be. If each sex could begin to acknowledge, both in verbally and non-verbally communicated expectations, that the other was probably going to be somewhat beaten down by the way things were structured, and not blame one's own particular partner for failures and disappointments that are built into the whole structure of the socially sanctioned asymmetries in the division of emotional and economic labor, we would have taken a significant step towards the recreation of trust that would make relationships both safer and more stable. With that trust, both men and women could then engage in struggle to change the social reality rather than settle for a lowered level of nurturance.

Many middle-class women face another manifestation of assymetry of power created by sexism. They have sacrificed themselves in some way to help their men achieve their goals. For example, the wife works at a lousy job to put her husband through law or business or medical school, or raises the kids and takes all the home burdens while the husband creates a career for himself in a corporation, university or government bureaucracy. The man becomes more "interesting" because of the stimulation and opportunities that he gets to develop in his professional career, while the woman who has removed herself from spheres where her talents might be developed and her thoughts refined appears less interesting. Ironically, the man now turns around and finds his wife to be a less fulfilling partner, and becomes attracted to some "independent" woman or simply puts his wife down for being boring. Thus the structure of sexism creates life experiences that continually work to undermine the possibility of deeper companionship in marriage.

While these problems are a direct legacy of the organization of work and the dynamics of sexism, they are typically lived through as "personal problems." It is easy enough, in the absence of an understanding of the social impact on personal life, for each partner to blame themselves or blame the other party. This kind of blaming usually makes little sense. We are all caught up in a set of structural arrangements that undermine loving relationships. We need each other's help and understanding so that we can engage in activity to change these arrangements. But instead, a much more common response is to oscillate between feelings of self-blame (I don't deserve a decent relationship) and feelings of anger at our spouses or lovers for having failed us ("You didn't make my home a haven from the storm," or even, "You said you believed in real equality between men and women and yet look at what you are doing now."). This kind of blaming often leads to the same kind of process of mutual estrangement that we discussed in the dynamics of the woman homemaker and her husband.

For an ever growing number of families, both those with women at home and those with women in the work world, the combination of sexism and the psychodynamics of work produce a set of relationships usually filled with more pain than fulfillment. The process of blaming the other can then lead quickly into a move towards divorce rather than towards any systematic attempt to work on the relationship, or to understand the social forces that are working in it.

The move towards leaving a relationship is encouraged by the whole ethos of the market society. We are taught to see ourselves as commodities in the world of work—and we groom ourselves to sell for the highest possible price, by having the best degrees, training, résumés, appearance and manner of self-presentation. That same thinking helps sell products in the sphere of "personal life"—we are taught to think that we will find a more satisfying relationship if we have consumed the right products, wear the right kind of clothes, drive the right kinds of cars, drink the right kinds of wines, or have completed the right kind of psychotherapy, growth process or exercise class. Once we see ourselves in these terms it is only a short step to seeing others as commodities. Our partners are no longer human beings, but the owners of good and bad qualities. We are driven to wondering if we couldn't get a better list from someone else. We are surrounded by what appears to be a supermarket of relationships in which you can buy one, try it out, discard it like last year's now outdated video games, and pick out yet another partner. If you have a problem it is probably that you haven't bought the right commodity, so go back to the marketplace and try your hand at it. And if you don't do so well, you might have to "settle"—probably because your own stock is no longer so high, you're not so attractive, don't make enough money, or are growing older.

The divorce option has traditionally been more attractive to men, because the economic marketplace rewards their work at higher levels of pay, and thus does not ensure that they will be thrown into financial trauma. Moreover, men are still less likely to take the children with them, thus giving them a greater degree of sexual mobility in the marketplace of relationships. Because women often feel the need to reestablish a more secure home for their children after divorce, they are also more likely to press for remarriage and the economic security attendant thereto. For that same reason, they are more likely to be prey to sexual exploitation by men who are willing to make false promises and fantasies of future commitment in return for immediate sexual connection.

Many of these men, victims of the world of work, take out their anger and feelings of powerlessness on the women who cross their paths, unconsciously acting out on others the very patterns of manipulation, humiliation, and exploitation that they have been themselves subjected to all day at work. All the male socialization towards violence and competition would not be sufficient to overcome our more natural tendency to recognize in each other a fundamental similarity and preciousness were it not for the fact that everyday these men are themselves subjected to a massive dehumanization process. The repetition compulsion is rooted in their own experience, each day, and will never be uprooted through psychotherapy alone or moral exhortation alone, as long as the structure of the work world makes this way of acting the one that is most highly rewarded.

But traditional roles are changing, and with it the picture of who does what to whom. The social structures remain in place, but new actors come to occupy the old positions, and begin to act in similar ways. So women who enter non-traditional jobs and have available higher levels of income begin to act like the traditional males of the past. "I'm going to get mine" quickly becomes the battle cry of the corporate woman—and she can show herself

to be every bit as ruthless as men in the work world, and every bit as manipulative in the sexual marketplace. There is a growing sanction for women to
exploit men, just as men have exploited women. But this new "fairness" does
not humanize relationships or make them work better, it only universalizes
the conditions of exploiter and exploited and makes them into roles that are
less sex-specific.

We should also not exaggerate how many women can avail themselves of
the options created by the movement for women's equality. A lot depends
on where you are in the class structure. Women entering professional or
semi-professional careers in law, medicine, nursing, engineering, science,
media, college teaching, business administration, public relations, psychology, and the arts may find a set of possibilities open to them that simply
were not available twenty years ago. Once the sexist barriers are down, these
fields discover that women make as many substantial contributions and bring
as much creativity and talent to their work as men. And the desire to appear
to overcome past sexist practices makes many of these fields available for
special opportunities for women. To women facing these opportunities, the
new possibilities will far outweigh problems from stress at work. And the
relatively high salaries in many of these areas will provide adequate compensation should they be facing lives without males. For such women, the prospect of a family breaking up may hold much less terror when the alternative
is staying in an oppressive relationship. Similarly, women who have these
options will be less prone to feel the need for commitment from a man, and
will be more available to play their own cards in the marketplace of
relationships.

It is quite different if you are a woman from a more traditional working
class background or a woman who sees her options primarily in terms of
the kinds of jobs that have been available to the men she has known. If your
option in leaving a marriage is to go to work on an assembly line putting
together micro-computer chips, cars, tractors, tv's, stereos, electronic equipment, working with dangerous chemicals, or working as an orderly for a
hospital or nursing home, serving as an operator at the phone company, a
salesperson for the local supermarket or department store, driving a bus
or truck, joining a secretarial pool, working a video display terminal, serving
customers in a restaurant or bank, cleaning rooms at a hotel, or any of the
hundreds of other similarly limited jobs that most working women still face,
then you may have a very different set of attitudes towards the marketplace
in relationships.

For many women who are not in the job market, the prospect of these
kinds of jobs is very unappealing. Many women would rather live in unequal
relationships than take these jobs. Many others who have those jobs are
willing to make compromises to get out of them or at least to not have to
depend on them for one's total living. All too often these women hear "the
liberated woman" with a good middle-class job putting down women who
have made this other choice, classifying them as "less conscious" or as "unlib-
erated slaves to men." The life of raising children and staying out of the job
market is seen as an indication of failure or lack of courage. It sometimes

sounds as if the women's movement is suggesting that every woman would be happier and more fufilled if she had a job. Yet this attitude could only be based on the expectations of the job market that are available to upper-middle-class women—and seems totally wrong to many women facing working-class jobs. Unintentionally, middle-class feminists may be projecting the message: "I got a fulfilling professional job. If you don't, it's your own fault because you are not wonderful like me."

These class differences also get expressed in attitudes towards sexuality and the sexual marketplace. To the extent that what is available to them is less exciting and fulfilling in the world of work, working-class women will feel more pressure to make compromises, more need for commitment from men, and hence be more susceptible to manipulation and sexual exploitation. For that reason, the marketplace in relationships and the sexual freedom that accompanies it will seem more double-edged, less a prescription for freedom. Having made the choice to stay out of the job market and do their work at home, they can hardly feel sanguine about sexual value systems that seem to discourage fidelity and seem to legitimate men to seek new sexual horizons with younger and possibly more physically attractive women—a path that might eventually lead to these women being abandoned or divorced, without any serious prospects for work, and without any long-term way to support themselves.

It is in this light that we can understand the attraction that some working class women find to the "born-again" movements in Christianity and to various right-wing anti-women's liberation causes. The appeal of these movements is in part explainable on the basis of the strong sexual morality that is preached. To many of these women, the new sexual experimentation connotes danger. The concerns about abortion and homosexuality, the concern about sexual licentiousness and even about divorce itself must be understood in part in relationship to their correct perception that if these women had to enter the job market or had to make a living without male help they would, given the realities of the class structure and the sexual stratification of jobs, enter into a reality far more oppressive than anything that they currently face.

Progressive movements should begin to acknowledge what is correct in these women's perceptions. Their fears are not irrational, and their concern about keeping their families together is not some atavistic or reactionary nonsense. But what such women do not understand is that the greatest threat to stable relationships is not the new "sexual freedom." If they wish to strengthen family life, they must start at a totally different point: by demanding a humanization of the work world. Similarly, the dynamics of sexism described here are a major obstacle to family life. Anyone who wishes to strengthen families would need to start with that concern. The women who are attempting to save the family through crusades against abortion, homosexuality, or sexual freedom have misunderstood the real forces that are working to undermine family life. Meanwhile, they advance programs that seem to tie "family life" to old and oppressive forms that many women will rightly refuse to accept.

In fact, it is the women's movement that could plausibly become the most effective pro-family force. The inequalities of power and respect experienced as oppressiveness in families leads many women to either be unhappy, or to leave families altogether. Any program that would equalize power, eliminate expectations that either party was there exclusively to serve the needs of the other, and insist on the need for full equality of respect would create the necessary precondition for relationships to work in the long run. It is only when people are in relationships out of choice and not out of desperation that they will stay in them and try to make them work.

Similarly, full economic equality for women in the job market is a precondition for strong and lasting family relationships. As long as women enter or stay in relationships for reasons of economic convenience, there will be an inherent instability in families, a chance that as new economic possibilities open up, these women will be tempted to leave, or that possible partners will come along who can offer even better deals. Love can only be based on freedom, not on coercion. Economic coercion is as poisonous as physical coercion. For that reason, sexism stands in the way of building a society in which love can be a guiding principle. And for that same reason, the elimination of sexism is only part of the program for creating strong family life. We must also include a fundamental restructuring of the world of work so that the experience there does not continue to create human beings who are impaired in their nurturing and relational capacities.

We need only remind ourselves of how debilitating it is for people to find that they cannot create for themselves satisfactory relationships for us to understand the centrality of sexism in generating Surplus Powerlessness. So often the pain that people experience when their relationships don't work is interpreted as further confirmation of their already deeply held belief that they are personal failures. Even though they may recognize that sexism exists as some kind of "external social reality," rarely do people appreciate how deeply sexism permeates and shapes the possibilities for finding and maintaining satisfying relationships. The inequalities of power and respect have helped shape the inner sense of themselves that both women and men bring into relationships. And the daily assaults on the dignity and equality of women that they experience in the economic sphere and in the media, coupled with the continued degradation of sex through its commercialization and through the exploitation of women's bodies to sell products, generates feelings and ideas in both sexes that interfere with loving interactions.

All of these seemingly abstract or external forces are internalized and become immediate both in the expectations that people bring into their relationships, and also in the set of choices that people have made throughout their lives that have shaped them into the people they are now. Yet typically we ignore all these factors when we assess our own personal experiences—and instead often end up blaming ourselves completely for the failures in our personal lives.

My point here, of course, is not to deny us any responsibility for what happens in our relationships. Certainly within the set of circumstances that we face we are still responsible for trying to do our best, to create the most healthy and life-affirming connections that we possibly can. Moreover, we are also responsible for getting together with others and working to change sexist conditioning and sexist social and economic arrangements. But when we make an assessment of how well anyone has done, how far they have come in transcending sexist dynamics, we need to heavily factor in the incredible weight of sexist conditioning and sexist institutions, and how massively they impact on each moment of our lives, each perception that we have about our possibilities, and each reaction we have to other people.

Here we make ourselves more powerless than we need to be if we think that the dynamics of sexism are so overpowering that they cannot ever be transcended (a mistake typical of those who choose to give up on heterosexual relationships). But we equally make ourselves powerless if we think that the dynamics of sexism can be overcome by a simple act of will, that once we have read all this and heard these kinds of analyses it is simply up to us to "ignore" or "overcome" all of the sexist forces we have described. This latter expectation can only lead to a new self-blaming as we find ourselves unable to make all the progress that needs to be made.

Just as the people who do not understand the way sexist forces may be central to why their own personal relationships are failing can end up blaming themselves inappropriately, and concluding that they are more screwed up than the average and hence more deserving of the unfulfilling lives that they have, so also the people who have been influenced by the women's movement to recognize sexism can end up blaming themselves inappropriately if they think that the whole weight of sexist conditioning will easily disappear just by virtue of naming it and recognizing how it functions. Or, they can end up blaming their partners for not having made enough changes (typically, men are charged with not having learned to drop their achievement orientation and get in touch with their feelings, or women are charged with not having dropped their fear of success or their fear of autonomy).

The thrust of my argument is that we need to develop a deeper level of compassion for ourselves and each other once we truly understand how powerful the forces are that work against loving relationships. It is not to say that there is nothing that we can do, that we are totally victims, or that we should merely feel sorry for ourselves. But it is to say that here, as in every other aspect of our personal lives, we must be continually aware of how very powerful the combined impact of the psychodynamics of work and the psychodynamics of personal life are, how much the world is structured in ways that undermine our sense of self worth, and how powerful are the forces working on our partners to make them be less wonderful than we wish they could be. If we approach each other with an adequately developed sense of compassion, we may begin to understand the other side of the picture: how truly incredible and powerful are the forces of beauty, dignity and worth within each of us.

Psychological Differences Between the Sexes

The social source of tensions between the sexes cannot be rooted entirely in the interaction between the world of work and sexist social structures. In the past two decades several writers have noted that fundamental differences in the way that women and men think about themselves and the world may be based less on any specific adult sexist conditioning than on the nature of childhood itself. Dorothy Dinnerstein, in her book *The Mermaid and the Minotaur,* points to the fact that women are the primary providers of love and authority, and the initial source for fulfillment and frustration of the child's emerging needs. Because women mother, the course of our psychological lives is shaped by our early-developed reaction to this powerful woman. And because the mother both fulfills and frustrates our needs, the relationship between mother and infant of either sex will produce a deep emotional ambivalence towards the mother.

The specific reactions to this situation differ for each sex. For the female child, there is no need to make a complete separation from the mother, because the primary identification with the mother does not create a role ambiguity as she grows older. For the male child, however, the role of developing into "a man" requires a dramatic break with the "female" within him, and a rejection of those elements of the female that he has acquired through identification with his mother. This very process allows females to develop their relational talents, because they do not have to fundamentally break with the first important relationship of their lives, while it encourages males to develop their own sense of autonomy and aloneness. So by the time they grow up, males and females have developed very different parts of their being—with women feeling most fulfilled precisely when they are able to build strong bonds of connectedness, and men often feeling both a deep need for that connection and a strong fear of it and need for autonomy and "not being smothered" in relationships. These differences in fundamental stance, of course, make it easier to place women in the role of primary nurturers and men in the role of primary strugglers in the economic arena.

The logic of this argument would suggest that if only men could begin to share in the tasks of parenting in an equal way, many of the problems of adult relationships would become less intense. If men and women were to share equally in mothering, there would be no similar assymetry in the process through which children go through their primary "separation/individuation" stage of development—because the separation would be from figures of each sex, just as the primary identification would be with qualities from each sex.

I have some doubts about how comprehensive an answer this is to the problem. While I can easily understand that shared parenting is valuable for providing a degree of equality in who gets to be the first object against which the child rebels, I doubt if it will significantly undermine the incredible forces that still tend to develop less desirable qualities in some adults. I expect that many of the "male" qualities like autonomy and aloneness and difficulties in making commitments and sustaining nurturance will increasingly show up amongst those women who are the most successful in getting better paying jobs in the economy. Just at the moment when these women will have partners who may be willing to do an increasing share of child-rearing, they may find that the personality-structure that they themselves bring to child-rearing has been deeply shaped by the competitive marketplace. Rather than find women suddenly "humanizing" the world of work, they may find that the world of work is making more women act and think like the "male" stereotype. Similarly, the males who begin to share parenting, however much they reject "male" stereotypes and sexist conditioning, still will be subject to the same competitive and dog-eat-dog pressures of the marketplace that play such an important role in shaping adult behavior. So while I am a strong supporter of co-parenting and even "shared mothering" (although I like to think of it as allowing fathering to be a more nurturing experience rather than mimicking the way that women do it), I don't have much hope that this in itself will do very much to change the fundamentals of how children turn out, as long as the people doing the parenting are themselves stuck in adult roles that are daily reinforced by the social world in which they live and in which they must sell their labor power in an unequal and competitive marketplace.

The feminist authors who have pointed to sexual asymmetries are certainly right that changes in the system of mothering may weaken the ease with which people fall into adult gender roles. But the frustrations in relationships transcend these gender roles anyway—as many gay couples report. And the distortions in child-rearing are as likely to continue regardless of what sex does the rearing, as long as both parents are subject to the pains and frustrations of work and family life that the previous chapters have described. It is to the dynamics of childhood that we must now turn to understand this process more deeply.

Chapter 7

Childhood and
Powerlessness

HENRY JACKSON WAS A 33-YEAR-OLD BLACK EMPLOYEE OF
a local utility company when he first came to my office in 1984. He had
worked for the company for over eight years, and had a relatively good
record from the company's standpoint. But in the past six months he had
a new foreman who had been "on his case," and recently Henry had been
having severe work problems, including headaches, absenteeism, and frequent outbursts at his foreman.

It might have seemed at first an easy enough case: stress at work caused
by harassment from the boss. As you can see from an earlier chapter, I
believe that many of the most important problems facing working people
are rooted in the way the world of work is organized, and the impact of
workers' understanding of that stress through the process of self-blaming.
Yet it would be simplistic to reduce all problems to one dimension.

In Henry's case, the issues were much more complex—and in ways that
are not atypical for most working people. Whatever the absolute righteousness of Henry's anger, however easy to understand his headaches as a product
of his anger, there was more to it. Henry didn't want to lose his job. But he
was particularly incensed at his foreman. The foreman was Black, and Henry
was furious that this fellow Black person had no sense of solidarity with him.
We explored in therapy the ways that some Black people are used by white
bosses to split the workforce, the psychologies of some oppressed people as
they try to mimic the very behavior patterns of those who oppress them,

116

and the understandable desire on the part of those who have been poor all their lives to try to get ahead. We discussed the way that this social system makes it seemingly rational for people to abandon each other emotionally and materially—and how devastating that is for all of us, how hard it then becomes to trust anyone, and how sad that makes us. We explored ways that Henry could fight back, using his union, and getting support from fellow workers. Finally, through a lucky accident, Henry's new foreman was transferred to another unit.

The case might have ended here, but Henry still wanted to come to therapy. He continued to be upset about the experience, and said he could think of little else. He persisted in fantasizing about killing the foreman, though he reassured me that he would never do so. The fantasies, however, interfered not only with his work performance, but also with his relationship to a woman friend that seemed to be working out very well in other respects. He reported constant dreams of getting out of control and hurting the foreman (who, by this time, was no longer even in the same city).

I no longer believed that the anger could be adequately explained in terms of the actual situation facing this worker. Actually, I had suspected this from a number of clues dropped in earlier sessions, but when I had attempted to pursue those clues, I had been effectively blocked by the client. Now, finally, in my eleventh session with him, he mentioned that the foreman appearing in a recent dream looked a little like his father. And when I asked him to elaborate, he began to tell me about his life as a child and what a wonderful and giving father he had. In glowing terms he talked about his memory of his father at Christmas time, bringing home presents that he had been hoping for, and how his father was now retired. He mentioned that he didn't see his father very much now.

In the subsequent session I tried a therapeutic technique that I find very useful: I asked Henry to shut his eyes and visualize the home he lived in when he was a child. I then asked him to see his father coming into the apartment, and asked him to describe to me his feelings. Henry began to shake, and then tears began to come to his eyes. He had suddenly begun to remember the feelings that he had when he was six, and the incredible sadness that he had about his inability to make contact with his father. His father had almost never been around—he was either out working, hanging out with friends, or drinking. When he did come home, there were terrible battles with his wife (Henry's mother), which would often spill over to both adults shouting at the kids (Henry had two older brothers and one younger sister).

We began to explore these childhood memories more concretely and in detail, and over the next few weeks Henry remembered many more such scenes. But he had a consistent theme to justify all of them: he insisted that he had been an "ornery" child, always demanding more attention than anyone else could reasonably expect to give him. He could not remember ever being angry at his father, and moreover he told me it would have been foolish—because "he would have beat the daylights out of me." I asked him about the use of the word "daylights" and he remembered a scene in which he had hid in a large closet for several hours, not sure when it would be safe to emerge without getting caught by his father's anger, and had then emerged only to find that it was already dark outside and his family was gone (to the movies, it later turned out).

Henry had become a problem child in school, often misbehaving and causing a ruckus. He was held back twice, and finally dropped out at age sixteen, but later completed high school through taking a series of evening courses. He had held a variety of jobs alternating with long periods of un-employment until he reached twenty-five, when he had been hired by the utility company.

The story may seem a bit unusual, but in many respects it has important themes in common with all people. My work with a wide variety of clients, mostly from traditional working-class and middle-income families, convinces me that childhood experiences are critical in understanding how adults be-have and understand their situations, and how they carry from childhood into adulthood ways of making themselves more powerless than they are.

Layers of the Self

Imagine a child growing up in the families that typically make up this society—families riddled with pain, denial, self-blame, repressed anger and emotional narcotics described in the previous chapter. There is every reason to expect that such a child will be emotionally damaged and malformed.

Children develop a sense of themselves and their own identities through a process of interaction with significant others. They come to know themselves by observing and internalizing how the important people in their lives re-spond to them.

What this means is that we form ourselves and our identities in a social process, through an interaction with those around us. But are we, then, nothing but products of social factors, molded into who we are by our social environment?

No. The process is much more complex. The child is not a "tabula rasa," but is from the start involved in a relationship. And that relationship has within it opposing and contradictory tendencies. Each of us as individuals, and through our relationship with others, has a tendency within us to be a fully conscious and loving being. But these tendencies get shaped and ac-tualized in different ways depending on the circumstances that we face.

I am very wary of the model that I present here, for one fundamental reason. This chart, while it will help you to follow some of what I am about to say about childhood, really distorts the reality because it cannot show the point that I think is fundamental: human beings are always and essentially in relationship to each other. Our being is not contained in "the individual," but is always in existence in the "between" that exists between human beings. Failure to recognize this point is one way that our language traps us into conceptions that are fundamentally egocentric. Yet my account here will use language, and hence participate in this distortion. With this warning noted, let us proceed.

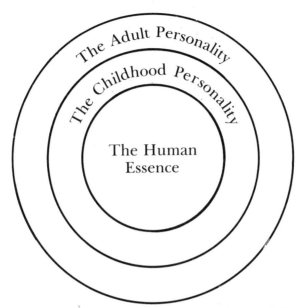

A Somewhat Distorted Image of the Individual

It will be useful for us to distinguish between three aspects of what are called "normal" adults within our culture. First, the core of such a being is the Human Essence—roughly the fundamental aspects of what it is to be a human being, our core capacities that are thwarted both at work and in family life. Second, there is the set of traits and dispositions, comprising a totally functioning personality system, that we have adopted in our childhood—call it The Childhood Personality. This is roughly the personality that we develop during our pre-adolescent childhood. Finally, there is the Adult Personality, the set of traits and dispositions we adopted to be able to present ourselves to the outer world, which we began to refine in our teen years and which now functions as our external self.

Let me hasten to add some important qualifications. Talking as though these were totally separate personality systems is potentially misleading. At every moment all three levels are in a carefully calibrated balance and mutual interaction; it is conceptually useful to separate these different levels of personality, but in daily experience they appear as one unified whole. They are always in a dynamic interaction, and who we "are" at any given moment is the result of an ongoing struggle among these three layers. We should also caution that many parts of the Adult Personality are simply elaborations and refinements of the Childhood Personality, and so it sometimes is difficult to know which part of the personality system we are dealing with. Perhaps it would be more useful to imagine these traits as "layered realities" in which a set of experiences had come to be exemplified and acted out. We might then talk about the childhood layer of that particular trait as the layer of that trait which first came to be part of ourselves when we were young.

Who we are at any moment is the sum total of the struggles among these different layers. In order for children to receive any level of recognition from parents (who have already been wildly distorted through their own socialization process in this society), they must lose touch with their Human Essence and adapt a series of traits and dispositions that don't succeed in winning the love and recognition that they so desire. For reasons that the child is usually unable to understand, the parents themselves have been trapped by their own lives into being people who are simply not available for fully loving and immediate contact. We explored some of these reasons when we saw what happened to adults in the world of work and then how this was compounded by their experiences in personal life. But the child does not have any awareness of this process, and so when the parents are unavailable for fully real emotional contact, the child begins to develop bad feelings about her/himself, and then attempts to compensate in some way. The first way is by adopting a Childhood Personality to please and win the parents' love. But when this seems to fail, the child begins to carry a terrible burden: "the knowledge" that s/he is really terribly inadequate—because s/he failed to generate recognition and love from her/his parents. In a desperate effort to cover up the pain of this "recognition" of oneself as a failure, by early teen years the child is developing an external or Adult Personality to cover him/herself up so that others will never discover the "inner person," namely this Childhood Personality that never succeeded in adequately pleasing the parents.

There are two struggles that are happening simultaneously in any given person. There is first the struggle between the Adult and the Childhood Personality levels. The adult level wishes to keep the child under control. The adult is afraid that the inner child will be "discovered" by others, and that then all the carefully constructed plans to show oneself to be a "together" and "OK" person will collapse. This inner child, most people suspect, is one's "real self"—and it is a very yucky and unattractive self that the people who know you best—your parents—found so unappealing that they couldn't even respond to you lovingly. So most people are sure that no one else will respond positively if this part is shown. The Childhood level, however, has never been fully suppressed. There are habits of acting, personality traits and dispositions, that were adopted in childhood as part of the child's desperate attempt to reach out to parents and get their attention, recognition and love. The unsatisfied thirst for this recognition still impels the child system, and gives fresh energy to these parts of the self to reassert themselves. The Adult Personality does its best to punish this child level and keep it hidden, repressed, and "behaving," but the Childhood level does not disappear and constantly threatens to disrupt the whole adult game. At any given moment how people "are" is a reflection of the current state of this particular struggle.

The second struggle is that between both the Childhood and Adult levels of personality, on the one hand, and the need of the Human Essence to find expression, on the other. At any given moment, there are fundamental human needs that were denied in childhood and are still being denied in adult life. These needs are fundamental to what it is to be a human being—

and they are articulated in the wisdom literature, religions and ethical and spiritual systems that human beings have built. But the entire process of socialization into a society of oppression is a process of denying and repressing these needs. We have already discussed how these fundamental human needs are systematically denied and discounted in the world of work. But human development begins in the family, and it is in the family, itself massively shaped by the impact of the world of work, that we first learn to deny and repress this fundamental level of our being. The repression and denial can only be partial—the impetus towards recognition and love are as much constitutive of what it is to be human as the tendency of objects to fall is constitutive of life in a gravitational system. Yet these tendencies threaten all the sets of compromises that people feel that they had to make in order to first get some recognition from their parents and then, subsequently, to function in the world. The implicit threat to our compromises, the challenge to remake ourselves and our world in accord with all that we could be and deeply need to be, challenges the entire fabric of self and reality that we have constituted. And so, both Child and Adult Personality levels are engaged in struggle to repress and deny any awareness of our Human Essence—and who we "are" at any given moment is partially a description of the current resolution of forces in that struggle.

This picture of inner life shall be filled out in the remaining part of this chapter. The model presented above is useful because it helps us identify how human behavior at any moment can be a result of an ongoing process that has been deeply affected by the world within which we live. The world, in turn, produces human beings who are remarkably well suited to fit and function in a world of oppression. But the model is distorted because it underplays the role of what I have previously called "The Social Unconscious."

To get the full picture, we would have to fill in the details of how at any given moment our perception of all the rest of reality, what is "normal" and what is "possible," shapes also our understanding of the meaning of what our parents are doing or failing to do, and what the meaning is of how other people seem to be responding to us. Moreover, we would also need to factor in the details of how all the significant people in our lives are acting towards us, including the ways that their own childhoods, adults lives and Social Unconsciouses shape the ways that they think it appropriate for them to respond to us. If we can keep these qualifications in mind, we can proceed to look at these dynamics.

Misrecognition of the Human Essence

When I talk about the core personality, or the Human Essence, or what Marx called "species being," I have in mind our tendency towards the actualization of our capacities to be:

(a.) Fully free and able to create ourselves and transcend the causal chains of past events and circumstances and produce ourselves and our world as new historical realities;

(b.) Creative and externalizing ourselves into the world through work and through art;

(c.) Fully conscious of ourselves and our physical, social and spiritual environment, understanding its dynamics and dialectical interconnections, and standing in awe of its grandeur;

(d.) Creating and discovering meaning and purpose in our environment;

(e.) Fully loving of ourselves and those around us, and experiencing other people as ends in themselves whose full realization is part of our own realization, and fully able to respond to their loving by loving them;

(f.) In full solidarity with other human beings, experiencing their pains as our pains, and their joys as our joys, and sharing the deepest intimacy and hope with them;

(g.) Deeply connected to the human past and to the human future;

(h.) Responding in radical amazement and humility to the calls of spiritual reality, and creating human responses to those calls.

It is this set of capacities, which I call the Human Essence, that is basic to all of human reality. I am arguing that there is a fundamental source of human energy that flows through the personality and energizes us, shaping our directions and generating counter-reactions on the part of other layers of our being. It is the human need for full recognition of the human capacities as listed above, and the need for the opportunity to actualize these capacities, that plays the fundamentally disruptive role in class-dominated societies. It is the drive to actualize these capacities which must be suppressed by systems of domination, but, while repressed, it nevertheless still presses towards fulfillment, manifests itself in our dreams, and unconsciously shapes some of our life-affirming behavior. Because the actualization of these potentialities is so completely in conflict with the maintenance of the present arrangements of unequal power fundamental to class society, the very recognition of these capacities must be denied—and this denial is communicated by the dominant ideology, but also by the very way that parents interact with children in family life.

Martin Buber captured part of the process when he described the difference between an I-Thou and an I-It relationship. An I-Thou relationship allows for the two participants to recognize each other as free, conscious, and infinitely precious subjects. An I-It relationship exists when one person relates to another as though s/he were an object that could be manipulated and controlled to satisfy one's own needs and desires. Though we are all fully equipped to experience ourselves as Subjects and to enter into I-Thou relationships, we find from the start of our lives that we are engaged in I-It relationships with those with whom we would want them least. We find ourselves misrecognized by our parents, who typically construe us as some set of roles to fill needs that they have. For example, we may be: (a) the thing that is going to make their own lives OK; or (b) the thing that is very entertaining and oh-so-cute; or (c) the thing that is going to keep the mother enslaved; or (d) the thing that will someday be a . . . (fill in the blank with the adult occupation that this family wants this child to be); or (e) the thing that is so very smart that it's going to learn to be toilet trained at a young age or read quicker than anyone else; or (f) be better at sports, or more charming, or more successful.

There are many theological accounts of why the original break with reality happened but I do not want here to try to account for origins. Suffice it to say, for the moment, that the initial fear of reality has been refracted through the history of class oppression for thousands of years and comes down to our parents as a fully integrated system of work, family life and childhood. Our parents themselves experienced this misrecognition in their childhoods. They came to feel that the only way they could make any contact with their parents was to deny their own sense of their human capacities and see themselves as their parents expected them to be seen. They entered work worlds in which their fundamental human capacities were hidden and denied. They, like us, have a dim sense that some part of themselves has been cut off. But they have done their best to make peace with how the world is, and by and large they expect us to do the same. The way that they respond to us is, for them, the best example they have of "real loving," and they would be astounded if they could experience again the initial confusion and terror that children feel as they attempt to situate themselves in relationship to the experienced phoniness their parents are projecting.

The child's relationship with the parents is from the start a process of misrecognition. The child's Human Essence is not acknowledged. Instead, the parent conveys to the child that the child is a set of roles and that anything more will be too much for the parent to handle. The parent offers an implicit deal: "You will get love and recognition from me of the sort I have available only if you will become the thing, the assortment of roles, in which I am seeing you. If you will be that thing, then I can give you as much love as I have to give." These are the fundamental terms of the basic agreement that governs family life. In some families the details are very rigid: You must act exactly in this way and that way. In other, more liberal families, the terms are much more flexible, and the child can find room for negotiations over specific roles to be adopted. But what both types share is that the child must lose its recognition of itself as having the Human Essence and must become the kind of partial being that will develop a Childhood Personality in response to the need for some level of recognition.

The Human Essence is repressed in the process, but it is not obliterated. Our fundamental capacities may be forced into the unconscious, but they are constantly pressing forward, undoing the best efforts of repressive social orders to permanently dismiss them from memory. They show up in our humor and in our irrepressible optimism, in our music and in our art, in our unconscious gestures and in our dreams, in our legends and in our rituals. They are a constant limit on how powerful or successful Surplus Powerlessness can ultimately be, because they challenge every ideological and emotional reality that purports to assume the inevitability of our flawedness.

How can this be? This Human Essence does not exist merely in some philosopher's platonic heaven, but in the actual experience of humanity. From the beginning, the child does not just face conscious misrecognition, but also unconscious recognition from its parents. The parent communicates in hundreds of subtle and unconscious ways that it really does love and recognize the child—even though on a conscious level it gives out messages that explicitly seem to deny recognition by forcing the child into a more narrow "thing-like" role. The child is faced with a double message: "If you want to be known by me, become thing-like and dead like I am" and a simultaneous unconscious message that, "I am still in here rooting for you, and for myself, so don't give up, because both of us are really more than we appear to be."

Much of growing up involves splitting off this latter message, repressing it to the unconscious, and learning how to deal with the parents' more conscious sense of themselves, which in turn requires that the child develop a sense of self that systematically denies its fundamental capacities. Contemporary psychoanalytic theory also talks about splitting and repression. However, it does not recognize that an important component of what is split off is the fragments of self that hold an intuitive grasp of one's Human Essence. Similarly, psychoanalysts rightly recognize the tendency of some people to seek a regression to early childhood states in which the person experienced more direct satisfactions. But, whereas the analysts sometimes describe this as a desire to return to a state of primitive narcissim in which childhood omnipotence was the dominant experience of the infant, I suspect that the desire is fueled at least as much by a wish to re-experience those moments in which one had not as completely repressed one's Human Essence. The desire to re-experience the Human Essence, far from "regressive," shows a continuing present desire for transcendence of an oppressive reality.

Individual differences among families are important if we are going to understand to what lengths different people may have to go to reclaim repressed parts of their beings. In some families the level of repression may be heavier, and the unconscious remnants less visible, than in others. These differences are themselves products of many factors, most importantly: (1.) How much repression do the parents have to engage in during their working hours? (2.) How much repression do the parents have to engage in in order to hold their relationship together? (3.) How much repression did the parents have to engage in in order to be able to make some accommodation with their parents, who were also products of the dynamic interaction between their own parents' adult life experiences and their own parents'· childhood experiences.*

There is a vicious trade-off in the process of developing a Childhood Personality. Children become active partners in shaping a personality for themselves that will in some way be a response to the demand of parents to

---

* My formulations here have much in common with views of Alice Miller, developed in her book *Prisoners of Childhood*, Basic Books, NY. 1981, itself much influenced by the writings of D. W. Winnicott, Margaret Mahler, and Heinz Kohut. Miller tells us that "the child has a primary need to be regarded and respected as the person he really is at any given time, and as the center—the central actor—in his own activity." I find Miller and the object relations and self-psychologists very stimulating. But I

be a false self. In adopting Childhood Personalities, we get some partial approval and recognition and love from parents, though not the kind of approval and recognition and love that we most deeply want. But even the love that we do get is tainted. We are always deeply suspicious of this love, fearing that whoever is loving us is not really loving us for who we really are, but only for the degree to which we are living up to their expectations. This perception often remains as the only still conscious fragment of our Human Essence. The initial experience of misrecognition and upset at this often predates our language so, as we increasingly become identified with our Childhood Personality, the alienation from our deeper level of being lives on in repressed memory, in dream fragments, and in a nagging sense that something isn't quite right with the world. This latter sense, often labeled "juvenile," may in fact be an important clue to the deep process of repression of our Human Essence.

Childhood Self-Blame

All this might not work so well, and the initial sense of misrecognition might explode into family disruption, if our sense that something isn't quite right didn't get filled in with a very different content. What is substituted here is self-blame: Yes, there is something not right in the world—and it is myself. The way this happens to us is that we are engaged as children in the process of creating a personality and identity so that we can inhabit the same world as our parents and find recognition and love. Most children do their best to mold themselves in ways that will fit their parents' expectations, as best the children can figure out. But no matter how hard they try, they discover that their way of being in the world doesn't fully generate the loving recognition that they need.

When children discover this problem, they typically begin to feel deep pain about themselves. The various roles and ways of being that they have adopted through these years were fine-tuned to meet what they thought their parents wanted. Although their Childhood Personalities are fabrications based on a constant struggle to suppress awareness of their Human Essence, children begin to think of these personalities as their "real selves"—and are then shocked to discover that these "real selves" don't generate the emotional reality that they seek. Most children become painfully aware that their parents aren't really there for them, emotionally alive, and do not recognize or love them for who they are (namely, these Childhood Personalities that they have adopted to please and connect with their parents).

Few children have any understanding of the deflecting conditions in their

---

differ from them in my description of what the primary need consists of. I see an important part of that need to be the need for being in relationship with other "Thou"s, whereas I often suspect these theorists of seeing individual I's as irredeemably and inherently separate when they are most healthy, and relationships as something that can be "achieved" with other "objects" (how revealing the choice of language) when autonomy has been won first. More on this problem in the next chapter.

parents' lives that keep them from being fully emotionally available. They know nothing of the world of work or the isolation of families, the generation of self-blame and the frantic efforts that parents are engaged in to hide from themselves their own bad feelings, with the resultant process of burying their emotions and dulling their capacities for intimacy. Children see how parents are responding to them, and believe that they are the kinds of children who deserve that response. Since children form their sense of self through a process of seeing how others respond to them, it is not surprising that this sense that they are the kids who have been unable to elicit emotional reality, recognition and real connection from their parents decisively shapes how they feel about themselves. Of course, there is a wide spectrum of responses, and the many hues and colors of meaning that are conveyed have a great deal to do with how deeply wounded children become. But the overwhelming majority of children experience some important degree of pain, and interpret the situation they face in terms of their own inadequacies. They feel deep shame about their own inability to elicit the kind of love they need from the people who know them best.

We have been describing all this from the standpoint of the child. Let's try to understand what is happening to the parents.

Parenting and its Distortions

The child discovers itself in the eyes of its parents, but most parents do not really see the child. Many parents are simply not open to the beauty, excitement, curiosity and wonder that they could experience with their children. It is not just that they have suppressed their own core Human Essences and hence find themselves threatened by the way that their own children remind them of what they lost and what they suppressed. It is also that the ongoing pain in their current lives keeps them from appreciating and being touched by their children's efforts to forge Childhood Personalities that would lovingly move them. Most parents are refugees from the pain of their work experiences and the pain of their childhoods. They enter each encounter with their own children in a state of inner pain and frustration. Their attention is scattered and their perceptions blunted by dramas that have been going on in their lives long before their children entered the scene.

The psychic costs of the world of work, I hope you remember, are not only impacting on the people in the most conventionally stressful jobs. While there are many people who have succeeded in repressing the awareness of the psychic costs of their jobs, the constant frustration of their needs to be creative and to use their intelligence at work still was an important impact. Similarly, the people who have spent their days molding themselves to be the "right kind of personalities" to win advancement in their corporations or more clients or customers for their ventures may see themselves as having an advantage over the clerical or assembly-line workers, and may even have time to read the latest best seller on how to be a good parent, but the embedded falseness in one's personality necessitated by competition in the economic marketplace inevitably carries over into the relationships at home. For most people in the society, the dynamics of self-blame and repressed anger are the legacy of the world of work—and we have seen how these emotions then play a role in generating a need for compensation that is sought first in one's spouse, and then in one's children. Many women bring with them the additional pains and frustrations generated by sexist institutions and sexist expectations in their relationships. Both parents bring with them the legacies of their own childhoods, and the pain that they still cause in adult life. All these interact as deflecting conditions, making it extremely difficult for most parents to see their own children's beauty and strength, pain and need. Too often parents respond to these children more as symbols of their own internal dramas, objects who will potentially shore up their failing senses of self or prove something to their own parents or bosses or friends, than as new human beings who offer new possibilities of relationship.

"Wait a second," you may want to object here. "I'm sure that there are some parents like this—perhaps the kind that need to come to therapy or the kind who come from very poor or very oppressed families. But this can't have much relevance to the kind of people I know, people who made a whole big thing of their kids, gave their kids lots of attention, and even took courses on child development or went to support groups for parents or read all the latest books on children. The truth is that in some parts of our culture parents are overly child-centered and yet you seem to be talking as though they were living in the Middle Ages."

My answer is that I am not denying how very much energy many parents put into their children, how much time they give them, or how hard they try to do what is psychologically best for them. All of this is completely consistent with parents being emotionally blocked in a wide variety of ways that prevent them from being emotionally real and honest with their children. All of this is consistent with the parent seeing the child through the frame of pain, self-blaming and anger that they have repressed within themselves. All of this is consistent with the child appearing through a symbolic frame as an "accomplishment" who will be used as part of the parents' own ongoing dialogue with their own parents about their own worth ("Now look at my wonderful child—so now, Mother, Father, will you love me and accept me, now that I've been able to produce this terrific child?"). In short, the distortions in our ability to be fully available and to authentically recognize our children for who they really are, are very subtle and completely consistent with the parent appearing to be "the perfect parent" from the standpoint of external appearances. You have to be there to know—and usually it's only the child who is fully there, knows, but misunderstands and blames him or herself for what is not happening.

Let us stop here for a word of compassion for these parents. Most typically they are people who are trying their hardest, doing their best, and entering parenthood with sincere desires to give to their children all the things that they didn't get for themselves in their own lives. Many of their best instincts towards giving and caring that have in other contexts been suppressed are given a chance to come out in their relationships with their children. Some parents find themselves rediscovering within themselves hidden resources of love that have had little opportunity to be expressed in the rest of their lives.

Most parents give as much love as they can to their children, and give it freely. The very act of giving this love is its own reward—it feels wonderful to the parents, reconnects them with parts of themselves that have been stifled, and re-awakens in them the suppressed feelings of being children themselves. While one might argue that in previous historical periods the bringing of children into the world was motivated in part by economic needs, in the contemporary period it is more often the incredibly moving experience of love and creation and wonder that contributes to why parents bring children into the world.

The existence of this powerful loving part of parents is a central fact of our lives. Split off and repressed parts of the Human Essence are temporarily reclaimed as parents allow themselves to feel parts of themselves that they gave up on even before they learned language. Children experience this bath of loving energy, even when it is communicated in unconscious gestures and indirect ways. The love we experience in childhood is so powerful that it becomes the basis for our search for adult-life relationships that can partially regenerate that wonderful experience for us. And if we are involved in repetitive compulsion of early childhood behaviors, it is in part through a desire to recapture some of the moments of real loving relationship that we experienced at that time, moments in which our Human Essences were allowed to be given some degree of real expression. Whatever the distortions in their loving, most parents offer real expressions of love and caring in childhood that should not be denied, and the real positive contribution that parents make to their children should not be forgotten just because we here focus on some of the limitations.

Moreover, the loving that does come through to us should be appreciated even more when we recognize the incredible array of forces that our parents were up against. Virtually the entire fabric of the social world mitigates against love. Daily life is massively shaped by principles of competition and struggle, and every human being must often accommodate to those principles to the extent that they want to survive in such a world. The degree to which parents have kept alive a spark of loving and caring is testimony to the incredible power of love and its ability to survive, though sometimes in the most distorted of fashions.

And yet, despite the best intentions, and despite these these real achievements, there is no way that most parents can totally escape the massive conditioning that they daily receive in the larger society. Most parents have been traumatized by their own childhoods and by the daily experience of living in a world that continually reinforces the message that it is their own fault if they are not happy. Their own interpretation of their lives makes them feel terrible about themselves: they see themselves as having been the kind of children who didn't deserve to get fully loved, and hence had parents who treated them the way they did; they see themselves as having not gotten to where they want in the world of work because of some deficiency in themselves; and they see themselves as not having created the perfect relationships because of some set of inner faults. So they must engage in a massive mobilizing of their own resources to repress the feelings that they have about what they wrongly perceive to be their own personal failures—and this depletes the energy that might be there to give to their children. The very need to keep their emotional lives under tight control so that the self-blaming and anger that they try to keep within doesn't explode and embarass them publicly depletes them of the strength and the talent to be emotionally real with their children.

Of course, the degree and intensity of this problem varies from person to person, depending on the specifics of each person's situation. Within the life of any specific person differences in a work situation, in a relationship, in the degree to which they have worked through some of their childhood feelings, can play an immense role in altering the specific details of how they will do their parenting. And there are huge differences between people based on the specifics of their own parents' situation, and how badly they were wounded in childhood. If we are to understand any particular person, we can't just rely on the general picture painted here: we need to know the details of their childhood and the details of their current situation. A lucky break that gives someone a better job, or a relationship with someone who helps undermine self-blame, or an experience in therapy or a support group, can have an important impact on how much a person is available to give to a child. These differences are important, but it is also important to see that the general picture is that most parents, despite all the real love they feel for their children, are so absorbed in the emotional pains inflicted by the world of work, the frustrated hopes of compensation in family life, and the legacies of their own childhoods, that they cannot give the spontaneous love and recognition that their children need to be able to allow their own Human Essences to develop and flourish.

Because the child lacks any understanding of these forces operating on the parent, the child usually forms a picture of him/herself as "the person who deserves to be treated in the way that I actually am treated." Their conclusion is that they are not totally valuable, their needs do not merit serious attention, and the people who are closest to them in the world, their parents, don't really see them as being valuable and important.

The story is not over at this point, however. If it were, children would feel badly about themselves, and would be permanently locked into that in such a way that we could close this book in despair of ever changing Surplus Powerlessness. But the reality is that the child has simultaneously experienced the unconscious communications of recognition and caring that have not been totally destroyed in their parents' being. Because children have an innate tendency towards being loving and connected, the experience of unconscious recognition from parents give the child a strong push towards keeping alive parts of themselves that can be given no conscious space in one's childhood families. The nourishment received from these unconscious communications helps sustain in the child desires that cannot be fully repressed and which will ever be pushing for acknowledgment, even in the most beaten down of adults.

The contradiction between the innate need for love and recognition and the actual experience of non-recognition causes the child to perceive that there is something fundamentally wrong in the world. This experience is often non-verbal, and it is felt as pain and frustration. Various writers on childhood have described it as the feeling of alienation, the discovery that there is a rupture in the natural order, a sense of estrangement from the way things are, a feeling of having been thrown into a senseless world, or a feeling that things just aren't right. In fact, it is this feeling of the contradiction between its own needs and the way the world is actually constituted that is the moment of most intense rationality and reality in the life of the child.

Unfortunately, the child begins to interpret this sense of "things not being right" as signifying that "the world is not right because I am not right. I am the source of my pain." This self-blaming runs counter to another intuition the child has: that its own integrity and legitimacy are valid, and that there is a problem somewhere else. It is the conflict between these two ways of seeing things that becomes the first serious inner struggle that children live through.

The very process of acquiring language weights the struggle towards the self-blaming alternative. The language of "reality," the language that constitutes the world for us, simultaneously proclaims to us that the world as constituted is justly constituted. The very act of entering the linguistic system means entering into a world of meanings in which the fundamental fairness of how things are set up is assumed and asserted. People, we are taught, are treated roughly in equivalence to what they deserve. The notion of what is "fair" is one that pre-school children have already mastered, using it to make demands on parents and siblings and childcare mates, and already understanding the limits that have been imposed by the established social order. And, at its most fundamental level, they learn that there is no point in getting angry or upset, because what they are receiving from their parents and from the world is what they deserve, a realistic reflection of who they are.

Ironically, it is your parents, the people who should love you most and who would be most reluctant to tell you anything hurtful or destructive, who are the primary messengers delivering this message. Most parents have themselves bought into the the dominant ideology of the society—so they believe that things are fairly ordered, even though this leads them to blame themselves for what is wrong in their lives. All too often, they convey in words and gestures, in explicit ideology and implicit formulations about how "things are," a deep and convincing sense of things as somehow rightly ordered and just.

The repression of one's Human Essence and the development of a Childhood Personality tailored to meet the child's perception of what the parents want is further impelled by the child's need for the parents' physical and emotional support. Imagine what would happen if the child were to consistently reject the misrecognition projected onto it by its parents, and instead stand up and demand to be fully acknowledged and dealt with without the constant interruptions caused by the parents' inner drama. Of course, the child lacks language through which it could make such a demand known—so it uses its own ways of communicating through crying, tantrums, disruptive behavior, "accidents," and "irrational" (from the standpoint of the parents) demands. The parent is in no position to understand what is being communicated by all this, and typically misses the meaning of the child's behavior, interpreting it instead as rebellion, anger, or lack of respect and discipline.

When the child acts out its upset to the parents, the parents respond through bodily cues, verbal messages of anger or overt violence in ways that discourage the child and communicate clearly that its behavior is unacceptable. The child, then, is forced to recognize that s/he can't really be heard. Its desire for recognition, communicated in the only ways that it has available, evokes in the parents a set of responses that are threatening to the child's continued ability to get physical and emotional support from the parent.

Gradually the child learns that its only real alternative is to repress its awareness that it is being misrecognized and, with that, to suppress the fundamental human needs that are not being actualized in this family. If the child can learn to "fit in" to the picture of reality that the parents project and become the person that can become a part of the drama that its parents are playing out, then the parents will respond with whatever love they have to offer. Given the relative isolation of children, and their dependence on adults, the compromise here seems to be the only possible choice, and one that has its rewards. But because the child knows that part of itself is being denied in the process, the love that comes never feels fully real and adequate—because what is being loved is not one's real self, but only a very partial part.

Becoming Like Our Parents

When children begin to adapt to parental reality, accepting their parents' way of loving as the standard of real recognition, they still face a great disappointment. For all the reasons we have outlined, parents are not fully available to the children, and are mostly absorbed in other dramas; and so, even though the child is doing its best to act in the way it suspects its parents want, it still does not get the deep connection and recognition it seeks.

At this point, the child begins a frantic and desperate effort to produce behavior that will satisfy the parents, and might then generate the kind of loving and caring that the parents seem capable of delivering. The child observes how the parents are in the world—their gestures, their ways of expressing themselves, their attitudes, their ways of treating their bodies, their ways of treating other people, their ways of looking at themselves, their moods, their sources of anxiety. And as this information is assimilated in every pore of the child's being, s/he begins to repeat the behavior. To some extent, of course, this mimicking is simply a learned socialization: this is the available model, so what else is there to use as a guide for behavior? But, to a large extent, the child is engaged in an inner drama in which it hopes to win the full attention, love, and emotional availability of the parent. "Look, Mommy. Look, Daddy. I'm being just like you. Now will you love me—I'm trying so hard!" And when it doesn't work, the child tries all the harder.

Much of the child's behavior in school and with friends must be understood in terms of this internal dialogue. A child may adopt behaviors and ways of being that seem to be weird or out of line to schoolmates or teachers or friends. But, in fact, the behaviors make total sense, because the child is fixated on trying to achieve the loving and caring that s/he so badly needs from his/her parents. So s/he acts out his or her parents' way of being, in the hope that this will finally get through to the parents and cause the parents to give the child more loving and caring. The more intense the deprivation, the more intensely the child ignores the setting and simply immerses him- or herself in behavior that is acting out the patterns that may, hopefully, win the parents' caring.

This drama often takes place on a totally unconscious level. Consciously, the child may be engaged in a very strong struggle to renounce the parent, and to consciously get away from all that the parent stands for. It is not unusual to see children rejecting parental belief systems, ideologies, and styles of life that were their first ways of identifying with their parents. This is the material from their parents' Adult Personalities, which children are very acute at "seeing through." What the child does not reject is the parent's Childhood Personality—the deep ways of being in the world that the parents do their best to deny in their public presentations of self. So, we may see a parent who fanatically believes in moderation generating a child who fanatically believes in some extremist ideology. The public presentation seems very different: the one might be a middle class respectable citizen, the other an outlaw on the Right or the Left. But the personality style of fanaticism, which the moderate parent tried to cover up with all kinds of external trappings, comes through in the behavior of the child. Or the parent may be a strong religious believer, and hold that everyone should love each other, but at home the parent secretly communicates deep intolerance. This communication may be very subtle, but it plays a critical role in shaping the child, who then may be equally intolerant with the parent, and thereby replicate the behavior. The child has no conscious knowledge of replicating the parent, and may even be horrified if this information were ever plainly presented to him or her. On a conscious level s/he may be convinced that s/he doesn't even care what the parents think or want. But unconsciously s/he is desperately still trying to win their love by adopting their ways of being.

The tragic irony of this story is that precisely the behavior that the child adopts is least likely to please the parents. The parents have been feeling bad about themselves for most of their lives. They feel that they were unable to win the love that they so badly needed from their parents. And they feel that they failed in their work world as well, mostly because they were not the kind of people who deserved to succeed. Moreover, they feel terrible about their failure to have created a meaningful and fulfilling life, and see this too as a reflection of their own personal inadequacies. But they have one hope left: that their children would somehow manage to avoid being like them and would be able to become more successful and accomplished in the world. Now, suddenly, they are forced to confront what they perceive to be an ugly reality: their children are just like them, having developed personalities and ways of being in the world that seem all too reminiscent of the things that they don't like about themselves.

Parents who experience their children as becoming similar to themselves are often shocked and depressed. Because parents typically are nourishing self-blaming images about their own inadequacies, they don't want their children to be like them. A frequent response is denial and avoidance: the parents try to pretend that it's not really happening, and to avoid situations in which they are forced to acknowledge the reality. Children, in turn, feel all the more perplexed and despairing when their parents don't seem to notice them even when they are doing their best to be like their parents. The tragic missing of each other at this juncture causes a legacy of pain that will be brought into adulthood. The child grows up with an increasingly shrill voice of inner desperation that dominates his/her consciousness: "Look, parents, look at me, see me: I'm doing my best to be just like you. Why don't you notice me? Please, if you'll only notice how very much I am like you then surely you will love me."

And the parents simultaneously become increasingly depressed as they see in their children the final "proof" of how much they have failed in their lives: "Not only did I fail at work and in personal life, but now I've created a child who is going to be inadequate in the same way I am." The parent may try to interface with this process by telling the child, "Don't be like me. Don't make these kinds of mistakes. Learn from what I did wrong. I don't want you to end up having the same kinds of pain and disappointments that I have had."

The child can rarely hear that message, because the child is focused much less on the content of any specific ideas or beliefs that the parent has. So, typically, the child becomes increasingly like his or her parents. Through their adult lives, these adults are acting out behaviors aimed at winning their parents' love. Not the love of the parents who are now older and may have changed considerably—but rather the love of the parents whose images still live vividly in their minds. It is this childhood image that persists—and we can easily say that within every adult there remains a part of his or her being that is still that emotionally undernourished child seeking recognition from the adult parent—the Childhood Personality. It is this dynamic that makes so many parents become just like their parents before them. And it is these very parents who are now providing the parenting for the next generation.

It is useful to think of parents as having a little child of their own inside them (their Childhood Personality), the childlike being that they were in the formative years of their life. It is this little child, the parent as child, that never got adequate loving and nourishment, and whose needs still determine the behavior of the adult parent. Though carefully kept under control and out of sight by the grown-up, this internal child is still experiencing pain and shaping the perceptions of the adult. Finally, in later years of life, the grown-up ego lets down its Adult Personality system, and that little child begins to speak again. It is not unusual in visiting nursing homes or homes for the elderly to find the very aged talking to their own parents (long since dead), and ignoring the reality around them. The pent-up frustrations and needs that have been so long buried are once again released, and the child tries once again to find love and caring that s/he never got in original child-hood. These poignant scenes only dramatize what is the constant reality of adult life: the ongoing drama by which adults still are engaged in the effort to achieve the recognition and love that they never got as children.

But why shouldn't the adults simply stop this frenetic and unsuccessful search for the love they never got as kids? After all, they realize they really are adults now, and that their children need something different from them. Now that they are adults they no longer see themselves in the terms that were inappropriately foisted on them as children. Why doesn't this "growing up" take place?

The answer is simple: most adults experience the same kinds of emotional dynamics in their adult lives that they experienced as children. Their work-places not only infantalize, but also confirm to them that they have made a mess of their lives and that it is their own fault. The structure of family and personal life mystifies the source of its own failure and strengthens self-blam-ing. The structure of adult life seems to confirm the messages of childhood, and to provide final validation of what one supposed all along: that one's failure to have a fulfilling childhood was in large part due to the same fact that made our parents not love us and not give us the attention and emotional honesty we needed: that we are in some fundamental way not OK. It is this apparently perfect fit between the experience of childhood and that of adult life that keeps us enslaved to our childhoods.

Hiding Our Inner Selves

The process we are describing operates to different intensities with differ-ent children, and it would be foolish to think that every family worked in exactly the same way. But before you jump too quickly to tell me about how free of pain your own childhood was, consider the following: it is often the best-behaved children, the perfect students in school and the ones who seem to be well-mannered and performing well in church or community affairs who have been most severely affected by this process. They are being "per-fect" little children precisely because they have internalized the fears most considerably, and have managed to repress their own feelings so completely that they no longer experience any overt contradictions on the conscious level in fulfilling their parents' fantasies, and in trying to fit into their parents' ongoing drama. Conversely, it is sometimes the children who have been least successful in adopting false selves who may be "acting out" in school (by not behaving or not doing well)—and the "acting out" is symptomatic of their inability to accept a world of phoniness and pretense, even though they may themselves be unable to articulate their feelings in that way.

Most commonly, however, children fall someplace between these two ex-tremes. By early teen years they are developing public personas, the Adult Personalities that to some extent fit the desires of their peers while simultane-ously developing separate inner realities in which they "know" themselves to "really" be the Childhood Personalities that never generated parental love. This inner self is valued as the "real" side that they can cleverly hide from the world, but simultaneously they may feel bad about it because this real self is, they believe, not so wonderful.

Although taking form in "healthy" egos by early teen years, the split begins to develop as soon as children enter school situations. Early schooling could be a place in which the emotional realities of home were discussed and shared, and in which children learned that they were not alone in facing the kinds of pain that they must endure. Instead, these central issues in their lives simply don't appear to exist—the school pays no attention to them. Nor do other children open themselves up to discuss their own pain—for they, too, are thinking that their problems from home are their own personal issues. Many children are loaded down with the burdens of anger and shame from home lives which have made them feel terrible about themsleves. They approach each other already so involved in their own inner dramas that they cannot be fully available for their peers. To protect themselves, children build up external personas that will permit them to function, to "pass" without being really noticed for the pain they are in, a pain rooted in their own self-perception as inadequate and not fully deserving of love.

This external facade eventually develops into what becomes the Adult Personality. The Adult Personality helps us present ourselves to the world in ways that we think will be acceptable—and it is also used as a defense against our own fears that who we "really are" is that Child Personality who has experienced such pain and disappointments. While we often think of people being "in trouble" when they can't let go of this bad self-image that they carry from childhood, I believe that the people who are in greatest trouble are those whose fear of that childhood reality was so great that they constructed absolutely impermeable Adult Personalities that are completely out of touch with the emotional realities of their childhoods. It is these people who become the "plastic" personalities of contemporary corporate and suburban life—the people who are so out of touch with their own inner lives that they don't even realize that their external facade is a defense against an inner pain that they still carry with them. The pain of that experience is so intense that they have managed to shut themselves off to all of its memories—and, in the process, to shut off access to most of their own deep feelings.

"Well," you might object, "so what's so terrible, as long as they avoid pain?" The problem is that they must also thereby avoid all emotional reality, as they fashion themselves to be appealing to others. They become the people who are most easily manipulated—by the advertisers and molders of the latest fashions in politics, clothes, food, and consumer goods. They are the very people who follow political leaders as they spend hundreds of billions of dollars developing instruments of mass destruction. Never batting an eyelid, these people will accept the contradictory logic of the leaders who tell them that they must support dictatorships in the name of freedom, or pollute the environment in the name of progress, or shut their ears to the cries of their suffering from others who aren't making it. In liberal political climates, they may be the same people who will quickly adopt liberal cliches, only to abandon them in later years when the winds of fashion shift. They are fiercely committed to their facades, and to the denial that there is anything underneath that hurts—though, as I mentioned in the chapter on work, these kinds of people who have never let anything get to them still end up frequently suffering from physical illnesses that are rooted in the stress of their lives.

Not everyone gets such a "successfully" operating facade. Many people are locked in a fierce struggle to keep their memories of the Childhood Personality out of consciousness. They are more "in touch" with these feelings of self-doubt and upset—though being closer to the pain does not always mean being closer to its actual transcendence. While it may be that someone who is closer to this pain may be easier to work with in therapy, most don't actually come to therapy. They deal with their self-doubts and self-blame through alcohol and liquor, through television and various born-again religions, or through lives of furious competition or consumption of material goodies—hoping thereby to divert their attention from the recurring feelings that they are really the same people who were always failing to get love as children.

Wherever you are on this continuum, it is likely that you share some of the key elements of this process. Most people feel isolated and alone, and believe that if they were truly seen by others, they would be seen to be that very self that had been rightfully rejected by their own parents. It is this belief which, when reinforced by our experiences growing up and our experiences in the world of work, makes us feel very unwilling to open up to others and share our pains with them. However helpful social support could really be, the dynamics of self-blaming are so deep that we feel sure that allowing people to get close will only allow them to discover what we think we already "know" about ourselves—that we are the kind of people who really don't deserve too much, that we really are a "mess" internally. While we have memories of another reality, our Human Essence, that are continually pressing forward and not allowing us to settle with this self-definition, we should not underestimate how very powerful are those other memories of ourselves as untogether and undeserving.

School

Our experiences at school typically confirm our worst fears about ourselves generated in family life. Children come into school with various degrees of upset from family life, but the teachers rarely acknowledge or focus on this central reality. Instead, schooling turns the children's attention to a "public life" in which the starting assumption is that everyone is just fine at home, and now all of us are available to learn and play together according to the requisites of this situation.

It is right here that we generate the myth of equality of opportunity: the school teacher will supposedly treat everyone equally, and how any child does in these cirumstances will be a reflection of the worth and talents of each child. By being "fair" in this way, the actual experience of the child in family life is "expunged from the record."

This seeming equality has no reality. The differing levels of pain that children bring to the school situation will have dramatic consequences on their behavior in school and their ability to pay attention to what is being taught. Even before manifesting in differences in academic behavior, the pains and problems of family life shape the roles children assume in social interaction with each other and the school authorities. The drama the child has been experiencing at home gets acted out in symbolic form in the child-care center, the schoolyard, and the classroom. So one child becomes the goody-goody, repeating patterns that have worked in getting a parent's approval at home. Another child is aggressive or angry—acting out in his or her relationship with little playmates the frustrations that s/he has felt but been unable to express at home. Another child just can't seem to concentrate—because s/he is "off in his or her own world," a retreat that s/he has constructed to avoid facing all the conflicting and confusing emotions that her family situation engenders and for which s/he has neither vocabulary nor people with whom it might be discussed.

The assumption that everyone starts out equally, because everyone is coming from a home reality that is just fine, seems to the teacher to be the way to be fair and not impose judgment on the child. But the structure of this fairness is to create a false reality in which everyone is supposed to participate. If any particular child were to interfere with this common reality by showing that things aren't so good at home (not by giving a sophisticated analysis of home life, to be sure, but by "acting out" his/her hurt in the school situation), s/he would be identified as "having a problem." So the child gets a very strong message from the very structure of the situation: "If you are having a problem, if you are upset, this is some personal issue, and certainly not shared by the rest of us, who are all doing very well. You had better keep control of what is bothering you, because your problems are more troubling than those of others. You would be making yourself look foolish to try to have your needs and your hurts be discussed with the other kids." The best move, it seems, is to hold back, to develop an external personality that can connect with other kids, and not to get too close. Learning to be the "right way" in school is learning how to deny one's real feelings and upsets, and to participate in a shared world that is distant from the real feelings that one is having.

If there were any hope that this might be overcome, that our natural tendency for love and solidarity would break through the falseness imposed by the structure of school reality so that we could reach out to the other kids we are going to school with, that hope is quickly smashed by another dynamic: the competitive structure of the learning situation. Schools are constructed to emphasize individual achievement, often at the expense of other kids. The competitive nature of sports and other "games" reinforces the competition built into the classroom itself, so that by the time the child has been in school a few years s/he has learned that this is "just how the world really is." And if their main energy is of necessity aimed at doing better than the next one, or feeling bad at having failed to do better, then there is less willingness to suddenly open oneself to others and begin to talk.

Meanwhile, students become increasingly alienated from school and from ideas. If the world of ideas is presented to children as radically divorced from their own set of feelings, they both learn to discount their feelings and, on a deeper level, to distrust ideas. Why should I put so much energy into learning ideas if they can't help me out in understanding my own daily reality? No wonder that anti-intellectualism has become a powerful force in our society. Ideas are presented in such a way that you have to be aliented from your feelings to feel comfortable with them.

An equally important source of anti-intellectualism is the set of feelings that a child begins to develop if s/he is not doing well in school. Once children have fallen behind others in the class, fears of failing become a factor in keeping them from learning. (Recent analyses have shown that the myth of Black intellectual inferiority has played a causative role in generating a fear amongst Blacks of applying themselves in school because of their fear of failing.) Students begin to hate ideas in part because they are fearful that they won't be able to "master" them and their true inner realities of failure will be revealed to others as they fail at ideas. So they want to stay away from anything that reminds them of this pain. They thus develop coping styles in which they put down ideas, pretend that they never cared about them anyway. In a society that glorifies power and money, these students can quickly find models of people who are successful (perhaps even Presidents of the U.S.) who have never been particularly good at mastering ideas.*

Because their own attention is being undermined by a series of noises in their own heads generated by the emotional upsets of their family lives, many students have problems giving adequate attention to their schoolwork.

---

* Understanding one's world is something we all intrinsically want to do, and there is no intrinsic reason why we all can't do so. This assertion should be distinguished from another assertion with which I do not agree, "Everyone would, if free, always want to spend their energies developing abstract ideas and pursuing them." This latter assertion makes it seem as if everyone has or should have the same interests in life. The totalitarian danger in this latter position is that it then demands that we create one kind of human being, and see every other type as pathological. There is an element of this in any social vision. We certainly do want to define as pathological those who enjoy exploiting or oppressing others; this is not one of the hundred flowers we hope to have blooming. But precisely because of the explicit value dimensions in these choices, we want to be very careful about imposing our values when they are not absolutely necessary for the survival of the rest of us. So, we can endorse creating the possibility for the fullest realization of an individual's desire to pursue an intellectual career, without thereby implying that everyone should do so or that it is a sign of an unhealthy society when some people prefer to go fishing or swimming or listen to music or talk with friends than to develop their capacities for abstract thought. But there is a limiting case: because we do want to insist that everyone develop their capacity for abstract thought well enough so that they can participate in the life of the community in ways that protect and expand their interests, we must have schools that foster a minimum level of competency in abstract thought about social reality.

There is no doubt that sugar, physiological problems, hearing problems, and perceptual difficulties can contribute to the problem in some cases. But the most widespread source of poor attention in class and poor performance is that the child is distracted by the pains that have been internalized at home. Nothing is more poignant than the scene of very talented and decent teachers, often quite idealistic, trying new and innovative methods of teaching year after year, finally growing frustrated and then angry at their students. These teachers keep on looking for a new gimmick or teaching strategy, not understanding how much of their supposed failure as teachers is rooted in the social structure that creates angry and self-blaming parents who then create children who have been deeply wounded by that home situation.

Because neither students nor teachers interpret the learning process in terms of larger societal issues (stress at work, the internalization of stress in family life), there is only one available interpretation: someone has failed— either the teacher (the answer of many irate parents) or the student (the answer that most children begin to believe). In self-defense, many teachers begin to think in terms of "learning disabilities" or some other category that makes problem learners simply "a fact" about the world.

Because all these dynamics proceed within a framework that presents itself as inherently unbiased and "neutral," the child who does well comes to think that s/he is getting an objective validation and the child who does less well comes to think that s/he has received this objective proof that s/he isn't really the kind of kid who deserves a full victory in the world.

This sense of self is reinforced by the class structures in different "tracks" within a school, and among different schools. The schools implicitly give out different messages to different sectors of the population. If they are training children who will grow up into the positions of power in the society, the schools will tend to emphasize self-direction, creativity, and a more holistic view of society and the interrelationships of its various parts. If the schools are training people for whom there will be few jobs, or people for jobs that require following bureaucratic leadership, they will tend to emphasize stricter discipline and less opportunity for decision making within the structure of their learning.

The individual typically experiences what s/he has learned as a reflection of who s/he is. If one has mastered a body of knowledge and learned how to succeed in the world of ideas, one often feels empowered and personally successful. Conversely, if all that one has learned has been preparation for not much more than a low-paying and barely skilled job, one interprets that as a personal failure. By appearing to be neutral while, in fact, providing class-biased education, schools create the setting in which most people learn that they don't really deserve to expect very much out of life because they aren't really that competent or together. To many, this is only an objective confirmation of what they suspected anyway, based on their disappointments and frustrations in making real connections and finding real love in their families.

The children who do "average" or "good" work in school may have work performance levels close to mastery without quite being there—and this may be even more tension producing, because many of these children feel themselves to always be on the edge of being discovered or found out for not being as smart or competent as they feel they ought to be. This dynamic becomes particularly acute among college-level working class students who have "made it" into a state university or even an elite college. No matter how smart they actually are, they often have to fight against a tendency to undermine their own performances by the fear that they will be found out and sent back to where the rest of the kids they grew up with still remain—in very unfulfilling jobs. It is this same concern that tends to make them more conservative than other students in taking risks for social change projects: without any sense of entitlement for being at the university, they certainly don't want to risk activity that might lose them their one chance to move out of the lower rungs of the working class. This same dynamic is an important reason why even demonstrations for the rights of minorities don't attract participation of those minorities—because of the minorities' correct assessment that they have too much to risk by losing this chance at economic advancement.

Many working class and minority students don't want to question the legitimacy of the university, because it is through the legitimacy of the university that they hope to overcome their own fears of not really being fully valuable and smart by having the objective validation of degrees. How sad for many of them when they enter the work force, now fully equipped with this supposed legitimation, to find that the kind of work available for most college grads (and even many with master's degrees in business and engineering) does not confirm but rather undermines their sense of self-worth and dignity. How quickly the little sense of achievement that some people manage to gain through their college experience can be undermined in jobs that provide few opportunities for them to really use what they have learned.

Ironically, even the gifted students or the students who are very popular at school often experience the same split between their inner "real" selves that they know to be unlikeable and their external adult personalities. These students have learned how to do all the right things and can now pull that off. They get credit and recognition. But inwardly they feel quite different. They have developed this external facade, and they are better at pulling it off than most people around them—but that doesn't make them feel valuable. On the contrary, many of these students are acutely aware that it is their external facade that is being loved, not they themselves. They can take some pleasure in how good they are at fooling those around them, but they know deeply that they don't really deserve the love, and that it will disappear the second their performances, or looks, or some other external features are no longer present. So they, too, are often living childhoods of pain—completely covered up by their abilities to project successful external realities. Moreover, they are often envious of people who are less successful, more "average", because they suspect that these others don't have to do something to earn admiration, or impress people in the way these winners feel that they must.

The False Group*: Legacies from Adolescence

The formation of the Adult Personality gets its clearest articulation in adolescence. The drive to create a personality that will be acceptable to our parents is now transferred onto the peer group as a whole. Its values and concerns will be adopted by each teenager with a passion and level of commitment that is fueled by desperation to achieve recognition and love.

The teenager enters the group with a deep hope that s/he will get recognition and validation that s/he has been unable to get in home life and at school. Yet each teenager has already developed a Childhood Personality in desperate hopes of achieving parental love, and has already experienced that personality as inadequate to generate the loving and caring from his/her parents that s/he sought. So the teenager has begun to develop the Adult Personality—a facade corresponding to his/her sense of what would be "acceptable". It is this personality that s/he presents to the group, hoping that thereby they will love her/him and not notice who s/he "really is." But, on the other hand, any validation that comes in this way is felt to be superficial, and the real underlying Childhood Personality still feels ignored and unloved.

Given the pain inherent in this dynamic, why would anyone choose to be with others in a group at all? Because the elements of the Human Essence that have not been totally undermined and which live on in unconscious communications between parent and child seek out other people for contact, love, solidarity. The impulse to be in a group is based on this unconscious yet powerful motive to be connected to genuine community. Yet the tremendous anxiety of being individually discovered to be the Childhood Personality, the undesirable one, leads each individual to be fundamentally false in the group. Convinced that no one else would possibly respond to their unconscious wish for full connection and real mutual recognition, people put forward myriads of signals to the others that indicate that they want them to keep their distances, maintain their facades, and recognize them only in the false forms.

For this same reason, many groups are intensely hostile towards anyone who threatens to break through the mutual confidence games taking place and force a moment of emotional reality. Potential leaders who do not reinforce the shared false consciousness of the group or who threaten to make the various facades less tenable are often discarded when they are not simply smashed. Couples who bring emotional reality into groups can find themselves subject to intense pressure to either break up their relationship, which is sometimes seen as threatening, or to "tone it down" to the emotional level that feels comfortable to the group. In general, the people who are most creative and emotionally alive are perceived as the greatest danger by these false groups.

---

* The idea of "the false group" is one of the many contributions to this work that developed through conversations with Peter Gabel, whose thoughts on the phenomenology of everyday life have taught me much.

The fear that a plague of mutuality might break out and pierce the veils of constructed falsehood leads people to quickly create an external project that can become the focus of everyone's attention. The fear that we might become aware of each other in some deeper way, a fear that is rooted in our perceptions that if people were to really know us they would know our Childhood Personality, lends energy to the frantic search for a shared external reality on which we can focus. Once it has been found, we can all sigh in relief, for now we have a justification for being together and that gratifies (if only in a distorted way) our underlying wish for true solidarity and unity, without risking the deeper level of mutual recognition that might shatter our carefully constructed ways of passing through the world. The phony togetherness of this group, however, requires that everyone stays fused in its false perceptions, and that everyone mutually validates that what is happening is the best possible emotional reality. We are furious and insulted by the person who is not part of the phony group and potentially see that person as an enemy. Meanwhile, we rigidly enforce internal discipline, careful to ensure that no one will disrupt everything by questioning whether we are being as real and as deep as we might be with each other. But the intensity of repression also testifies to the fact that the deeper needs for genuine solidarity and recognition are so strong that they may break through, confronting us all with a desire for the kinds of human connections that are rarely available and which the false groups were designed to conceal.

We all know that this kind of a group can feel both oppressive and reassuring to its members. Though it may be oppressive in allowing no space for our own individuality and thinking for ourselves, it has the good feelings of safety that come from knowing that one's "bad parts" are completely hidden from view. No wonder that teenagers who have been working so hard at finding a way to be accepted in the world and to not show their Childhood Personality find that it is a relief to be part of the pack, with everyone mutually supporting secure boundaries that will never pierce the veil of phoniness.

The reassuring aspects of the false group are sought in adult life as well. The mass flight into an unreal togetherness both expresses that underlying need for real community and simultaneously, out of fear, creates a false reality that undermines the possibility of real togetherness even as it allegedly seeks to create it. Television news reporters are often attempting to create that kind of feeling when they report on a natural disaster or the death of a famous person or the events at a national political convention or the Olympics. And so hungry are we all that we often respond. Nationalistic events or wartime memories are fondly nurtured for our fantasy that we were part of a "WE." I have seen numerous areas in which people clamor for this false unity: a religious community that projects itself as having direct access to the divine will; a city of lonely and alienated people suddenly coming alive in a moment of joy because "We won the World Series"; or a country merging in collective fantasy that "We have worked together to beat Communism somewhere in the world." Nor is this phoniness confined to the groups defending the established order—I have seen a group of workers in an alternative

is painfully inflicted by reality. I see the child as fundamentally in relationship from the start, and it is the historically conditioned distortions in these relationships that provide the basis for the initial struggles between the child's Human Essence and actually developing being. Every "internalized object" reflects this tension in ways that psychoanalytic thinkers often miss.

In this regard, I want to restate the point made at the beginning of this chapter that part of the Human Essence that is being repressed is the fundamental need to be in deeply loving human relationships. And while that need is partially repressed precisely in the process of forming an "individual" identity under conditions of parental misrecognition, it is nevertheless an abiding factor in human life, always pushing us beyond the levels of alienation that we have been taught to accept.

One final technical note: In terms of traditional psychoanalytic language, the preponderance of self-blaming might be seen as a continuation into adult life of the phenomenon Freud describes as childhood omnipotence. Just as the infant acts as though the world were an appendage of its own desires and wants, the self-blaming adult sees the world as product of his or her own will and choices. Hence, things are going badly because one has made it bad—not because there is an independently existing world that may be constructed in an unfair or destructive way. Psychoanalysts and culture critics have talked about a growing epidemic of both clinical and social narcissism— but the grandiosity and loneliness of the narcissistic personality can be understood as a product of a society whose fundamental premise is that each person gets what they deserve in childhood, work and family. Indeed, the discovery of childhood omnipotence may be a reflection of our tendency to read back into childhood both the ideology and the social realities of the adult world—realities that may affect how we interact with infants, and which certainly shape the way children interpret their parents' behavior.

Chapter 8

Anger

The Tyrannical and Terrified Child Within Us

IT WOULD BE USEFUL TO IMAGINE OURSELVES AS HARBORING a little child within, a child that has been terrified of pain and rejection, and that is desperately trying to hide itself from our Adult Personality. Thus the Adult Personality takes shape, and most people gradually lose awareness of their Childhood Personalities. The painful experiences of childhood that formed this little child within us are "forgotten" or repressed—and we identify ourselves with the external personality we have developed. But while that little child may be repressed, it has not been defeated. Many seemingly incomprehensible behaviors of adults can best be explained in terms of the control that earlier child-like personality continues to exert. People are continually acting in ways that are self-defeating, and there seems to be no adequate account of why. But if we look at those forgotten childhood experiences and the meanings that the child assigned to those experiences we can make more sense of much that otherwise seems just "irrational."

Consider Henry Jackson, whom I mentioned at the beginning of the last chapter. Henry was a "responsible" worker from the standpoint of his employer. So when he began to act in troublesome ways, it was quite unexpected. Surely, an important part of his response was simply a covert form of resistance to an oppressive new foreman who was "on his case." But Henry was troubled by his own behavior and by his continuing focus on the foreman even after the latter had been transferred. Again, we might have sympathized with Henry's sense of outrage—but wished that the energy were channeled into union activity or political work designed to change the stressful work situation. Instead, Henry became obsessed with his feelings, and they interfered with the rest of his life. The outrage did not make him more powerful, as it migh have, but instead made him less able to function both on his job and with women.

What was diverting Henry, and undermining him, was a set of unexpressed and unworked-through feelings about his childhood. Obviously there was a way in which the foreman reminded him of his own oppressive father. But why didn't he simply say to himself and to me, "Part of the reason I don't like this guy is because he reminds me of the way my father was unfair and destructive to me when I was a child." The answer, I believe, is that Henry couldn't integrate into his adult consciousness the feelings he had as a child—though they still played a determining role unconsciously.

Henry didn't want to think about his childhood too clearly, because he remembered himself as having been a terrible child, someone who had made a mess of his own life. While we as adults could understand that Henry's father acted irrationally, Henry as a child had come to feel that he, Henry, had brought this behavior on himself. He firmly and resolutely blamed himself for whatever had been done to him. At the same time, Henry may have been seeking out new adult situations like those presented by his father, so he could work out again what he had failed to work out as a child.

When I dug deeper, I found that Henry had often abused his younger sister, sometimes simply teasing her, but by the time he was eight he had actually hit her a few times under the pretense that *she* was "misbehaving." Henry also told of an incident in which he had stolen a dollar bill that his mother had left on the kitchen counter, and then had falsely sworn that he hadn't done it. These behaviors were part of the repetoire of behavior that had convinced him that he really was an "ornery" child who deserved whatever was coming to him.

Henry was no longer shocked by his childhood behavior, and his Adult Personality could say "No big deal" about those incidents. But he nevertheless felt convinced that he had screwed things up for himself as a child, and that's why his father was always angry at him.

I have seen this same pattern repeated in many clients—the strong self-blaming about one's own childhood, complete with documented cases that the child has drawn up against him/herself, much like a jailhouse lawyer. The case appears very strong to the prosecutor who has developed it. It may take months or in some cases, years to get the individual to see that the little child once was itself a victim, and not the cause of his or her own unhappiness. The feelings are so strong and so deeply embedded that it often takes a very careful and sensitive helper or therapist to assist in unwinding the various strands of self-blaming. After all, they are based on years of experience in which each event was interpreted through the frame of the child who thought that s/he created his or her own pain and emotional isolation.

Henry carried this image of himself to school. He was above average in intelligence, but he did terribly in school. His explanation was simple: he was a mean kid, and he was always getting into fights. Eventually, through therapy he became aware of the anger that he brought with him from his house, anger that he worked out on other children.

But the anger got him nowhere. In the nine years of drifting between ages sixteen and twenty-five he had come to understand how that anger had to be controlled if he was to keep a job—and eventually he succeeded in molding an external personality that made it possible for him to "make it" in his present job.

It was very painful for Henry to discover this underlying anger—because he thought that anger was a complete confirmation of how awful a kid he really was. He suspected that he had a great deal of anger that might explode in any possible way—and this both scared him and gave him strong reason to "keep the lid" on things by staying away from that seething cauldron of feelings that he experienced as a child.

The encounter with the supervisor threatened to blow the lid off Henry's accommodation to this childhood. Here was a perfectly legitimate reason to feel anger—but once those emotions were tapped, they threatened to get out of control. Henry used all of his resources to contain his feelings, and the resulting struggle showed up in his fantasy life, in his dreams, and in various irrational and self-destructive behaviors. But why was it so necessary to keep away from those angry feelings?

In part, Henry was making a realistic assessment that he might do something that would endanger his job. But there were other ways to deal with angry feelings—e.g., by becoming an outspoken activist in the union. Henry couldn't deal with those feelings at all because they brought up a whole picture of himself that he still held within him. In that picture he was the irrational bully who picked on his sister and who couldn't make it at school, the little kid who messed up his own life. Ironically, much of his adult behavior was aimed at warding off those feelings—so they still remained an important part of his life, only they were out of his conscious control.

Once Henry got to this point he began to understand that the feelings of fear that he had about his anger could be dealt with. Here was a case of rational anger at an adult situation mixed with irrational anger from a mixed-up childhood. Right? No. The anger that Henry felt in his childhood was quite legitimate, and not one bit irrational. But Henry had never allowed himself to fully feel that anger, and had never understood that he as a child had been dreadfully wronged. Once he could feel that internal child was justified in feeling hurt and anger, once he could see that child-system within him as a poor innocent victim, he began to develop some compassion for himself. And that compassion became a critical element in redirecting his anger in more constructive ways.

Redirecting anger is quite different from dissolving anger. On the contrary, Henry had much reason to be angry. Even when the "bad" foreman was transferred, Henry was in a job that was oppressive in all ways that we have come to understand. While his new foreman was not specifically picking on him, he still acted in the way that many foremen do, and made most workers feel terrible about their work. Henry began to think about the work situation he was in, and once again he began to feel strong anger. But this time he wasn't particularly scared by the anger—it made sense to him, and he reported feeling better about it. After eight months in therapy Henry became an activist in his union and a shop steward, helping fellow workers to articulate their grievances and giving them emotional support to do so.

A few months later Henry was asked by the union leadership to run for a position in the union that would have made him a representative of his shop on the union's executive board. Henry refused, telling me privately what he hadn't said to the union leaders—that he thought the union was not that good, not representative of the members, and that he hoped eventually to run in opposition to the current leadership. However, he had no specific plans on how to do that, and reported to me that some of the people he thought should be running things were in fact now standing for election to the executive board.

I had mixed reactions to his decision. Henry was talking about the union as if it were one of the famous corrupt unions, in a way that was both mystified and abstract. I knew some of the people in the current leadership, and knew that they really had decent intentions and a desire to serve their membership. True, at times they seemed aloof or distant, but I knew that some of this flowed from their being overworked and feeling unsupported by their own membership. Moreover, their move to involve Henry was not simply some co-optive device—instead they were recognizing and trying to utilize Henry's talents for the best interests of union membership. On the other hand, I had a certain pride in Henry's refusal—after all, he was standing up for his own perceptions of the situation and acting in a decisive way. Wasn't this precisely the kind of leadership that the unions needed—people who would refuse to go along with a path that they disagreed with, and instead would provide alternate leadership? I even allowed myself to fantasize that my own good work as a therapist was leading to the development of a rank-and-file movement that would ultimately win power.

Because I had both reactions, I was careful not to provide any feedback that would appear to be supporting or subtly questioning Henry's decision. Perhaps in a few months something would turn up that would help make more sense of what was happening. In fact, however, it was the very next week that Henry came back in with a series of dreams to report. Several months earlier Henry had begun keeping a pad near his bed, and when he woke up in the morning he would write them down. In the course of one week, Henry had several dreams that were all startlingly similar in their major theme. In each dream Henry had taken power, felt powerful and effective, and had then botched things up in ways that made him feel ashamed and frightened. And there had been a series of figures, sometimes resembling his father, who had looked on in shock and disapproval.

I wondered if these dreams were connected to the union elections. At first Henry strongly denied any connection—and then, in a dramatic turnaround in the middle of the session, suddenly he said, "Yes, alright, I admit it, I admit it, I'm scared!" Henry began to cry—the first time since he was a child. I told him it was OK to cry, and that it was OK to be scared, and he cried even more. When he stopped, he began to tell me of a football game that he had played with neighborhood families when he was eight, and how he had dropped the ball. He had been terrified that his father would punish him for being so clumsy, but his father did worse—he gave Henry a look of disdain and disappointment that crushed this young boy. Of course, it wasn't this one "critical incident" that had shaped Henry. The incident was a representative memory of a set of behaviors that had eventually shaped Henry's internal self.

Henry's refusal to run for office was tied to this fear. He was sure that he would flub things if he ever got to a position of responsibility. Some of his criticisms of the union were correct, and his suspicions of being coopted were plausible. But the reason they had as much weight as they had with him was because he was scared of winning, and then being shown up for a failure. It would be much easier to be the lone critic, saying in his heart, "I believe that these people are screwed up, and I could do it better, but I have a good reason not to try."

When I say easier, I don't mean that Henry was lazy or irresponsible—but rather that Henry was afraid that he would be really seen through by people in his union if he were to allow himself to be in the public spotlight, and allow himself to be in a potentially vulnerable position. He would be discovered for who he "really" was—The Childhood Personality that had been formed in response to his father's pattern of rejection.

Loyalty to Powerlessness

There was another level of Henry's resistance to running. A part of Henry did not wish to have too much power and felt more comfortable seeing himself as not being able to run for union office. There existed in Henry, as in many clients I have seen, a fierce loyalty to powerlessness, developed in part out of the many accommodations to real powerlessness that they must make. But there is more to this dynamic. I have taken pains to explain that no childhood can simply be the product of rejection and misrecognition. Even as the child represses its awareness of the Human Essence, s/he receives unconscious and sustaining communication from the unconscious manifestations of the Human Essence in his or her parents. At the very moment that s/he is being misrecognized on a conscious level, s/he is being recognized unconsciously—and this provides some of the basis for the ability to continue to feel gratified through his or her parents. Because these feelings are not just painful but also gratifying, the child develops a loyalty to this mode of connectedness. By remaining the child that was a failure and powerless, one also remains in connection to one's parents. So it is partly out of loyalty to his father that Henry did not want to succeed, because Henry was connected to his father precisely in his own powerlessness.

This same pattern applies to our connections to the adults in our life—the people whom we care about at the workplace, and the people with whom we make our long-term loving commitments. We have known them and become connected to them through various accommodations of our own powerlessness. So, part of the fear of changing our positions of powerlessness comes from a fear of shaking loose from those connections. We have no real basis for believing that their worlds could be changed along with our own, so that our empowerment would be mutual. And we are very scared that, in becoming more powerful, we will abandon them, betray them, and then be both subject to their rage and also responsible for their pain. Out of loyalty to those whom we love, we refuse to seriously consider making ourselves more powerful, and instead fall back into the very personality styles that have been the inadequate but the only real bridges that we have to them.

I have seen this same pattern repeated in countless incidents amongst people in the progressive movements. There is an underlying fear that the individuals really are not OK—a deep sense of personal knowledge of who they "really" are, based on a childhood experience of rejection or isolation or parental discounting of the child's reality. This fear then colors the individuals' reactions to adult life situations. They begin to feel uncomfortable in situations where they might actually win, have power, and be able to exercise determining voices. So they adopt strategies and political viewpoints that are guaranteed to protect them from the risk of ever winning, of ever being exposed, of ever having to be seen through. They adopt a language, a style of relating, or a political viewpoint which is sure to alienate others—and in doing so, they feel as if they are being true to themselves. On a conscious level this sense of being true is based on the content of their elaborately worked out political ideology—but on an unconscious level, they are being true to their own feelings that they deserve to be isolated, that they have always made a mess of things, and that they are the kinds of people who would never generate real love and caring if they were known in the same deep way that their parents knew them.

Much of the thrust of this book so far is to show that these self-blaming attitudes, though originally developed in childhood, are not simply remnants of childhood. The whole emotional thrust of the world of work is geared to reinforce and regenerate those feelings. And the ideology of family and personal life, the fantasy of compensation and fulfillment, are powerful daily reinforcers of this process. It would be a serious mistake to think that all one had to do was to uncover the childhood system to uproot the whole problem. But childhood systems do play an important ongoing role—because our inner child still exists, often in fragmented forms, under the cover of the external Adult Personalities, that are our public presentations of self.

Given all this, is there any hope that Henry could ever escape the painful legacy of his childhood? Yes. But Henry first needed to deepen his caring for the wounded child inside him, to really and more fully accept that child. What was holding Henry back was that every time he would begin to love and care for himself as a child, he would simultaneously begin to feel feelings of anger that scared him. He had never worked through his feelings of anger at his father, and he was afraid that if he came close to them he would lose control. Yet, there was no way to proceed without a significant release of anger. The grieving for himself as a child could never be thoroughly accomplished until Henry dealt with anger.

The Positive Emotion

Just as human beings have a natural tendency to actualize their capacities for love, cooperation, sharing, intelligence, freedom and self-determination, so we also have a natural and healthy psycho-physical response to situations in which these capacities are being frustrated. That response is anger. Anger is a powerful emotion, and a positive emotion. In a healthy human being, anger results from frustrated human capacities, and leads to action to change the situation that frustrated the expression of those capacities. In this way, human beings have a built-in mechanism that leads them to change the world in ways that make it more conducive to human self-realization.

But anger can also be destructive when it does not get a chance to be released in healthy ways, or when it does not lead to action. In these cases, anger builds up, gets to levels at which it can no longer be completely contained, and then bursts out in inappropriate ways and at inappropriate objects.

Self-blaming is the classical instance in this process. The anger that we rightfully feel at some external impediment to our self-actualization is directed inwards, with very destructive consequences. While research to date is undeveloped and inconclusive, there are many health scientists who believe that anger directly effects bodily processes, causing or intensifying bodily stress reactions that damage internal organs and that weaken the immune system. On the experiential level, anger always feels terrible, and the pain of it needs to be alleviated in some way.

We explored some of the results of holding back anger in earlier chapters— the frantic efforts to bury the awareness of this pain through alcohol, drugs, tv or frenetic social, political or religious activity. Most of us have encountered people who were obviously engaged in this struggle to control their anger. The sports coach who yells at his or her team, allegedly to get it to "do better" on the field, sometimes is simply releasing anger that has little to do with helping the players. The parent who explodes at his or her children, supposedly to "teach them a lesson" so that they won't mess up their lives, is similarily engaged in the process of self-deception. We have all seen the religious fanatics who let out their anger by oppressing the members of their own sect who don't live up to the prescribed "correct" behavior, or who lead intellectual or physical crusades against those who have not yet accepted the correct doctrine (ironically, in the West, this is usually tied to verbal behavior about "loving your enemies.") In the anti-war movement I was particularly startled by some of the pacifists who volunteered to be "monitors" at the demonstrations, committed to keeping the crowd from erupting into violence: they were often themselves quite obviously filled with anger and hostility which they let out on fellow demonstrators who weren't behaving in the "proper" nonviolent and orderly way. (Could their pacifism be a product of their fears of what would happen if they ever allowed any of their anger to be released?)

I mentioned these examples not to cut these people down—because I believe that *everyone* who has grown up in this society has much reason to feel anger. When we don't have any good ways to let it out, the anger builds up. And the more the anger builds, the more that people get very scared of it. Often they fear that it is so destructive that once they let down the constraints they would "go crazy" or kill someone. So keeping it under control is often experienced as a life and death struggle.

Ironically, it is the very fear of letting it loose that actually helps make it look so dreadfully awful. Very few people would go crazy or kill anyone if they actually let their anger go, and particularly not if they could regularly let their anger express itself in words and in action. It is precisely the storing up of the anger that becomes destructive in words and in action. When anger can't be released in natural and healthy ways it sometimes seeps out inappropriately—in a massive outburst against a loved one or child, in a destructive rage against some inanimate object, or in some other scary way. The tighter the controls, the more massive the eventual eruption. In some cases, the need to control the anger becomes so extreme that the person has to hide from him- or herself any awareness that the anger exists.

But if anger is expressed when it actually is experienced, and if it is not internalized and directed against oneself inappropriately, it can be a health-producing and cleansing emotion. The release of anger can be positive when it is allowed to be coupled with appropriate action, action aimed at transforming the conditions that generated the anger in the first place. In my view, neither the anger nor the action are, apart from each other, sufficient: both parts go together. When that actually happens, anger is a positive and valuable human emotion.

My research, described in the chapter on stress, also showed that when there was a decrease in self-blaming there was an increase in anger that is externally directed. However, it is important to look at the kind of anger if we are to understand specifically how anger functions. We distinguished between anger that was problem-focused and anger that was generalized in the environment (random anger that gets directed irrationally at friends, co-workers, family members, random strangers). Using the Hostility Score from the Brief Symptom Inventory, and the Anger and Hostility Score from the Profile of Mood States, we found that this random anger and hostility that is so destructive to everyone significantly decreases when people have gone through an Occupational Stress Group emphasizing externalization of anger at societal structures that are oppressive. On the other hand, as might be expected, problem-focused coping and problem-focused anger increased! In short, our empirical work completely substantiates the value of encouraging anger that is directed at real oppression. It discredits those who fear that anger is a kind of faucet which, once opened, will pour out in every-which direction without any possible control. People in the experimental group said that they felt much more in touch with their anger, and much more comfortable about expressing their anger, and much less afraid that their anger was too explosive. But these very same people decreased on the scale of random hostility—their anger increased, but only anger that was focused and channeled toward concrete action to change the conditions that initially caused the anger. Hence, the important increase in problem-focused coping.

Anger Has A Bad Reputation

If anger is potentially positive and healthy, why has it gotten such a bad reputation? The primary reason is that anger is an emotion which is particularly threatening to those who have power in this society, because it could be directed against them. Precisely because anger would lead people to feel strong and would potentially be associated with action to relieve their oppression, it is an emotion that is always seen as threatening by the ruling class. For any ruling class, the message that they want the oppressed to hear is a message that emphasizes putting up with oppression rather than fighting it. They much prefer the message that says "Turn the other cheek" to the message that says "Uproot the .evil from amongst you." For that reason, ruling classes have always favored religions that taught people that evil was something that had to be endured, either because it was inevitable, or because its punishment would happen in some future world. And they have always supported an approach to culture that saw anger as ugly and destructive.

Creating an anti-anger bias in the culture is not a matter of giving good arguments against anger, but rather of indoctrinating people with feelings of guilt and shame about the anger that they felt, and associating anger with everything that is repulsive and disgusting. It is more a matter of getting people to internalize a sense that "good manners" requires the suppression of anger, and that showing anger is somewhat analagous to spitting on the lush carpet of a living room floor or defecating in public. To the extent that ruling classes succeed in getting a population to internalize these feelings, they can maintain their rule without excessive dependence on force.

Yet the force of the powerful always lies behind the injunction against expressing or even allowing oneself to fully feel anger. The bottom line has always been that when anger is expressed, those with power will not hesitate to use that power to cut down those who are angry. There is, in most situations, a remarkably short space between the expression of anger to those with power and some form of retribution, often quite excessive, that puts the angry person in his or her place and shows others that it doesn't pay to be angry. Whether the retribution comes in the form of torturing, killing or jailing the angry oppressed, or "merely" in firing or suspending someone from a job, the message is usually quite clear: "If you express anger at me, you will be in deeper trouble than you bargained for."

The expression of anger becomes unsafe—unless you are prepared to go all the way, to follow through with action that overthrows the system of power that you are angry at. This reality provides the experiential base for the fear of expressing anger, rooted deep in the collective history of the peoples of the world, embedded in the common folk stories and family wisdom that gets passed from generation to generation. The idea that if you get into your anger you won't be able to control it and it will run away with you actually makes sense in a social order where you are often prevented from expressing total anger and backing that up with force. The social reality of class-dominated society ensures that you are not allowed to get into anger at all unless you are ready to let it dominate and become the major emotion determining all of your experience. This perception becomes incorporated in the Social Unconscious.

In such a social reality, it becomes quite understandable why people become afraid of their anger, and feel a strong need to control it and keep it well hidden. The various ideas that justify repressing anger, the styles of etiquette and manners that reinforce that suppression, must be seen as cultural expressions and supports to what is fundamentally a strategy for survival in the face of oppression.

It is precisely because parents love their children and want them to be able to survive in this world that they teach the children to suppress their anger. Nurturing families and communities encourage their members to suppress anger because they fear that children raised to express anger will be destroyed.

Unfortunately, this very good and clean motive is often mixed with another less attractive parental motive: the unconscious acting out on children of behavior that is a response to trauma the parents experienced in childhood. Equally important: Parents, because of the pain of their own childhoods coupled with the pains they experience daily at work and in the frustration of their hopes for compensatory relations, often are not lovingly available to their children in ways we described in the previous chapter. Without any larger social view of the causes of their parents' behavior, the children simply see their parents as doing things to them that make them angry.

Their parents, as we know, have often come home from a world of work that has been frustrating and destructive. These parents have no place to vent their anger. And they have received no real appreciation for who they are and what they have been trying to do. When they find that their children are venting anger at them, often for reasons that they don't fully understand (because they are not always fully aware of the way their behavior is being experienced by their children), they become even more frustrated and upset. Rather than understand what is happening for their children, many parents experience their children's anger as a final stab at their own self-respect and dignity. Here they have been struggling all day to pay for the food and shelter and clothes and toys and vacations and sports equipment and everything else to make a nice home for their children, and their children don't even appreciate them. In fact, no one appreciates them. All the pain and daily upset that they have to put up with at work seems all the more difficult to bear if your children are angry at you. And what right, anyway, does a child have to get angry when things aren't going right—do they have any idea of how much anger you've had to repress all day just to keep your job and your life from falling apart? These reactions are not always so conscious, but they are strongly there. The fragile edifice of daily life that most people have put together may have a sweet and pleasant appearance, but not too far below the surface lingers all the pain and frustration we have described in earlier chapters. And this is precisely why the children's anger can suddenly ignite such intense responses.

And parents do typically respond quite intensely. Children's anger may be dismissed in ages one to three as "temper tantrums", but if these tantrums continue, most families give very clear messages to their children aged three to six about the necessity of repressing and containing their anger. Quite often, those messages are communicated through physical violence (quaintly described as "spanking"), through shouting at the child, and through menacing gestures and language. Parents quite often respond with excessive anger: all the pent-up anger that has no other place to be expressed can now be transferred onto one's child. Sometimes there may be a "good reason": the child is being irrational, is acting sullen or disrespectful, is refusing to do things that s/he ought to do. But parents pick up the anger underlying these various acts of resistance to parental authority, and they respond with an anger far out of proportion to anything that has been expressed to them.

It is through this process that parents manage to do to their children what the ruling class has done to them: repress the legitimate expression of anger. After all, children are not born angry, but they are born needy. They need love, attention, caring, and the opportunity to actualize their human potential. When this is interfered with, they feel angry and express it (though not always in the most articulate ways that can be fully understood by adults).

Parents rarely respond by legitimating that feeling of anger. If the parents could take that expression of anger less personally, if they could see that their children are right in feeling anger (but wrong to think that it is their parents' fault that they are being kept from actualizing their potential as a human being) there would be a basis for a real alliance between parents and children. But this requires something that most parents are not prepared to do—because, in fact, parents do blame themselves for what has been happening to their children. Parents have learned in the world of work and in family life to blame themselves for all that is not happening in a humanly satisfying way.

When their children begin to feel anger at them for not being fully available and giving, the parents could respond by saying to themselves, something like this: "It's too bad that my child is feeling angry at me—but I know that my lack of full emotional availability is not my fault, but a product of an oppressive social reality at work that I have brought home with me and of my own childhood. When my child gets older s/he will understand the stress that this inhumane system produces, and the psychological consequences it has for me, consequences that make me less of a parent than I would otherwise want to be. But in the meantime, it's good that s/he is allowing herself to feel this anger, because s/he has plenty to be angry about. And, although her anger is misdirected at me, since I too am also in part a victim of this order, that anger can't really hurt me now. Once s/he is older, having learned to express that anger, s/he can join with me and others to direct that anger against the forces that have really been responsible for making me so beaten down and exhausted and stressed from work, so pained in not getting more satisfaction in family life, that I ended up making serious mistakes in relationship to my children." But, instead, most parents feel terrible that they really *are* to blame. That feeling is so painful that it hurts to experience it. One way to escape that feeling is to scare the child out of expressing its anger. In some families this is done through violence or threats of punishment, in some families it is done much more subtly through the implied threat of withdrawal of love if the child isn't "nicey-nice" and doesn't put on the act that s/he is ever so happy with his/her parents. But whether through overt force or gentle coercion, most children learn quickly that they must suppress even the awareness of their own anger to survive in their families.

The impact of this on children is quite dramatic. Children become frightened of their own anger. They are frightened, in part, by the obvious danger that their anger produces: the possibility of being shouted at, spanked, beaten, or more subtly rejected and denied loving energy. But they are also frightened of their parents' fear. Their parents' reactions have been so out of proportion, so excessive, that it is clear that their parents are scared. Most children do not reason, "My parents must be scared of being reminded by me of the ways that they have failed in their lives, and that's why my anger produces such an extreme result." Instead, most children come to believe that the reaction of their parents must be appropriate in some way—which means that they must be more yucky or awful than they had previously understood, because look at what they are eliciting from their parents. Most commonly, the children begin to feel that their anger is really something scary, that their anger may get way out of control, and that if it does, it may really hurt or destroy something. After all, if their own parents, who know them best, are so scared by the child's anger, it can only be because they see this anger as something very powerful and destructive that must be repressed. Something that powerful within them must be carefully contained. So, if the children are not immediately successful in containing their anger, they become scared of it themselves, and adopt various strategies for blocking these feelings from their consciousness.

It is precisely this fear of one's own anger (an anger that has been so powerful that it even "got to" and "shook up" the most powerful people in their world, made them act hateful and irrational or violent towards them) that makes it so hard for grown-ups to remember the feelings that they had as children. They have systematically repressed these memories because they were so painful, and because they made them feel so terrible and ashamed of themselves. They believed that the world was just, and so came to feel that their parents' heavy repression of their anger was just—and that there was something terrible about how they were as children. When people tell you that they can't remember too much about their childhood, very often the reason is that they unconsciously fear that their memories of even non-anger-related events might open up a flood gate of emotions that would bring them back into contact with these feelings about themselves as kids—feelings that they were really terrible for having anger, feelings that they were so ugly that they justifiably provoked negative parental reactions. People who will tell you that they had completely wonderful childhoods with deep connections to their parents sometimes will simultaneously tell you that they can't really remember very much in detail—and have no idea why! In other respects they may be psychologically sophisticated, know Freud's work, even use Freudian theory when analyzing other people, and yet they may feel perfectly unconflicted and unperplexed by their failure to be able to remember many details of their childhood experiences!!! It is my view that many of these people are still nurturing a picture of themselves as fundamentally "not OK," and that they can never get beyond this feeling about themselves until they are able to look in depth at their childhood, re-experience the anger that they were forced to suppress at that time, and now realize that the child that still lives within them was right, that its reactions were legitimate, and that it was deeply wronged as a child. The reason its anger was repressed was not because it was irrational, crazy or ugly, but because it constituted a threat to parental reality which parents were unable and unwilling to deal with, given their own situations.

All these dynamics are compounded in many working class and poor families, or in families of oppressed minorities, by the desire of children to take care of their parents. While unable to articulate this in any clear way, many children unconsciously pick up on the neediness and vulnerability that their parents are feeling, even though that vulnerability and neediness may be covered and masked as parents become oppressive and domineering. So the children suppress their angry feelings because they feel this vulnerability and don't want to hurt their parents. They understand that their parents are really terribly fragile, and that beneath the huffing and puffing through which parents try to show how tough and "in control" they are, beneath the irrational outbursts of emotional distancing, really very scared and vulnerable people who could very easily feel pain. Few children can articulate these feelings—but many act as if they were in touch with this deep understanding of who their parents really are. So they often try to rescue the parents, take care of them, protect them. One way they do this is by not allowing themselves to feel their own anger at their parents, and to even feel guilty if they do feel anger. Ironically, some of these same children may proceed to moderate their anger and then use it manipulatively to control parents through threats of being angry.

School and Work

The need to repress anger is greatly reinforced by the dynamics of school. Teachers, faced with overcrowded classrooms, rigid instructional curricula, and harassment from school administrators, are often not able to be fully available to the children, not able to give them what they need in the way of nurturing and support and individualized attention. Children often need that attention because they come into school full of sounds in their head about how inadequate they are, noises that in any event tend to distract them from giving full attention to their school work. But far from getting the emotional nurturance that they need in order to learn, students can't even get individualized attention for problems that they are facing with specific areas of the curriculum. Caught between the expectations of their parents that they will succeed in school (expectations that are often emotionally charged with the fantasy that this will be a way for their children to avoid the stressful work that these parents have to endure daily) and the frustration of not getting the help they need to make it possible for them to succeed, students often feel angry and upset at school. The anger is often quite justified—because the schools do not give the students what they really need. But the moment that the anger comes out it is met with fear, anger and repression. The teachers and administrators take the anger personally, and it raises for them a set of fears about their own failures to be the kind of educators that they want to be.

Given the lack of adequate staffing and the strain on people's time, there just is no time to give individual attention to the needs of students to express their anger. "After all," they reason, "this isn't therapy, this is school, and if the kids can't fit in here, then let their parents deal with it." This attitude is unrealistic and denies the actual reality of parents' lives. But it is forced on teachers and administrators who would quite quickly lose their jobs if they were to attempt the creation of a different kind of learning environment, one that helped children deal with their anger and legitimated it. No one would be quicker to react than most parents, who would be outraged that their children were being taught that anger was OK. So teachers fit into the constraints, and become enthusiastic disciplinarians, teaching children how to keep their feelings to themselves and threatening the children who express anger with the possibility of being sent home from school, suspended or even expelled.

With these dynamics in place, children can grow up and fit into the world of work. They have already learned that their anger is dangerous and must be repressed. And lest they forget, they will be quickly retaught the lesson, often at considerable personal expense, should they express that anger at work, challenging the right of the bosses to run things their way. If anger gets expressed, it often leads to problems, harassment, not getting promotions, and sometimes getting fired. But mostly this process doesn't have to take place; many people have learned their lessons so thoroughly by age six that they have difficulty remembering what anger feels like, because they are so good at repressing their awareness of it. The anger that does threaten to break through is quickly turned into self-blaming, and is felt mostly as pain.

No wonder then, that rediscovering our Child Personality isn't so easy. In remembering the ways that we formed ourselves as children in order to win our parents' love, we are also in danger of rediscovering our anger. And in having compassion for who we were as children, we are in danger of recrediting our initial feelings of outrage at the ways that we were treated. So there is a tremendous counter-force to any desire we have to become archaeologists of our own pasts: the fear that we will let loose our previously contained and buried anger. And this frightens us not only because we are afraid we might not be able to control ourselves, but also because feeling this anger makes us feel bad about ourselves, insofar as we feel that having anger is a further confirmation of how "yucky" we really are.

The Subtleties of Anger

There are important qualifications I must add in any discussion of anger:
(1.) I am not suggesting that people should go around in this society letting

out their anger whenever and wherever they feel like it and on whomever they please. This is silly because anger gets dissipated only when it is expressed at the correct object of the anger. People don't get to feel better if they let out their anger on random bystanders—on the contrary, they feel bad about themselves, and this increases their self-blaming.

Moreover, therapies that suggest people should just let out their anger at whoever is causing them upset rarely understand the actual constraints faced by people in a class society. Most working people exist in working conditions that both generate anger and that prohibit its expression. It is not some psychological hangup that keeps most working people from expressing their anger to their supervisor—it is fact that they would be suspended or terminated. Therapies that don't recognize this, and that base themselves on the greater freedoms available to upper-middle-class and ruling-class clients, can actually create a new source of self-blaming: "I'm not OK because I can't even express my anger the way that all these other healthy people can."

But whereas you may not be able to do it by yourself whenever you feel the anger, we can do it together. It is appropriate for us to let out our anger—but we need each other's protection in order to get away with it. This is one of the potentially health-producing aspects of the labor movement, and of political movements. Unions and political movements can create a social space in which people can fully express their anger, and may even be able to make it possible for workers to express their anger directly to their bosses without risk of reprisal because of the strength and shared anger of that movement or union.

(2.) Anger is positive when it is linked to action. Otherwise, it can wind in on itself, produce new levels of frustration, and become for some people an end in itself. Of course, in any therapeutic process, the freeing of our ability to express anger may be an important step. Sometimes in order to learn to do this, people may have to temporarily abandon any specific thoughts about how to direct their anger. The demand that anger must be goal-directed or "responsible" may be perceived as continuous with the demands parents and institutions have always made on children to be "reasonable" that effectively delegitimate their feelings. But getting in touch with anger is only a step in a process and must be completed by being linked to concrete and specific steps to change the sources of our stress. To make our anger effective, we must learn to link our anger with each others' anger, see that we share a common set of problems and a common source of anger—and then use the anger as part of what binds us together. Anger, when linked to action in this way, becomes a central part of any program for empowering people, undermining self-blaming, and creating social movements that can potentially change the world. This is why it is so central to work through all the levels of self-blaming, to discover the repressed anger, to teach ourselves how to feel once again the feelings that we had as children but were afraid to fully experience.

Both because anger needs to be expressed at the real sources of our anger (not just at who we happen to be feeling anger at in any particular moment), and because anger needs to be linked to action for changing the conditions that created the anger (and not just changing the conditions that may have elicited our anger recently), we need an analysis of the underlying structures of the society and how to change them. That is, an appropriate release of anger requires a theoretical understanding—not just a response to "what feels good."

This is a far cry from those pop therapists who tell you that all you need to do is to express any anger you feel whenever and wherever you feel it. It is a far cry also from those who think that all our problems will disappear when we can feel our feelings.

(3.) Part of our reason for being upset about anger is that when it can't get expressed in an appropriate way it gets expressed in destructive ways. A world in which people are acting out their anger violently against each other is not the logical outcome of a position that legitimates anger, but rather the outcome of a world that tries to suppress anger where it is appropriate. We call this "Random Hostility" rather than "Problem-Focused Anger." It is precisely these acts of gratuitous violence that scare all of us, and make us more afraid of trusting the people around us. And for that very reason, the people with power will do their best to constantly remind us of every such act of violence, highlighting it in their newspapers while giving no sustained attention to the hundreds of acts of love and caring that also surround us in daily life. The message implied is: "Everybody had better keep their anger under control, or you will be living in a world dominated by violence."

This same phenomena shows through clearly in the way that elites deal with violence in low-income communities; it is often tolerated when it is directed at other non-elites. The acting out of anger against each other in poor or oppressed communities is one of the factors that keeps people separated and depoliticized. We know how debilitating it is, for example, in the Black community for Blacks to act out their anger against each other—and the constant shows of "macho" strength in neighborhood corner fistfights and in family violence creates a level of mutual distrust that undermines everyone's ability to participate in the larger communal struggles for justice. The expression of anger in random ways against each other has nothing to do with the kinds of expression of anger that I advocate, precisely because it is done on an individual basis, done towards inappropriate objects, and done in ways that only accentuate one's helplessness rather than transform it.

That is why I think the results of our study, cited earlier, are so important. Encouraging people to trust their right to have anger, encouraging them to express that anger against specific aspects of their work world that are oppressive has the effect of decreasing random hostility against inappropriate objects. Nor does anger become so consuming that people can do little else. The widespread myth that people will be taken over by their anger and lose control of their lives was belied by our study. Most of the people in our Experimental Group felt fearful about their anger at the beginning of the group, and were very resistant within the group to allow themselves to get in touch with it. In this respect, they were very typical of most people in the society. This is not to say that they didn't ever have outbursts of anger in

their lives—they did. It was precisely these outbursts that made them feel
upset with themselves for being "irrational." Some people boasted about
their anger at bosses or spouses, but when they began to talk more deeply
they quickly revealed that underneath the bravado they were really quite
afraid of their anger and ashamed of themselves. It was only by the eighth
or ninth session that people began to feel different about their anger as they
began to feel that they really did have a right to be angry at oppressive work
conditions or at oppressive societal realities (e.g., racism or sexism). Once
that anger was experienced in a safe context, it did not get out of hand.
Workers did not either "go crazy" or "lose control" as they feared. On the
contrary, in many respects they became more able to focus on their work
and the problems in their lives (hence the increase in "problem-focused
coping"). The ability to express their anger made them more competent to
handle their daily problems, not less so.

In this light, it is no surprise that alcohol consumption by workers in the
experimental group decreased. As the anger gets externalized, and the self-
blaming decreases, the use of various narcotics to deaden the pain is less
necessary. Alcohol, used to suppress the anger or to give it legitimation ("I
was drunk—so my anger is excusable"), has less of a role to play in the life
of a person who thinks it is OK to direct anger at oppressive social realities.

(4.) There has been a tendency in Humanistic Psychology circles in the
past twenty years to emphasize the importance of experiencing one's anger.
Unfortunately, because Humanistic Psychology rarely discusses issues con-
cerning class and the organization of the world of work, its prescriptions
seem class-biased. Who could afford to go around in daily life expressing
their anger when they feel it? Who could allow their defenses to be broken
down completely and then go through a process of slow reconstruction of
their personalities? Certainly not most working people, who have to show
up at work the next day in functioning condition. Though well-intentioned,
the pop psychology prescriptions of many humanistic psychologists often
seem quite remote from the daily life realities of most working people, and
serve to further alienate many workers from the world of therapy.

The vulgarization of Humanistic Psychology by those pop writers who
wanted to make a buck off of it, combined with the class blinders worn by
many of its practitioners, contributed to a strong negative reaction in the
1980's to any approach that called for the expression of anger. This anti-anger
reaction, fed in part by the simplistic ways that those who had advocated
anger were misunderstood, was also a reaction to the inability of those previous "anger advocates" to understand the class nature of the society and
the ways that class structure both shape childhood experience and also constrain many adults from experiencing anger without immediately putting
themselves in danger of loss of job.

For all these reasons, I want to emphasize that we need to create safe ways
for people to express their anger—and not to encourage random expression
of this emotion whenever it is felt. The Occupational Stress Groups were
one such format. I believe that union meetings could be another such format.
And there will be a need to create other contexts in which people can articulate

their anger together and then move with that anger to work collectively for societal transformations.

(5.) Anger is a central repressed emotion, but it is not the only thing that is repressed, or the only emotion that needs to be recovered in a process of becoming emotionally whole. Coupled with the anger there is also pain. The pain of misrecognition, the pain generated when one recognizes that no matter how hard one tries one is not fully getting through and winning parental love, the pain of not getting the kind of contact one wants from childhood friends or not being successful in school, the pain of feeling that one is really a deep failure—all these pains must be uncovered and re-explored.

In the development of any specific child, the anger and the pain are complicatedly inter-related, and no general formula can describe the specific way these feelings will be inter-layered. Part of why the process of unlayering and undoing the web of self-blaming is so difficult is that each person has had his or her own unique story of the ways that the pains were experienced, the ways that anger manifested, and the specific ways that s/he then buried these feelings. One of the mediating factors was the stage in development that the child experienced different pains. Children develop conceptual tools through which they sift their experiences at different points in their developmental histories. A particular pain may take on quite different meanings depending on what categories are available to children to understand what is happening, and what categories children have for storing memories of that pain. All this is simply to say that knowing about the pains and angers of childhood in the abstract is no substitution for the complicated and detailed process that each person needs to go through of unraveling his or her own personal history.

On another level, the pain that one rediscovers by unpacking childhood is not rooted solely in the failure of the Childhood Personality but also in the primal rupture that occurs as the child originally discovers that it is being systematically misrecognized by its parents. The frustration at not being able to actualize our basic Human Essence, creates a common legacy of pain that underlies much of early childhood experience.

(6.) One current reason for the anti-anger reaction is that those who control U.S. industry have succeeded in convincing working people that it is the workers' fault that Americans have been losing jobs and hence they have no right to be angry. The myth suggests that if workers were more disciplined and had less of a sense of entitlement (for decent wages and working conditions), they would be more productive. This view ignores the actual sources of American economic decline, including the vast over-expenditures in armaments and instruments of destruction, the failure of corporations to modernize their industrial plants until foreign capital had developed a competitive advantage, the squandering of huge amounts of money in nonproductive investments (particularly in the mergers of one large corporation with another at huge costs with no corresponding increase in productivity), the refusal to engage in rational planning of production and allocation of resources, and the unwillingness to draw upon the wisdom of working people in designing how work should be organized. Instead, it focuses workers' discontent against each other. It is particularly useful for the corporate elite in discrediting the anger that workers might otherwise feel at plant closures and large-scale cutbacks of social services and "take-aways" in contracts. What right do they have to get angry when they have been too self-indulgent and self-centered all along? Far from being right to be angry, if workers now face difficult work situations it is only the price they must pay for their own supposed previous failures.

(7.) I have noticed a profound anti-anger bias amongst people who are involved in various spiritual disciplines and religious traditions. Religion and spirituality need not be fundamentally opposed to anger—as the biblical prophets make clear. God's anger is both fierce and justified. My teacher, Rabbi Abraham Joshua Heschel, taught that God's anger denotes what we call Righteous Indignation. God is aroused by evil and determined to not be either passive or patient in the face of evil. The God of the Prophets urges His people to not be indifferent in the face of evil. Far from those who teach spirituality as a way of becoming detached from the world of suffering, or as a way of keeping one's equanimity in the face of oppression, the God of the Bible refuses to restrain His justifiable indignation at the way the world has become. We too are enjoined to be impatient and angry with a world of injustice and oppression.

It may be that the whole discussion so far would have been much easier had we earlier distinguished between irrational anger and righteous anger and righteous indignation. I did not do so because I think it all too easy to rush in with a set of criteria that will quickly disenfranchise most anger—in the name of a "Higher Anger." I think it's more important for us to understand how much even displaced and inappropriately expressed anger is itself a product of righteous indignation, anger that was appropriate originally but which was not allowed expression and which was detached from any possible action to change the conditions that produced the anger. People are significantly empowered when they begin to re-understand their own lives and feelings about themselves in terms of the suppressed anger that they felt, the legitimacy of that anger, and the way that anger sometimes got displaced in irrational ways. In particular, we all need to understand how the anger that we felt as children was legitimate, how it was generated by an unhealthy and humanly destructive social order, and how we came to feel bad about ourselves for having that anger. Even our irrational anger as adults is typically rooted in the displacement of anger from places where we have a legitimate right to feel it, where it is really righteous indignation, but where it is still too unsafe to be expressed. A movement to change any aspects of an oppressive order must teach people to feel less afraid of their anger, and less afraid of experiencing the pains of childhood with which that anger is often linked.

Spiritual disciplines must be very careful here. They can extol love and sweetness in such a way that people become more afraid of the feelings within them that are not filled with love and sweetness. This can only force those feelings into an underground existence that gets played out in destructive ways. Even the more sophisticated disciplines may teach people how to observe their own anger without getting "hooked" by it—thereby rupturing the valuable connection between anger and action. If we talk about righteous indignation, as the biblical spiritual tradition does, we must be careful to insist that feeling those feelings and acting on them is a spiritually high path that is to be valued and passed on to our children.

I also reject as without foundation the claim that anger must necessarily cloud our vision or lead us to act irrationally or self-destructively. There are moments when this can in fact happen. Particularly if one has had a lifetime of controlling or denying one's anger, the few moments when it is allowed to emerge may feel so overpowering that we lose sight of the larger picture. But that happens when we get overpowered by an emotion. Love, for example. We all know that people can sometimes be so overwhelmed by feelings of love that they lose sight of the larger picture and act in irrational and self-destructive ways. But we would hardly use this as an argument for why we should stay away from making love a central part of our lives. Rather, we would talk about integrating love into our beings in ways that make it so regular and central to our daily experience that we could still carry on a rational daily existence. Anger, too, may need to be destigmatized and integrated into our lives in ways that make it seem less overwhelming. But until oppression is eliminated, the suppression of anger in a systematic way has largely destructive consequences.

Why So Much Focus On Anger?

When anger is repressed, it most often is directed into self-blaming. The anger that we might feel at an oppressive reality is directed against ourselves. We feel terrible about ourselves, and unable to imagine that we have a right to change things in the world.

I have attempted to show how deeply the pattern of self-blaming and repressed anger flows, how we have a very complex and inter-related set of experiences that act together to make us feel terrible about ourselves, and completely despairing of any right or power to change things. While Surplus Powerlessness is a dynamic that involves our ideas and our feelings, a central source of its power comes from the way that we discount and repress anger from childhood through retirement.

I hope that this discussion can also suggest to you the great importance of anger in dissolving Surplus Powerlessness. I believe that it is absolutely necessary for us to re-experience our childhoods, rework those experiences by legitimating the anger that we never allowed ourselves to feel, and basically side with our Childhood Personality and see how its needs were fundamentally legitimate. The child within us that was experiencing anger was quite right to do so, and it was wrong of others to delegitimate that anger. When we can understand the many ways in which this is true, we are then in a position to more deeply understand our right to anger at an oppressive work reality and an oppressive social structure that continues to function in our current lives. Feeling this kind of anger can then free us to channel our energies into changing things such that we no longer have to feel angry.

I believe that feeling anger in this way, feeling real Righteous Indignation, is an important part of a deeper strategy for freeing ourselves. That strategy, the development of true compassion for ourselves and each other, will be discussed in the last part of this book. For the moment, it is sufficient that we recognize that anger is an important and necessary step, though not the full answer in the struggle against Surplus Powerlessness.

Chapter 9

The Creation of the
Isolated Individual

THE EMOTIONAL ROOTS OF SURPLUS POWERLESSNESS ARE not the products of any single experience or set of experiences. These roots have been produced by the dynamic interaction between childhood experience, adult personal life, and the world of work—all mutually informing and shaping each other.

Reality is a seamless whole. It exists as a totality, and every part of it shapes and is shaped by every other part. We can, for the purpose of describing it, break things up into analytically separable parts as long as we understand that this is just a way of speaking about reality. At any given moment all of our experiences in the economic world—our experiences of competition and betrayal, of self-blaming and anger, of playing along to keep our jobs and of wishing to do more than we can—all of these are present in our interactions with our families and friends. And all that happened to us—how we felt about ourselves as kids, the ways that our parents and teachers treated us, the ways we got disappointed by friends, the experiences on the first dates we had, the movies we have seen, the books we have read—all are present and shaping our understanding of this particular moment and every other particular moment.

If we keep this in mind, it becomes much easier to understand how people come to believe that (a.) We cannot trust anyone else; that (b.) We are completely alone in the world; and that (c.) We have made a mess of our lives. I will try to summarize here what we have learned about this from the last few chapters.

167

We have experienced pain from early childhood, a pain generated by our need to abandon parts of our fullest potential so that we could receive recognition from our parents, who both wished to have real contact and simultaneously felt connected to us only through the set of roles that they had learned and inherited. Our parents had a need to make us "wrong," so that they could avoid the pain of recognizing how they were emotionally abandoning us. Had they understood how their supposed "failure" was itself a product of circumstances out of their own control, had they had real compassion for themselves and their limitations, they could have realized that it would be OK to acknowledge the ways that they were not able to be real for us, the ways that they had themselves been deformed by the legacy of their childhoods, family life, and the world of work. With such an understanding, they might have experienced genuine anger at a world that was now even deforming their relationships with the very children whom they most wanted to love—and their anger might have led them to struggle to change the world. Failing that understanding, they felt terrible about themselves, tried to hide those feelings from themselves, and ultimately participated in a process of making us feel guilty about our anger at them, to the extent that some of us even had to deny to ourselves that we ever even felt such an emotion.

Lacking memory of the source of our anger, we began to feel terrible about ourselves. We tried desperately to break through to our parents, in the process becoming more and more like them, adopting their personalities as our own in an attempt to capture their love and attention. But we never quite succeeded, and we came to feel that this personality that was our "true" self, was really not very wonderful or deserving of love.

These dynamics were continued in school, where our feelings were systematically ignored and discounted, while we were increasingly trained to see ourselves as deserving to be in whatever part of the class structure we were being trained to fit into. Finally, we came to work situations in which we could not have real fulfillment, but in which we were taught that we had shaped our own reality through our own merit or lack of merit. And while we nurtured fantasies of finding deeper fulfillment in personal life, we increasingly became aware of how personal life wasn't working—a final confirmation of our own failures, which, after all, we "knew" we really deserved.

The outcome of all this is an individual increasingly isolated from other human beings and increasingly afraid to make deep and real contact. Because every contact with another is an opportunity in which our supposed inner awfulness will potentially show through, precisely what should be our most satisfactory experiences, our connections with other people, are permeated with anxiety. We distance from each other out of fear. And we experience each other's distancing as a confirmation of our own worst fears of ourselves—they are smart because intuitively they have recognized what we "know" is our inner yuckiness and, hence, they are keeping their distance from us.

It is critical to understand that this is not just some individual pathology, but a collective social process lived through by each individual as personal life. To each of us it appears that the world just *is* a certain way—because everyone acts in that way. We develop a Social Unconscious: a way of perceiving the world that shapes each individual perception according to our shared understanding of isolation and powerlessness.

No wonder, in this context, that many human relationships feel ultimately unsatisfying. Even good friends have, as a kind of cantus firmus or psychological framework for their closeness, the deep belief that the other can't really be counted on for very much, and that if things got really bad there would be no one there for us. Moreover, there is a deep and seemingly intractable belief that abandonment and isolation are somehow fitting—that it is the way the universe was meant to be. Nowhere is this more striking than in the biggest risk most people are willing to take: the risk of connecting with another in marriage. It would be very nice to believe that if people learned better communication techniques all the distancing would disappear. But human beings socialized in the ways we have described will have to recreate themselves in very profound ways before they can hope that their marriages will come close to providing them with the levels of deep intimacy that they both yearn for and need.

At the same time, the existence of our distrust of other human beings which generates so many of the pitfalls of marriage, will simultaneously act to strengthen marital bonds: because, having taken the leap into commitment of some sort with one person, we are sure that we cannot allow ourselves to trust others even this much. Often couples that stay together do so not so much on the basis of having overcome the obstacles to deep trust, as from a deep conviction that no one else outside can be trusted, and so they need to rely on each other as a kind of fortress against the rest of the scary world.

Every aspect of our lives is governed by this distrust and its resultant isolation. We can't stand up to the boss because we know that we will be alone in doing so. We don't speak up at union meetings because we don't want to call attention to ourselves. We are certainly not going to call for militant action through our unions when we know that workers throughout the society will view us as selfish, and will go about their own selfish interests without giving us the support we need to win our struggles. We drive home on crowded freeways, frustrated by the ride but knowing that we can't stand up to the powerful auto and oil lobbies that have prevented the creation of adequate mass transportation systems. We watch violence-filled television programs, because our choices are even dumber situation comedies—and we know that no one is ever going to listen to us about what kinds of shows we would really like to have (which we demonstrate by giving serious shows like "Roots" or "The Wall" the highest tv ratings in television history). We enjoy attending or watching on tv large events at which tens of thousands of people like ourselves are present—but we think it impossible that we could ever organize such events ourselves around activities that we more deeply believe in than rock concerts or football. If we are political people, we put our energies into making very small changes, convinced that nothing larger is possible and seeing few others who would join in more transformative social movements. If we are religious people, we make compromises with established groups, even though they miss important things that we believe in, because we don't think that we could ever get people to join us to create spiritual lives in the ways that we believe would be most fulfilling. We accept schools for our children that we know are overcrowded, uncreative, or which fail to teach the values that we know children need to learn. And we accept chemicals in the air and in our foods that we know have not been adequately tested and which may be shown to cause cancer at some future time after we have already ingested unsafe amounts. In our most relaxed moments, we sit with our friends and fantasize about how we would like things to be—but we immediately retreat from the excitement such visions generate, because we "know" that they are impossible, that no one would ever join us in doing what needs to be done to make them happen, and that even our friends would probably not really want to do it with us.

But is this all really Surplus Powerlessness? Isn't it really true that if one person were to try to act differently, she or he would not suddenly change it all or even very much? Yes, that is true. But the key here is "any one person." Alone there is very little that can be accomplished by "any one person." But together, most of this reality could eventually be changed. True, only eventually, and then only after prolonged and intense struggle. But it could be changed.

What keeps this from happening, in part, is that we can never allow ourselves to become part of this potential "WE" that could transform things. We look at the world with our carefully developed "realism" and we see that everyone is acting only for their own self-interests and consequently that we would be foolish to trust them. We feel deeply convinced that our isolation is inevitable, and that no real basis exists for transcending ourselves and connecting with others in a deep way for any length of time. It is this deep conviction that keeps us from trying, and keeps everyone else from trying or responding when someone does try.

The process that creates us as separate individuals is very powerful. But by the time we get to be adults we are no longer making judgments about what we can change and what we cannot. Instead, typically, we are simply accepting as "common sense" the way the world actually is, including both our isolation and our belief that the world is simply made up of a conglomerate of isolated beings like ourselves.

Theories of Selfishness

To make any kinds of changes in the world, we need to trust each other and rely upon each other. So one way of convincing people that no change is possible is to convince them that they can't trust anyone else but themselves—because everyone is out only for themselves and will inevitably take advantage of people around them who are too naive and trusting.

There is something compelling in this account. In a capitalist society based on competition those people who do not act competitively often end up hurting themselves while those who are most vigilantly self-interested often end up with all the material rewards. You don't have to postulate some inner drive towards selfishness to understand why people would act as egoists in this social order. In fact, what is striking is the surprising amount of self-sacrifice and the continuing impulse towards higher values. While there are always opportunists in any institution or social movement, it is remarkable how many people participate in the Left, the Right, the religious communities, the self-help communities, and the organizations devoted to charity, community improvement, health care, and education of the young with essentially altruistic motives and intentions. Daily life is suffused with little acts of kindness, unexpected acts of generosity, moments of people giving of themselves to others that are a constant source of hope and reassurance. It is these acts that the philosophies of selfishness must either ignore or explain away.

Acts of generosity, commitment and love are the expressions of our Human Essence. They are the residue and expression of our internal urge to be loving, giving and in solidarity with our fellow human beings. Our daily acts of distrust and exclusiveness, our daily betrayals of each other's needs and interests, are completely understandable in terms of the societally sanctioned system of rewards and punishments.

"But society must come from somewhere. True, we live in a competitive society—but isn't this merely the expression of a deeper egoism that is rooted in our very natures?" This way of thinking would have seemed quite incomprehensible to most people living in most societies throughout history. Almost all societies have been based on a much higher degree of mutual caring and cooperation than our own. Societies that were organized around the hunt, societies that depended upon the planting and harvesting of sometimes unreliable crops, societies that shared water sources and fields for grazing of animals, most often were populated by people who recognized communal bonds as primary. If we claim that societies are merely the outgrowths of some more basic human traits, we would be led to assume that the human traits of altruism and mutual care were primary through most of human history, and that egoism is a recent historical invention.

Of course, if we look carefully to the past, we are bound to find many examples of people who were motivated more by selfishness than by compassion and love. But what is astounding is that in most past historical periods this kind of selfish behavior was seen as an aberration, a rare and often horrifying exception to the general expectations of righteousness. When the Bible talks of God's injunction to the Jews to be a "nation of priests and a holy people" there is no sense that this requires some fundamental transcendence of their human nature. When Greek or late Roman plays begin to depict the irrationality and self-centeredness of their ruling classes, it is most often in the context of an explicit (the Greek chorus), or implied (Roman humor) assertion that the larger community finds the behavior to be a violation of the generally accepted expectations of what it is to be human.

What changed this was the emergence of a new class within feudal society, the bourgeoisie or trading class, that put forward its own idea of what it is to be human. Trade itself tended to be an isolating way of living. It involved taking things that had been made, mined or grown in one place and selling them at another place for a cost higher than that which it had cost to make them and transport them. The trader was often seen by the rest of society as a potentially dishonest person charging more for things than those goods were really worth. The trader was not a part of the larger society—he was often the outsider, the one set apart who had been uprooted from the natural rhythms of the seasons that still governed the lives of most people. Alienation was even stronger amongst those who became bankers and moneylenders—engaged in making profits off of wealth that they had not themselves created, and in ways specifically forbidden in the religions of many traditional societies. It is not so hard to understand why people engaged in this way of making a living would begin to develop ideas that were based on the assumption that the larger community's values and needs should not be the highest guide to life and that individuals should be able to determine for themselves what was best. Theories of egoism were a necessary tool in emotional and intellectual survival for this group.

The pressure faced by these people was intensified by the restrictions placed on them by religion. Traditional religions severely limited their ability to function. Through most of history, these limitations were seen as correct and reasonable. But as more and more of these people began to come together in associations, forming towns alongside the medieval castles of Western Europe, they began to develop a sense of their potential strength, and a sense that they should be entitled to live lives free of the restrictions and prohibitions that the larger society placed upon them. They insisted "private" or "personal" needs should be equally legitimate with communal needs, and that the goals of the community should include the fulfillment of the needs of the individual.

This kind of development was an extremely valuable and important contribution. Too often the communities of the past had not been real communities, but instead had been dominated by small groups of people who managed to sell their own special interests as the general interest of everyone. To assert that the needs of individuals should also be taken into account had the potential of being an important corrective. But this is not where it stopped. The rising class of traders and moneylenders met with tough opposition from the landed aristocracy and the church. They were forced to define themselves and their "rights" even more clearly. In the ensuing struggles from the 14th through the 18th centuries this class began to posit the needs of the individual as the highest goal, and to demand that all external constraints on individuals maximizing their own interests be removed. Eventually this included the demand that religion, ethics, and philosophy be purged of all elements that could challenge the rights of the individual to do whatever she or he chose to do, regardless of its effects on the larger body politic. Emphasis was shifted from the community to the individual. The larger society was seen as valid or deserving of allegiance only to the extent that it served the needs of the individual.

These ideas were regarded as very antagonistic to the established religious and economic elites. For hundreds of years ideas about individual rights were seen as revolutionary. But eventually, through the triumph of the American and French revolutions, and less bloody conquests of power in

England, the bourgeoisie became the new ruling class, and its ways of regarding reality became enshrined in the universities, churches, and instruments of mass communication. One important part of that process was to establish the pursuit of individual wants not only as something which should be protected from state intervention, but as the very embodiment of the highest ideas, the very goal of life, and the criterion by which all other activities should be evaluated. To provide a foundation for this approach, theories of the world were developed from Hobbes to Freud to contemporary economists that were based on the assumption that the pursuit of self-interest was the "natural" inclination that people would follow if left to their own devices, and that egoism was not simply an historical aberration but a biological and psychological necessity. Indeed, the whole discipline of psychology developed on the assumption that individuals' needs were the primary unit of analysis, and that one could be "value-free" in investigating the ways that individuals sought the fulfillment of personal wants and the things that got in the way of their fulfillment.

From here it was only a brief step to the position that has been a key prop to the self-justification of competitive societies. This involved the proposition that while people all pursue their own self-interests, there are some people who are better at it than others, because they are smarter, more energetic more motivated, or more something than others—and these people end up being the ones who get the greatest rewards in society. The whole psychology of self-blame follows immediately. If you aren't good at pursuing your own self-interest, you have nobody but yourself to blame, and your anger should be directed at yourself. The retributive aspect of this position, the "It's your own fault—so now live with what you made" kind of tone, seems morally fitting, precisely because it is based on the assumption that, "You were just out for yourself anyway, trying to get what was best for you without regard to anyone else, so you can't come crying to the rest of us if you don't do so well in the scramble for self-interest." And this in turn flows from the view that this way of being is the core of how humans are, the essence of our very nature.

Of course, there is a way of stating egoism that makes it almost true by definition: "Everything a person wants is wanted for his or her own motives, to fulfill his or her own needs." The very fact that someone wants something is usually seen as strong proof that it flows from their own motives. But this is quite different from a version of egoism that has much more destructive consequences if true. "All that individuals want is to take care of themselves, to satisfy their own pleasures and to avoid pain for themselves regardless of its effect on others." In this latter version, we are being told that human beings only have one kind of motive and that all their other wants or needs can eventually be reduced to satisfying their own pleasure.

The problem with this view is that it flies directly in the face of our experience. We have much knowledge of people who sacrifice themselves for their beliefs in an ideal of justice or for a religious belief or out of love of their children. Even if one said, "Well, this is just another kind of pleasure seeking, because people get pleasure out of making these sacrifices," one would still have to concede that human behavior has a much greater range within it than was first implied by saying that people are basically selfish. If being self-sacrificing and idealistic is just another version of selfishness, then it may be that there's nothing so awful about saying that people are basically selfish, as long as it now is meant to include the fact that they will sacrifice themselves for each other to achieve a better society and will give of themselves selflessly to take care of other people.

But this is exactly the point that so much of contemporary ideology is meant to deny. The underlying theme of much of psychology is that human beings are only out to please themselves, and that they are driven to do this by a set of internal urges that they can only barely control. In the traditional Freudian model, the infant is largely uninterested in the outside environment except insofar as it can satisfy basic instinctual needs. Child development is seen as largely about learning how to get those needs satisfied from the external world, with all of its frustrations and limitations. Later ego-development and Piagetian views understood that human beings are also motivated by curiosity and desire to explore and master their environments. On this account, the self evolves in part as a result of a desire to achieve mastery and control over a set of tasks that becomes available to it as ever higher levels of comprehension become accessible. But on both accounts, the model starts with an individual self that has a set of internal needs, and then attempts to account for human behavior as the consequence of vicissitudes in the struggle to deal with these inner needs.

In trying to understand childhood, I talked about a basic core level of human reality in terms of the human need for loving, caring, and solidarity with others. Human beings are fundamentally and inherently social. We come into the world in relationship to our mother, who, in turn, is supported and associated with a whole network of human connections. The food which we eat in utero and emotions that are absorbed into the structures of our nervous systems are themselves the products of a complicated set of social arrangements that reflect the fullness of human experience. From the moment that we emerge from the womb, we are surrounded by a world infused with human meanings and intentions that shape our experiences and call forth our emotions.

I don't mean to be merely suggesting that as human beings we are affected by other human beings. My claim is stronger. Our fundamental essence, our core being, exists in relationship with others, as part of a community of meaning, love and solidarity. The basic reality is, in the words of the theologian Martin Buber, to be in an "I-Thou" relationship, in which our subjectivity itself is a relational subjectivity.

The existence of the "individual" is merely an ideological construct, an idea that was invented to make sense of the modern reality in which people began to act in very self-centered and self-serving ways that negated their common togetherness and solidarity. But, in our essence, we are connected, and our fulfillment depends completely on each other. We have a basic need for the fullest realization of each other's capacities, precisely because our own being is fully tied to all those around us.

No wonder that the quest for individual fulfillment is always so frustrating. The very terms within which it is framed are so heavily infused with the ideology of the "individual" that it is bound to lead to impoverishment. We can only find fulfillment by reconnecting with our human essence, and that would require a full and deep connection with a loving community of others. But, instead, we are surrounded by human beings who have been similarly estranged from their essence, similarly alienated, and similarly seeking their own fulfillment in ways that will inevitably frustrate and disappoint them.

Getting back to our original nature is no simple task. One key step is to recognize that our deepest needs are not selfish, that needs for love and caring and solidarity take us directly into the deepest levels of human connectedness. A second step is to become aware of the things in our world that keep us from total fulfillment. A third imperative is to engage in a struggle to change the world in order to make it more supportive of our being together in loving communities. Yet one of the things that gets in the way of that struggle is the ingrained belief that our deep needs for loving community are actually individual aberrations and holdovers from childhood fantasies or immature yearnings for utopia that the mature individual will eventually overcome.

One of the most sophisticated articulations of the philosophies of egoism is a version of contemporary psychodynamic thought that aims at shoring up ego boundaries. From the correct perception that there is a special class of people who have problems in separating their own needs and desires from those of others, many clinicians have begun to popularize the idea that a major problem facing most people seen in therapy is the problem of getting adequate boundaries. Their notion is that healthy individuals have managed to define their boundaries in such a way that others do not impinge upon them. They can stand by themselves and function well as autonomous beings. From that standpoint, they can enter into relationships at will, making free choices about what suits their desires and when their boundaries may be "permeated." On the other hand, the unhealthy individual supposedly acts out of compulsion and need, is not able to separate him/herself from the needs of fellow humans, and hence is compelled to be in unhealthy relationships.

A part of this account is compelling. There are certainly many individuals who enter into unhealthy relationships out of a desperate fear of being alone and who act overly dependent and needy, often frightening their partners who begin to withdraw in fear of being swallowed up by this neediness. The fact of this withdrawal then confirms the first partners in the fear that they are going to be abandoned. They become all the more desperate in their attempts to merge with others. This behavior is pathological to the extent that it does not result in either partner getting what they want. It becomes equally pathological when one of the partners begins to lose her or his own identity altogether in an effort to avoid losing the other's affection and support.

Yet the real questions we should be asking here are quite different. Why is it that people get so desperate about being abandoned and left alone? Is it merely an irrational concern?

My answers are quite different from those put forward in the psychological mainstream today. I believe that it is totally rational for people to be very worried and upset about being abandoned and lonely because our society creates a set of conditions in which people are always being abandoned, and in which it is extremely difficult to get the nurturance and support that are essential for psychological health. It is certainly true that this worry can be self-destructive when the desperation it engenders undermines the possiblity of finding more fulfilling relationships. But it is also true that when we assess our options we do so in a society characterized by competition and conflict, pain and self-blaming, which typically lead people to act in hurtful ways towards each other. The dynamics that we have explored that undermine family life and personal relations are real—and the fear of physical or emotional abandonment in these circumstances is quite often based on this reality.

The cure to the problem is not producing "healthy" individuals who can stand alone. This ideal itself emerges from the bourgeois tradition of egoism and has little to do with the basic human reality. Human beings need each other, and our very essence is to be in relationship with others. The healthy human being is the human being who can allow him/herself to be vulnerable and who rightly rejects any notion of a life lived in fundamental separation from other humans.

We need each other, we are mutually interdependent, and the height of pathology is persons who have convinced themselves that they can be autonomous from others. We do not enter into the world as a matter of free choice; we enter into the world as products of other people's already existing social relationships. We get a language, a set of categories and a material and emotional support system from others and the ways we have come to understand and feel about ourselves is largely shaped by these others.

Egoism emerged as a mass ideology because the fundamental humanity of people was already being denied. Using the rhetoric of community and solidarity, land-owning ruling classes in feudal societies traditionally dominated the lives and fortunes of everyone. It was this misappropriation of human ideals to cloak domination that led the masses of the oppressed to look with hope towards the worldview being articulated by the rising class of traders and moneylenders who talked about individual fulfillment and an end to subordination of individual needs to the alleged higher goals of the community.

This same dynamic has been repeated in the past two hundred years in the sphere of personal life. While the new ruling class rejected the right of larger communities to impose their wills on individuals, they often believed that the key unit of individual survival was the family. Yet within families they recreated the very dynamics of domination that this bourgeoisie had theoretically rejected in the larger community. In families, the women and children were to subordinate their needs to the needs of "the family" and were to give primacy to creating loving households. But the "needs" of the families were defined by the fathers, the patriarchs who were supposed to be the best "guardians" of the interests of all the others. No wonder that women and children rebelled against this reality, identifying instead with various strains of egoistic ideology that asserted the primacy of individuals' rights above the needs of the community. If patriarchy was the reality of community, then down with community!

People were right to reject the older forms of community because they were pseudo-communities that masked domination. But they mistakenly brought the glorification of autonomous individuals and their needs into a new ideology, which has created an equally oppressive new reality.

The call to return to community and to loving relationships flows from the essence of our being—and it challenges the theories of selfishness and the psychologies of individualism that predominate today. But it is not a call to return to the oppressive communities and families of the past, whose togetherness was phony because it was based on fundamental inequalities of power and respect. Instead, our common humanity requires the development of new communities and new forms of loving relationships that are inherently equal in power and respect. This is the positive side of the effort to support people to feel strong and independent. Loving relationships can only work if they are conceived as the expressions of people who can acknowledge the places in which they are weak, people who can accept that "no man is an island," people who do not feel that they are any less full because they need and want each other, people who feel that they can be most fulfilled when the others around them are also fullfilled.

Does this require some fundamental transformaion of human beings? On the contrary, the fundamental transformation would be required if people were to make themselves into the independent egos that bourgeois ideology tells us we already are. What is most crazy-making in this society is the demand that we be able to stand by ourselves, that we deny our needs for love, that we interpret our neediness and mutual interdependence as problems, that we learn to look on others as objects for manipulation and control. Many of us get very good at doing this. But it is a corruption of our very being and requires the continued suppression of our Human Essence. That is why people end up feeling unhappy and unfulfilled. They develop physical diseases like cancer and emotional diseases like narcissism which accentuate how ill-suited humans are for the self-centered life that they are all thrown into. They experience stress and despair and interpret them purely on individual terms as further confirmations of their own personal problems, rather than as the natural warning signs of an inhuman, sickness-producing environment. A society based on selfishness and egoism requires a transformation of our beings because it is bad for us. The world must be reconstructed on the basis of human solidarity and love, and purged of the elements of manipulation and control that discredited these ideals in the past. The basis of this new solidarity already exists in the loving connections that still remain the emotional underground of this society, the experiences of fullness and solidarity and altruism and idealism that continually threaten to erupt and destroy the false selves that we have all constructed as our best way to deal with the reality of life in a competitive society.

Why doesn't this deeper reality burst forth more clearly? Because of our real powerlessness. Our world has been constructed in such a way that these parts of ourselves are constantly battered down. Those who act upon their lovingness are treated poorly. Because of Surplus Powerlessness we don't believe in ourselves and our right to fulfillment. We get scared that our best selves will turn out to be crazy, isolated, and subjected to the same disappointments that we experienced when we were children. And because we have been taught to believe that selfishness is the reality, and all else mere fantasy, we are encouraged to ignore or discount those fleeting moments when we get a temporary glimpse of all that we could really be.

The Limits of Autonomy

The discipline of academic psychology helps strengthen our belief in the isolated individual as the bedrock of human reality. Psychology has had a very strong impact in reinforcing the prejudices of common sense, dressing them up in academic or clinical garb, and making the world as it appears in our daily experience into the world that must be, the world that is the inevitable product of basic psychological drives. The way this is done is simple: the psychologists start out from the perspective that the actual way people are in the world today is the way that they probably should be—i.e., normal or healthy. They take the majority features of that existence—our isolation, the strong divisions among people, the occasional breaking down of those divisions between husbands and wives, the ability of people to function effectively in making a living in the economic marketplace—and analyze them as the features that make for acceptable people. Not surprisingly, they decide that strong boundaries between people is one of the central aspects of strength. They locate the highest goal as autonomy and, while they are not loathe to see people involved in relationships, they insist that healthy relationships are ones in which each individual maintains his or her autonomy in virtually every respect.

From this standpoint, we get an elaborate description of "normal" child development as the set of things that must happen in childhood in order for the isolated individual to emerge. It is an intellectually clever and sophisticated system in which the adult is written back into childhood, and childhood mechanisms are invented in order to explain what must have happened in order for individuals to become who they have in fact become in our society. Pathology is seen as the failure of this process at some point in the developmental scheme. Because these accounts see the isolated individual as the norm for adult development, they fail to notice the disruptions that take place in everyone's childhood that stem from the fundamental misrecognition of our Human Essence, and the resulting process of frustration of the children's desires for deep and real connection with those around them. The whole process by which the child denies to itself who it really is in order to establish contact with its parents through the mode of their own denial of themselves is not noticed. The way that the child accommodates to the parents' denial of their own essence by denying its own essence, while simultaneously communicating unconsciously with the unconscious desire of the parents to be fully actualized and authentically recognized, is absent from these mainstream theories of child development.

"Now wait a second," you may object. "Are you now asking us to believe that there is something wrong with the idea of autonomy? I thought that was the whole point of your critique—that human beings didn't have real autonomy in this system. If you now are denying that that is the goal of human liberation, maybe I shouldn't get too involved in this thing after all. I don't wish a clever way to be re-enslaved. In fact, that's one reason why I've stayed away from so-called progressive ideas in the past—because they seem to end up like the Soviet Union, with everyone losing their own individual freedom and submitting to an oppressive collectivist state!"

This is a good objection, and quite a legitimate concern. But I think that these are not the only two options. Let me briefly sketch out yet a third way of considering what it is to be a human being.

Human beings, I want to suggest, are fundamentally and intrinsically social. This is not only because we develop a language and a set of categories to analyze our experience that is socially shared, and not only because no human infant could possibly survive without other human beings to nurture and support it. We are social in a more fundamental sense: we are in need of each other. We need each other not just on a material plane, not just because none of us could live without the accumulated wisdom and experience of the rest (even Robinson Crusoe depended heavily on the contributions of all of humanity to provide him with categories of understanding, technology, etc., that he could use to survive as an individual). More importantly, we need each other to actualize our human beingness, our essence, as loving, giving, and connected beings.

Imagine the world in this quite different way: that it is not a sign of weakness and incompleteness and imperfection to be in need of each other. Rather, to be able to acknowledge our neediness, our mutual dependency, our intrinsic connectedness with each other is a sign of great strength and power. The healthy human being is not the human being who can stand alone and who then, if the opportunity should happen to arise, enters into relationship. Rather, the healthy human being is one who deeply needs to be connected and in strong relationship with other human beings. The basic reality is not "I" but "we"—and every reality that denies this "we" is a falling away, an alienation, a being less than we can and need to be.

In this alternative way of seeing reality, the development of the isolated individual is actually a falling away from health, a creation of a being that will be alone and afraid and will call this fear "having a good sense of boundaries."

No wonder, then, that the world of autonomous individuals does not feel so fulfilling for those who claim to occupy it. No matter how therapized they have been, no matter how much they have worked through their Childhood Personalities and come to accept important aspects of their split-off childhood parts, there is still a worm gnawing at the core of existence. The reason? Because the Human Essence is still not fulfilled, and cannot be fulfilled until the world is rebuilt in accord with a new principle, a principle of mutual interdependence and need, mutual recognition of our abilities to be free, creative, loving, giving, and in solidarity.

Recognizing our Human Essence and the frustration of it within this world generates a different way of recognizing our common humanity. To be fully human is to be in need of each other's fullest self-actualization. I need you to be all that you can be in order for me to be as fully human as I can be. Your development, your fulfillment, isn't something that I recognize as an external good, something that would be nice if it happened but intrinsically your personal problem. Rather, once we see the mutual neediness of human beings, our mutual dependency, we can also see that each other's fullest flowering is a personal need that we have. But it is a personal need that is systematically repressed in the process of becoming "an individual" with strong ego boundaries and a strong separateness from each other. Yet this same need is fundamentally incompatible with totalitarianism. The Soviet Union may have manipulated the language of collectivity, but it never even attempted to build a society based on this kind of mutual love and caring. Because the actualization of human potentialities requires democratic participation in political and economic life—precisely what every totalitarian society must necessarily oppose.

That the separations among people are somehow based on falsity and misunderstanding and alienation is not a new insight. I believe that it is the same truth that underlies much of the continuing attraction of the spiritual traditions. We spend our lives in a world of illusions, believing in the fundamental divisions among people, and in the inevitability of loneliness and isolation. But all these divisions would be seen as illusions if we were to achieve the true enlightenment. As enlightened beings we could come to see how the world is based on a fundamental unity, and would no longer be overcome by the separateness of all things.

One reason people are still turned on by these mystical traditions and spiritual disciplines is that they embody a fundamental truth about the world. They pull at a place that is very deep within all of us, and a place that remains part of every experience. No matter how deeply we have come to believe in our isolation, no matter how deeply every interaction is colored and interpreted by our sense of the inevitability of separateness, there remains a part of our being that calls for a radical restructuring of the world so that our Human Essence can be actualized. That call is continually renourished by the unconscious communications that go between people. Just as the initial desire of recognition between infant and parent was both denied consciously and unconsciously reconfirmed, so every human interaction potentially communicates a different message on an unconscious level even as it simultaneously communicates a push-away message on a more conscious level. The Human Essence may be suppressed, but it cannot be extinguished and remains a constant force and factor in human life.

"And yet, aren't these mystical traditions themselves just another variant of a totalitarianism in which the individual is lost because s/he must submit to the arbitrary authority of someone else who runs the community? Isn't this just another oppressive variant of the same thing that I wanted to avoid in Orwellian fantasies of totalitarian control?" All too often, the answer is "Yes." The reaction against the extreme individualism and isolation of contemporary society makes it possible for many individuals to rush into organizations, movements, spiritual disciplines in which one can suspend one's own intellect entirely, and merge into a community that is in fact controlled and manipulated by a guru or a central committee. And, not surprisingly, many people who experience this reality as the only alternative to the isolated individual in society, end up returning to the mainstream with songs of praise to the life of the individual as isolated and hence as uncontrolled by oppressive vanguards of enlightenment. Indeed, it was against these very kinds of communities that people rebelled in the past, allowing the emerging class of shopkeepers and moneylenders and traders to lead them into a society that would guarantee individual freedom even if it simultaneously required isolation and mutual distrust.

The point here is that part of the experience of people in communities in the past has been oppressive. Not everyone who shouts the word "we" can automatically be trusted. But when we look at the source of the problem, it turns out that those communities that have been repressive have been so precisely because the "we" was actually a cover for a dominant "I." That is, too often "communities" have been ruled and manipulated by ruling groups or individuals, and within those groups there were some who were more equal than others.

A liberatory community, then, is necessarily based on the full equality of power of all participants, not just equality in rhetoric but equality in real power. And this flows from our understanding of the Human Essence—we need every person to most fully actualize their human potentiality. Now, one of the most important ways that people get to actualize their capacities is through politics itself—through the mutual fashioning of a social world together. In this very process of creating our joint reality, we begin to become the embodiments of our potential, because we are actually doing what we have the creative potential to do. A community governed by others stunts this capacity, and necessarily leads to us becoming less than we could be. Moreover, in order to ensure that some people maintain power while others do not, an oppressive community will have to mystify reality for us, make us focus away from what is happening in real human relationships, and hence focus us away from the real here and now. With such distortions built in, spiritual truth that arises in this context becomes a distorted truth.

We can build a different kind of community, one based solidly on democratic principles and guarantees of individual rights to participate fully in the shaping of the community. But the basis and goal of these rights is not to maximize any one individual, but to foster the fullest development of all by valuing each. Is this a contradiction? No. Not any more of a contradiction than to suggest that we highly value and treat with respect our livers or our hearts, not because we think that the liver or heart is of value in and of itself apart from the rest of the body, but because we value them as part of the totality. Even this analogy doesn't quite get it, because it misses the sense in which each part must be understood to be intrinsic to the whole and permeated by the whole. It is not that we have a community made up of so many individual building blocks or organs, but that each part is wholly suffused by the totality, and the totality is a dynamic product of the interactions of the parts. In such a community, it makes no sense to think of the individuals who make it up as "expendable"—on the contrary, they are of ultimate value, precisely because they participate in and are constituent of the valued totality. It is this understanding that led the Talmudic rabbis to correctly declare: "He who saves one life is as if he saved the entire universe."

We don't have such communities at the present time. Our attempts at building such communities are distorted, because they take place within the context of a society that produces individuals who do not believe that they can trust each other. So every attempt at building these communities has within it a tendency to reproduce the distortions of the larger society—and to give further evidence to our pessimism and despair.

"But if every attempt to build something new reproduces the distortions of the old, then are we not in fact stuck? And, in this case, isn't pessimism quite rational?" No. The tendencies to reproduce the oppression of the past are not absolute—and there is a counter tendency. In each of us there is a very strong tendency to break out of the ways that we have been oppressed, to reach out to each other, to connect in loving and trusting ways, to become the creative and conscious and free human beings that we are capable of becoming. Much of these past chapters have described how that tendency gets undermined or prevented from finding adequate expression in daily life, but the tendency is never finally subverted or defeated.

"Fine, it's not subverted or defeated. But still, you admit that whenever people actually attempt to build a different kind of community, what they end up with reproduces the distortions of the larger society. We can be optimistic that in the very long run things can be changed, but in the short run, the next hundred years, the distortions will still dominate. And if that's true, then it's quite rational for all of us to pursue our own individual needs, and to relegate the hopes for transformation to a quasi-religious belief system that should not interfere with our daily life activities."

It would be silly for me to try to talk in terms of how many years it would take to transform reality—because there is no way to say until people are engaged in the activity of trying. How long would it take for Chinese peasants to make a revolution? In 1938, it would have been very hard to argue whether it would take ten years or fifty. How long would it take for a people decimated by the Holocaust to create their own State? In 1945, it would have been hard to argue that the Zionist dream would take three years or one hundred. How long would it take for a small group of activists to build an anti-war movement capable of stopping the Vietnam war? Few of the few thousand of us who asked that question in 1964 could have dreamed of the rapidity with which we would become tens of thousands, and then millions. Nor could we have dreamed of the incredible vitality and desire to question all institutions that would become a by-product of our movement, within ten years. While it would be wrong to underestimate the difficulties of the tasks of undermining self-blame, liberating anger and creating communities of people who could give primacy to their senses of "we-ness" and to their needs to actualize their Human Essences, it would be equally wrong to dismiss such developments as impossible or even improbable.

Retrospective on the Emotional Foundations

This part of the book has been dedicated to showing how complex are the sources of Surplus Powerlessness in our daily experience. I have wanted to show that it is quite silly to dismiss Surplus Powerlessness as "merely" psychological—something that could, perhaps, be overcome through a good therapy experience or even just a better attitude towards oneself. We have seen how carefully interlayered are the levels of self-blaming, repressed anger, and individual isolation—and how powerfully these ways of being are supported by the entire fabric of social and economic life.

I have also highlighted that at its roots this entire system is fundamentally unstable. It depends on repressing a fundamental aspect of what it is to be human. As such, it can only function through an ongoing struggle, and that struggle has severe physical and emotional consequences for most human beings. At any given moment, our more fundamental human needs threaten to reassert themselves, and even when they are "successfully repressed" they are never so far from the surface that they can't be mobilized should real opportunities for significant change arise. Most of us become aware of the contradictions between our own inner selves and the way that we have been living our lives at some point or other. But when we do so, we look out on the society and it appears that we are very alone. So most people dismiss these thoughts and feelings as some personal craziness or misperception, and return to living more deadened lives. But the threat always persists that these "moments of awareness" could happen for many millions of people at the same time—and in that case, they would recognize all the others as potential allies and supports. We have been analyzing all the factors that make this unlikely. But precisely understanding how all the feelings that make us feel unworthy and isolated actually work are themselves factors that tend towards the creation of more such moments of awareness. The process need not be spontaneous—it can be created by a movement that sees itself as dedicated to such a task. But before such a movement can become powerful, it must first confront not only the feelings but also the ideas that generate Surplus Powerlessness. So before we describe the strategies for potential empowerment, we must examine in Part II the ideological supports for powerlessness.

• Part II •

Ideas That Generate Powerlessness

Chapter 10

Evil Humans,
Transcendent Technocrats

T HE CONVICTION THAT WE ARE FUNDAMENTALLY POWER-
less to shape our world in ways that would be more fulfilling is a central
element in what keeps us from engaging in the struggle against real powerlessness.

The conviction, of course, is held because it articulates our feelings that
we do not deserve to have power and do not deserve to have a world shaped
in accordance with our needs. As such, it is merely the expression of feelings
that we have been exploring in the previous chapters. But there is never a
neat distinction between feelings and ideas in our lived experience—the
feelings are interpreted through a particular idea frame and the ideas usually
rest upon deeply held feelings. Equally important, we have seen that the
Social Unconscious operates to shape our perceptions of any given situation,
deeply affecting how we will experience and think about reality. The Social
Unconscious is itself formed through a developmental process in which certain ideas and feelings, mutually informing and reinforcing each other, begin
to appear to be so natural and real that they frame for us what parts of
reality are worth considering. But, conversely, as we grow in this society, the
Social Unconscious takes on a life of its own that then makes us pay attention
to certain ideas and discard others. In lived experience, these processes are
always mutually interacting, but in this sector of the book we will artificially
separate out the sphere of ideas and explore those that have gained popularity
precisely because they reinforce our sense of powerlessness, making our

186

belief that "nothing fundamental can be changed" appear to be "the common sense of the age."

Most of the new ideologies and world views that have been "taken seriously" by the media, publishing houses, public opinion shapers, educators, and journalists have in common the notion that while the present social order has serious social flaws, these flaws are inevitable—given the nature of the world. Their underlying message is that there is something about what it is to be human, or in the nature of societies, technology or science, indeed, in reality itself, that makes it impossible for things to be significantly different and better than how they are. Change is seen as utopian and fanciful. Theorists who espouse change are dismissed as "naive" and "childish," and those who help popularize the doctrine that nothing new is possible are praised as "serious-minded," "sophisticated," and "realistic."

Of course, these ideas could not be accepted and made popular if they did not appeal to something real in people's experience. The collective memory of attempts at social change that failed, union strikes that were defeated, organizing that got nowhere, protest marches against armaments that had no impact, and individual acts of courage that never got recognition and led to personal setbacks—all these are part of the real powerlessness that sets the stage for receptivity to ideas that seem to justify powerlessness as inevitable. Similarly, the entire set of experiences in childhood, the world of work, and family life that interact to generate Surplus Powerlessness plays an important role in creating people who will feel that the ideas which articulate the inevitability of powerlessness are merely statements of Common Sense.

But the ideas have a power of their own. There are moments in most people's lives when they are so distraught by the conflict between what exists and what they deeply need to be fully human that they begin to consider the possibility of becoming involved in social change. At that moment, these ideas, always a backdrop, play a formidable role in generating the conviction that such activity would be a waste of time. A host of ideas comes forward to argue that we are indeed being foolish because nothing can fundamentally change, except for the worse. These ideas feel powerful and often decisive to a population whose emotional infrastructure has already been so deeply shaped by Surplus Powerlessness. In the next few chapters we will explore some of these ideas.

Human Beings As Evil

Perhaps the oldest, and still one of the most powerful, arguments against human beings taking power into their own hands is the assertion that we are fundamentally evil. The source of that evil has changed in different periods. Sometimes it is attributed to fundamental defects in human reason, sometimes to the dominance of emotions over reason, sometimes to inherent evil inclinations. The conclusion remains the same: "It is folly to rebel against the established order, since no other order could be any better, because human beings are evil creatures and their social products will surely recreate as much evil as exists, no matter what changes are made. The inherent evil of people will be certain to make the new society every bit as humanly destructive as the present one."

The conviction that human beings are fundamentally evil entered the West through the Christian notion of original sin. Human beings were thought to carry with them from birth an essential sinfulness that can only be partially restrained and can never be eliminated. Whereas the earlier Jewish culture had enjoined human beings to remake the world in such a way that it conformed to certain ideals (e.g., "Justice, justice, shalt thou pursue"), the Christian perception was that life in this world was fundamentally tainted, and that the best one could do was to seek personal salvation in the world to come. The vehicle for that salvation could not be the individual or collective efforts of human beings, since the works of their hands would inevitably go astray. Rather, God, out of the goodness which is one of His defining characteristics, decided to redeem the world by sending his son Jesus to us, and salvation is obtained only by those who establish a certain kind of relationship to Jesus. Whether that relationship is to be direct, as the Protestants later argued, or whether it is to be mediated through an established Catholic Church, the central point remains: human beings can only make things OK by relying on Jesus, whose bounty they will taste in the afterlife. There is nothing that they can do in their own lives apart from this relationship to God that will in any way alter their fundamental sinfulness.

The notion of original sin can accommodate within it some of the most morally sensitive and decent human beings who see themselves as forced to accept the moral corruption of the established order because they believe that nothing can be done about it. But, on the other hand, the rulers of a society, can also join in the denunciation of Evil in the world, because they are confident that such denunciations will never lead to any political action, since Evil is an ontological reality. No matter how bad the present world looks, original sin ideas help to promote the belief that there are no human acts of political, economic or social restructuring that would likely make things much better.

The idea of original sin was important historically in transmitting the conviction that human beings are fundamentally evil. However, with the rise of the bourgeoisie in the 17th and 18th Centuries, this concept became less popular. The bourgeoisie pushed the idea that if the feudal ruling classes were discarded there would be major positive changes. The doctrine of "unlimited progress," articulated by 18th Century philosophers and political activists, became the rallying cry of those merchants, manufacturers and bankers who sought the overthrow of the old feudal order. Their message was that they would shape a new social order which would deliver all that people had been denied under the previous ruling class. But once in power, they began to promulgate ideologies that would convince the newly emerged working class to temper its own fantasies about remaking the world. The new rulers preached moderation, decreasing expectations, and "realism." Original sin was revived—both in its religious incarnation (as many bourgeois leaders attempted to revive the very religious worldviews that their predecessors had fought so hard to dislodge), and in a new "scientific" garb in which "original sin" was dressed up to fit the new metaphysical systems of the 20th Century, particularly the metaphysics of science.

In the "scientific" versions, aspects of human behavior or psychological structure take the place of metaphysical evil. Sigmund Freud, writing in the wake of the unprecedented human destructiveness of the last World War, discovered a "death instinct" and found that human beings would act this out through aggressive impulses towards each other. Aggression, on this account, is a fundamental and inevitable outcome of an instinctual feature of human nature. Though Freud himself may have changed his position on this question, many of his followers and popularizers enthusiastically drew the conclusion that any human civilization must necessarily be flawed—and that those who seek to remake the world do not really understand this inevitably "tragic" aspect of reality. All the professional apologists for inaction and human estrangement, from the professors of literature and the marketers of highbrow culture to the essayists and newspaper columnists who teach people what is "proper" to think, found solace and profound affirmation for their political passivity and knuckling under to the status quo in the "scientific" findings of a Freudian tradition which, for that very reason, quickly became a cornerstone of 20th Century "common sense."*

Another "scientific" formulation was given in the 1960s by Konrad Lorenz, who argued that human aggression is an instinctive part of the human makeup, and that it is built up within the organism until it explodes, often in irrational ways. Through extensive studies of animal behavior, Lorenz argued by analogy that human behavior was dominated by a fundamental aggressiveness that originally had served the survival of the species, and which now remained as part of our instinctual nature even though it no longer plays a functional role.

Freud, Lorenz, and many other "scientific" explanations of innate human aggressiveness are the latest formulations of the "original sin" concept. These views are plausible only because they restate in seemingly scientific language something that we have been conditioned to believe as a fundamental part of the ideology of the society. When looked at in detail, they are no more than oversimplifications and conceptual confusions strung together with

---

*Ironically, some modern Leftists and critical theorists have sought to revive the pessimistic elements in Freud's instinct theory as a necessary counter to their correct perception that some post-Freudians were too quick to discard the deeper unconscious forces that stand in the way of human salvation. The American mind has always been quick to gravitate towards philosophies of cheerfulness in which human redemption would be right around the corner. The many sellers of psychological or religious "quick fixes" cannot be countered by reviving a metaphysic of dark and uncontrollable human forces. The "evil side" of human experience should not be ontologized—rather, it must be understood concretely in terms of its actual roots in the interaction between the unconscious forces that were shaped in our childhoods and the continuing legacy of pain and anger that explodes in irrational ways as people are continually frustrated and misrecognized. Those who save a Freudian death instinct from the superficial humanists bring back too much dirty bath water with the baby.

fancy-sounding language. For instance, aggressive behavior as a defense reaction to threats to the vital interest of the organism are quite typical of animals and humans. But it is not at all appropriate to conclude that human beings are aggressive in any other sense. If an animal is aggressive to defend his/her life, or his/her requirements for sex and food, or for adequate physical space, it does not follow that that animal is basically or fundamentally aggressive. We might even say that the animal is being "rational" to act aggressively in these circumstances. And it is precisely these kinds of circumstances that exist for most human beings in society today: it is quite rational for people to be aggressive, given current institutional arrangements. And, as we saw when looking at irrational outbursts of anger—even that makes sense, given the history of childhood repression, and need not be accounted for in terms of some fundamentally flawed aspect of human nature. I shall not try to prove this point in detail—it has already been argued quite effectively by Erich Fromm in *The Anatomy of Destructiveness*, a wonderfully definitive refutation of many of these modern versions of original sin.

In a capitalist society, each individual is encouraged to compete for better jobs, more money and power. Those who win are already decisively shaped by class background and the economic and political connections that class background generates. It is still true that within the limits of one's class position competitive behavior is rewarded, while cooperative behavior is rewarded only if it is cooperation with those who have more power. Children are taught that they ought to compete fiercely, and that they will have a more fulfilling life if they can develop those traits that are sometimes labelled aggressive. Is it any surprise when children so socialized begin to manifest aggressive behavior?

Aggressive behavior is the rule in corporate life. Corporations are engaged in constant struggles with each other for markets, and with political entities to ensure minimum supervision and maximum profits. Individuals within the corporations try to make it up the corporate ladder, competing for jobs. We don't usually even call these behaviors "aggressive"; behaviors which are accepted as normal and ordinary in the lives of ruling elites will not be singled out for comment. However, behavior that threatens the established order will be termed "aggressive." Yet so-called aggression makes as much sense for the lower class as it does for the elites, at least when understood in terms of the alternatives that are available.

Much of what passes for criminal behavior is a plausible, if usually ineffective, response to poverty or material deprivation. Crimes of passion and violence are not rational—but if we understand the anger and rage that many people carry around with them as the legacy of innate frustrations of work (or the lack of it), it is somewhat surprising that there isn't a higher level of irrational anger and aggressiveness. Once we understand the kinds of pressures and tensions people are typically subjected to, and ways in which tension is often directed inwardly at oneself, we do not have to go to any hypothesis about "irrational" aggressiveness.

"But that isn't adequate," you might object. "Maybe an individual's behavior is rational given the larger society—but isn't the whole just made up of individuals, and a product of their aggressiveness?" No. Society is not the product of all of us equally and we do not have equal power to shape it. There is a small sector of the population that has vastly more control over societal outcomes than the rest of us. And when we look at them, their aggressiveness seems quite rational. Class rule has always been maintained by violence—and while ideological control is now becoming much more important, it still has not eliminated the need for violence as a backup. So, if these people who shape the society depend on violence to keep their power, we need not attribute to them some fundamental irrationality. And it is rational for them to encourage a certain degree of aggressiveness in the rest of the population—because the society needs people who can fight its wars, and because this aggressiveness can then be used to divide people up against each other and to promote the kind of disharmony and fear of each other that will prevent them from ever forming a solid united front against the rulers. I don't mean to suggest any conscious conspiracy here. This is an arrangement which works with outcomes that are objectively in the rational self-interest of ruling elites, but that doesn't mean that anyone ever chose them or created them with this in mind.

"But why did ruling classes emerge in the first place? Isn't this where innate evil emerged?" I do not know the full answer. There was certainly some fundamental misrecognition of each other's humanity. A blindness to who they really were or could be. However, it might be appropriate to label "fear" as the founding "instinct," not aggression, and then to talk about ways that the fear might be overcome. Our response would be one of compassion for people who had originally developed that fear, mixed with anger that that fear had later been compounded in ways that led to evil. Exploring this hypothesis may be a direction for future research. For now, our task is to demystify the fear, recognize it as a moment in human history that must be overcome, and proceed to build trust-constituting ideas and patterns of human relationships.

We can also think of ruling classes as emerging in the context of a need to secure a life devoid of material scarcity and meaningless toil. Throughout most of human history, there has been a drastic material scarcity, such that an even distribution of goods would have left everyone sharing the same misery. In such a situation, we need not postulate any inherent evil or aggressiveness to understand why some people would see that they could have a much better life for themselves by subjugating others. That such subjugation felt questionable rather than a simple manifestation of one's natural aggressive tendencies is shown by the elaborate set of justifications people went through to explain this behavior away (e.g., by defining the other as non-human because they looked different or spoke a different language). Most often class societies emerged by one group of "have nots" conquering another group of "haves" and subordinating the latter primarily as a way of getting access to land and thereby avoiding starvation.

What is remarkable about our own period is that for the first time in human history, it is possible to eliminate material misery and replace it with human comfort for all humanity. What stands in the way is not the actual

material conditions, but the social and economic forms of societal organization.* Whatever rationality we might attribute to aggressiveness and domination in the past, it is no longer rational or necesary if we changed the society.
But the very belief that such aggressiveness is inevitable forms a major part
of the obstacle to eliminating the societal conditions that generate aggression.
This is because our belief in the inevitability of aggressiveness makes us fear
changing societal conditions, and because we don't trust each other to really
be different than we are now.

   I think we see here part of the seductiveness of the ideas that generate
and sustain Surplus Powerlessness. They are not groundless ideas. On the
contrary, they are often quite descriptive of some aspects of the way things
are set up now. But what they do is make us think that the way things are
now is the only way things can be. And to the extent that they ignore the
historical sources, they get us to believe that things are fixed in a particular
way. Once we have that belief, we see no point in trying to use our energies
to change things.

Post-Industrial Society

   A major argument used to convince people that they are powerless to
change their world rests on the notion that we have entered a "post-industrial
society" whose structures and forms of organization are required for
maximum efficiency. Unlike the older industrial world in which workers as
a class battled owners, today's economy is producing individuals who gain
power by their scientific or mechanical expertise. What is critical is one's
mastery of complex technology, rather than mere physical ability to do work.
Large-scale bureaucracies have emerged which control production and
within which ownership assumes a diminishing role. Guided by the necessities
imposed upon them by science, the newly developed technical and professional personnel increasingly make the basic decisions of the society.

   The effect of believing this is to further disempower working people.
Whatever powerlessness individual workers experienced in their own lives,
they were potentially capable of coming to see themselves as part of a class,
and that class stood in a pivotal place in the running of industrialized societies.
But now, a scientific and technological revolution has taken place whose
effect has been to replace labor power and the working class which delivers
it with science and the technocracy that delivers it. As Daniel Bell puts it
(*Post-Industrial Society*, 1973, p. 127): "What counts in post-industrial society
is not raw muscle power, or energy, but information." In this line of thinking,
the central person is the professional, who is equipped, by his education and
training, to provide the kinds of skills which are increasingly demanded.
Moreover, the present hierarchical and bureaucratic forms that have

---

*For example, American society could retain its military security and still take two
thirds of its military budget and use it for the purpose of creating a worldwide system
of growing and distributing food that would eliminate world hunger.

emerged are necessitated by science itself. The present organization of work does not derive from the needs of capital, but from the dictates of scientific intelligence. In fact, there could be no better proof of this than to turn to the Soviet Union, a totally different social system, which has followed the logic of science to organize production hierarchically and bureaucratically in ways fundamentally similar to the American system. Why bother struggling to change things, so the argument goes, when the most basic features of society will remain the same in any society that is governed by scientific principles?

This analysis is wrong on most major points. The distinction between managers and owners fails to hold, since the vast stock holdings of managers make them the largest group of owners. More importantly, managers and higher level technical and professional staff have managed to get where they are precisely because they can show to the owners that their work is useful on the basis of the criterion of profitability. It is not that the scientists or professionals suddenly grabbed power, or that they snuck in without anyone noticing, or that they were brought in by capitalists who were impressed with their intellectual credentials. Rather, the new rising class of scientists and professionals has power only within the context of promoting the interests of the owning class, and the owning class still remains a tiny percentage of the population. Imagine that the scientists and technicians of a given firm develop a very cheap way in which to produce a product that would undercut sales of a major revenue producer of that firm—and that this new product could not conceivably yield an equivalent profit. Not only would such a product not be marketed by the firm, but those who had developed it would almost certainly be disciplined. The example is fanciful only because the scientists and technicians simply would not have even begun to put their energies into a venture that would lead them into conflict with their employers. Internalizing the values of the world in which they must work, most scientists and technical and intellectual workers have already disciplined themselves to develop the kinds of products that make sense in the capitalist market. The power of owners remains, though now embedded in the logic of the firm, and not usually implemented by some direct show of power.

The limitations of this thinking are even more obvious when it comes to industry-wide planning and development—the supposed key areas for scientific and technical workers. No large capitalist firm typically decides to cut into its profit margins in a substantial way for the purpose of improving the environment or bettering the conditions of its workers unless proposed changes can be shown to benefit the long-term profitability of the firm. This does not suggest anything about the decency of the people who run the corporations; they are constrained by the logic of the capitalistic market. If they were to cut back their own profits, they would be seen as betraying their investors (who, after all, put money into the firm because it generated high returns), because they would eventually be placing the whole enterprise in danger. Other firms, not similarly inclined, would tend to undersell them and cut into their share of the market. So even though scientific and technical workers have input into planning and development, they do not have much power in determining policy because of the nature of capitalistic enterprise.

What has really happened in the economy is not a takeover of firms by different people (the scientists, technicians, and managers), but rather an extension of participation within the basic structure of capitalism. We now have a larger number of technical, scientific, and professional personnel who are given the opportunity to use their talents and intelligence to perfect the profitability of the firms, and thereby serve the capitalist class more efficiently. That those people increasingly think of themselves as having real power within the system is a tribute to the ideological grip of the system, and in no small part due to the acceptance of theories like those of "post-industrial society."

But the actual experience of most scientists and technicians supports an opposite conclusion. The owners are not becoming less powerful, but in fundamental respects scientists and technicians and professionals, once thought of as independent from the forces of the capitalist market, are becoming increasingly proletarianized. They find that their research and the applications of their work are increasingly being dictated by "higher ups," so that they have less control over their work. Increasingly, they find they have no say over what happens to the products of their work (something which has increasingly bothered many of those whose products become appropriated for new methods of warfare). Though they sometimes form "work groups" within their corporations, they are engaged in fierce competition with other groups within their own firms and in competing firms, and so they lose any sense of being part of an intellectual or scientific community that transcends parochial interests. Increasingly there is the threat of their firms closing and moving abroad, leaving them without employment and often without adequate pension or survival skills. Far from being the new rulers of the corporate world, they are just higher- paid guns, equally dispensable, and equally precariously situated with most other workers.

The fundamental point here is that these new kinds of workers are still workers and, in the long run, they have very similar interests to those of other workers in the firm. I do not mean to deny that in the short run these workers think of themselves as quite different from other workers. They are harder to organize, more likely to identify with the interests of the owners, less likely to express solidarity with other workers, and even more likely to see themselves as individual entrepreneurs whose success has validated for them the very myths of the Meritocracy that are so damaging to everyone else. In the short run, they are likely to have more bargaining power within the firm, and more autonomy in their work. But fundamentally these are just the same kinds of differences that exist between white and Black workers, or between men and women, or between skilled and unskilled workers. They represent major forces for disunity and mutual antagonism; but they are not so great as to fundamentally alter the essential unity of interest that workers have in democratizing the firms and democratizing the economy. Whatever short-term benefits all these divisions provide to some, in the long run they only serve to keep in position a system which is fundamentally dehumanizing.

There is nothing "scientific" about the current organization of work. It is a system whose primary goal is to recreate hierarchy and control by the management, so that it can extract relatively predictable long-term profits.

A society that was organized according to democratic principles would not have to worry about preserving profits and control for the owners. For that reason, it could consider restructuring work. It would no longer benefit from workers feeling bad about themselves or unfairly blaming themselves. Society could be organized differently—and even more efficiently—in a different social order. But efficiency would be judged in different terms—in terms of human health and satisfaction, and not just in terms of profits and power for a small section of the population. So the theory that everything would be the same has little "objective" validity. Its function is to keep us from trying. And this, as we shall see in the next few chapters, is precisely the function of so much that parades as intellectual sophistication in our society.

Chapter 11

Failed Socialism

THE OPINION THAT, "IF THE SOVIET UNION REPRESENTS socialism, I want no part of it" is a quite reasonable response to the actuality of the Soviet Union. There is an inordinate amount of repression and fear in the Soviet Union. There is no freedom to express dissenting views. Anger cannot be expressed freely, and the resulting alcoholism is legend. Absent political freedom, human capacities are often stunted and repressed. And the Soviet Union acts to discourage the development of freedom and democracy in the countries that it effectively controls on its borders.*

But the word "socialism" has an honorable tradition that should not be abandoned just because it has been misused by identifying it with the actual practice of the Soviet Union. The goal of socialism is to establish a society in which working people own and control the means of production, and thereby control the larger society. Control here is the central category. It makes no sense to call a country "socialist" if the rulers of the society simply proclaim that everyone owns the means of production, but then continue to make the actual decisions about how the resources of the society are going

---

* From the vantage point of the late 1980s, it's hard to imagine how this will change short of a genuine socialist revolution in Eastern Europe. Nevertheless, I am hopeful that Western-style liberalizations will eventually make the Soviet system more like the West, with all of the more gentle forms of powerlessness that this book is attempting to expose.

196

to be allocated, how production is going to be run, and how the profits are going to be distributed and where they will be reinvested. Just because a dictator pops up and calls his regime "socialist" doesn't make it so, any more than America's policy of arming for nuclear war can be regarded as "democratic" when no one ever gave the people the ability to directly decide the issue.

The Soviet Union is not a socialist society, though it uses that term. Part of the reason America's rulers accept that designation is that they are all too pleased to let socialism be identified with the Soviet Union because it is an excellent way to discredit socialist ideas. But it is not socialist because the working class does not control the society. The same must be said of many Third World countries whose ruling elites similarly misuse this word.

Apologists for the Soviet Union sometimes answer that the working class does have control and that control is exercised through the Communist Party (CP). It is argued that the Communist Party is an expression of the will of the workers. But this argument doesn't work. There is no democratic way in which the workers can select who gets to join the Communist Party and no way that those who are selected can be de-selected by the workers that they supposedly represent. The CP members are supposed to intuitively know the will of the workers. But there can be no "will of the workers" until workers have been allowed to participate in a process of discussing the alternatives, hear vigorous debate by all possible sides, and then come to a conclusion.

Similarly, there is no real democratic process within the Party itself. In order for there to be any meaningful participation by Party members in the decision making process, they would have to have the right to form factions, debate issues in public, and try to win over fellow members to their position. To do this, minority positions would have to be protected and those holding them even given special opportunities to contact the majority and present their ideas. Without these structures, the CP becomes an organization of camp followers, everybody seeking to learn the "correct line" from those above them and then to reflect it lest they lose credibility and eventually lose their positions. So in no sense would it be reasonable to suggest that the Communist Party provides a way for the people to shape the society.

Great accomplishments and advances have been made by Cuba and China. In many respects they do not have the same uncreative rigidity and belligerent bureaucracy that rules the Soviet Union. However, no matter how humane these societies are with respect to care for the most weak, no matter how well intentioned their social welfare programs that benefit the majority of their citizens, no matter how committed they are to eliminating sexism and racism, these are not "socialist" countries in the critical respect because the working people do not have democratic control over the economies and the political structures.

The same is true for the countries of Scandinavia and Western Europe. They have instituted social policies that are responsive to the needs of their citizens. They have healthcare programs and retirement programs and childcare and educational benefits that are in many ways more humane than those in the U.S. They have provided workers with a more humane workplace and greater protection against arbitrary actions by employers. But these are just benefits, not fundamental changes in the system that would allow workers to democratically control the economy and the society. Only a fundamental change in social structure that democratized key decision making would make us call these countries "socialist."

Many people have given their best energies and intelligence to fighting for socialism, and then have become discouraged. Part of the reason why many got discouraged is that they felt that the very ideals they were fighting for had been put to test by the Soviet Union and had been found to "not work." The discrediting of the idea that people could democratically shape their world and create a better and more humane reality has been a major source of despair and disempowerment. But the despair is not warranted. It is quite different if we recognize that the idea has not been tested, because people have failed to create a socialist reality anywhere in the world up to this point. For example, it would be unfair to say that Christianity proved fundamentally wrong because instead of creating a society of love and charity it created a society of oppression and unfreedom. Rather, we would say that people misappropriated the word "Christian" and applied it to a reality in which the ideals of Christianity were not really tried.

"Perhaps," one might argue, "it is right to say that the high ideals of democracy and socialism have never really been tried. But millions of people thought that is what they were fighting for when they created the U.S. and when they created the Soviet revolution and the Cuban revolution and the Chinese revolution. If these ideals never quite get tried, that too is a basis of despair. Ideals are fine—but whenever you have to deal with reality the ideals always get lost. Maybe human beings can't quite live by ideals, or maybe they will always allow themselves to be subverted by some clever Stalin-type leader, or maybe they will always end up defeating their own higher purposes. So it makes no sense to dedicate one's life to trying to change things—because one's ideals are always going to not quite make it."

This argument avoids examining the actual historical context within which the revolutions in Russia, China, Cuba, etc., developed. There are specific reasons why these societies didn't make it. Karl Marx accurately predicted that socialism would only be possible in an industrial society whose material base—the technology and factories and self-developed work force—was sufficiently advanced to make possible the elimination of scarcity. As Marx correctly saw, the advanced industrial societies had all the prerequisites necessary for abolishing forever the domination of humanity by irrational forces. But the countries that now call themselves "socialist" were backward peasant countries, often prevented from developing their own economies by the capitalist countries that controlled the international economic marketplace. The main task of these "socialist" revolutions was to build up the industrial bases to the point where it was possible to talk about the elimination of scarcity. And this is not just a narrowly "economic" task; it also must involve creation of the conditions within which workers can develop the internal sense of themselves that allows them to become conscious of their own potential power and their own need for self-actualization, solidarity and creativity.

But in trying to industrialize, these countries faced a hostile capitalist world which attempted to isolate and destroy them. In 1919, for example, the last remnants of the economic infrastructure of Russia were destroyed by the crippling civil war that was spurred by the United States, Britain and France. The United States actually invaded Russia that year, but the American working class was opposed to this invasion, refusing to load cargo for the "American Expeditionary Force." The Russian working class was so mobilized that the U.S., Britain and France were forced to retreat and allow the Soviet Union to live. Lenin himself realized that socialism could never be built in one country, and expected that a European revolution would soon occur which would enable the working classes of the advanced industrial societies to aid in Russia's economic development. The revolutions did not succeed, and the Soviet Union was forced to industrialize alone. The tremendous hardships that this imposed on the Russian people, coupled with the extra burdens of Stalin's ruthless and paranoid dictatorship, rivaled the sufferings faced by the people of England, France, Germany and Italy over the several-hundred-year period of their capitalist development. It seemed worse in the Soviet Union, both because of the concentration into a few decades of what had taken several centuries in the West, and because of Stalin's obvious and unnecessary evils. The suffering bears comparison to what it took to build the U.S.—the hardships suffered by millions of slaves in the course of America's history of capitalist accumulation, which in turn provided the basis for America's quickly emerging economic strength.

After the civil war in Russia, there were those who advocated that the Russian people should continue the fight to spread socialism around the world in a continual revolution. But the people were exhausted, their resources depleted, millions had died of starvation. Instead, they followed Stalin, who preached "socialism in one country." Stalin's vision of self-protectiveness seemed to be more "realistic" precisely because he appealed to the Russians' fears that no one else would ever come to support them and that they would always be isolated. He played on the moment of fear, on the Surplus Powerlessness of the revolutionaries who were tired and discouraged. He could make good economic and material arguments but, in the end, these arguments were not decisive. What mattered was the certainty of abandonment, the belief that because the workers of the West had not yet rebelled they would never rebel, the sense that one had better watch out for oneself and forget others—in short, the legacy of Surplus Powerlessness. Ironically, it was this very choice made in the 1920s that set the Soviet Union on the course which would eventually lead it to abandon everything but its socialist rhetoric, and transform it into a vicious and totalitarian state. This decision was shaped by real powerlessness—by the failure of the workers in the West, by the death of many revolutionaries and the destruction of much economic life during the 1919–1924 civil war, and by the general level of fatigue of the Russian people. Yet it can only be understood in the end as a decisive moment of fear.

Similar stories could be told about the Chinese revolution, the Cuban revolution, the Vietnamese revolution. How ironic, for example, to hear the U.S. posturing about the lack of freedom in Vietnam after the U.S. spent ten years bombing that society to smithereens and leaving hundreds of thousands dead, millions homeless, and large sections of the countryside destroyed by chemical warfare. In each case of failed revolution, we do not have to postulate some fundamental urge of people to abandon their ideals. Instead we have to look at the actual historical context within which people were forced to make their choices. Then the moments of fear become more understandable, not a matter of inevitable evil or dereliction but the exhaustion of courageous people who were pushed beyond endurance. I do not applaud or apologize for what resulted—I have little sympathy for any country that does not maximize democracy. But I don't have to falsely conclude that their failures were inevitable or likely to be repeated in vastly different realities.

"Fine," continues my pessimist, "but what is to guarantee that the same thing won't happen when we try to change things? It always has happened that way, so what makes us so special that it won't happen again?"

There are no guarantees. Precisely because human beings are fundamentally free, they can choose to not go all the way, to act out of their fear, to succumb to despair. But neither is there any reason to believe that they always will do so.

The choices that people make are shaped by the sets of conditions that face them, and their own understandings of those conditions. That's why it is so important to emphasize the specific ways that people have organized their lives, and how this affects consciousness. People who have been starving are more ready to accept unpleasant choices. When people come from a society where they have never had any opportunity to make choices, they may be more ready to give up some of the democratic aspects of their revolution. When people have never been prepared to work cooperatively, they may be more prepared to accept hierarchy as inevitable. Even though their inner beings will present them with a different tendency, a tendency to demand the fullest realization of all that they could be with each other, their past practices will make it easier for them to make compromises. With this in mind, we can understand why the Russians, Chinese and Cubans reacted in the ways they did and understand that it is not inevitable that people in advanced industrial societies would make similar choices.

There are many reasons to think otherwise. The fierce commitment of the American people to civil liberties and to democratic forms has been a constant pressure on the rulers of this society. It has forced important concessions throughout American history. The rich web of small group activities, churches, unions and community organizations may not be sufficient to force America's corporate elite to be responsive to the needs of America's working people—but it is sufficient to create a deep experience of participation and self-development that provides an experiential basis for an expansion of democracy. The stress that people experience daily as a result of the stunting of their capacities at work provides a strong motivation for participating in a different kind of social order. The high level of education and literacy of the American people provides a basis for expanding the intellectual quality of people's participation in a democracy. Advanced capitalist societies develop capacities in people which are simultaneously thwarted but which also make it possible to envision a new kind of social order that would really be based upon human potential and ways of being that had been prefigured in the existing society. We need not fantasize any miracles to understand that people could be very different if social conditions were changed appropriately. The qualities that we wish to see developed already exist, even if sometimes they only manifest in the form of dim protests against the dominant forms of conditioned behavior.

"Sure, it may be possible," insists the voice of pessimism, "but aren't you forgetting that our fear also is already a reality that we would bring with us and might lead us to make our own kind of disastrous mistakes, just as people have always done in the past?"

This is not a senseless doubt, and it may in fact happen that way. But it is this same way of thinking that keeps us from ever becoming fully loving. We could always be abandoned. No wedding ceremony, no present act of commitment, no current sense of love and certainty and hope can ever guarantee that fear won't crop up again in the future and lead to behavior that will destroy the love. That's just what it is to be a human being. To have freedom means to always be subject to the possibility of fear. There will always be the possibility of shared visions turning into less loving and less humane paths based on mutual suspicion and distrust. This is the abiding kernel of truth in the cynic's challenge. It is why examples of past failures cannot be dismissed as totally irrelevant.

But this should not leave us powerless, and need not lead us to pessimism and Surprlus Powerlessness. We can recognize the likelihood that moments of fear will arise—as they always do in human relationships. We can prepare ourselves and others for those moments by talking about them in advance and planning how to handle them. We can establish ways to help and support each other through those moments, recognizing that sometimes they might last for years. We can learn to anticipate the political and economic realities that most often generate our deep fears: poverty, unemployment, loss of home, state repression, and disruption of meetings by undercover agents, for example. We can reach agreements on how to deal with these circumstances. We can plan how to reassure each other when we get scared— and how to reassure whole sections of the population when they get scared. In short, we don't have to be overwhelmed by the moments of fear. We can get beyond them. The Occupational Stress Groups, Family Support Groups and other strategies to foster Compassion described in the last section of this book provide a context in which those moments of fear can be overcome.

And even when we don't get beyond all of those moments, even when our fears become so intense that they lead us to make incorrect decisions that have bad consequences, we can still correct our mistakes and move on. Too often those who wish to make social change have the view that there will only be one cataclysmic struggle and then the struggle will be over and it will have either turned out all fine or all bad. I think that this is a narrow historical perspective—one that comes from people who have lost all sense of the ongoing flow of the human endeavor. Most likely we will be engaged in a cataclysmic struggle to overcome nuclear war and militarism, racism, sexism, and the undemocratic structures in the economy and the workplace. After that struggle, we will have a much more democratic society. There will still be ongoing struggles against the tendencies to give up on our democracy and cede our power to some new elite. We will probably make many mistakes. There will be people who will be angry and unhappy and want to change things. There will be freak-outs and there will be problems, and history won't be over. It may be easier to struggle, to sacrifice one's life and fortunes, if one believes that in victory will come the messianic era in which all things will be fine. But I think that we may have to settle for something less; for a marvelous and incredible new social order within which the forces of repression will have been decisively defeated though not permanently eliminated. The forces for human liberation will have shaped a new daily life situation. There will still be deficiencies, but they will also be amenable to improvement. In short, we will be able to have moments of fear without worrying that they lead to nuclear holocaust or to genocide or to extremes of poverty and repression. And we will be able to work through the problems, to move beyond them, to get through that fear. That is what will be possible. There is no way to guarantee more.

We know what we have now. It is not nurturing the best in humanity. It may lead to our destruction, quickly through nuclear war, or slowly through cancer, heart disease, alcoholism, crime, and lives of quiet desperation and despair. The alternative is to do our best to keep alive the parts of us that are most hopeful, loving and giving—and to build a world based on the assumption that though we will fall into fear we can get through it and come back to the moments of real mutual recognition, love and support. And in studying the specific ways that we have made mistakes in the past, either individually or collectively, both in personal life and in social movements like those that attempted to build socialism, we can learn ways to prepare ourselves to do better when we make mistakes in the future.

Failing this kind of thinking, failing to understand the deep importance of psychological sophistication that we must constantly bring to bear in politics so that we can help people overcome their moments of rationally based fear, as well as fear based on Surplus Powerlessness, we can only fall back into despair. The previous failures of those who attempted to build socialism can then become a source for our own Surplus Powerlessness. But it need not be thus. A new psychological sophistication is developing and can be creatively applied in political life. This book is a contribution towards that effort.

Chapter 12

Science Legitimating Domination

The Experts

SCIENCE HAS BECOME A TOOL FOR DISEMPOWERMENT IN THE way that it seems to legitimize the rule of "experts." Science is seen as having all the necessary answers. Scientists and technical experts are validated as the modern sages, prophets, or priests who will tell us how to live our lives, order our society, and plan for the future.

The impact of this domination by "experts" is that most of the rest of us are taught not to use our intelligence and not to rely on our intuitions. Instead we must consult with the "experts", and follow their advice. For many of us this experience leads to greater passivity. We wait for some expert to tell us "the right answer", and since the advice of "experts" is contradictory, we wait for their disagreements to be resolved. Most important areas of our lives can't wait for this, so we proceed to make our choices anyway. But we are surrounded with a feeling of illegitimacy, because we haven't adequately consulted with the experts.

Moreover, many people feel even more unsure of themselves, because they can't quite understand what the experts are really saying, garbed as it often is in a language of obscurity. And so the decisions ordinary people make feel even more unsupported and illegitimate since they derive from the mistaken notion of their intellectual incompetence. So many conflicting answers: Marry young or old, send children to be raised at childcare centers, insist on their staying at home for the first five years, insist that they learn to read early, avoid pressuring them until fourth grade, move to a city for better employment, stay rooted and hope for new economic policies, buy stocks or invest in a home, take a new training course in computers or a course on starting your own small business, buy a big car for safety or a small car for fuel efficiency, and in each case feel that you just don't know what you are doing. Feel bad no matter what you do because you ought to have known better and followed the advice of the experts, whatever it was.

But who constitutes the experts as experts? Supposedly this is done by some entity called "Science." But science is not a thing. It is a kind of activity and it is pursued by individuals. These individuals have to make a living. They sell their labor power to those who can employ them. And typically these are big corporations, or universities that see themselves as "service stations" to the large corporations. They justify themselves by asserting that knowledge should be for the benefit of humanity, and that human welfare is best served in this period by helping the corporations, which are the backbone of the economy, to succeed. Such experts have a wide variety of differences amongst them, but they tend by and large to share a sense of loyalty and responsibility to those who feed them. So their perspectives and the thrust of their ideas tend to reinforce the dominant ideology and the dominant scepticism towards the possibility that life could be fundamentally different.

It is not primarily the content of their views that makes experts a conservatizing force. There are some experts who understand the need to change things and use their expertise towards that end. But the impact is often similar. The meta-message that is communicated is the same: "You are not bright enough to figure things out for yourself, and you should distrust the intuitions and insights that you already have and instead listen to me. After all, I have science on my side, whereas all you have is your own ideas and feelings." People never fully buy this message—but it plays a role in the panoply of emotional and intellectual messages we get throughout our lives whose cumulative impact is to make us feel that we can't really trust ourselves and that we aren't really bright enough to figure out our own world anyway.

Perhaps the most obnoxious examples of this "expertise" come in the form of television pre-digestion of the news. Instead of showing us what happened, the newscasters shape the information to fit neat little packages that conform to their previously held categories. When the news can't be neatly pre-digested, as when they are covering a presidential news conference or a political party convention or a raucus demonstration, the media will be right there with instant analysis to tell what you have just seen, to make it fit, and to sanitize it. The hidden message is that the rest of us couldn't possibly figure out what's going on without these "political experts" who will make sense of a reality that would otherwise be far too complicated to understand.

The experts are there, too, to tell us what to consume. The advertisers use the latest scientific findings to validate the superiority of their products, to prove that they work most quickly and most safely—hoping thereby to convince you that you needn't think any more about it. The myth of expertise becomes an excellent way to avoid having people discuss with each other what their actual experiences have been with the products. They, not the experts, are probably in the wrong—or so the advertisers would have them think. Perhaps if their experience wasn't what the ad said, they didn't use it right.

The emergence of "experts" as a way of validating the established order, with its consequent passivizing of the population, is not the deepest reason to be concerned about science. After all, one might argue, this is just an unfortunate misuse of the scientific enterprise. If experts stuck to the actual domain of their expertise there would be no problem. A nuclear physicist might know how to split an atom, but not have a clue about whether or not we should build nuclear weapons. An army general might know how many troops it would take to fight off an assault by an enemy invasion, but have no special expertise on whether the enemy intends to invade, or whether or not we'd have better morale if more money were spent to alleviate domestic problems.

The problem goes deeper than just a misuse of expertise. The experts are experts because they have mastered this realm called "facts". Facts seem to be the sum total of how things really are, so we need to know facts in order to understand and cope with reality. And scientists and those who are legitimized by science are our vehicle for knowing these facts.

Yet "facts" are very problematic. It is we human beings who constitute facts by the way we approach the universe. The totality of our experience in the world is immense. Every moment we are taking in a huge amount of experience from our surroundings in tactile, auditory, and visual stimuli. If we paid attention to everything we would be overwhelmed by it all. But we don't pay attention to everything; we organize our experience in accordance with our needs. We pay attention to what we need to pay attention to.

First and foremost, we pay attention to what we need to do in order to survive. Through history, those humans who survived were those who tended to pay best attention to the aspects of their experience that were related to survival. This goal has tended to organize our experience. The community of humans that we enter has already developed its language system and its behaviors in order to assure survival. We become human through the process of learning their accumulated wisdom. Facts are constituted by a human community. They are the products of asking certain kinds of questions related to goals that have been shaped by the previous history of the community. What we discover as facts have historically been shaped by the struggle for survival in the face of material scarcity. Yet today we have arrived at a point in human history when the struggle for survival could be eliminated and abundance made the rule for everyone. This means that our whole way of organizing our experience could be changed as well, and new facts would emerge.

"But, in the meantime, here we are now, and we need to organize our experiences according to our current needs. If science does that, what's the problem?" Well, the problem is that science is not the only, or even the best, way to organize our experience according to our current needs. In failing to understand the real limits of science as an approach to reality, we tend to disempower ourselves.

Science is the systematic organization of knowledge around the concern to predict and control the physical world. In that pursuit, science looks for aspects of reality that are observable and repeatable.

But, through most of human history, the human community found that what it needed to survive was much more complex than that. There were aspects of reality that could be publicly observed that would repeat themselves in predictable ways. But there were other aspects of reality that were not accessible to our senses, and/or that could not be repeated at all. The unique, the special, the marvelous—these were aspects of existence that were also found to be needed, and every society developed its knowledge or science in conjunction with its knowledge of the unique as well as the repeatable.

Who Defines What is Real?

The emergence of science as a separate discipline and a special approach is a relatively new phenomenon, roughly corresponding to the ascent of the bourgoisie. This was no coincidence. Traditional feudal societies tended to rest their claims to legitimacy on their own special interpretations of established religions and mystical systems. Ruling classes appropriated the religious traditions and used them to control the behavior of everyone else. The newly emerging bourgeois class found itself at odds with many of the aspects of those religious traditions, particularly those parts that limited its ability to charge however much it wished for its goods, or to lend money for interest, or to engage in commerce on the wide variety of religious holidays that covered almost one-third of the medieval years. Although at first the challenge to this order was very limited, the bourgeoisie over the next several hundred years increasingly began to formulate its own self-justification in ways that opposed the spiritual foundations of feudalism. If the church was the guarantor of salvation in another world, the bourgeoisie could provide concrete results in this world. It could provide material goods that were verifiable by one's own immediate experience. If the church would look at the special and unique, the bourgeoisie could not compete on spiritual terrain with the feudal order. What it could do was to deny the importance of the spiritual altogether. While the old feudal order talked of the realm of the spirit, of good and evil, of the higher responsibilities and refinements, the bourgeoisie talked of the material needs of the body, of immediate gratification, of making the evidence for its success clearly visible where it could be seen, rather than in the sky or in some future life.

It was this insistence on material gratification of the needs of the body in the here and now that spurred the growth of the bourgeoisie and won for it growing support from other sectors of the population. The church had asserted certain economic and social constraints as spiritual values. But, since these values were not vindicated by the experience of justice in people's lives, they became increasingly rooted in an other-worldly interpretation of "the spirit." Because the church could not really allow itself to go with establishing a spiritually sound order in this world, tied as it was to a corrupt system of power, it could only compete by promising reward in a future world. The bourgoisie was increasingly effective in exposing how this spiritual order was a cover for the material wealth that the feudal nobility and church hierarchy extracted from an oppressed peasantry. Even those who sang the praises of the spiritual were really only concerned with their own material well-being, so why not give power to the emerging class of traders and manufacturers and bankers, which could make that material realm flourish for greater numbers of the population once they were unleashed to follow their own unbridled self-interests?

The struggle against religion was never absolute. At every stage in its development, the bourgeoisie tried numerous compromises with the spiritual order, most notably through the development of various Protestant denominations. Even when its most advanced spokesmen in the 17th and 18th centuries completely ridiculed the church and developed a thoroughgoing materialism that denied the very existence of the spiritual realm, much of the rank-and-file bourgeoisie still held to religious practices. And when the old order was defeated and the bourgeoisie became the new ruling class in the 19th Century, there were frantic efforts to revive religion as a suitable way to contain the potentially disruptive demands of a new rising class, the workers. Nevertheless, the logic of its position led it to champion a new way of looking at the world that was aimed at domination and control of nature as the highest goals.

The science that developed in this context was often a practical expression of the materialism of the bourgeoisie. In its interests and concerns, this science seemed to validate the bourgeoisie's worldview by suggesting that what was important was what could be presented to the senses and publicly observed and manipulated. Moreover, science seemed to undermine the basis for belief in the biblically sanctioned account of the nature of the world.

The mechanistic model of the universe developed by science was justified by the promise that it could account for everything there is. But later, "everything there is" was reduced to those things that the model could account for. So if one complained, "You have left out the force of spiritual effort," the answer might be, "If we have left it out, it must not really exist." No critical experiment ever disproved the existence of the realm of the spirit, nor were the metaphysical foundations of the rising science ever totally validated. The triumph of science was ultimately political. It was based on the ability of the rising class to convince people that focus on manipulation of the physical world would produce a better and happier life for them than any that would be otherwise available. Science was the vehicle and the bourgeoisie the force that would allow it to develop unconstrained by outside forces.

Ethics, human freedom, religion and spirituality are left out by the world view of science. These are the very elements of our experience which empower us as human beings. Their elimination has been one of the great contributions to deeply engraining Surplus Powerlessness into the way we think about ourselves and our world.

There were two stages to the process by which the scientific worldview discarded ethics. The first was the insistence on a fundamental dualism between the world of outer publicly observable reality and the separate realm of subjectivity and inner life. Adapting itself to the already existing dualism of feudal thought, science claimed primacy for itself in describing the facts of "external" reality, the world that could be observed through our senses. In the feudal order, the realm of the spirit and ethics was never seen as "private." It was the central organizing force within the public arena and the sphere of production. The bourgeoisie struggled to banish it to a place where it would have no direct control over the public life of the community. Supported by a growing revulsion at the endless battles among religious communities that reached their peak in the battles between Protestants and Catholics in the 16th and 17th Centuries, the bourgeoisie appealed for a new order based on mutual toleration of "individual differences." This had the effect of removing ethical and religious considerations from the public realm.

While early Protestantism may have attempted to fuse spiritual elements with the public life of the community, the protest against the Catholic community tended to emphasize the private spiritual life of the individual. Individual moral conscience and the freedom of individuals to personal beliefs came to supercede the previously held goal of "the politically moral commonwealth." Freedom increasingly became a matter of isolated individuals actualized in the personal sphere and not through the collective life of the community. The public life of the community, on the other hand, was to be guided by the dictates of science. The only shared value in this public sphere would be increasing the domination and control of the universe. The rising bourgeoisie was particularly apt at this task because it could provide for the expansion of material production and wealth based on trade. So its class rule seemed almost "scientific."

When all ethical considerations were relegated to a private realm, the only public goals were those that seemed to derive from the facts themselves. And the facts seemed to show that if they followed the path of science, they could have greater and greater control over the world, with a consequent increase in material abundance. Ethics were fine in their place, but they had no business in questioning the "real" world of public life. Commerce and industry, after all, were merely the extensions of science into practical human affairs, and one would have had to be "reactionary" (trying to reinstate feudalism) if one wanted to bring ethics into this arena.

The second stage in this development was the dismissal of the private sphere as based on nothing real. After all, if what was "real" was the domain of publicly observable and repeatable experience, then the private sphere was merely a matter of personal taste or choice, a reflection of subjective whims. But how could subjective whims have any legitimacy in shaping public life? So the common sense of the modern period became, "Ethics is merely subjective, having no objective validity." And, of course, this is true if "objective" means based on "facts," and "facts" are seen to be those things we discover already existing in the world through the observation of our senses.

Ethical Relativism

The subjectivity of ethics, or ethical relativism, was proclaimed by many radicals of the past as a triumph over oppressive forms of constituted morality. Since the dominant forms of oppression used the language of ethics to justify their existence, the radicals thought they had dealt a blow for freedom once this language was destroyed. But the opposite is the case. Today it is sufficient for ruling elites to justify their existence simply in terms of their contribution to scientific progress. If the current organization of society produces material goodies, and those goodies are generated by an application of scientific technology, then nothing else need be considered. The costs to human beings of our societal organization are dismissed as "unfortunate" side effects, and we are told that any challenge to the current order is really a challenge to science and progress.

In face of this, we can articulate a critique based on our sense that human beings have fundamental needs that are not being actualized in the present order. We can point to the way that the present social order generates crime, disease, and the estrangement of human beings from each other. We can show how this accommodation creates a human reality which is much less fulfilling than it could be. "All very nice," responds an establishment critic, "but that is merely your personal way of seeing things. Your account is suffused with ethical insights and intuitions which you hold but which I disagree with. Your assessment of alienation is based on your values. But I disagree. And my freedom to choose my own values is well worth the cost that there may be inequalities in the outcome in this society. You are entitled to your ethics, and I am entitled to mine."

At this point we want to respond, "No, this is not just a matter of subjective choice. A society that systematically destroys the lives and fortunes of others in order to enhance its own material well being, a society that promotes racism and sexism, a society that encourages people to see others as threats and enemies rather than as allies and friends, is an unjust society that must be changed." But once ethics has been relegated to the realm of subjective choice and relativism is the coin of the realm, we are faced with a very difficult situation. We have no "objective" basis upon which to build our response.

Enter here the philosophers of tolerance. "It is fine for you to have your own feelings, just as it's fine for those who oppose you to have their feelings. Our community is built on a wide range of different feelings living in harmony with each other. What is not fine is if you think you have a right to trample on others' rights, on their ways of doing things and their ways of living their lives, in order to change the world to make it correspond more closely to the way you want to see things be. When you start to do that, you become a moral fanatic, and in order for us to keep our community of differences functioning harmoniously, we have the right to repress the moral fanatics who would otherwise ruin the whole thing for everyone."

It was with precisely this line that the elites of wealth and power confronted the anti-Vietnam war demonstrators of the 60's and the anti-apartheid demonstrators of the 1980's. "Sure, you can have your disagreements, but you have no right to disrupt our activities, which flow from a different ethical position from yours." The logic of the position could be extended to say something like this: "Some people like to be flower children or religious pacifists and some people like to napalm Vietnamese or support inequalities in South Africa. Since everyone is entitled to their own ethical perspective, we should allow all these activities to proceed unimpeded."

The obvious problem here is that the world is already constituted according to a specific distribution of wealth and power, and it already functions to oppress most of us for the benefit of the few. But if we no longer have a moral right to challenge that oppression through action, we feel less able to do so. It's not as if were we to leave things alone, they would remain neutral. Somebody's values are already being imposed on us, and we have the choice to either accept their values and the world that it has created, or to challenge those values in the name of another set of values that we know to be better.

Ethical relativism is a powerful tool for disempowering people. Once we are weighted down by a sense that what we know to be right may only be our own personal opinion, we are much less able to struggle to change things; whether it be the German people facing the rise of Nazism, or all the peoples of the world watching the superpowers charge ahead furiously squandering the world's wealth in the production of armaments. The belief that our reactions to the irrationality of our rulers may be illegitimate or merely subjective preferences tends to passivize us. We may wish that things were different, but when faced with a reality that can only be changed through confrontation, going to jail, possibly even risking one's own life, then the doubts generated by ethical relativism and its call to "tolerance" have a subversive effect on our willingness to act in accord with our own moral sense.

There has been a traditional dilemma facing those who believe that there are basic ethical truths. Once science established its hegemony as the key to all truth, it seemed that other truths should function in the same way. If science could solve its disagreements by some critical experiments, so the argument went, then certainly ethics should be able to do the same thing, or else admit that it has no validity. What this argument conveniently ignored, however, is that science can't resolve its fundamental disagreements either. The difference between Copernican and Galilean views of the heavens, or Newtonian and Einsteinian approaches to physics can never be solved by mere observations of reality. Rather, a dominant way of thinking, a paradigm, emerges which seems to make more sense to people than the previous way of thinking. The new paradigms amass experiments and observations to their credit, but so did the old ones. The structures of scientific revolutions were not simply based on observation, but on changing world views. It is the same with ethical views. Many of the changes in ethical perceptions themselves have been based on the emergence of new paradigms of thought that seemed to fit into new historical needs of given societies.

Furthermore, ethical intuitions do not change so dramatically as it might sometimes seem. There has been remarkable consistency in the vast majority of religious and ethical traditions in terms of underlying values. Human beings, they all believe, are precious and valuable—and their capacities for love, intellectual and emotional development, freedom, creativity and solidarity should be given the fullest encouragement and opportunity to develop. What has most dramatically changed through the past several thousands of years has been an understanding of how to implement this intuition in concrete daily practice. In that area there has been, and will continue to be, wide levels of disagreement. Ethical argumentation has most often been about this latter point, and not so much about the fundamental ethical intuitions upon which this latter point rests.

When it comes to figuring out how to live in accord with the ethical intuitions, the disagreements are not so puzzling. There are serious moral questions. Can a just society be created by legislating morality? Can people become more moral by reminding them of their moral obligations through the imposition of specific religious rituals? What kinds of behavior, sexual ethics, table manners, or forms of dress are most likely to reinforce our moral sensitivities? These involve complicated factual judgments; and it is no proof of fundamental ethical relativism that people have disagreed in trying to answer these questions.

Ruling classes traditionally have had stakes in creating ethical systems that would not challenge their rights to rule. They have employed poets and singers, magicians and priests, educators and social scientists and psychologists to provide moral bases for their rights to rule. But they have also introduced repression and fear to keep people from listening to those whose moral intuitions led them to challenge the established order.

The involvement of fear or danger is central to understanding why people have had difficulty in recognizing, much less trusting, their own ethical intuitions. Certain intuitions can require us not only to challenge the established order, but even to challenge the authority of those who are close to us: our parents, our husbands, our religious leaders, our union leaders. Moreover, these intuitions can lead to thoughts that would re-awaken our anger, with all the attendant fears generated by our childhood experiences of righteous indignation against a deforming world. At times we don't want to take the risks and the dangers that would be involved in acting on these perceptions or re-experiencing them. We correctly assess some of our real powerlessness, but we also believe incorrectly that our powerlessness is inevitable. We find it safer and more convenient to lose touch with our ethical intuitions, to not quite trust them, and to experience them as "confusing." In this way, Surplus Powerlessness plays a role in generating our lack of clarity about ethics.

Lack of clarity in turn generates Surplus Powerlessness. If we can't trust our ethical intuitions, then we are all the less likely to believe that we have a right to struggle. Indeed, following our own beliefs begins to appear like so much egoism. How dare we think that we know the truth about what the world ought to look like? It is only our grandiosity, our fanaticism, or our monumental self-delusion that can allow us to think that we know better than others. So we had best shut up, go along with the program that has been established, and attribute our discomfort to personal problems.

Any challenge to the established order will require that we make sacrifices, that we are willing to endure some suffering, that we be prepared to lose some of what we cherish. No one wants to engage in that kind of struggle unless they have to and unless they have a deep feeling of the rightness of so doing. The incredible power of the scientific worldview comes from its ability to take away from us the sense that we have a right to challenge how things are. After all, if the only thing we can really know are facts, and facts are the kinds of things we learn about through public observation of repeatable phenomena, then the whole realm of ethics is not based on facts.

Science vs. Human Freedom

If we accept the scientific account of truth, we are obliged to develop a "science of man" that is concerned only with that which is observable and repeatable in human behavior. Many scientists began to think that they could explain all human behavior in terms of internal chemical or physical or biological processes. They believed that everything unique about human beings could be factored out entirely. Human reality could be considered solely as if it were another object in the material world. All human intentions and meanings could be ignored and human beings could be "watched" as if from some objective standpoint.

The first problem with this is that the scientists doing the observing quite forgot that they were themselves human beings, and that their own interests and needs and goals were primary factors in what would be observed and described. Human reality has existed for at least 50,000 years. An attempt to describe it exhaustively would take at least that long. So there must be some principle of selectivity that decides which parts of human reality really are important and which are not. The criterion will always be related to some goal or end that the social scientist has. Certain facts will be taken as significant if s/he wants to achieve one end. Other facts will be significant if s/he wants to achieve another end. There is no possibility of neutral description, because principles of selectivity that say that "x" is important but "y" isn't are necessarily value laden. Social scientists who talk about their enquiries being value neutral are typically taking the dominant values in the intellectual environment in which they live as their guiding light.

"Yes," responds the social scientist, "we do have a goal and and a value—but that goal is only to be able to show casual connections. And that goal is quite neutral." But showing casual connections in social science is not so straight forward, if casuality is conceived of in the same terms as the physical sciences. The physical sciences attempt to provide experiments where phenomena can be observed and repeated. It is much more difficult to do this in the social sciences. When it comes to prediction, normally a criterion of casuality, there is almost no successful social science.

The difficulty is not one that can be overcome. The reason is not in the lack of inventiveness of social scientists, but because they are trying to make human beings into something that we are not. What is fundamental to human reality is the fact of human freedom and change. We are able to understand our present situation, its ethical implications, and then to transcend our present in the direction of what we believe ought to be. Social science can't adequately encompass human freedom and the implications of human transcendence. As long as social science is built on the foundation of a "science" that requires that everything "real" be validatable by publicly observable and repeatable experience, it will always miss the most real aspects of human life.

Such an obvious point has been overlooked because our paradigm of knowledge and reality was itself determined by the struggle to validate a new world view that eliminated the basis for religious worldviews. In this ideological struggle to give the bourgeoisie a solid intellectual footing, all aspects of reality that did not fit the new "hard" sciences were discarded as "not grounded in fact."

Unfortunately, the pressure of the dominant class has acted to make humans more quanitifiable. The actual behavior of human beings has become more standardized and rigidified as the dominant society has succeeded in molding the internal lives of its citizens. We have pointed out the incredible ability of Surplus Powerlessness to keep people from believing that they can have any power to change the larger society. Unlike previous epochs in which the major force keeping people subordinated was some external oppression, today we face a society where even the most oppressed have internalized beliefs about themselves and their world that keep them from attempting to struggle. In this context, people begin to act in ways that are increasingly uniform, increasingly constrained by dominant ideologies, increasingly predictable. The very power of the dominant society to generate unfreedom, then, becomes the pre-condition for the possibility of a social science. In a reality in which people have been contained and have been socialized to be unfree we will find much higher degrees of regularity in behavior and may even be able to predict behavior. In such a society, human freedom seems to be a útopian. concept.

We are encouraged to minimize the possibilities of human freedom to enhance our Surplus Powerlessness. If human beings really are like the complex laws of physics, then it is rather silly for us to be engaged in struggles to change things. Our struggles are themselves predictable, and just as they have always failed in the past, they will fail in the future as well. "Just name a successful revolution that has produced a real transformation," we are challenged. "You can't—and the reason is that social science has already established that these kinds of dramatic changes are impossible. So stop kidding yourself."

The impact of this kind of thinking should not be underestimated. Not everyone goes to college and takes courses in which the political scientists, sociologists, economists and psychologists attempt to teach us about the predictability of human behavior. But the ideas from these disciplines seep out into the public through endless newspaper articles and editorials, magazine accounts, and popular books that all share the same perspective on human beings as predictable and regular in their behavior. Many people adopt this kind of thinking as proof that they are "sophisticated" and conversant with the truths about social science and the forms of human behavior. And, precisely because they believe this way of looking at human beings, they act in ways that are constrained by the "common sense" of their society. And to the extent that they do so, their behavior becomes predictable, and hence seems to confirm the very "science" that helped to mold the behavior it pretended merely to explain.

In an unfree society, social science can be successful to the very extent that its citizens have been forced to give up their freedom. The conditioning process is always only partially successful with most, and only marginally successful with others. Human freedom is never fully extinguished in even the most repressed human beings. In most people it is always popping out and ruining the carefully developed "science" of experimental psychologists, sociologists, political scientists and economists. These social scientists then scurry about busily making up new theories to account for "unpredictable" behavior, studying "deviance" in these individuals or groups, and acting much like the Ptolemaics who tried to save their hypotheses about the sun revolving around the earth by inventing many new and skillful explanatory schemes.

Social science looks most ridiculous when people begin to act together in a political way to change things. Their activities are rarely anticipated, and their choices often create new realities that defy the established systems of social science.* As people begin to taste the possibility of their own freedom, they move to actualize that possibility more and more. And the more they do, the less their projects and moves can be anticipated or explained in terms of "laws of human behavior."

On the other hand, until a new social order has been created in which human beings are fully free, people will continue to be subject to forces that pull against their freedom. Childhood conditioning is very powerful. People become convinced that they do not deserve to have power. This sense is reinforced by adult life experiences in work and family. These emotional forces do not magically disappear. They tend to push people back into patterns of mutual distrust and fear that will reinforce their powerlessness. Similarly, many of the beliefs that people hold about the world are still operative even as they respond to their deep needs for a more humanly satisfying reality. To the extent that people retain their older emotional and intellectual patterns, they are describable in terms of social science categories, even though they are engaged in struggles to realize their fullest potentialities. To the extent that they succeed in becoming more free, the social science of the past will fail to comprehend them. The extent to which social science

---

* It is always amusing to watch the social scientists scurry for cover when political activism emerges immediately after the social scientists and their journalist populariz- ers have solemnly proclaimed the final death of student activism and the dominance of campus conservatism—as they did in the mid-1960's and once again in the mid- 1980's. They then discover some overlooked factor to explain what has happened. But they sigh in relief when this activism is defeated—and they can once again return to a more harmonious view of their world without having unruly elements act in free and, hence, unpredictable and unscientific ways.

does work is the extent to which people are unfree. To the extent to which people think of themselves as entities which are subject to the laws of social science, they will emphasize those aspects of themselves that are least free. Their belief in their "object-ness" will play a causative role in their further enslaving themselves. They will act the way they believe they are "supposed to act."

Human beings are not things in the world like other things. But to the extent that we think we are things, and base our actions on the expectation that we and those around us act like things, we will create a world which has so much of a "thing-like" quality that it will be comprehendable in the terms of social science. And, as long as we accept the dictums of those who believe that what is real is equivalent to what can be shown, the possibility of becoming quantifiable will remain. Once the population has completely accepted this approach to social science, those who speak about the possibility of meaningful social change and that which could only be established through human transcendence will be dismissed and isolated as though they were fools. The social universe is then closed off from real growth and development. It becomes what Herbert Marcuse called "one dimensional." This is very desirable for the elites of power. If that which exists already is used as the only arbiter and standard of reality, immortalizing the rule of those who are already established in power, there is an inevitability to everyone else's powerlessness and degradation.

In mass consciousness, this outlook takes the form of "common sense." It becomes the only standard for what is "real." Trying to change things comes to seem not just utopian, but silly—because it denies the common sense of the times. No wonder, then, that people are dubious about social change, or even about any real deep changes in their own personality structures. Specific short-term reforms may seem plausible because they can be immediately verified in practice. But any longer-term struggle, involving a vision of the new world to be struggled for, seems to be fundamentally misguided. In this way, the "scientific" approach becomes a powerful instrument of social control. Its spacious insights come to be built into the very language we use. They are reinforced by continued daily re-affirmations of our belief in science and the nature of reality. In the end they become a way of looking at reality that makes us far more powerless than we need to be.

How Many Forms of Marxism Disempower

It is doubly ironic that even the Marxists, who are most explicit about their commitment to change bourgeois society, have fallen into this same trap. Marx made a brilliant critique of bourgeois ideology as a political doctrine, but gave little attention to the role of science as part of this ideology. And he sometimes talked as if he thought a science of society could be developed that had similar dimensions to the physical science of the 19th Century.

Insofar as we have a society in which human beings have been prevented from exercising their own potentialities for freedom and creativity, we can develop regularity and perhaps even "laws" that describe that context. For example, within the structure of a capitalist society based on the initial conditions of material scarcity, it is possible to describe the process through which capital is accumulated, the likely transformations that occur in the concentration of capital, the development of monopoly, the creation and then expansion of a working class, the conflict between capitalist and worker, the tendency towards imperialism, etc. The development of such a science is an advance over the traditional forms of social science because it uses categories that are not simply derived from the constituted society as it presents itself to the naive observer. Its conceptual schema sees the present as the product of past class struggle and looks to the present as a source for discovering tendencies that will, in the future, transform the present into something qualitatively different.

Yet there is a serious limitation to this kind of science. It cannot adequately account for that which makes a real revolution possible, at least not for revolutions that would move us to an order of genuine freedom and self-development. It may proudly proclaim the demise of capitalism, but it can't account for that demise.

Imagine trying to construct a science that empirically predicted the collapse of capitalism and its replacement by socialism. It would have to reason thusly: "In all past instances where capitalist societies have broken down and material conditions have made possible a conquest of scarcity, socialist societies have emerged." But, because there have been no past instances upon which to make any such generalizations, and because human beings are not governed by laws that make them always act in the same ways, this reasoning is necessarily fallacious. Moreover, there is no reason to believe that the same set of external conditions will always generate the same set of responses by human beings. This hasn't been true in our personal lives, and even less is it likely to be true in our collective lives.

Marx could predict in a very general way that the property relations of capitalism will come into conflict with the development of human needs. But this conflict comes because people perceive that there is a conflict and then act according to their perceptions of the situation. If people's perceptions can be shaped by the dominant ideology, they may not even see the conflict. Or, they may note the conflict and still feel unable to do anything about it because of Surplus Powerlessness manifested in a belief that nothing can be done or that they are too weak to attempt to do anything.

Marxist theories of determinism have actually played a negative role in the process of developing a social movement to challenge existing forms of oppression. As this determinism has appeared to people in the form of a notion of the "historical inevitability" of socialism, it has made people feel less desirous of taking any personal risks for social change. If what we all want is going to happen anyway through a law-like process that can be predicted with scientific precision, "whether or not men are conscious of it" (in the words of a St. Petersburg reviewer of Marx's *Capital*), then it makes sense for individuals to withhold their own personal participation and sit back and watch the inevitable march of history. For people socialized in a society that has always stressed self-interest and maximization of personal gain, it seems nothing short of silly to take personal risks to advance a process that is seen as inevitable. And when large numbers of people reason in that way, there is no chance of building the kind of political movement necessary to overthrow capitalism. So the idea of the "historical inevitability of socialism" becomes a causative factor in preventing the development of socialism. Now, a good social theory must account for its own impact on the social reality it purports to describe, but Marxism failed to do this adequately. Had it done so, it would have noted that the very belief in "inevitability" and "scientific determinism" of social life has a conservatizing impact.

There is another related problem. Just as science has developed in a hierarchical manner, with "experts" who understand and interpret scientific laws to the rest of us, so if there are special laws of revolution, there seems to be a special role for an elite that can understand and interpret these laws to the rest of us. Hence, the power of a vanguard party which claims to be in a unique position to tell us what actions we can take at any particular moment.

Some people will stand out as more experienced and be seen as having a better feel for events and how to move within them and turn them in potentially revolutionary directions. It is in this way that the art of revolution may produce a vanguard. But the alleged existence of a "science of revolution" makes possible a quite different kind of vanguard. Those who claim that their power derives from their ability to read the laws of history do not keep their titles by the creativity they show in leading revolutionary struggles, but rather by their sophistication in explaining to people why the time for struggle is or is not ripe. Through this process, these vanguards actually pacify people. They make them believe that the vanguard has all the knowledge, and that the people need not figure out for themselves when and how to engage in struggle. It is very similar to the way that unions too often make their members passive.

The plausibility of the Marxist notion of "inevitability" was dramatically undermined by the failure of capitalism to "collapse" under the strains of the economic depression of the 1930's. True, the system created mass unemployment, starvation, economic dislocation, psychological and physical pain—but that in itself did not generate a final collapse.

What is needed is for people to conclude that "there is no point in giving any energy into trying to make it as individuals within this system and that the only thing that makes sense is for us collectively to fight to replace it with a socialist order." But that consciousness has not been produced by economic crises in the past, except for a minority of the population, and even a political movement that articulates this idea does not necessarily become popular or listened to. This is not to say that no such movement can be created. It is only to say that it is not a law of history, or of social science, or of "scientific socialism" that such a movement will appear and succeed.

What makes a revolution possible is precisely what empiricism and "science" leave out: human freedom and the decisions of human beings to actualize the potential to be free, conscious, loving, creative and mutually supportive creatures. Because these qualities are suppressed in this society, no empirical science will be able to adequately describe them and plot the dynamics of their emergence. The continuing pressure executed by our Human Essence does not appear in some easily recognizable external form—nor are the moments in which people transcend their fears to provide each other with real recognition and renewed trust themselves predictable in advance or subject to objective third-party observations. The struggle to create a new social order involves the development of the very aspects of our beings that empirical science typically ignores or negates.

The irony is that Marxism, to the extent that it shares the empirical approach with bourgeois social science, cannot account for the revolutionary process that it predicts. And to the extent that it attempts to attribute these processes to describable, regular, law-like behaviors (namely, what happens within the context of bourgeois society to the economy), it actually mystifies and obscures. Marxism's revolutionary thrust was that it demystified capitalism by helping people see the human reality behind rigidified economic·categories. Capitalist ideology distorts our perceptions precisely because it makes us treat ourselves as though we were objects. Yet Marxism, to the extent that it represents itself as a science of revolution, actually participates in this same process of reification. When the development of consciousness and revolutionary struggle is presented simply as a product of external circumstances, it becomes a "fact" external to us and our choices. Marxism, then, provides another source of powerlessness and another way in which we come to see our lives as beyond our control.

When the New Left collapsed in the middle-1970's, there were many activists who attempted to assess past mistakes and chart new directions. But the view that prevailed was that the collapse of the New Left was inevitable, given a certain set of economic conditions, or "social forces." While there was considerable argument about what the specifics of these conditions or forces were about, there was widespread agreement that what had happened was inevitable, and nothing could be done about it.

The comfortableness of this kind of approach to politics must be noted. The political sophisticate can give an elaborate political analysis of what is wrong with society and then back away from any potential risk involved in political activism by pointing to economic or social forces that are beyond our control and which must be played out. Or activists can point to some other oppressed group (e.g., Blacks) who must, given a scientific account of how things will develop, play the central role in the development of revolutionary struggle. Conveniently, they can cheer on these others from the sidelines, well armored against any enticements to involve themselves directly in the strategizing and program building of a political movement. The more scientific their analysis about the inevitable path that political movements must take, the more secure their defense against personal involvement, except in the curious way that academic revolutionaries now participate— through reading left newspapers and journals, and joining left organizations that do little more than provide forums for these analyses.

Of course, this is not to put down those who try to make a serious analysis of what is happening in society, and attempt to incorporate that analysis into their thinking about what should be done. But an analysis must focus not just on "objective social forces," but also on people's current understanding of themselves, on ideology, and Surplus Powerlessness. And it must do so with a strong focus on the ways that the current realities were created and the potentialities that exist for changes as people choose new ways of understanding themselves and their world.

Some Western progressives may have used these scientific approaches to revolution as ways to avoid the risks involved in the real possibilities for social change. They may have also reinforced the general passivity and defeatism of many of those who have come into contact with it. But the results have been much more devastating in societies where "scientific socialism" has allegedly taken power. There, the governments which have institutionalized themselves over the people without democratic processes, and often with only marginal public support, have managed to use Marxism itself as the ideology to repress popular dissent. The revolutionary thrust of Marxism as a movement that urges people to become active agents in taking power for themselves has been lost, and what has emerged instead is an account of the inevitability of certain stages in the revolutionary process (to which the current Party leaders happen to have access). Lip service is paid to the fundamental importance of the working class, while the reality is that the working class's wishes and needs are ignored. And all this happens under the guise of a scientific management of the society according to principles that are based on the "laws of history." The tragedy is that certain strands within Marxism give justification to this behavior and also allow Marxism to be used as a justification for oppressive regimes in Eastern Europe.

Though I don't think Marx would have intended what actually has happened, Marxism has become a way of dealing with reality that has fostered an excessive focus on "objective conditions," and a focus away from the sets of beliefs that people hold about themselves and the ways that those beliefs can be transformed. It has, as a popular political practice, tended to undermine rather than support the spontaneity and political innovativeness of people struggling to make social change. In Third World countries where revolutionaries have described themselves as Marxists, there has often been a re-interpretation of Marxism that has emphasized the voluntaristic and freedom-oriented elements of this tradition, even when it meant dramatic twisting or fanciful interpretations of the original sacred texts.

While Marxism is the deepest and most telling critique of capitalist society, and is an especially rich and deep methodology for studying societies in their phase of domination and oppression, it fails to the extent that it does not emphasize human freedom as the fundamental social reality which underlies the possibility of social transformation. And to the extent that it has legitimated thinking of human beings as things that can be subjected to scientific laws, it has strengthened, rather than weakened, the ideological hold of capitalist society and increased Surplus Powerlessness.

• Part III •

Breaking the Stranglehold

Chapter 13

The Primacy of Politics

Politics has a bad name—and for good reason. Politics has become the arena within which individuals pursue their own private advancement without regard to the public good. Sometimes it is opportune for a political leader to appear as if s/he cares about the general welfare—and the appropriate words will be spoken. But in general, the public has come to expect that politics will be dominated by self-seeking individuals who are as likely as not to be deceptive and misleading in what they say to the rest of us about what they believe in and what they are for.

But there is another kind of politics—though it is rare enough and hard to find. That is the politics of mass movements struggling to achieve social justice. In those mass movements, people commit themselves to ideals that transcend their own individual self-interests, and fight for a higher good. These struggles are quite different from electoral campaigns to elect particular individuals to office. While elections, too, can take on the flavor of a "cause," they are usually limited by the personalities of the "candidates," and they have the self-limiting aspect that the communities formed around them usually disappear once the elections are over. But a social movement has a very different feel, and the experience is shaped by a goal that transcends winning a particular election, and addresses the possibility of changing history, remaking the social world in some respect.

Of course, I don't deny that some people enter these social movements and use them for their own ends. I have seen many ego-trippers moving successfully into positions of power and attempting to gain fame or personal gratification without regard to the needs of the larger social movement. But having personally known thousands of people involved in such movements, I am strongly convinced that the self-seekers represent a small minority, and that the internal dynamics of the movements are usually set by people with real commitment and dedication. For most of the people who participate, their own individual careers, pocketbooks, and egos would have been better served had they taken the same time and money that they gave to the movement and singlemindedly pursued their own advancement. They are drawn to remain active in the movement because it speaks to a part of them that transcends self-interest and that recognizes the possibility of a new kind of world.

Through this kind of political activity, people can experience real freedom. Politics here becomes a concentrated experience of what is possible, of what daily life could be like in a different social order. When human beings come together to reason out the possible lines of action, when their goal is both to figure things out and to then convince others of the truth of their perceptions, to listen to others and work out a common plan based on sharing each other's ideas and understandings, and, finally, to engage in activity designed to implement their plans—they actually participate in a lived experience of being free. When a political movement allows people to come together in this kind of way, politics becomes a true arena of emancipation.

I want to explore first why politics has too often become the arena for the first kind of activity described above—where individuals go to seek their own fortunes. To do that, I shall talk more about Real Powerlessness. My point here is that when people have become convinced that nothing fundamental can be changed in the larger society, it then becomes perfectly understandable why they give up larger social visions and become involved in dog-eat-dog struggles for their own individual good. After all, that is what everyone else is doing, and all that is really possible. Politics then becomes just another extension of the competitive economic marketplace—another arena in which everyone can get for themselves at the expense of others.

In this chapter I shall discuss why a different kind of politics—based on a movement orientation towards achieving fundamental social change that would better everyone—is an activity that can have important empowering effects. In the next chapter I will show that even when people engage in this movement kind of politics they are at great risk of defeating themselves unless they explicitly address the ways in which Surplus Powerlessness becomes involved. My point here is to show that while I can describe a higher and more empowering kind of politics than that which dominates in the contemporary American power arena, and while I can talk about how this politics has a strong tendency towards empowerment, I must also acknowledge that this tendency towards transcendence and human freedom can easily be undermined by the psychological baggage that we bring to politics. It is for that reason that politics, empowering as it can potentially be, must be reshaped through a new vision that incorporates as a central political activity the struggle against Surplus Powerlessness.

Real Powerlessness and Opportunism

You don't have to think that human beings are fundamentally self-centered or egotistical to understand why they get involved in self-interest politics. Most people have concluded that nothing can really be changed in the society. They see the wealthy and powerful using the political arena very successfully for their own goals. Sure, they have heard the sermonizing of those who talk about "the common interest" and "the needs of society"—but this seems like so much fluff to cover over the reality that the way it actually works is that everyone is out for themselves. They have seen social movements come and go—but what stays are the people who seek to take care of themselves.

We have studied the way that this worldview gets inculcated into people. Once they have this view, it seems perfectly rational to use politics to advance their own self-interest. Before assuming that politics just "naturally" brings out the bad in people, or that it must necessarily corrupt people since it is about power, we should first acknowledge how very important real powerlessness is.

Of course, people are not totally powerless. In the past decades we have seen millions of people, when they engaged in activity together, put real restraints on the ability of the warmakers to do what they wanted in Vietnam. Also, people forced even the greatest militarists of the Reagan administration in the 1980's to justify a fierce arms buildup in terms of how they would eventually lead to what the people wanted (disarmament agreements and de-escalation), and they even forced President Reagan to reverse his opposition to sanctions on South Africa and accede to popular will. Yet, in each case, people won far less than they sought—and only in the context of mass movements that involved many people spending huge amounts of time and energy. It is no surprise that many people give up on this kind of politics when their larger goals (e.g., real and total disarmament or full protection of the environment from corporate avarice or real equality for minorities and women) are still successfully blocked by the entrenched interests of wealth and power.

The corporations and those who own them can draw upon their tremendous financial resources to defeat most reforms that do not conform to their interests. Unlike the majority of the population that must engage in seemingly endless expenditures of time, money and energy, the corporate elite often does little more than hire the right public relations companies, use their lawyers, economists and lobbyists placed in the right positions, and use their congressional connections.

Even when people band together in social change organizations and pool their resources and energy, they find that their collective financial resources are considerably less than those of the corporate elite. But shouldn't they, by strength of numbers, be able to elect representatives who share their views and thereby get power? This, too, is considerably more difficult than the theory would suggest. Because of their control of the media, elites of wealth and power are able to define "responsible opposition" as only that opposition which does not call for significant transformation of the current distribution of wealth and power. Any other worldviews are dismissed as so far outside the mainstream that they don't deserve publicity or consideration. The public may hear that there are these more radical ideas, but they never hear them presented by their exponents in an intelligible and reasoned way. Even when people organize mass demonstrations, the media tends to cover the fact of the demonstration, how many people were there, were there any arrests or any windows broken, but not the content of what people are saying.

Even within the Democratic Party, candidates who have positions more critical of the established order find that the media rarely discusses the content of their ideas, but mentions them only to discuss how likely it is that they will get elected. When a presidential campaign is launched by a candidate backed by a particular social change movement, the media does not tell us the ideas and worldview that is being articulated in the campaign, but rather how many people were there, and how likely it is that this candidate can win the nomination. Given that kind of focus, new ideas are very unlikely to be heard by most Americans, unless the candidate already has so much money that s/he can buy huge amounts of advertising. But the only way that can happen is if tens of millions of people already agree—and that is unlikely if they have never really heard the message articulated. Should such a candidate turn to a particular social change organization, e.g., the women's movement or the labor movement, to get stronger backing and financial support, s/he is labelled by the media as "merely" a representative of "special interests,"—a tactic that the media never uses against those candidates who represent the interests of the corporate elite. The public is encouraged to think that these "special interests" are cleverly manipulating them for narrow and self-interested reasons, and so the very groups that got into politics to counter the dominance of self-interests find themselves the victims of the legacy of the previous corruption of the political sphere.

The most important reason why corporate interests tend to have disproportionate power in the political sphere remains their disproportionate power economically. The corporations, when they work in concert, have the ability to threaten all of America with economic havoc should their interests be threatened. The most idealistic legislator must realize that if s/he pushes legislation that seriously curtails the rights of a corporations to pollute the environment, or requires corporations to treat their employees with greater respect and economic fairness, or that funds health care and childcare in ways that require higher corporate taxes, those corporations may simply move out of their states or out of the U.S. entirely, exporting jobs and causing serious economic dislocations for the domestic population. Precisely because the legislator cares about his/her constituency, s/he must always weigh in every specific piece of legislation the needs of pacifying and accommodating to corporate power.

The Power Picture

It would be a terrible mistake to think of American corporations or the elites of wealth and power as somehow acting in a unified way as an organized conspiracy. The ruling class is usually not united on anything except its right to maintain disproportionate wealth and power. But since that point is rarely challenged in American politics, the daily life experience of the ruling class is usually built around intense struggles between different corporations about which is going to get the larger part of the consumer market, and between different sectors of the economy about which is going to get most assistance from the government (either through direct purchases made from the defense budget, or through bailouts, tax benefits, import protections, subsidies to build transportation and communication facilities, funds to develop scientific and technological research that will later be appropriated by the private companies, funds to develop training for personnel that will then be employed by the corporations, funds to offset mortgage costs or to subsidize housing and construction, or guarantees for loans or new investments). The battles over how the budgets of city, state and federal government agencies are to be spent are real battles—and they represent conflicting interests on the parts of different sectors of the ruling class.

Corporate battles are fought out directly in the economic area through clever advertising, marketing, and price struggles, as well as through corporate mergers and consolidations. These battles absorb the talents of millions of Americans.

I emphasize these battles both in the economy and in the political arena so that we can understand that the subjective experience of most corporate leaders is that they are continually engaged in a world full of fierce competition. They must either expand and conquer larger parts of the market or they will contract and die. For them, talk of a "ruling class" is belied by their daily experience of struggle against competitors—so they rarely feel any solidarity with fellow capitalists, and think that those who talk in these terms simply don't know "the reality" of life in the shark-filled waters of capitalist competition. Since the system they have created so effectively disenfranchises those who challenge their collective interests, they rarely experience themselves as sharing a common class interest.

Nevertheless, it would be a mistake to overstress this lack of solidarity. There are several institutions, e.g., the Trilateral Commission, the Foreign Affairs Club, the Bohemian Club, and Boards of Trustees of major universities, in which the corporate leadership does, in fact, get together and attempts to work out common strategies, both on the national and international levels. They have often worked very effectively to back proposals that benefit their shared class interests (e.g., huge tax cuts for the wealthy that the Reagan Administration engineered in the 1980's). But since there has been little effective opposition to their interests on the domestic scene for the past fifteen years, they can afford to focus their primary energy not on what unites them but on what divides them. It is only when threatened by a powerful mass movement that they are able to unite. Even then, they tend to split into two major camps: those who argue for repression and those who argue for concessions aimed at co-opting the challengers.

Working Class Power

The ruling class does not have unlimited power. It is not a total dictatorship. American working people have fought and won many battles, and have institutionalized many countervailing powers to that of the ruling class. The most important of these are enshrined in the Bill of Rights and in the rights of the labor movement to organize and strike.

The working class is not without its own power. "Without our brains and muscles not a single wheel would turn" is a line from a union song that reflects a vital truth: in the final analysis, the working class, united, can withdraw its labor and cripple the economy and paralyze the capitalist class. But this is not a power that would be easy to exercise, for the suffering caused would be inflicted very directly on the workers themselves.

All workers know this when they go on strike. They will be faced with the inability to pay mortgages or rents, with consequent potential loss of housing, inadequate money to pay for food and medical expenses, and potential pressure from children and spouses for needed financial support. If settled quickly, of course, strikes can feel like a short and happy vacation. But if they drag on for months, because the owners or bosses refuse to accede to workers' demands, the costs to workers and their families will usually be very high, often resulting in strikers going into debts that will be a burden for years to come. The costs are also reflected in the resulting family quarrels, for years to come. The cost is also reflected in the resulting family quarrels, violence, and even break-ups of marriages. Working people know this, and for this reason they often settle for oppressive contracts rather than go out on strikes.

Of course, there is a much more powerful weapon: a general strike of all workers. But this weapon is even harder to use, both because it would require that all workers agree to act together on their grievances at the same time (something that has never happened in the U.S. on a national level) and because the immediate impact would be hardest on those with least stored up resources. It is important to emphasize that this potential power is there, and that people can work to find ways to actualize this power. But it would be foolish to blame workers if in their day-to-day assessment of how much power they have in a given situation they did not give too much importance to their long-term potential to mobilize a general strike.

The relative power of workers at any given moment is partly a function of how much real damage they can do to a corporation should they engage in some form of action (e.g., strike, sit-in, slow-down, seizing expensive technologies, etc.). Depending on the industry, the particular historical moment (e.g., Is this moment one in which the corporate reserves are great and could withstand a strike or are low and would hence require quick settlement?) and the likelihood of government intervention on the side of the bosses (e.g., by declaring that the strike hurts "the national interest" and using injunctive powers to force workers to give up their strike), different workers will have different real possibilities. But their power is also a function of their own level of willingness to struggle. To the extent that workers are prepared to struggle, that itself becomes another part of the "objective conditions" that must be added in to assess their relative power. That preparedness becomes a factor in the calculations of the powerful about how ready they must be to give in to worker demands.

Many of these same issues apply when people act directly in the political sphere. For example, when it is clear that people are willing to engage in both electoral and non-electoral activity to accomplish a particular end, e.g., sanctions against apartheid in South Africa, that becomes a factor in the calculations of the ruling elites about what policy to pursue. When they are convinced that the population will stay relatively quiescent, they can afford to ignore public opinion polls that show massive support for policies that run counter to the desires of the ruling elites. But when people show that they're willing to become seriously involved in a struggle, new calculations are made, compromises are struck, and sometimes even real changes are accomplished.

For the elites of power, the most important goal is to keep people from becoming too politically mobilized. They understand the very point that I will argue in the latter part of this chapter: that mass participation in politics has the potential of creating in the participants a new sense of their right to have power, and that sense is very threatening to the established order. It may sometimes be more important to concede on a particular issue (Vietnam, South Africa) than to allow a continued politicization of the ordinarily quiescent masses. For this same reason, ruling elites are made uncomfortable with mass movements from the Right—because even though these movements do not support policies that are fundamentally at variance with the purposes of those in power, they do potentially empower people, awaken desires for a different way of being in the world, and, hence, have the potential of awakening desires that might eventually lead to real conflict with established interests.

A Practical Step

Because people's willingness to be involved in real struggle is such an important factor in their level of real power or powerlessness, the struggle against Surplus Powerlessness becomes an immediate political necessity. Yet this can't be done in a vacuum, and would be most effective if conjoined with struggles for political reforms which, if won and implemented, could really make a difference. Let me suggest one such step that could form the basis for political struggle in the 1990's.

Consider the following scenario: A majority of Americans are determined to remake power relationships in the society. They are not yet ready to engage in a revolution to redistribute wealth and power totally, but they do want to put serious constraints on the power of the ruling elite. Within four to six years they could elect state legislatures and a Congress and President committed to a program of serious reforms that would include:

(1) Prohibition of any firm moving out of the country, or closing its operations or reducing its level of investments, without paying reparations to the

community whose social environment had been negatively effected by plant closures—with reparations being close to confiscatory levels where necessary, coupled with jail sentences for corporate leaders who threatened or acted to significantly reduce levels of employment in any given area without being able to show significant successful efforts to provide alternative employment for the vast majority of their employees who would be at risk. Eliminating the threat of moving or closing businesses takes away part of their trump card.

(2) Massive taxation on incomes over $80,000 a year and on personal wealth over $1,000,000 (in 1986 terms, figures to be adjusted for subsequent inflation). The additional revenues would be reinvested in productive enterprises, democratically controlled, which would employ people already laid off or those who had never been able to find work. The reduction of excesses in personal wealth also limits how much ruling elites have as disposable income to support candidates of their choice.

(3) The imposition of strict spending limits on any electoral campaign, coupled with a practice of having any party that can muster ten percent of the electorate to sign their petition or vote for them be given weekly free tv, radio, and newspaper space to advertise their positions, with a requirement that no party be allowed to use any monies to buy more tv, radio and newspaper space than this equal allocation allows.

(4) Legislation requiring every corporation to have a worker-elected safety and health committee with power to mandate changes in work conditions and operations of the firm to make it more healthy and less stressful. Workers would be mandated to have more power to engage in long-term decision making and planning as part of the anti-stress aspects of this safety and health program.

(5) Using the decreased power of capitalists to threaten a "capital strike," people would then likely vote for increased social benefits, including locally controlled free health care, childcare and massive housing subsidies to increase available housing units and decrease their costs; rebuilding of the cities and beautifying of local neighborhoods according to plans determined by local residents; and a dramatic increase in monies available for community arts, recreational facilities, and leisure activities as defined by the local communities.

(6) Legislation requiring all firms employing ten or more workers to lower the work week to thirty hours a week maximum, with no forced overtime, but retaining pay at the forty-hour level (annually adjusted for inflation).

(7) Drastic overhauling of the defense budget so that only the minimum defense necessary for U.S. survival was allowed—but then the extra funds used to guarantee full employment of all those who work in these industries, including full employment for any who may be temporarily dislocated as the factories shift their foci from production of unnecessary and wasteful arms systems to useful domestic products.

None of this is meant to be exhaustive of what people would want to accomplish, and it is far from a total vision of a new society. It is a scenario that is accomplishable even without a total revolution—just by using the existing social order effectively should people overcome their Surplus Powerlessness. That such a scenario can reasonably be envisioned suggests that, although real powerlessness is never to be ignored in the short run, in the long run it is really parasitic on Surplus Powerlessness.

The problem is that we all live in the short run. And here the massive power of the corporations plays an incredibly powerful role in ensuring that these ideas are never even seriously considered, much less fought for. Those who advocate these ideas will be ignored or denounced. Nor does this have to be done for us externally—because after having grown up and internalized the way things are done here, every bone in our bodies cries out that these ideas are "unrealistic." At every moment, facing every decision, each of us includes in our judgment, usually unconsciously, our sense of the totality, and this Social Unconscious tells us that nothing is possible, and that everyone else will abandon us and leave us alone, standing out on a limb and in a precarious position. So immediately we moderate our own commitments accordingly—and the very people who would most benefit from these proposals move quickly to dismiss them as impossible without even bothering to allow themselves to experience how much they would wish them to be true. It is almost too painful to know that you want these kinds of changes when your Social Unconscious is telling you very clearly that nothing like this is possible.

Here we reach the limits of politics. We can see that some very plausible moves could be made. But we are also aware that as long as we live in a society that shares a dominant attachment to Surplus Powerlessness, the potential struggles against real powerlessness that could be won are unlikely to be fought.

So we are back with the chicken and egg. But not totally. Because the very act of being in a political struggle can itself be part of the process by which Surplus Powerlessness gets defeated and transcended, at least partially. To this aspect of politics we now turn.

Politics as Empowerment

While self-interest politics further confirms us in our distrust of each other, mass movement politics can generate a new sense of human possibilities. Participating in mass meetings at which different positions are rationally argued and then democratically voted on, engaging in struggles for shared ends, going door-to-door and talking to new people about our ideas and listening to their ideas, developing tactics and strategy and testing them out in practice and then modifying them in the light of our experience, and watching as a relatively small group begins to get much larger support—all these can give people new hope and trust.

Politics is a kind of community production—and the product that is being produced is the future. No longer accepting the passivizing and pacifying theories about how things work, people begin to act as though what is going to happen in history is not independent of what they do. They can play a decisive role in the outcomes.

Something else is simultaneously produced—namely, ourselves. Through politics, human beings can participate in the process of shaping ourselves. The very activity of freely choosing what we will do together is also simultaneously a choosing of what we want human beings to become—beings that can actualize our capacity to be choosing and self-defining. But this self-definition is done in a way that recognizes our mutual dependency and need, and that hence respects every other person's choices and tries to create a community that does not obliterate anyone but incorporates everyone.

In this important sense, politics can be the sphere in which we collectively reclaim our Human Essence. Of course, there are many tendencies to fall back into the fear that we have experienced all our lives that turns groups into "false groups" in which everyone is responding to everyone else's need to be reassured that nothing real will actually happen, and that their isolation and mutual distrust will not be disturbed. But mass movement politics around shared ideals can sometimes create a safety for people to begin to trust each other, and the more that happens, the more that people find aspects of themselves that have been suppressed from childhood suddenly re-emerging. It is not at all unusual to find people in these movements discovering strengths and courage that they didn't know they had in them, and making connections with other people whom they would formerly have defended themselves against. It is not unusual for people in these movements to be filled with desires to actualize their capacities for freedom, understanding, and solidarity that had previously been suppressed. In periods of upsurge in these movements, we find much higher levels of intellectual and artistic creativity, and also much higher levels of loving, sexuality, and shared belief in the possibility of possibility.

This kind of politics is the embodied defeat of Surplus Powerlessness. To the extent that we become actively engaged in consciously shaping our future, we are simultaneously rejecting the teaching that we have neither the power nor the right to take history into our own hands. The experience of making choices in concert with many other people is an experience of the possibility of freedom that dramatically counters all that we have learned about the inevitability of our passivity and powerlessness. While this experience is constantly being undermined by the voices from our childhood and by current economic and social realities that tell us we really don't deserve this and will certainly screw it up, to the extent that it is happening we are often deeply moved and our belief systems shaken. That is why people who participate in these kinds of political movements talk about experiences of transformation that are every bit as powerful as anything that comes from the spiritual and psychological communities. They experience themselves as part of a community that can transform the world; as part of a "we" that can make history.

A moment of deep and profound illumination occurs when a mass movement suddenly begins to discover that history is not something fixed and alien, but is rather something that can be shaped by conscious intention. It is the struggle that creates freedom, not the "having won the struggle." Of course, we don't have total power. There is still an existing system of power that must be fought against and transformed. Disillusionment can quickly set in if we do not fully acknowledge the power of the ruling elites—because in our intoxication with freedom, we may choose unrealistic goals, and then suffer defeats that will be interpreted as undermining the validity of our movement. But systems of existing power can be fought against and beaten, if increasing numbers of people become convinced that they are part of a growing community of people who are choosing to remake the world.

Some people have disparaged the experience that people have in political movements as merely a new taste for the kind of power held by traditional politicians. This is profoundly mistaken. When people experience the possibility of shaping the world in accord with their highest ethical visions, they are rejecting the kind of power that politicians have—the power to get personal wealth, security and fame at the expense of others. The kind of power available in a mass movement for social transformation is the power to be part of a "we" and to affirm oneself as part of a community.

Democratic participation in the process is absolutely critical and necessary. No matter how many good feelings of community one can get temporarily in a large social movement that is not democratic, ultimately the contradiction that is at the heart of such a movement emerges. Unequal power always means that some people's needs are being treated as intrinsically more important than others. Eventually, people realize that this creates only the appearance but not the substance of a loving community. When they do, of course, many people despair of politics—because they think that their experiences in these undemocratic political movements is all that politics could be, or that, having seen their own fantasies fail, every possible political movement will always end up being undemocratic.

A democratic community in politics is absolutely essential—because the self-realization and freedom that we seek can only be accomplished together, with each other. The process of self-creation that I have described cannot be sustained unless it happens as part of a larger social reality. That is why the counter-cultures have always collapsed shortly after political movements have been defeated. Individual creativity for a few may be possible at any moment—but to sustain it on a mass level, there must be a climate of creativity and openness that the political movement generates.

Equally important, realization and fulfillment depend on the self-realization and fulfillment of those around us. Human beings are irredeemably social. We are always forming ourselves in relationship to others and their responses to us. Our own fulfillment can be achieved only when we are surrounded by people who are able to respond to us with love, play, creativity, emotional honesty and spiritual depth. But to get a world like that, these other people must themselves be engaged in the same kind of process of making themselves and of developing their own self-transcending capacities. The democratic process provides the format through which people learn to create themselves freely, and thus become the kinds of people with whom we could build a loving community. Unlike individual creation of art, for example, the democratic process requires that in the very act of creation we create together, taking into account the needs and values of those around us. In thus generating a new kind of creativity, a creativity infused with love and caring for others, it also generates people who are more sensitive to the realities of others around them. While democratic processes are frustrating sometimes because we don't get what we want as quickly as we might want it, they are the most efficient means for creating what we ultimately want—a community of loving human beings who can provide us with the companionship and nurturing that we need.

No wonder, then, that mainstream politics seems so dead in comparison. In fact, people who have only experienced the politics of political parties dominated by mainstream assumptions ("the sole goal is to get our candidate elected, without regard to any movement that gets created in the process") find it difficult to even hear the word "politics" used with any honorable and exciting connotations. Yet my own personal experience, and that of hundreds of thousands of the people in the 1960's and 1980's, demonstrates that politics can have within it elements of art and creativity, playfulness, deep emotional reality, thoughtfulness, theory-building, action and risk-taking, connectedness, love and sexuality. A political community can have thousands of different tasks, and thousands of different ways to do each task, and space for each participant to shape his or her own path while still participating in the path that has been collectively shaped in democratic process. No wonder, then, that so many of the people who were most involved in the political struggles of the 60's claim that they felt more alive and real then than at any subsequent or previous time in their lives.

But if this were true, why didn't those movements sustain themselves? If the feelings of aliveness and the creation of community are so powerful, how come people eventually get disillusioned.?

The short answer is: Surplus Powerlessness. All the psychological elements that we discussed in the first part of this book, and the hammered-in ideological conditioning discussed in the second part of this book, continue to reassert themselves in destructive ways. Only a political movement that explicitly and self-consciously attempts to combat these phenomena can hope to succeed.

No matter how powerful the experiences that people have in collective political bodies, the lifelong conditioning to feel bad about themselves is still very powerfully operative. We have explored all the ways that people have come to believe that they do not deserve power or success, that they are fundamentally not OK, and that they cannot trust other people. These feelings don't magically disappear the moment we become part of a political movement. On the contrary—we bring them into politics, and they shape how we perceive what is happening. For example, you are in a political meeting and someone says something critical of what you have just said. The experience isn't received simply for what its content says—because the experience of being criticized in public may have a host of meanings and associations from childhood, from your family life, and from your contemporary work situation that make it seem much more frightening and upsetting than it might normally feel. So you may respond with an escalation of political rhetoric or emotional anger that is out of proportion to what you are facing. Suddenly, the pleasant dynamics of the meetings get changed, people become more tense, there is a feeling that people can't trust each other, that here too they will be exposed and hurt if they are too open and vulnerable. In short, it is very easy to have the legacy of one's outside conditioning directly interfere with how good political life will feel.

Nor are these simply legacies from some distant past to be overcome through a good psychotherapy process. Any political movement that is going to succeed will have to incorporate the tens of millions of Americans who are daily involved in making a living. The stress and emotional degradation, the anger and self-blaming, that these people experience at work each day will certainly effect how they act within the political movements that are being built. People will come into these movements with all their imperfections and all their yuckiness, and not just with their beautiful parts showing. A political movement that is to succeed must expect this, be prepared for it, and build a strategy to help people deal with these emotional dynamics. If, instead, the movement thinks that these problems are merely "personal" and should be worked out by the individual outside of any political context, it will only help to reinforce the dominant message of the society: that people have no one but themselves to blame for not being the fullest embodiment of wonderfulness and for not having created wonderful lives for themselves. And this, in turn, leads to quietism, or to people thinking that what they really should be doing is going through therapy rather than engaging in political activism.

Nor will this be a side problem for a few "problem individuals." The Surplus Powerlessness generated by our conditioning in the rest of our lives will dramatically manifest itself in any political movement. At the very core of these movements, people will act out their beliefs in their own lack of worth. They will overestimate their powerlessness, they will act in ways to confirm the isolation that they fear is inevitable, and they will create dynamics that turn most people away from politics. Each generation will have its own unique ways of expressing its Surplus Powerlessness, and the lessons of the past cannot be mechanistically applied to the problems of the future. Nevertheless, it is very instructive to look at how the dynamics of Surplus Powerlessness manifested in the New Left of the 1960's and early 70's, so that we can see in detail how the factors we have described come together to limit even the most powerful political movements. It is to that task that we turn in the next chapter.

Chapter 14

Snatching Defeat from the Jaws of Victory

A Case Study in Surplus Powerlessness

To MANY PEOPLE THE CREATION OF A MASS PSYCHOLOGY and a mass movement dedicated to creating mutual confidence and trust and undermining Surplus Powerlessness may seem like an unnecessary diversion. "If this society works on so many levels to cripple us, then surely the most immediate and appropriate target is the society itself. Surely nothing meaningful can be accomplished without that larger social change, so let's put all our energies there."

But this is impossible because any such struggle would necessarily involve tens of millions of people who had grown to self-consciously identify with the movement for change. These people would invariably bring with them all the deformities that have been generated by their experiences in the world of work, in family life, and in childhood. The social movement itself would, no matter how wonderful it was in other respects, also serve to provide a location in which all the Surplus Powerlessness that they had inherited would get played out against each other. Unless people were to directly and consciously incorporate into their analyses and into their expectations an understanding of Surplus Powerlessness, they would be overwhelmed by the problems that are endemic in such movements, and they will be driven back into passivity and cynicism. Without negating the transcendence-producing aspects of mass politics described in the last chapter, we must also acknowledge that these factors are not, in themselves, sufficient to defeat Surplus Powerlessness.

The Possibility of Social Movement

We have seen that there are many factors in our intellectual and emotional conditioning that would lead us to reject politics. Nevertheless, it is frequently the case that people do get involved in movements for social change. This may happen for any number of reasons, most typically because:

1. A small group of people begin to struggle, and if they are not defeated very quickly, they begin to experience the joys of feeling hope. That feeling is contagious, and the more the first group insists on the possibility of possibility, the more that others are attracted.

2. Our society constantly shatters our sense of justice. Yet, precisely because this system relies on all of us believing that where we have ended up in the class hierarchy is really a fair reflection of our ultimate worth, it must portray itself as fundamentally fair. The civil rights movement, the women's movement, and the anti-apartheid movement challenge this sense of fairness. Ironically, it may be our very deep belief that our own failures in the society are really fair that leads us to feel so charged up on these kinds of fairness issues and simultaneously allows the media, normally fully committed to the status quo, to be more pro-change when these kinds of issues are raised. For, at some deeper level, everyone may be afraid of discovering just how deeply unfair the economic system is—and, for that very reason, we may all be willing to give attention to this "minority victim" level of consciousness. When reforms have been made, the system can congratulate itself, everyone can be reassured of the ultimate justness of the society, and we can then all continue to blame ourselves for the ways that we are personally inadequate. This is the severe weakness and limitation of civil-rights politics. But, of course, the other side is that people's experience in these kinds of movements can be empowering and lead them to feel the desire to struggle for even larger and deeper kinds of changes.

3. There is a realistic possibility that our very survival may be threatened unless we become involved in politics. This has been the basis of anti-war movements, anti-nuclear movements, and even ecology movements.

4. Our Human Essence exerts a continual push towards politics. The pervasive sense that "something is wrong" derives from a deep knowledge that our needs for love, connection, freedom and creativity are being stunted in this society. No matter how layered over by beliefs in our own personal failures and inadequacies, our Human Essence exerts a continuing push in a different direction—and if a social movement appears and begins to grow, we may be attracted to it, whatever our consciously stated reasons, because we need to give expression to these underlying needs.

The Aroma of Defeat

Just because people have overcome their Surprlus Powerlessnes enough to become engaged in politics does not suggest that the massive conditioning they have received throughout their lives has magically disappeared. On the contrary. Most often they bring with them into politics a sense of their own inadequacy, a deep commitment to the inevitability of their own failure, and an abiding belief that nobody will really love them as they are. Our deep belief in the inevitability of powerlessness then comes into immediate conflict with the supposition of politics that one is in it to win something.

The dynamics here are often very complicated. On the one hand, we may want to win. We may feel that it is only because we might win something that we are willing to take risks, spend money, give time away from personal pursuits. The anticipation of winning may be very pleasurable. But it may simultaneously, in the very same person, be very unpleasurable and scary. Most of us feel wildly uncomfortable with the position of winning. It feels completely out of sorts with who we "know" ourselves to be, our inner Childhood Personality. It may also stir unconscious fears of disloyalty to our parents, whose lives were firmly enmeshed in powerlessness. So we act in ways that will ensure our defeat, continued isolation, and rejection by the very people that we need if we are to make the changes that we want.

Here we have the primary inner contradiction of progressive politics. People both do and don't want to succeed. On the one hand, anybody who has been part of a movement for social change cannot fail to be impressed by the sincerity, dedication and willingness to sacrifice that are characteristic of many movement activists. Outsiders who dismiss these activists as self-seeking or selfish don't know what they are talking about. With rare exceptions, most of the core activists in movements for progressive social change tend to be intelligent, caring and giving people. They are usually motivated by strong desires to achieve justice and peace and freedom not just for themselves but for others as well. Very often they are people whose talents, if applied in a more self-centered way, would have brought them many more rewards at the level of money, power and recognition from the marketplace of capitalist society than they could ever achieve by being part of a social change movement. Yet, at the same time, they are also deeply committed to losing. Over and over they will choose paths of action that are guaranteed to estrange those who would potentially listen to them. They become experts at seizing defeat out of the jaws of victory. The double message of progressive politics is to be strong and visionary, but act in ways that prove you are going to lose.

Because progressive social change movements are dominated by Surplus Powerlessness, they give off an aroma of defeat. People who want to make serious changes in the world quickly learn that these movements are so entwined in their own internal dynamics and their own commitments to alienating rhetoric that there is only slight hope of them becoming effective. On the other hand, people who are more enmeshed in their own Surplus Powerlessness will feel quite comfortable in these movements—precisely because they pick up the unconcsious message that this is a safe place for those who wish to remain isolated and defeated.

All too often, these social movements become havens for people who are too afraid to engage in real struggle. They get together with other people and look down on everyone else who isn't smart enough or pure enough to join the struggle. This behavior, guaranteed to keep people away, is actually quite effective for recreating isolation, and thus assuring people that their ideas will never have to be taken too seriously. Secure in their own isolation, many a social movement can then articulate the most visionary and "radical" visions without ever confronting the real Surplus Powerlessness that cripples their participants. If we now focus on the movements of the 60's and 70's to see how these dynamics manifested themselves in a real movement, it is not through any disrespect of the real power and accomplishments of that period. As an activist who participated in the movement, I found it a profound and extremely valuable part of my life. Yet the problems that emerged there will continue to dominate and disrupt any movement for social change in the future that has not developed a sophisticated strategy for addressing Surplus Powerlessness.

The New Left and Anti-War Movements

We have seen that a major source of Surplus Powerlessness is the way that we come to blame ourselves inappropriately for not having created a more fulfilling life. We have seen how our experiences in childhood, the dynamics of personal life, and our experience in the struggle for economic survival shape us to believe that we have failed and that we have no one to blame but ourselves. Because we believe that we are simply reaping what we have sown, we have no compassion for ourselves.

It is in this context that we can best understand America's quest for the ideal self. The dominant ideology of the society tells us that our lives are the direct result of our merit and our efforts. So it is reasonable to believe that the pain we experience is a reflection of these individual inadequacies. The solution seems clear; we must better ourselves as individuals, and each become more of what we ought to be. If we all take these individual actions, we will all be OK and all our lives would be better.

Now imagine a social movement made up of people who hold this kind of belief—the belief most likely to be held by people who have grown up in this society. They are likely to shape that social movement to be a public expression of this private but deeply held belief.

This was the core dynamic of the New Left and the anti-war movements of the 1960's. They were dominated by people who believed that things would get better if the people in society could be transformed. They were convinced that this transformation was a matter of people overcoming their individual inadequacies, largely through acts of will. Failure was blamed on various forms of "false consciousness," acts of moral cowardice or self-deception.

New Leftists were brilliant in pointing out the contradictions of the dominant society. They pierced through the illusions of the Democratic Party. They coined the term "corporate liberalism" to expose the way that many liberal leaders were more interested in protecting the interests of corporate capital than they were in promoting a society where human needs came first. But when it came to analysis, they tended to talk about co-optation rather than social structure. The supposition was that individuals had succumbed to the corruptions of material pleasures that were available through capitalist consumption, and thereby had lost their own senses of moral vision. Individual weakness was rarely seen as the product of a sophisticated social-economic-psychological reality, but rather as a manifestation of some inner defects. Conversely, the way to change this was to force people to live up to their inner higher selves and to renouce the materialism and false values of the society. A moral transcendence could be achieved by any given individual through an act of will. Those who failed to do so were hypocrites who espoused one set of values but lived another.

It was to take aim at hypocrisy that the New Left engaged in confrontation demonstrations. The confrontations were aimed at exposing the contradictions between what the "liberal establishment" said it believed and what it was really doing in practice. The universities were confronted for failing to live up to their stated ideals of free speech and rational inquiry. The liberals in Congress were exposed as two-faced because they preached "peace" yet voted for appropriations for the war. The New Left was filled with moral outrage at the distance between stated values and actual realities. And these were seen as failings of the individuals involved. "Never trust anyone over thirty" was rarely understood to mean that one must be sensitive to the structural constraints on people as they attempted to build families and make livings in the society. Rather, it was typically understood to refer to the moral weakness that seemed to plague people as they became older. As a Phil Ochs song said, "If I've got something to say, sir, I'm going to say it now"—and the "now" was important because at some future time one might oneself become coopted as well.

Lacking a social, economic and political analysis of real powerlessness, and its impact on Surplus Powerlessness, New Leftists tended to blame individual weakness for collective failures. They were extremely perceptive in showing the ways that the Old Left had made fundamental mistakes in building a social movement. Yet there was no compassion for the actual constraints facing the generation of the 30's.* Old Leftists were thought to have failed because they allowed themselves to be coopted by the New Deal, because they weren't smart enough to see through the dangers of the undemocratic forms of the Communist Party, and because they were afraid to call for socialism instead of merely backing reforms and building the labor movement. Instead of asking, "What were the social and economic conditions that prompted people to follow less courageous and less revolutionary paths than they should have?" they condemned the activists for having been "co-opted."

---

* For example, the mass fear generated by the Depression, a fear that led as much to conservatism as it did to radicalism; the growth of fascism in Europe and the consequent possibility of a defeat of progressive forces on a world scale; the resiliency of the American political system with its appearance of listening to the pain of the unemployed; the powerful hold of bourgeois ideology, particularly its message of self-blame; and the continued power of the State, which made membership in the Communist Party illegal and dangerous.

Similarly, in analyzing the failures of socialism in the Soviet Union and elsewhere, there was the same tendency to focus on individual failings rather than the consequences of social structures. The Bolsheviks were seen as having paid inadequate attention to democratic process, a correct criticism, but without any acknowledgement of the social conditions that might have made this seem plausible. Stalin's rise to power and the defeat of Trotsky were seen in terms of their personal strengths and weaknesses and rarely in terms of the social forces they represented. In general, Bolsheviks were faulted for allowing their revolutionary ideals to slip away into bureaucratic forms—as if this had happened solely on the basis of personal failings, stupidity or weakness of these revolutionaries.

. How could they avoid making these same mistakes? What would ensure their ability to not recreate an oppressive and bureaucratic state in the future should they win? Lacking a deep social analysis, most New Leftists turned to the focus on quality of personal commitment, individual authenticity, and virtue. The solution, they insisted, would be found in the quality of the movement itself. They would build a movement that reflected in its very essence the values that they held for a future society. The reason, so the logic went, was that such a movement could be trusted because it would itself embody the values of the future by living them in the present.

This was totally consistent with a psychology of self-blaming. If we have no one to blame but ourselves for all that goes wrong, we can only look to ourselves to ensure that everything will go right. If we are the right kind of people, and we are truly dedicated and not phony in our commitment, then of course we will build the right kind of movement, and that movement will build the right kind of society.

Just as in personal life, in politics this supposition has different consequences depending on the class realities one faces. For a small percentage of the population, many of whom are in college or in their twenties, the problems of making livings and raising families have not yet become the dominant foci of attention. There is always the possibility of dropping out of college or a given job, and then returning at a later point, or going in a totally new direction later on. Without the obligation of supporting children, or paying for mortgages, economic responsibilities are much less confining and these young people have more freedom to experiment. Most people, particularly those from the more traditionally defined working-class backgrounds, never get this moment of privilege and resent those who do. Those who talk about the freedom to create new ways of living are often seen as an elite whose opportunities are resented by everyone else.

In the 1960's, the economy as a whole was booming. It led President Johnson to decide that he could make war in Vietnam and still mount a lavish program of domestic spending to achieve his version of a Great Society. The economic boom meant that there were jobs available. One could drop out for a few years and still drop back in. One could find others who had enough surplus in their earnings to share their wealth without rendering themselves impoverished. In these circumstances, young people had the luxury to take risks, and the call to take personal responsibility for social change produced incredible creativity in this section of the population. New Leftists experienced heights of productivity and self-actualization that they had never dreamt possible. The experience of the movement brought out their most giving, courageous and transcendent selves. In this way, it became self-validating. Yet, lacking any theory that could help them understand the economic constraints on those who could not "drop out" and join a movement, they could only see the rest of the population as somehow morally deficient for not having been willing to take the same risks to fight for their own ideals. The very ideology of the Meritocracy that they had learned in their childhoods and had been reinforced in their colleges now made them see themselves as a moral elite.

New Leftists responded to the rest of the population in the very same way that upper-middle-class people tend to respond to working class people. Those who were not part of the New Left were disparaged as being on a lower moral plane. They had made "wrong choices"—perhaps because they weren't as "smart" or meritorious as the New Leftists. Because every New Leftist knew someone of his or her own generation who had not become part of the movement, joining was seen as a matter of insight and moral courage rather than a structural reality based on class or social circumstances. While this may have had some validity in relationship to some of their school-mates, it was a decidedly uninformed view of the bulk of the American population.

Eventually, this idea would be articulated in the notion of "white skin privilege." White working people were alleged to be reactionary because they had been bought off by the rewards of imperialism. The American public not only could not be trusted—it was in fact the enemy. The only ones who could be saved would be youth who had not yet been corrupted by having bought into the established order. All the rest of the population was really "the enemy."

The goal of creating a movement which is the living embodiment of the goals you hold for the future was a monumentally difficult task. It seemed plausible to those who had no social understanding of the forces that keep people from achieving self-realization. But gradually the unreality of that demand undermined the New Left.

The New Left attempted to live up to the belief that if one was to embody the future, one had to be as selfless and self-sacrificing as possible. There should be no limit to how hard one worked, or how many hours one gave to the movement, or how many risks one took with one's schooling or job, or how often one went to jail. These kinds of expectations had unfortunate consequences. They meant that those who had the greatest freedom in their lives already, the upper-middle-class youth, would be those most honored, the heroes of the movement. Working-class youth who had to work their ways through school or who had to support themselves with jobs were less able to live this kind of life. They were also less likely to be able to walk back into secure futures once their movement experiences were over. Such unreal expectations meant that movement people were likely to "burn themselves out" in intense years of struggle. One can go at full speed for only so long, and, as individuals reached their limits, they found themselves put on the defensive by newer recruits whose energy had not yet been dissipated. Since there was no place of honor or respect for those who had been worn out in the cause, veteran activists were often squeezed out. The movement had a very high turnover. Any attempt to plan for one's own future and prepare to make a living was seen as "selling out" and "counter-revolutionary." The very idealism of the movement thus precluded people from integrating a long-term commitment into their movement activity. The pace made sustained involvement inconceivable. No wonder, in these circumstances, so many dedicated people felt themselves pushed out of the movement.

To avoid what they saw as the mistakes of Stalinism, the New Left tried to ensure democracy by enshrining it in the daily activities of its organizations. The movement became a floating meeting, requiring lengthy discussions of every possible topic and concern. The attempt to achieve consensus in these meetings required endless patience. Only those who had no jobs and could stay up every night could participate. Those who could not were seen as less dedicated and, hence, their opinions didn't matter as much. In the name of being democratic, forms were established that guaranteed participation only by those who had little else to do in their lives, while those whose lives were filled with other real world commitments such as raising children or making livings, were effectively excluded from the democratic process.

To ensure that there would be no manipulation of the movement by totalitarian leaders, a culture of anti-leadership was developed that effectively precluded New Leftists from learning from their own accumulated experiences. In the mid-'60's, the main New Left organization, Students for a Democratic Society (SDS), had a tradition that its top leadership could remain in that position for only one year. By the late '60's in the New Left organizations it was not unusual to hear people who had been in positions of local leadership for six months referred to as "the old leadership" with a hostility mixed with impatience that the democratic process was failing as these old-timers were likely to consolidate their "power." The cult of anti-leadership made it very difficult for committed activists to play an effective role for very long within the established organizational confines of the New Left. So, many of them began to act outside the formal movement structures and organizations.

Unrestrained by the New Left consensus mentality, these activists could then play much more effective roles as national leaders. They could talk to the press, call demonstrations on a national level, and propose strategies directly to the growing mass of New Leftists who were unaffiliated with any organization. But many New Leftists saw these national leaders as elitist and unresponsive to democratic forms. The very fact that national leaders were operating without accountability reinforced the conviction of local activists that leadership had to be viewed with suspicion and strictly controlled. And the persistence of this approach guaranteed that leaders would have to seek ways of operating outside the official New Left circles, because there was no legitimacy granted to them within. Not allowed to lead through the organizations, they often sought media notoriety as an alternative way to get their ideas heard—and this only reinforced the distrust felt towards them by the masses of New Left activists.

New Leftists thought that the problem of leadership could be dealt with by a correct internal attitude, a culture of anti-elitism and anti-leadership, instead of by development of structures that would guarantee democratic accountability within the context of leadership. The very cult of anti-elitism made it inevitable that the only way leaders could lead would be in elitist ways because they would not be allowed democratic ways to present their ideas and their leadership as legitimate.

Actually, good leadership deserves to be rewarded. It is no sin for someone to get gratification out of being accepted as a good and creative leader, or to enjoy the fame that comes with having good ideas that others validate. But this notion of legitimate gratification of ego was totally inconceivable in a climate in which the very idea of "leadership" was suspected of having anti-democratic overtones.

Closely aligned to anti-leadership was the strong anti-intellectualism tradition in America. Anti-intellectualism was greatly strengthened by the experiences of many New Leftists in universities when many academics supported the war in Vietnam and refused to recognize that American democracy was controlled by corporate interests, or that racism and sexism pervaded many American institutions. Many students saw intellectual activity at the universities as an immoral obfuscation of power.

In my view, intellectualism in itself is not a vice. Intellectuals can use their talents to demystify just as readily as they obfuscate, though they are likely to have difficult times retaining their jobs in universities if they do. Many New Leftists, however, dismissed all intellectual activity as fundamentally elitist, and touted the value of spontaneity over thought and action over reflection. If you were "coming from a head place" rather than "from a heart place," you were likely to be inauthentic. The reliance on ideas, it was thought, would tend towards an undemocratic reality. Any idea was thought to be as equally valid as any other, as long as it was expressed with deep passion and personal commitment. Otherwise, ideas would have the tendency to select out those who were more advanced, more trained in certain skills, and more able to articulate what they thought.

Since New Leftists did not want to live in a society where there would be inequality, they believed they had to have a movement with no inequality. Everyone had to be equally wise. The quickest way to accomplish this was to discount all ideas which were not manifestations of feelings. And since all feelings were equally valid, the people who expressed them could be seen as equal. In such a climate, sustained intellectual activity was seen at best as an inauthentic way to spend time, and possibly dangerous.

This was based on the mistaken belief that the movement must already embody the values of the future. An equally humane approach to unequal knowledge would have been to structure ways in which those who have more knowledge and more theory at their disposal would be able to teach what they know to those who have not had equal opportunities to develop these strengths. Sharing strengths could have made it possible to gradually eliminate inequalities. But this would have been possible only if one could recognize that asymmetries in talent, experience and knowledge did not reflect differences in fundamental human worth, but differences in past history and opportunities. An ideology that requires that everyone be viewed as a fully actualized revolutionary subject of the future, where there is no place for weakness, intellectual under-development, or any emotional lack is doomed to failure; it prevents the movement from developing techniques and support systems that gently help people take the necessary steps to move from who they are to who they want to be.

Racism and sexism posed similar problems for the movement. Since the movement already had to embody the values of the future, there was no place for people who had sexist and racist attitudes. Instead of recognizing that anyone socialized in this society would certainly have these attitudes, and developing plans to gently assist people in self-transformation, the movement simply declared that anyone with these attitudes was a traitor or a deviant. The result was a wild set of manipulations. Every possible crazy scheme that anyone came up with could be justified if the proponents merely proclaimed it to be "objectively anti-racist." For example, "Revolution and armed struggle should be on our short-term agenda!" If you didn't agree, you were a racist yourself.

This line of argument was used by a group of undercover agents who were part of a Black caucus at a convention of anti-war activists in 1967. Their demand was that the whole convention accept the program of this particular group of Blacks or else be labeled "racist." The same tactic was used by those who tried to coerce New Leftists into supporting various middle-of-the-road Democratic Party candidates ("Blacks benefit materially from the Great Society, so if you try to start a third party you are really 'objectively' racist because you would hurt the Black community.") It was also used by those who wanted the New Left to become totally identified with the fortunes of the Black Panther Party ("If you don't support revolutionary violence, then you are racist, because that violence is what the Black community must engage in to defend itself.") Otherwise intelligent people were completely bamboozled. Almost never were these manipulations confronted and stopped in forthright ways. The reason was that people in the movement *knew* at some deep level of their beings that they were all in fact racist and sexist. Rather than acknowledge that this was an inevitable result of growing up in this society, and attempting to figure out compassionate and supportive ways to change themselves, they tried to deny what they knew and covered their denial by actions designed to prove how very unracist or unsexist they were. They were forced to deny their problems because they had framed their expectations of what would make a good movement totally in terms of an imperative for that movement to already embody the goals of the future in its present actuality. But if we must already be unsexist and unracist to start with, there will never be an opportunity to create the safe context within which one can work through and transcend the racism and sexism. There will never be the opportunity for people to take partial steps at overcoming their previous conditioning—because they will be too much on the defensive for not having taken even larger steps.

The demand to embody the goals of the future in present practice. does not allow for the actual limitations of people. It demands instant transformation, without any understanding of psychological constraints, without any sense of Surplus Powerlessness. Hence, it has no room for the one feeling that is indispensible for transformation: Compassion. Moreover, it gives no recognition to real powerlessness, to the structural factors that reinforce Surplus Powerlessness. Such demands are set-ups for failure. People join a movement thinking that they will become new people. Instead, they find the same kind of behavior that exists in the larger society. They are unprepared for this and believe that it is an indication that either they or their fellow movement members just aren't serious enough, haven't tried hard enough, or just aren't the right kind of people.

For some people, trying hard for instant transformations has startling positive results. For most, though, it produces a greater sense of failure and despair. People become very hard on each other. Lacking any analysis of why others are not living up to the highest ideals, they start to browbeat each other. "I'm less sexist than you," or "I'm less racist than you," or "I'm less egotistical than you," or "I have more collective spirit than you," or "I'm willing to take more risks because I believe in my ideals more deeply than you," or "I'm more serious about changing myself than you are." These are expressions of the kinds of interactions that begin to dominate a movement which has no compassion for its own members and their inevitable limitations. People are driven out of such a movement because they can't stand the incredible backbiting and power-playing that goes on in the name of creating a new humanity and a more loving reality. Unfortunately, people who have gone through this experience, instead of understanding the distortions that were introduced by the expectation of instant transformation, conclude that social change itself is impossible because people will inevitably recreate these same destructive games.

This dynamic can only be understood as a product of Surplus Powerlessness. The expectation that they would achieve the perfect personhood as an immediate result of their political commitment came from a set of misunderstandings generated by a society that emphasized that everyone can achieve whatever they want if only they have the will and talent. The lack of compassion for weaknesses that is learned in socialization gets translated either into a sense that we can accomplish nothing and, hence, that politics is totally useless because we are always certainly to fail, or into a set of utopian demands on ourselves and others that are bound to lead us back into despair about politics.

These were the most important manifestations of Surplus Powerlessness in the New Left, but there were many other important ways worthy of mention. One of the most striking was the absolute determination of New Leftists to see themselves as losers. Of course, as with many individuals who attempt to compensate for their feelings of inferiority and insecurity by projecting a false grandiosity and superficial self-confidence, there were those in the New Left who talked about revolution as something they expected to happen in the next year or two. There were people who projected an inflated sense of the movement's accomplishments, most typically to cover their own fears that what actually had been accomplished was not quite enough. They believed they had to inflate their achievements to keep the troops loyal. But the dominant sentiment in the movement was that nothing much had been accomplished, and that even what had been accomplished was probably not very important. The social psychology of discounting oneself and secretly suspecting that one's "failures" were a product of some internal problem showed up in how New Leftists assessed their actual achievements.

The rapid growth of the New Left and the anti-war movement from 1965, when it held the loyalties of an estimated 50,000-75,000 people with a core of not more than 5,000 activists around the country, to 1970, when it held the loyalties of over 5 million people, with a core of over 300,000 activists, was nothing short of phenomenal. Yet the core activists who held positions of dominant influence in this period continually acted as if the growth of support was a great danger, portending the possibility of co-optation as a more likely result than winning change.

This was particularly true in terms of the relationship between core activists and the large periphery of supporters who could be counted on to show up at peace marches, vote for peace candidates, sign petitions and donate money and occasional time. The core activists worried intensely that their movement was being taken over by liberals. As a result, they continually upped the level of involvement and radical vision necessary to be accepted as "OK." This thinking culminated in the New Left's reaction to the defeat of the McGovern campaign. Instead of acting as if the vast support for an anti-war candidate reflected a potential mass base that they could build upon and consolidate, a possibility made all the more real by McGovern's unwillingness to retain leadership over his own movement once he lost the election, New Leftists acted as though they themselves had been solidly defeated. Similarly, I remember attending many national meetings of New Left activists in 1971-1972 which were dominated by a sense of defeat and despair at precisely the moment when opinion polls were showing the greatest mass support ever for some of the positions and programs that New Leftists had been advocating for the prior seven years.

A continued effort was made by movement activists to redefine the criteria of success in such a way as to ensure that their own New Left would be one-down and seemingly impotent. At every stage in the growth of the movement from 1964 to 1970, new and more expansive goals replaced those that were in danger of being accomplished. By the time it became obvious that the anti-war movement would soon be in a position to elect sufficient Congressional support to ensure a cut-off of funding for the Vietnam war, the New Left had expanded its definition of success to include an end to American imperialism around the world. But even when in post-Watergate days very significant constraints were placed on direct governmental intervention in other countries, some New Leftists had already outpaced that development by insisting that nothing short of total revolution and the creation of a democratic socialist society would mean anything.

Now, I do not want to put the blame totally on the New Left. Precisely because important elements in America's ruling circles have an intuitive understanding of the importance of Surplus Powerlessness to ensure their continued power, there was a constant attempt on their part to discount any accomplishments of the social movement. Just as they had already learned ways to re-interpret union victories as gifts that management had "given" workers, so, for example, ruling elites in the United States took great pains to redescribe the victory of the Free Speech Movement in Berkeley, as a gift from the faculty and regents. The passage of Civil Rights legislation was propounded as proof of an enlightened establishment, and the expansion of programs for the poor was not related to the growing radicalization in the streets of America's cities. When it became obvious to the most politically astute and influential circles within America's corporate elite that the war in Vietnam would have to be ended, the major attention was focused on how the war could be ended in ways that would not credit the anti-war movement itself. Systematic and sustained efforts were given to discredit the movement at the very moment when the movement's program could no longer be resisted. An important element in this was to infiltrate the movement with FBI, police, and other paid government agents, and to have these agents incite and execute violent acts, which could then become the centers of attention for media coverage thus discrediting the political contributions of the movement.

The Watergate tapes reveal a dramatic instance of the execution of this strategy aimed at denying the importance of the movement. During the November, 1970, anti-war demonstration in Washington, D.C., over one million people assembled to challenge the war-makers. Demonstrators peacefully surrounded the White House at one point. President Nixon came out on the lawn and spoke to one demonstrator. The president asked him where he went to college, and then began to talk about football. The press gave this little incident major play because it showed how little the president cared or was influenced by the size of the largest demonstration in American history. The message was clear: "You can peacefully demonstrate all you want—I won't pay any attention, and we are carrying on our policy without regard to your activities." But the Watergate tapes reveal that President Nixon spent the entire day cloistered with a host of assistants getting frequent updates on the progress of the demonstration and planning how to deal with it. The public appearance was calculated to discount his concern—but the reality was that the top leadership was worried.

Similarly, the tapes reveal that major military decisions were shaped by their anticipated impact on domestic dissent, and that the use of tactical nuclear weapons was rejected only because of the potential resistance that it would engender from the powerful anti-war movement at home. My point is that if New Leftists discounted their strengths, it was not without the assistance of ruling elites, but it was a discounting that was fundamentally misguided.

I must acknowledge that there was something rational in the process by which New Leftists moved to redefine the criteria of success. After all, as people became more engaged in serious political thinking and action, they began to discover that American problems were less ad hoc and more systemic. As long as the owners of the society's wealth have the option of not investing their money, or even shipping their investments to another country in the face of liberal reforms that try to "humanize capital from within," every set of reforms is likely to be woefully inadequate. Reforms cannot be allowed to antagonize the corporate elites. When all else fails, the elites simply create large unemployment, high prices and shortages of important goods to bring the people once more under their heels. Looking to larger social transformation was not irrational. What was irrational was the failure to allow actual accomplishments to be counted as having deep meaning and importance. The struggle to change society is a long and complicated one— and requires that people feel an increasing sense of strength and accomplishment as they pursue this goal. But if all a movement does is focus on the larger goal as if it were the only thing worth accomplishing, no one can achieve any sense of accomplishment with anything less. No movement can survive that way. A rational approach would validate each important step and help participants reflect on the value of what they had in fact accomplished. It would not pretend that the steps were all that was necessary, and it would certainly continue to articulate the difference between what had been achieved and the full vision of a better society.

Without such a focus, movements will tend to be overcome by the Surplus Powerlessness that its members bring with them into the struggle. The New Left activists could never feel any real pride for their accomplishments. They were so sure that they were inadequate that they framed their politics in ways that would make their failures self-evident. Thus, they compared their accomplishments not to where the American left had been at five or ten years before, but to what had been accomplished by the Vietnamese, the Chinese, or various other revolutionary movements. They found themselves to be insignificant in comparison. Much has been written about the glorification of the third world by '60's activists—but rarely has it been mentioned that an important reason for this glorification was precisely so that New Leftists could see themselves as inadequate in comparison. Criticisms of these foreign third world movements for their lack of internal democracy were never taken seriously, not because New Leftists didn't care about democracy, but because they felt they had no right to be criticizing people engaged in these courageous struggles, unlike themselves who were mere grasshoppers in comparison. It was this felt lack of legitimacy that was the legacy of Surplus Powerlessness in the larger society that, in turn, caused people to make self-destructive errors when they engaged in political struggles.

Some theorists have argued that New Leftists felt a lack of legitimacy because they were middle-class youth facing a society that no longer offered the economic opportunities that the ideology of the society had promised them. They were thus facing downward mobility while holding an ideology of upward mobility, and this disparity created an identity crisis which motivated their activity. Others have argued that these were people who were about to enter the professional/managerial class, and that they were thereby divorced from "real production" and, hence, from any potential ground for identity with real achievements such as those of both working class and ruling class people. I find these explanations intriguing, but ultimately unsatisfactory. Most New Leftists had very little sense of where they were heading in the economic market, and even less focus or concern about it. Nor could class of origin distinguish those New Leftists who were suffused with powerlessness from those who were less affected by it.

New Leftists were no exception to the rest of the society in relation to the issue of powerlessness but, rather, had ingested the same sources of powerlessness as everyone else. If anything, they were less infused with Surplus Powerlessness than most because they were able to participate in a relatively successful social change movement.

Unfortunately, they brought with them ways of viewing themselves that had been forged in the larger society, and which caused them to act in ways that would guarantee the very isolation and defeat that on a conscious level they hoped to avoid. Trapped in the liturgy of self-blaming whose functioning we explored in the first part of this book, New Leftists could find no basis for compassion for themselves or others.

Nothing dramatized the self-negating irrationality of the New Left so much as the collapse of Students for a Democratic Society. SDS had grown from a few hundred people in 1962 to an organization with a membership of close to 100,000 in 1969.

Yet the people at the core of the organization were obsessed with how little was being accomplished by the organization. Many of them had been elected to leadership as representatives of the anti-leadership tendencies within the organization. But once in those positions their perspectives shifted. From the vantage point of the national organization's office in Chicago, one could see that President Nixon was embarked in a systematic effort to suppress the New Left and the emerging Black Liberation Movement. Yet SDS was so dominated by a fear of leaders and manipulation and by an obsession with democratic procedures that it prevented its leaders from developing national strategies and coherent responses. The national leadership could have responded by developing a program to show the membership how destructive the fear of coherent national strategy and the attachment to "local control" actually was. Simultaneously, they could have developed a national strategy to prepare for a unified response to the likely escalations in violence that the Nixon Administration would likely bring both in Vietnam and at home.

But the leadership did no such thing. Instead, it emphasized how unimportant SDS itself was as an organization, and how little had been accomplished by the anti-war movement. Mass demonstrations and campus disruptions were described as "meaningless," mere distractions that served to make people feel good and avoid the real issues of seizing power. This would be a time to escalate the level of the struggle, to become "real revolutionaries" like the Black Panther Party, the Vietnamese, the Chinese. And the only way to do that was to form an organization that was geared for fighting in place of a cumbersome democratic-styled organization like SDS.

Moreover, it was claimed that SDS members themselves could not really be trusted. Too many of them were simply interested in maintaining their own "white skin privilege." Too few of them were willing to take the risks that were needed in this period. So, when this leadership was elected to run SDS in 1969, it proceeded to dissolve the very organization with whose leadership it was charged. In its place, it formed "The Weathermen," which was quickly to slip into bombings, violence and self-destruction.

All of the anti-leadership localists, instead of understanding how their own myopia had helped create a climate in which those who saw the need for national strategy would feel frustrated in SDS, used this betrayal by the Weathermen as proof that any national leadership, even that which was elected on an anti-leadership ticket, would ultimately become elitist and un-democratic. This reinforced their belief that national leadership was a bad idea. Any new leadership that would have attempted to reconstruct SDS would have been suspected of trying to amass personal power and prestige, hardly the kind of emotional reward to entice anyone to engage in what would have been a very difficult task. The most important reasons why the Weathermen were able to get away with their destructive act were rooted in the fact that most SDS members systematically discounted their own achievements and did not understand the incredible importance of their own organization. Even at the absolute height of New Left influence and support, they were beginning to explore other life options for themselves now that "mass politics had failed." By the time the Kent State demonstrations unleashed a nationwide student strike, and the Hatfield-McGovern amendment to cut off Vietnam War funding had led to the successful capture of the Democratic Party by anti-war forces, most New Leftists had already opted out of national strategy. Some concentrated all their activities on local reformist struggles, already despairing of winning national power. Others "went to the land" and set up rural communes in which alternative lifestyles could be created. Others undertook personal quests in the areas of psychology or Eastern spirituality. These moves flowed from a conviction of failure formed at the very moment when, by any objective criterion, the movement had achieved its greatest success and had every reason to look forward to even greater success.

I do not want to underestimate other factors involved in the ultimate collapse of the New Left. Certainly the degree of repression generated by the Nixon White House was effective in scaring people away. Yet this alone would not have been sufficient, since in earlier moments in New Left history people had faced jail and even murder. The deeper reason was that people no longer believed in the value of what they were doing—their Surplus Powerlessness had led them to discount their actual achievements. The risks no longer seemed worth it. It was not the repression itself, but a climate of self-derogation, that played a critical role in weakening people's resolve.

Another important factor was the emergence of the women's movement. Like the Black movement before it, the women's movement caused a significant crisis of confidence for the New Left and for the anti-war movement.

The analysis of sexism was so transparently correct and important that it raised new doubts about the legitimacy of many of the current political struggles. It seemed that if the the New Left itself was infused with sexist practices and sexist men, how could it possibly hope to be an embodiment of the future society? And, if the movement was sexist, why should one risk going to jail fighting against Nixon on its behalf? Since the movement had accomplished very little anyway, why put one's energy into struggling with its internal dynamics, when they had been exposed as destructive to women? Here again, it was the Surplus Powerlessness of its members that led them to respond in this self-negating way to the emergence of a women's movement. In fact, the women's movement offered an incredible opportunity for the movement to strengthen itself and broaden its base. Had the New Left moved to incorporate the women's movement's understanding and approach within the context of a broader New Left framework, it could have both transformed itself and offered a new hope for the larger society.

A rational response would have been to acknowledge the women's critique, and to understand that people in the movement, socialized in a larger sexist society, would likely have deep sexist scars, and to recognize that what was needed was a compassionate program for helping people overcome their sexist conditioning. Such a program would have encouraged women in their absolute right to anger at sexism, and would have helped deepen and sustain that anger by encouraging women to understand the other aspects of society that also merited anger. It would have encouraged men to engage in profound reevaluation of their sexism without making them feel so defensive and worthless that they would run for cover without even allowing themselves to explore ways in which they could make serious change.

But all this would have only been possible if the participants in the New Left felt basically OK about themselves and their achievements. And this was precisely what was lacking. Instead, New Leftists responded in a variety of self-destructive ways. Some experienced instant conversions to feminism. They added "women's issues" to their list of societal demands but without ever experiencing the deep inner reevaluation of their beings that the original feminist critique made possible. Others simply quit politics altogether—using the critique of their own sexism as an excuse to "work on their own heads." While many women moved into feminist activity and carried on the social activism of the New Left, still others retreated from politics, overwhelmed with disappointment now that they saw their male comrades as so clearly untrustworthy.

Much of the inwardness of the 1970's amongst people in their twenties and thirties must be understood as an outgrowth of these same dynamics. Lacking any compassion for themselves, suffused with Surplus Powerlessness, the political activists of the '60's were overwhelmed with their own inadequacies. It was not just that they had failed in their own estimations. They "discovered" precisely what every aspect of socialization in this society had prepared them for: they deserved defeat. This consciousness was summed up in the saying, "We have met the enemy and it is us." The larger society had been able to get even these courageous people to think that the

basic problems they faced were internal, functions of some personal inadequacies. This was the reason that so many chose to quest for personal salvation
by attempting to become perfect enlightened beings through Eastern spirituality, or "open and honest" graduates of growth programs like Erhard Semi-
nar Trainings (EST), or the "healthy" products of psychotherapies, traditional or alternative. The focus of these movements on the individual's inner
being was a product of the pessimism that played a key role in the movement's
demise. Yet this pessimism was only the reassertion, now in collective form,
of the self-blaming and self-directed anger that is a critical aspect of Surplus
Powerlessness that we all experience throughout our lives. Conversely, once
people became more immersed in personal growth activities, the very self-
blaming generated by the larger society gets reinforced, since these activities
teach a metaphysics in which individuals alone, apart from all social forces,
are responsible for creating their own realities. So a social movement that
does not succeed in limiting the self-blaming of its members will inevitably
face defeat and dissolution-as its participants begin to "rediscover" the basic
alleged truths that seem to be acted out by all the movement's participants:
that they are all too undeserving to be able to transform anything, and all
they can do is tend their own gardens.

The Lessons for Politics in the Twenty-First Century

Surplus Powerlessness is not just some "other" problem in politics—it is
central and critical. No movement can succeed for any length of time without
confronting the ways that its participants have been shaped by Surplus Powerlessness. We should recognize that every political decision will be influenced
by the ways that the Social Unconscious shapes our perceptions of what is
possible. And this is not going to be true only in the sense of affecting our
choices of strategies and tactics. It is also going to be true at the micro-level
of experiences: how much people enjoy and feel nourished and not ripped
off by their experiences in politics will be directly affected by how the movement deals with the Surplus Powerlessness that gets expressed in every interaction between movement participants.

For this reason, I believe that any social movement that intends to sustain
itself must take the struggle against Surplus Powerlessness to be a central
focus of its activities, in addition to whatever topical area that movement is
addressing at the moment. Whether it be a movement against involvement
in Latin American wars, or a movement against apartheid, or a movement
for nuclear disarmament, or a movement for equality, or a movement against
racism or sexism, or a movement to preserve the environment, or a movement
to create greater power for workers, or a movement to provide jobs, childcare
or health care, any sustained political activity must also and simultaneously
create forms for dealing with the Surplus Powerlessness that permeates the
people who will be part of it. While it is my guess that ultimately these social
change organizations need to be fused in a more effective political party
form than they have available in the 1980's, my concern is not with the form
of organization, but the way that any organization creates a need for some

internal activity to combat Surplus Powerlessness.

Here are some of the steps that should be taken by any movement for political change.

(1.) It must educate its members about Surplus Powerlessness from the moment they become involved. This education must start with an open discussion of a point that cannot be repeated too often in the life of any movement: that the movement to change the society will be composed of people who are radically imperfect. Some of the ways that people in this movement will be manifesting their radical imperfections will be: (a.) Discounting their real achievements; (b.) Over-inflating their achievements because they can't feel satisfied with what they have actually achieved; (c.) Despairing of democratic process and thinking that people who don't yet see things the way they should will never change; (d.) Setting themselves up for battles they are sure to lose, and using those failures to conclude that they should really give up; (e.) Acting as though the people around them in the movement are "not enough" in some important ways, and then acting to make them feel inadequate or unworthy—perhaps because they haven't done enough to overcome their sexism or their racism or their elitism, or haven't taken enough risks, or are not morally pure enough, or sincere enough, or don't trust other people enough or are not humble enough (I can already see people baiting each other about who has done enough to overcome their Surplus Powerlessness!); (f.) Putting down or being condescending to people outside the movement, which will ensure their continued isolation and reconfirm their fears that they will always be discounted; (g.) Putting all their energies into reforms that are much less than what they really believe in, and toning down their full visions in the name of being "practical" or not wanting to scare people with their full vision; (h.) Shoving their full vision down people's throats before they've had a chance to make deep contact—also·as a way of losing contact with people and thus proving to themselves that they will always fail, just as the suspected they would. This list also suggests the problem; no specific position will always be a manifestation of Surplus Powerlessness—all we can do is sensitize people to the fact that this dynamic is going to exist in their movements, but we will still need sensitive evaluations of Surplus Powerlessness in any specific circumstance—and we must beware of those who use this analysis as yet another club against themselves or each other to perpetuate their own powerlessness.

(2.) A central message of any political movement must be that it aims towards the creation of a society based on Compassion. That Compassion must begin with the members of the movement itself—and the movement must encourage people to re-understand themselves and their lives in terms of the various factors that have kept them from being all that they could be. But it must move to articulate a doctrine of compassion towards all who are outside of it. How to do this will be the focus of the last part of the book. For here it is sufficient to say that the movement must see the generation of compassion as equal in status to the specific goal-directed tasks it seeks to accomplish in the world.

(3.) To establish this focus as equal in status to any of its other goals, any political organization or movement must sponsor autonomous support groups for its members in which they focus on eliminating self-blaming, liberating righteous anger, and learning mutual trust. Autonomy is critical to ensure against manipulation of these groups for narrow power ends. These groups are not for "indoctrination" into the latest ideas of the movement. On the contrary, they must provide places for people to express their doubts and upsets about the ways the political movements are proceeding. Like the Occupational Stress Groups, these support groups should provide safe places for people to express their doubts and their anger, to look at their own roles, to begin to assess what happened to them throughout their lives and in their contemporary home and work situations that tend to make them feel powerless. Indeed, to make these groups safe, they must also be places in which people can role-play ways of challenging the people in leadership in the very political movements that help create these groups in the first place. While this is risky for leadership, it is the best way to create movements composed of people who have the inner strength to struggle for social change—because they have come to feel supported in their right to have their feelings and ideas respected. As these groups allow people to explore the ways that they have been making themselves feel powerless, they begin to transform the people who have joined political movements—and to make them more ready for the long run. Moreover, the trust that any movement has in its members, manifested in its willingness to sponsor these small groups and allow them to be genuinely autonomous, would almost certainly communicate itself to outsiders, and would become one of the reasons that people would be attracted to the movement. The feeling of respect for its members that such a movement manifested would be in such striking contrast to the manipulations that people typically experience everywhere else in the society that they would want to find out about the rest of the political messages of the movement.

(4.) To give Compassion such equal weight is really to raise the question of re-shaping what politics should be about. I believe that the success of the Right in the 70's and 80's in the U.S., no matter how short-lived, was based in part on their having touched a set of needs that liberals and progressives seemed to be ignoring—needs for a deeper fulfillment of our Human Essence. While the Right's programs could never deliver a society that actually provided such a fulfillment, even articulating the ideals spoke to something deep in the beings of many working people whose economic interests might have inclined them away from the Right. Without discounting the importance of each of the specific programs and demands that liberal and progressive forces are concerned about, I believe that ultimately they must all be put in a very different political context than that which has dominated the thinking of the past decades. In the past, progressives have framed their political issues in terms of an abstract notion of fairness or equality. While this notion is valuable, it is ultimately inadequate. The ultimate basis for our struggles must be posed in terms of our understanding that human beings deserve love and caring—and that the way this society is built retards Compassion and undermines love. A practical politics is one that articulates precisely and in detail the ways that current arrangements undermine our abilities to love, and projects a vision of how to create an alternative society based on the possibility of love. So talk of love leads to talk about stress, families and childhood.

But doesn't my fourth point here simply constitute a re-raising of the very kind of utopian hopes that so hurt the New Left? To deal with this objection, we need to offer three important qualifications: First, the focus on love must be accompanied by a strategic focus on Compassion—specifically, helping people understand how not to blame themselves or each other for not being adequately loving; and how to understand the complex interactions among the work of the world, family life and the legacy of childhood that make us less loving than we want to strive to be; and understand the many ways in which our moments of transcendence are undermined by the pressures of an existing social reality that is based on exploitation, competition and mutual manipulation. It is critical to avoid the creation of a church-like flavor to a political movement by having articulate goals that everyone believes are unrealizable and utopian. For that reason, the movement that puts forward a vision in the name of love must be clearly articulating why it expects that its members will not be the full embodiment of that ideal, and why it is nevertheless crucial to change those aspects of existing reality that tend to undermine our ability to be more fully loving.

Also, we don't need a new form of totalitarianism in the name of love—the very manipulation of that ideal by right wingers gives some people reasonable grounds to be suspicious. So we need to specify our vision of love in society in terms of what it means concretely: encouraging cooperation and rewarding it, encouraging mutual interdependency, and providing options for people to treat each other lovingly without fear that they would thereby lose out economically—a fear that is justified in our society. We don't want a society that will claim a right to tell people how they should live, with whom, when or if they should marry, when or if they should have children. So we must insist that our vision is for a society that provides possibilities, but that simultaneously guarantees freedom so that people can determine the specific ways they want to use those possibilities.

Likewise, a society structured to promote loving relationships will not be a perfect society, one in which everyone will always receive all that they want or have all their needs always fulfilled. There is always the risk that in talking about love we project expectations that can never be fulfilled, and this will then engender a deeper level of disillusionment. There is something deeply true in the conservative temperament and, though it wrongly articulates this through ontologizing some fundamental flaw in human nature, it is correct in warning us to stay away from fantasies of humanly constructed utopias. We must always be careful to acknowledge what is true in its concerns—that the new societies that we can construct will still not feel as good as one's mother's womb, that people will still feel rejected in love affairs or disappointed in how deep are their friendships, or befuddled by the fact that other people don't "understand" things as deeply or truly as they do. There will still be instances in which people act out of their fear—and in fact, the possibility of regressing into fear on a large scale, while significantly reduced from our own society, will always be present as long as human beings have freedom. To acknowledge all this is not to say that fundamental change isn't worth fighting for—but to understand that even a society based on love will have imperfections, doubts, elements that aren't wonderful, and the permanent possibility of slipping back into a less loving reality.

If we keep all three of these qualifications at the forefront of our articulation of an ideal of love, we are in a much better and stronger position to fight for a really loving society, and to win the hearts and minds of many people who today are very distant from progressive or liberal politics. A movement that seems to be focused on these issues in personal life, that cares about how people treat each other, and gives real space for people's inadequacies, would command the attention of many millions of people who today want to have nothing to do with politics.

It may seem discouraging to have spent so much time on how a particularly vibrant mass movement could go astray. But there is much to learn from this example. As I argued in the last chapter, the politics of mass movements have a potentially liberatory effect. They open up possibilities of mutual trust and the excitement of creating ourselves and our futures with other people. What we have seen here is that these movements inevitably come up against Surplus Powerlessness. But we have also begun to articulate a way to deal with this problem—through the generating of Compassion. If self-blame is the unifying theme of our self-defeat, Compassion can be the theme of our transcendence.

In talking about love and Compassion as central to politics, we quickly come upon another concern. After all, religious communities have for millenia promised to bring about a world of love and caring. Yet many people today are disillusioned with the whole religious enterprise and see in it a mere trap and a set of delusions. Indeed, religion has often played the role of increasing Surplus Powerlessness. Perhaps all this talk about love and compassion will just re-legitimate religious worldviews that make for powerlessness. These objections, I believe, are worthy of consideration, though I disagree with them. As we will see in the next chapter, religion can play either a destructive role or a constructive role. It is my contention, indeed, that some of the fundamental insights of religion can help to undermine Surplus Powerlessness. Just as politics, when dominated by self-interest, can lead to an intensification of isolation, cynicism and despair, so religion, when used as a tool for legitimating unjust social orders, can lead to a quiescence and acceptance of the social irrationality. But just as politics can also be much more, a sphere for real empowerment, so religion can strengthen our capacity for compassion and deepen our sense of power by enlarging the sphere of our understanding.

Chapter 15

Religion Versus
Powerlessness

T HE SUMMARY DISMISSAL OF THE INSIGHTS OF RELIGION BY
many of those engaged in social change movements is a serious mistake.
Religious traditions have developed insights and ways of understanding reality that can make an important contribution to a struggle against Surplus
Powerlessness.

It is no surprise, however, that many people are unwilling to even consider
the possibility that religion could play a progressive role. Many religions
hold onto their members by inducing deep fears about engaging in non-
sanctioned activities. Others induce a deep sense of guilt that impairs adult-
life functioning. For example, many of my Catholic clients need to rid themselves of much of their conditioning around sexuality before they can have
a loving and spontaneous sexuality in their adult relationships. Moreover,
many children are taught religion as part of an effort by their parents to
rigidify their behavior and limit their spontaneity—and so they find it critical
to break from religion as part of the normal process of separation and
differentiation that is required for a young adult to develop his/her own
internal sense of self.

Adults breaking out of negatively imposed religious patterns often retain
high degrees of resentment towards the religion in whose name they received
negative or hurtful training as children. I have watched this happen to many
of my Jewish friends. The specific way that Judaism was imparted to them
as children seemed to convey the message that to be a good Jew was simply

to be a successful American, say some prayers in Hebrew, eat certain kinds of food and celebrate Chanukah instead of Christmas. But if this is all that Judaism was about—then why bother? Why inconvenience oneself to learn to read Hebrew, participate in rituals that take up time, and set oneself up as different from other people?

There are deeper reasons to be suspicious of religion as well. There is no doubt that religion has often been used to keep people enslaved to oppressive social systems. This became obvious in the mid-1980s when Christian fundamentalist preachers became public apologists for racism in South Africa, just as many other such preachers have used religious justifications to support militarism, racism, and imperial plunder of one society by another throughout human history. This may be more than just a temporary misuse of a tradition. There are fundamentally oppressive ideas in some religious traditions. For example, the idea that human beings are fundamentally evil or born in sin has been used as an argument against people building a just world. The injunction to "Render unto Caesar what is Caesar's" is only one formulation of a theme that has been central to many religious and spiritual traditions: namely that this world of oppression isn't what really counts, so don't spend your time struggling to change it when it makes more sense to put your energy into preparing yourself spiritually for life on a higher plane of reality, either in this world (the way of many Eastern spiritualities) or in the world to come (eternal bliss or eternal damnation awaits you). Use your time here to prepare yourself for this higher reality and don't get involved in the politics of the present.

But this may be too quick a victory for those of you whose bad personal experiences with religion make you want to believe that religion is reactionary or anti-political. After all, to be fair we must also notice that many of the contemporary alternatives to religion have also been used to justify both apolitical or reactionary positions. Marxism has become the official ideology of repressive states around the world. Feminism is sometimes misused to justify racist or classist positions that have alienated many feminists from the majority of American women. Democracy has become an excuse for one country to impose its will on another by military force. Tolerance is a value that is invoked to explain why it is never correct to impose your views on others and, hence, to invoke passive protest when the people constructing the apparatus of human destruction will only pay attention to something more forceful. Science and progress become justifications for the construction of the weapons of war and environmental harm. There are few ideologies that have not been used in ways very different than they were originally intended. Once we understand how any set of ideas gets misused, we need to drop the automatic self-righteousness that so many people bring into their negative attitudes towards religion.

My point is that any set of ideas is a historical product and subject to forces outside of itself. Religion is no exception. The themes and traditions that become dominant within religious traditions at any given period are in part the products of internal struggles that go on within the religious community. At various points, those with secular power enter into such struggles, helping to support those tendencies within the religious world which are most likely to support and give cover to the established system of domination. That support comes by giving financial aid, protection and public sanction to the safe tendencies within the religious world, while suppressing, ostracizing, ridiculing and denying financial support to the more "irresponsible" elements, those whose ideas might have the tendency to undermine established social realities. This process is just the same as the process within the intellectual world, where monied interests create universities and think tanks populated by those whose thoughts are deemed useful and safe; or the publishing world, or the world of psychology (where tendencies critical of the established order are marginalized); or the world of social movements (where the intervention of the powerful, through their media and through their police, selects out who will be deemed "responsible opposition leaders" and who will be relegated to the "irresponsible fringe"). In all these arenas there is a tendency to take ideas that might have originally had a critical impact and to transform them until they become accommodated to established reality. How much this tendency actually succeeds in any given period is often as much a reflection of the relative power of the alternative forces as it is an indication of how inherently progressive the core ideas really are.*

It is particularly ironic and sad when we see religious traditions that had their origins in a struggle against oppression become useful tools for a new oppressive order. Yet it is no secret that religion played a particularly powerful role in sustaining feudal aristocracies in the West, just as it continues to play a role in sustaining many oppressive regimes around the world today. This role was not hidden—and when a new class of shopkeepers, merchants and bankers began to take shape in the 13th–16th Centuries in Europe they were faced with a religious ideology that supported the rights of feudal landlords and severely restricted the possibilities for the kind of economic activity that this new class needed. Yet this rising bourgeoisie, as it was called, did not initially try to challenge religion. Eventually, it sought religious reform that would allow its economic activity greater opportunities—and the various Protestant denominations that they supported provided greater latitude to their desire to accumulate capital. But, even when the bourgeoisie in the 18th Century became so fundamentally aligned with anti-religious metaphysics (empiricism) that no reconciliation was possible, there were still many who hoped to save religion by divorcing it from the world of scientific phenomena and creating a different arena for it—"noumenal reality," the realm of the spirit, within which religion might still be said to be valid, while no longer interfering in any way with the "right" to unlimited accumulation.

It is my contention that the main thrust of contemporary ideologies of

---

* No content is immune from this process and struggle. The deconstructionists thought that any attempt to programmatize progressive ideas would necessarily lead to the creation of new false unities—so all we can have is critique. But critique is quickly marginalized and absorbed into intellectual islands that have been constructed precisely to keep these people busy and safely away from the majority which would be necessary to transform reality and not just merely lament it.

domination has been to discard all aspects of reality that are not quantifiable and publicly observable. As I argued in the discussion of science, it is the shrinking of the world of discourse in the way that science makes possible that allows for the most sophisticated control of the social world. And it is the failure of Marxism and psychoanalytic thought to recognize this disempowering aspect of scientific thought that has made them less radical in their actual application in the 20th Century. The Marxist and psychoanalytic traditions rail against religion, thereby winning battles of previous centuries, but, in that very act, miss the very different meaning that religion may have in a society whose ruling forces so successfully have adopted the religion of science and technical rationality to strengthen their system of domination.

The foundations of one-dimensional thinking in our society may be more fundamentally questioned by a religious world view than by a more narrow critique that focuses on specific inconsistencies or hypocrisies within the dominant ideology. We are witnessing a dramatic turnaround in the role that various ideologies fulfill. The very progressive and freeing ideologies of the past, including science, Marxism and psychoanalysis, are today frequently assimilated into cultures of domination—while religion, still reactionary in some contexts, may be the most solid basis for a critique of contemporary society that is deeply founded and not merely trendy. In short, we need to look at a given social reality in considerable detail before knowing whether a particular thought system plays a progressive or conservative role within it—and we cannot rely on our experience of the past.

Certainly there are still many communities where the continued prevalence of religion has destructive consequences because the religion that is preached tends to emphasize those aspects that lead towards fatalism, acceptance of constituted authority, and sexist ideas. These are, in my understanding, the communities where the bourgeois revolution has still not taken place or gained any deep hold. In these communities, I am supportive of the ideology of the bourgeoisie—the emphasis on freedom, individual responsibility, loosening of repressive boundaries, destruction of traditional roles, rejection of communitarian ideals and practices. I support this as a transitional corrective to the repressiveness of feudally based communities and feudal ways of understanding reality. As opposed to societies within which individuals were systematically degraded and within which individual choice was impossible, I support the process of disintegration of social ties and the fostering of ideals of individual autonomy.

I want to emphasize this point, because I do not think it is possible to create a new kind of community and a new kind of mutual interdependency without first going through the steps of rejecting the old. The fears that people have about communitarian values and the transcendence of individualism are in large part based on their concern that this older feudal reality not be reestablished. It is not only important to assert that the bourgeois revolution was in fact an advance, but also to insist that people must incorporate bourgeois society's insistence on the dignity and autonomy of the individual into any program that would transcend bourgeois individualism and create a new kind of human being who is at home with values of mutual interdependency and communitarian realities.

In that same spirit, I want to insist that the kind of religion that I believe to be empowering must be distinguished from religious communities and practices that have not yet gone through the process of grappling with the Enlightenment, the rise of science, the dominance of empiricism, and the rejection of authoritarianism. It is only those who have already absorbed what is plausible and compelling in these developments who can then move beyond them to see what is crippling and destructive in them as well. To religious fundamentalists I recommend a good dose of modernism, not because it is ultimately more true and satisfying, but because it represents an alternative set of distortions and insights which, when passed through, opens up the possibility of constructing a new kind of religious community that is not simply a reversion to the oppressive aspects of feudal religion.

In this process of constructing a new religious community, I think that we can draw upon aspects of religious thought and life which coexisted with those aspects of religion which were more oppressive. Within monasteries, spiritual sects and oppositional groupings, insights were kept alive that form the basis for a religious tradition that is committed to the struggle for full human liberation. It is not my contention that this religious tradition constitutes an existing reality that must simply be rediscovered and revitalized. After all, no matter how liberatory any aspect of religious ideology might have been within its historical context, it always embodied sets of understandings that were limited by the specific period.

Moreover, having an understanding of the necessary limitations in any given historical period may also alert us to the necessary limitations of our own solutions. We, too, are likely to be producing theories that are both a reflection of the limitations of our historical situation while they are also a manifestation of some transcendence. Compassion for our limitations is an important ingredient in any enterprise that aims to construct a new reality. With this in mind, it seems appropriate to say that we can construct a new kind of religious community that draws upon the past and also confronts the specific realities of oppression built into a society which rules by convincing its members that they cannot construct and do not deserve to have—a more fulfilling social world based on mutual love and mutual caring.

My talk about building "a new religious community" need not mean building a new religion. Within Christianity, Judaism and Islam there are enough bases for constructing new communities that could be part of the social struggles of transformation*. A new religious community within Western religions could unite Christians, Jews and Moslems around a shared effort to reclaim what was liberatory within their traditions. It could bring them together to foster mutual ties and joint activities that respect their differences and are. built on their points of unity.

Jews, Christians and Moslems could consciously and intentionally build shared events, celebrations and intellectual enterprises within which the

---

* I have no similar confidence about Eastern religions, but could be convinced.

emancipatory visions that they each hold could be refined and developed.

"But why even bother with these religious traditions? If they have to be reconstructed, then why not start afresh and construct a community that does not have religious content and which would therefore be able to include all the many millions of people who have been totally alienated from the religious world? Isn't religion just an additional factor that will divide people and make it less likely that a community of hope can be constructed to challenge the philosophies of despair that dominate contemporary thought?"

At one level, the answer is simple. There are many millions of people who hold onto a religious perspective, and whose worldview is deeply attached to that tradition. If we hope to ever reach these people, we must speak in a language that is appropriate. To the extent that the progressive forces write these people off as a lost cause, they also guarantee their own continued isolation. Indeed, I believe that the dismissal of the religious community is a misguided and potentially dangerous strategy that must be challenged. It flows in part from the Suprlus Powerlessness of people in the progressive movement. It is their very fear of other people that makes these progressives dismiss or caricature so many people who might otherwise be open to listening to progressive ideas. Ironically, progressives often point out that religion is based on a fear of the unknown. In my view, it is the fear of being discovered as not really worthy, a fear that all of us have from our socialization into this society, that shapes the way that progressives approach religious people. If this were to change, I believe that many of the insights of the movements of social change could be expressed into the languages of religious communities, and receive significant support there.*

But this is an argument for how the progressives could bring *their* truth to religion. I believe that the more important consideration is that religious communities have something important to contribute to defeating Surplus Powerlessness and that it is the progressives who must *learn* from the religious community. I shall present some aspects of biblical religion that can provide a necessary counter to the dominant ideologies today and discuss how they can provide us with alternative ways of viewing reality that break the cycle of domination of the establishment ethic.

An Alternative Reality

Religions ask us to look at the world from an entirely different perspective from that of the dominant culture. In contemporary capitalist societies, the criterion by which we judge all things is the way that we can use them for our own purposes. The world is seen as an endless set of opportunities for satisfying our desires, and each individual is encouraged to do his or her best to get as many personal desires satisfied as possible.

This same approach is then extended to the way that we deal with other

---

* These ideas are merely programmatic; a future work will explore this in more detail.

human beings. They too are there to satisfy our desires. We have the right to use them for that purpose. People become commodities, not just in the economic sphere, but in our personal lives as well. We have already seen how this way of understanding reality makes it extremely difficult to build loving relationships.

Most religions have a different perspective. They tend to emphasize the notion of stewardship, believing that human beings have a sacred obligation to take care of the world, to use their intelligence to create a harmonious order, and to respect the universe. The biblical injunction for man to rule over the universe was sometimes misinterpreted by apologists for the rising bourgeoisie as a justification for their wanton destruction of the physical environment. But, in fact, most people within the biblical tradition emphasize the need for human beings to shepherd and to care for, not to transform and remake. Insofar as human beings are meant to interfere, it is only to make the world more deeply based on an understanding of the ultimate harmony and moral imperative within the universe. Thus, Noah is said by the Rabbinical tradition to have spent much time on the ark trying to quiet down fighting among the animals—but never to have been involved in throwing any species off the boat for not fitting his ideal. Stewardship involves reporting to a God who created the whole universe and decided that it was good.

The orientation towards the universe preached by most religions involves the notions of awe, wonder and radical amazement. Human beings are encouraged to understand that they are not the creators of the world, and that their interference with the natural order must be governed in rational and ethical ways. The earth has a sanctity and value that cannot be appropriated. In biblical tradition this results in a prohibition against private property: people may inhabit the land, but the whole land belongs to God, and cannot be divided up and sold in any permanent way. Every fifty years the Jubilee eliminates all transactions that have resulted in exchange of property, and everything reverts to the original biblically prescribed equal division of land.

It is not just that the land is not available for ownership in the sense that we mean in capitalist society—but that human beings are required to spend time focused on the celebration of the grandeur of the world. Every week people are enjoined to dedicate an entire day to leaving the goal-directed world of daily life and regarding the universe not from the standpoint of control but from the standpoint of reverence and appreciation. The Talmudic rabbis specified that all "melachah," all interference with the natural order, was disallowed on the Sabbath. It was not just hard or heavy labor that people were to take a rest from; even the pleasure of planting a garden or creating a nice little bonfire was outlawed. This was to be a day when the universe would be approached not from the standpoint of how we could transform or use it, but how we could simply appreciate it.

This idea is an important counter to the dominant worldview. It challenges the fundamentals of capitalist ethics, and the way that we have come to view the world. It is particularly powerful when coupled with another aspect of biblical religion: the notion of the sacredness of human beings.

Human beings are created in the image of God. As such, they are of ultimate value. They cannot be treated as means, but only as ends. Human beings are not simply "capital" or "human resources·" It is foreign to the Bible to talk as if the reason for taking care of other people were that it would pay off for all of us in the future. Human beings deserve respect because in their essence they are mirrors of the Divine.

Here, then, is a language and worldview which can provide a real alternative to the contemporary approach to reality. It adds a dimension to our understanding that can never be generated out of the technocratic mind.

It is important to emphasize how radical a break this is with the thinking of contemporary societies of domination. The critique of capitalism inherent in this approach is not civil libertarian. It does not say that capitalism is bad because it doesn't allow for free speech or free choice. It doesn't criticize capitalism for not being fair to everyone. It criticizes it on a much deeper level. Capitalism is unacceptable on moral terms because it does not treat human beings as if they were created in the divine image and because it allows and encourages us to think of how we can manipulate and control each other. Capitalism has at its root the notion that it would be OK for some people to dominate over other people.

The same critique also pertains to communist societies. Precisely because they do not base themselves upon a real understanding of the divinity within each individual, East European societies adopt a way of treating human beings that reflects the same logic of "using" and "manipulating" that is so frequent in capitalist societies. I do not believe that this would happen in a true socialism or communism—a society in which working people had real democratic control. Obviously, my faith here is not based on any existing society—since there is none in which this kind of democratic socialism actually exists. Rather, it is based on my understanding that in order for such a society to be created, we would have to build a social movement that treats human beings with this kind of respect, and aims at the creation of a world in which the true dignity of human life was the guiding criterion for decision making. Hence, it would embody the spirit of biblical religion, rather than the spirit of secular science. To the degree that existing "communist" societies have seen themselves as instantiations of the scientific approach they have tended to reinforce some of the worst aspects of the capitalist societies they were allegedly aimed at transcending*.

I personally think that the religious perspective helps us understand reality

---

* Of course, it would be unfair to condemn the attempts at socialism just because they failed. A deeper understanding would lead us to have compassion for the millions of dedicated social change activists who tried to build a better society in the midst of a peasantry that was illiterate, an economy that needed to be built from scratch, incredible levels of devastation from the First and Second World Wars. They were faced with the active hostility of capitalist states which did everything possible to increase the misery of the people in these lands in order to foment rebellion against the newly emerging regimes. We must have compassion for their failures, and respect for their efforts. But we must simultaneously recognize that within such conditions it was possible for liberatory voices to be drowned out by those who merely

in a way that is more true to the basic nature of human beings. But let us leave aside that claim for a moment. For the main claim that I am trying to pursue is something different.

The religious perspective is really an alternative way to view reality. It is much more of an alternative than perspectives that critique capitalism on its own terms, or than those whose greatest problem with the capitalists is that they don't live up to their own ideals, that they are inconsistent and hypocritical and unfair in their own espoused values. As an alternative, the religious worldview helps to challenge the dominant society's attempt to frame reality as "that which is" at the moment. We have already seen how powerful a constraint such a worldview is on any thinking about social change. The religious worldview opens up the social, intellectual and emotional space to imagine a quite different way of approaching reality. It may well be the case that not everyone who is religious succeeds in experiencing the world in this different way, and it may be the case that everyone who is religious fails to experience the world in this different way much of the time, but the very fact of having this alternative accessible stands as a limit on the power of domination of our psyches by the established order. To the extent that religion provides us with a fundamentally different reality, it inhibits Surplus Powerlessness by keeping alive the possibility of alternatives.

"Oh great," a skeptic might respond, "Now perhaps you'd like to justify every form of religious obscurantism on these same grounds. The next thing we know, you'll be justifying Catholicism or orthodox Judaism or fundamentalist Islamic tendencies."

Yes and No.

I have already said that I agree with the content of the biblical view of the dignity of humanity, and that is one reason I find it attractive. I reject the specific way that women are treated in the Catholic and fundamentalist Islamic traditions, and that is why I would have trouble "justifying" them in any ultimate sense. But, yes, I do see even these religious positions which on other grounds I do not accept, as valuable in regard to the struggle against Surplus Powerlessness within the context of societies where they are *not* the state-established religion. Precisely to the extent that they keep alive an alternative that is fundamentally different from the logic and experience of contemporary societies dominated by ideologies of empiricism, they put a check on the total domination that ruling elites seek. No matter how many sermons may be preached in the names of these religions which seek to

---

sought to improve material conditions, and who rejected democratic ideals and replaced them with an oppressive and manipulated reality. The people most dedicated to creating a new world have been rightfully critical of what has actually emerged—and, while having compassion for those who tried their best under impossible conditions, we must reject as inexcusable the attempts to define what actually exists in these societies as forms of socialism. Those who claim that in order to avoid being utopian we must embrace "actually existing socialist experiments, however imperfect" do the work of the capitalist class: they take our hope and identify it with an oppressive existing reality, thereby making it harder for us to even imagine that anything could ever be different.

justify this or that oppressive regime, the underlying logic of the religion stands in contradiction to the one-dimensionality of the dominant advanced industrial society.*

To understand that the way things are is not fixed and to experience a whole different way of experiencing reality is subversive. And it doesn't matter if the whole other way isn't completely ideal for it to have this subversive effect. Its radical otherness is sufficient to offer an experience of Possibility. Once that space has been opened, political progressives may fill in a different content. The question of what kind of alternative reality, what way we want to rebuild the world, remains open. The discussion can be carried on amongst people who have the intellectual and emotional capacities to experience the possibility of Possibility.

A Sense of History

Religion also can teach us a sense of history. In school we learn facts, mostly about kings, queens, presidents, dictators, and rulers. We learn who fought whom for what. We rarely are taught to experience or understand history as the struggle of human beings to achieve more of their essence under conditions that have been systematically distorting. The only "logic" that we are taught about history is that it has all been building up to its final culmination in contemporary society—and that what we have achieved today is the final flowering of rationality, or the best of all possible worlds, and that history is now over because our society has set in motion processes that will solve all the remaining problems that can in fact be solved.

Religion has two important dimensions to teach us about history. First, it can teach us that things were once actually quite different. It does this not just by talk. Religious symbols and prayers actually capture experientially the feeling of past ages. There is no other social practice that enables masses of people to regularly re-experience the past, and hence enables them to feel in a deep way how things might in fact be different than they are. Its subversion of our powerlessness comes from its ability to teach us on the

---

* It is so easy for Western liberals to dismiss Christian or Islamic fundamentalism as irrational, and to think of their adherents as dupes, rather than to ask themselves, "What real needs are these religions answering, that liberal capitalism and modernism have failed to satisfy?" As much as I detest the anti-women and anti-Israel aspects of Islamic fundamentalism, I can also see that its growth is in response to a rational rejection of the kind of modernizing that Western-educated elites were making available—a modernizing that benefitted some while ignoring the material needs of most, while simultaneously negating the spiritual realities that remained the only area in which most people could feel any sense of wholeness or purpose to their lives. Instead of dismissing these people as crazy, we should instead ask, "How can we find ways to satisfy their legitimate needs and dissociate that fulfillment from the anti-women and anti-Jewish components in their religion?" In the meantime, we should understand that part of their appeal is precisely that these religions articulate a critique of the modern capitalist world and its values—a critique that has some important and reasonable elements within it.

experiential level that things have been really different, and might be different in the future.

Second, religion tends to focus on the future redemption of the world. Whether it be "the Second Coming" or the first coming of the biblical messianic period, Western religion is unabashed in its determination to teach people to think in terms of how things may one day be quite different. We might fill in the content somewhat differently from various religious communities, but, nevertheless, many religious communities have regularized their membership to think in terms of historical transformation. All philosophies of hope benefit from the ability of people to think in terms of a future quite different from the present—and this is an important contribution of many religious communities. It is therefore not surprising that when the trendiness of a political movement passes, it is often the religious radicals who remain committed even in the "slow" periods, unlike many disillusioned secularists.

Liberation is Possible and Necessary

Biblical religion is insistent on the point that real liberation is possible. The central event of the Bible is the exodus from Egypt. The event sums up a message that has as many revolutionary implications for today as it had then: the order of oppression is not "natural" and can be overthrown.

God is constantly reminding the Jews throughout the Bible about the fact that they once were slaves in Egypt. Therefore, they have an obligation to identify with people who are oppressed. The widow, the orphan, the stranger—these are their special responsibility. The tone is quite the opposite of what we accept in contemporary society: "You were oppressed once, so now it's your turn to get yours, and forget about those who remain oppressed. After all, nobody took care of you, so why should you take care of everyone else?"

The centrality of the overthrow of slavery is emphasized by the fact that it is commemmorated all year long. Just as one reason the Bible gives for Sabbath is the celebration of creation, it gives a second reason: Sabbath exists to remind us of the exodus from Egypt.

In fact, the idea of the Sabbath is the celebration of the first great workers' victory over their bosses. Of course, oppression is not totally ended by having a day off from the economic realm. But when a whole people sanctifies one day as a day in which the economic powers of the world cannot touch them, in which the still existing class divisions within their own society will be suspended, and in which people will collectively celebrate the victory of moving from a very oppressed position to a less oppressed position—this is a light and inspiration to other peoples.

Among the ancient peoples there was no day in which everyone stopped work. Slaves were required to work on most religious holidays just as though they were not human and had no rights. The Sabbath idea articulated in the Bible is quite different—it specifies that no one may be required or even allowed to work on the Sabbath (i.e., it's stronger than the demand for time-and-a-half for overtime; it prohibits "forced overtime," it is an absolute demand for the right of all people to rest and free themselves from any struggle to survive and any whims of those who have economic power in the society). Even housework is forbidden, including cooking, cleaning, mending, planting, or any other work that might in a chauvinist society be assigned to women. So this biblical idea is one that recognizes all forms of labor as dignified, and insists that the labor of the rest of the week be celebrated by honoring the workers and instructing them to refresh themselves (literally: "get back into breathing again") and relax.

The whole story of the exodus, read and reread on the Sabbath, still needs to be learned. It tells us that there is nothing natural about oppression. Once, people were free, but this was undermined when certain political and economic conditions led oppressive rulers to create slavery. Once enslaved, the Bible tells us, people began to act as slaves, so that when some of them got the idea that slavery should be fought against, most of the rest already believed that any change in their condition was impossible. Nevertheless, the whole system of slavery was overturned, as the Jews left Egypt not just with Jews, but with other peoples who had also decided to join them in the exodus.

So here is the central message being preached by biblically based religions: "Those who are oppressed need not be oppressed. And let us tell you our story—because we were once slaves, and now we are free. And this same thing can happen to you. Oppression can appear to be natural and necessary, but this is just false consciousness that accompanies being enslaved. In fact, everything can be totally different, just as it was for us." It is a revolutionary message.

"OK," you might respond, "I can see that this message is important. But doesn't it always get lost when it gets enmeshed in a religious system with all the silly and distracting rituals?" No. Ritual can in fact be a powerful force that draws us out of the mesmerizing and self-absorbed life of contemporary society. We need to give rituals a new looking over.

The Power of Ritual

Rituals can be stultifying and de-energizing. So many rituals are carried out in ways that deaden consciousness. The term has almost become synonymous with "rote and unconscious behaviour." But religious rituals can also function in a quite different way. When people are alive to their own religion, ritual is a direct way to re-experience the central messages of the faith. Rituals are usually connected with important ideas or experiences in the life of the community, and allow people vital access to those ideas and experiences.

When I was a younger man, I thought that my ideals did not need to be ritualized and they could be articulated in verbal patterns that I could share with others. My community was defined by those who liked to engage in these exchanges of words in political meetings. Unfortunately, these meetings were not always exhilarating experiences. The main justification for anyone to speak was to articulate differences. But there was almost no form for people uniting around agreements, and no way that those agreements could fully be expressed. This only happened when a Bob Dylan, Phil Ochs, Joan

Baez or John Lennon would sing a song. The song stated in ritual fashion what we all shared.

Eventually, some of us got the idea that we really needed some kinds of rituals to be part of our lives. I was part of a flurry of activity in the early '70s of those who thought that rituals could be intentionally constructed. We would have gatherings in which some kind of ritual was used—but there was no prior agreement on what ritual. In fact, each week someone would try to introduce some new kind of ritual in order to be creative. We couldn't agree on which new rituals to adopt, so we kept on experimenting, kept on discussing or even arguing about ritual. But ritual isn't ritual when it is something new and different every week. Part of its strength is that it is a vehicle to a unifying underlying unity—and the vehicle needs to have a transparency that is gained through continual usage.

I began to realize that the power of ritual is that it is an agreed-upon form. And once you agree upon the form, you can get to a deep central meaning that transcends the form. For example, we all wanted to have rituals to celebrate our community. We wanted a deeper contact with each other than the society normally promoted. But to the extent that we were focused on creating new ritual every week, we tended to recreate the divisions among us, because everyone had different and often conflicting ideas about how to do it.

Now, I am not against the democratic process. In fact, I believe that it is often a very empowering process and must be cherished as such. But there also needs to be moments in which the task is not democratic construction, but celebration. Celebration of that which we have already achieved, of victories, of the grandeur of the universe. We need rituals, agreement about the ways that we can jointly enter into the experience of celebration, rather than constantly debating about what is the best way to celebrate.

Rituals establish community. They provide us with a way to share our deepest essence. No wonder, then, that the vioce of "modernity," which is the voice of the capitalist marketplace, finds rituals to be offensive, old-fashioned and oppressive. Precisely the way the dominant society keeps its power is to nuclearize and isolate every person from each other. Precisely to the extent that the rituals reconstitute a "we" they become potentially subversive to the established order.

Of course, it matters what this "we" is about. I don't think that the rituals of various male social clubs are necessarily subversive. Religious ritual is important—because religion develops a particular content of what the "we" is about—a content that potentially challenges the priorities and worldview of the dominant order.

Whether or not they are part of a religious community, people who are interested in combating real powerlessness must create a community of people who are committed to that struggle. And that community will need to have rituals. It will need to have forms that are more than "meetings" at which those who are best at articulating and those who are most adept with words can dominate and define the reality. In constructing the rituals for such a community, social change agents can learn from the religious community. These religious communities have thousands of years of experience in the issue of constructing rituals that speak to the actual needs of people, their daily life experiences. While their rituals cannot be adopted mechanically and automatically, I think it would be very wise for anyone who is seriously interested in building a successful mass movement to study and learn from the rituals of religious world.

"But aren't those religious forms suffused with authoritarianism and sexism and other values that must be fought?" Some are, and they need not be preserved. Many rituals, however, remain very powerful when (with some slight alterations to eliminate oppressive or destructive legacies) they are re-adopted by people who continue to seek meanings that are not reducible to the common sense of a capitalist and empiricist society*.

Ritual has another dimension that makes it particularly important: it conveys our meanings to our children, and makes it possible for the insights of the past to be taught on a non-verbal level. Progressive movements often stumble on this point. They are based on a sophisticated articulation of ideas. But this isn't something that everyone feels comfortable with. It is particularly difficult for children. With only words, the values and ideals of parents can be inaccessible to the next generation. Ritual activities can change this. If the meanings and history and ethical values of the progressives' ideology can be instantiated in ritual form, it will be possible to pass them on to children who often can respond to symbols and music and celebration and pageantry long before they can master these same ideas when presented in a more linear form.

In defending the importance of ritual, I want to distinguish between the deadening rituals, or a ritualized way of using rituals, and rituals that can serve a very different function. The rituals that I want to preserve must be judged by whether they have the consequence of re-awakening in those who use them their conscious or unconscious connections to their own deepest selves, their Human Essence, and the deepest levels of connection with those around them. Does the ritual remind us of our fundamental humanity? Does it awaken in us a longing for transcendence and a transformation of the world? Does it help us express our joy and celebration of the universe and our awe at the grandeur of creation, and our desire to face pain, suffering and death together rather than as individuals? Does the ritual challenge us, does it make us more alive and more real, does it allow us to be playful, or does it allow us to experience our experiences in deeper and more immediate ways? If so, the ritual can be a vehicle for collective empowerment.

---

* The rituals that have developed through history have had many different meanings to those who have used them. There is no reason why the meanings imposed by that section of the religious movements most closely aligned to established ruling elites should be the meanings that are fixed forever—particularly when the rituals themselves were often understood in different and more subversive ways by people in the past.

The Atman Project and the Fear of Death

Many of our problems in the political and economic world, asserts Ernest Becker, in this book *The Denial of Death,* derive from our desire to transcend our own death. Human beings can't accept the fact that they are going to die. So they create social realities to overcome their finitude, and to hide from themselves their own frailty. They construct systems of power hoping to convince themselves that they will somehow escape the finality of death. Whether it be through the construction of cities and monuments, empires and corporations, or whether it be through the creation of religious views of immortality, human beings are engaged in a frenzied mission to escape and deny reality. This quest is the psychological underpinning of the accumulation mode of capitalist society. It is the same motive that helps explain "the urge to stand out as a hero, to transcend the limitations of the human condition and achieve victory over impotence and finitude". Honesty, says Becker and the existentialists with him, requires that we admit the radical solitude of human beings, the finitude, and the inevitability of our own obliteration from the earth.

From the religious standpoint, Becker has only gone halfway in his analysis. People do hunger for the infinite and for utter transcendence, but this is because they intuit that their true nature is to be part of the infinite spirit. The real hunger for immortality is based on a hunger for a unification with the totality—a hunger that is systematically denied and hidden.

An important formulation of this position is articulated by Ken Wilber in his book, *Up From Eden: A Transpersonal View of Human Evolution.* Wilber argues that every person intuits that the basic nature of human beings is a wholeness, and that s/he is ultimately,

> "all of a piece with the universe. . .when one rediscovers the ultimate Wholeness, one transcends—but does not obliterate—every imaginable sort of boundary, and therefore transcends all types of battles . . . But this does not mean that one loses all egoic consciousness, all temporal awareness, that one goes into blank trance, suspends all critical faculties and wallows in oceanic mush. It simply means that one rediscovers the background of egoic consciousness. One is aware of the integral wholeness and of the explicit ego. Wholeness is not the opposite of egoic individuality, it is simply its Ground, and the discovery of the ground does not annihilate the figure of the ego. On the contrary, it simply reconnects it with the rest of nature, cosmos, and divinity" (pp. 12-13).

Wilber insists that every human being constantly intuits that his/her prior nature is infinite and eternal.

The problem, says Wilber, is that each person is terrified of real transcendence, because transcendence entails the loss or "death" of the isolated and separated self. So, each person wants true transcendence, but each person fears the loss of the separate self, the "death" of the isolated ego. People want wholeness, but they resist and fear it (since it would involve the death of their separate selves). Human beings want transcendence above all else, but they seek it in ways that are substitutes for the real transcendence, because they are afraid to lose their separate selves. They fill up their lives with the pursuit of sex, money, fame, knowledge, power—and all these are ultimately substitute gratifications for true release in Wholeness. Similarly, the focus on oneself as the ultimate reality is a distortion of the prior intuition. Instead of being one with God, we try to play God. Wilber calls this attempt to regain a consciousness of the Whole in ways that prevent it and force symbolic substitutes, "the Atman project."

I believe that looking at human history from this perspective can add an important dimension to our understanding. Human beings are not driven just by the material needs for food, clothing, shelter, and security. Many of the historical struggles can be understood among cultures, nations and peoples as symbolic substitutes for what people most deeply want—a return to fundamental wholeness and connection with the entire universe—a substitution necessitated in part by the fear of losing one's own self and dissolving, dying, disappearing. The Atman project helps explain some of the more apparently irrational aspects of human history and culture, because it shows how human beings can at once articulate some of the most sublime goals and aspirations and simultaneously act in destructive and oppressive ways. Their behavior reflects the fundamental double-bind between our aspiration towards transcendence and our fear of death and dissolution and loss of the only reality which we have been able to construct for ourselves: namely, our own individuality, with all its frailty.

But why have human beings had such a hard time in merging with the whole, why have they been so reluctant to lose their own individuality? After all, if the experience of being part of the totality is so much part of who we really are, shouldn't its compensations be enough to outweigh our individual fears? Where do these individual fears come from?

It is at this point in the discussion that a spiritual worldview may be strengthened by an understanding of Surplus Powerlessness. The way that the spiritual worldview sets up the answer to this problem is in terms of some fundamental flaw or weakness in human beings. Poor sad creatures bound by a world of illusions, we are unable to transcend our illusory selves and to realize our full identity with the totality. In some religious traditions, at this point, God shows himself to be merciful by intervening in the process and sending some special help, e.g., Jesus or Muhammed, as saviors and guides who can help people escape the follies of this world (though often these views themselves are tied to a notion of the individual surviving in some other world). In Eastern religions there is a greater sense that individuals may ultimately achieve a unity with the totality in this world, though the superconsciousness that it requires may not be possible for thousands of years, except for a few gifted individuals. Nowhere in these views is there any understanding of the social conditions that make this step towards unification with the whole so difficult, nor of what could be done to change that reality.

If we look back to our analysis of the fundamental alienation that human beings experience in this world, we may be more optimistic about how to achieve the kind of transformations that spiritually based religions seem to be seeking. What we saw is that the individuality and separateness that we hold onto is imposed upon us by the fundamental misrecognition in child-hood, and is sustained by a well-functioning social order whose goal is to keep us apart and separate. That goal is a rational one from the standpoint of ruling classes, whose need to dominate the society requires the elimination of fundamental solidarity and connectedness.

With this understanding, we get a clearer picture of why human beings find it necessary to hold onto their individuality and separateness. The reason is that with the emergence of class-dominated societies some eight to ten thousand years ago, the original experience of wholeness and connectedness to the universe, an experience manifested in human communities, was funda-mentally torn asunder. Whatever its compensations in terms of the develop-ment of agriculture, the elimination of the constant insecurity of the hunting and gathering societies, and the creation of scientific understandings that could make sense of what was previously a terrifying unpredictability in the world, class societies also posed a fundamental ontological rupture with the moral harmony of the universe. Human communities increasingly were dominated by ruling classes which shaped the dominant ideologies. These ideologies proclaimed the importance of a new merging with the larger whole.

The fact is that one part of the community was ruling over the rest of the community, and the majority was giving its creative energy for the sake of the minority. In this context, the actual experience of "merging with the whole" took on a different meaning. The "whole" was now a reality of oppression and humanly imposed pain.

In this context, the experience of submitting to the established order and not keeping oneself separate is an experience of pain and not simply of fulfillment. The mutuality and reciprocity that are fundamental to our nature are thwarted, in the very name of community and connectedness and totality that we fundamentally need. It is in relationship to this class-dominated reality that people begin to differentiate themselves, to create their own separate identities that are not seen as connected and integrated with the totality. Indeed, the very essence of human beings is denied in the class-strat-ified communities—because the very essence of human beings requires that they be united in loving and mutually affirming communities. Yet these communities, while articulating such values, are actually systems of oppres-sion in which most human beings are not being fully affirmed.

It is in opposition to these pseudo-communities that individuality becomes most strongly developed—not as some irrational "fear" of being part of the totality, but rather as a way of preserving the spark of divine within us in the face of an alternative that is to merge with an unjust and humanly destructive totality.

The kind of individuality that can be achieved, however, will have its own set of distortions, because human beings are fundamentally social, fundamen-tally need each other, and need to be connected in loving and mutually affirming ways. Individuals are created who are incomplete and longing for a connectedness that the social order has no ability to offer at the present moment. The fear these individuals have of reconnecting and integrating themselves into some larger whole is not simply an irrational hangover or an ontological weakness. It is, rather, a response to the actual powerlessness that we experience in class-dominated societies. Because some people have inordinate power and wealth, the society as a whole is distorted. So, no wonder that people hold onto their individuality and hope to attain some personal or private solution to their desire for wholeness—because any larger solution appears to be impossible so long as the social order is dominated by forces that create an evil reality. And no wonder that so many people rejoiced at the collapse of a feudal order that ostensibly justified itself in terms of larger cosmic realities.

The problem is that holding onto our individuality creates an impossible double bind. Human beings fundamentally need each other and need a way of becoming integrated into a totality that is loving and supportive and that provides a way for our capacities to be actualized; but human beings are afraid to take that kind of a step because all our experience leads us to believe that the rebuilding of communities will only regenerate the same disappointments and distortions as before. All our experience of communities has been an experience of class-dominated communities. So we seek a variety of substitute gratifications—and none of these can possibly work to replace the kind of loving communities we need.

A just world, then, is not just a nice ideal; it is an ontological necessity for us, and without it, human beings will engage in all kinds of acting out, on the individual and societal levels to achieve the kinds of feelings of wholeness that actually cannot be achieved as individuals.

Yet there appears to be no way out, once we accept that our actual powerlessness makes it impossible to fundamentally change the world. The established order does everything it can to reinforce this sense both on an intellectual and emotional plane.

Through most of human history this perception has been fundamentally correct. Any struggle to re-order the world would have been merely a struggle to re-distribute poverty and would therefore have had only limited impact on the daily experience of most people. But in the past three hundred years, the development of industrialization, scientific technology, and the consequent advances in material goods have made possible a redistribution of wealth that would potentially involve a dramatic increase in the material well being of all people. Moreover, the development of printing and electronic communication makes it possible to envision the mass participation of the human race in its own self-development in ways that were hard to imagine only five hundred years ago. What this means is that the struggle to transform the world becomes much more rational today than it was in previous class-dominated societies.

It is precisely at this point that the struggle against Surplus Powerlessness becomes so central. What was previously a rational assessment of limitations is today a mistaken carryover from a previous period. For the first time in human history, the question of creating a fully loving and humanly affirming and just society is completely on the agenda. Moreover, the society today relies primarily on the internalization of the impossibility of social transformation and the necessity of our alienation and isolation as key props to maintaining the established system of domination.

It is within this historical context that we must assess the Atman project. Yes, human beings have been denying their fundamental nature, and, yes, they cannot achieve real fulfillment as long as they maintain the kind of individuality that class society offers. But what Wilber and various Eastern religious thinkers leave out of their schemes is that human beings do not just need and crave a fundamental integration with the totality, but rather they need and crave an integration with a just totality. This is the special contribution of biblical religions: the insistence that the universe, in its essence, has justice and love as the fundamental basis, and that it is our alienation from a potentially loving and just totality that is the real basis of our frustrations with the constituted order of the universe.

The world can now be transformed, and the set of ideas and feelings that made us feel that it was impossible are in fact the primary obstacle to that transformation. Primary, but not sole. Because, if people were to feel empowered intellectually, emotionally and spiritually to transform the world, they would still have to engage in a powerful struggle with ruling elites, a struggle whose outcome would by no means be guaranteed from the start. Yet, a strong possibility exists for winning that struggle, if people were engaged in it wholeheartedly. In fact, we might even expect as a possibility that such a struggle would not ever have to be fought should ruling elites become totally convinced that the majority of people were willing to engage in such a struggle with all their energies and all their creativity.

What the religious perspective has to offer us is a framing of the problem that allows us to see the ultimate cosmic significance of what might otherwise appear to be "merely" psychological and "merely" political. We begin to see that the most fundamental realities of human life could be transformed, if we could overcome the parts of us that convince us that we are totally and inevitably powerless. Our fear of death, our very relation to the cosmos, would be transformed if human beings could exist as part of a community that had overcome its legacy of fear—a fear generated by the experiences of childhood, reinforced by the daily realities of adult life in class society. Creating that reality requires more than a transformation of consciousness— it requires a rebuilding of our social reality. That process requires a decrease in fear and an increase in Compassion. As this is accomplished, we will start to take decisive steps to create a community which affirms what it is to be human beings, including our mutual dependency, our neediness, and our joint need for the fullest realization of all people. In the absence of that kind of community, individuals will always seek some partial solution, whether it be individual "eternal life" in heaven, individual acts of glory, or power of conquest, all of which are bound to fail us in achieving what we most deeply want. But the overcoming of the Atman Project requires a collective process in which we actually create a new "We"—and not just perform individual acts of self-transcendence and spiritual growth.

Does Everyone Need Religion?

Couldn't much of what I have attributed to religion be achieved by a community of people intentionally constructing a secular or non-God-oriented reality in which the most important dimensions of religion were integrated with the most helpful insights of psychology and class analysis?

In theory, Yes. But I don't think such a community will be constructed. The historical momentum of religious communities is so strong that they will continue to be the places where the ultimate questions are debated most seriously. The very way that empiricism and scientism have come to dominate contemporary thought make it likely that religious communities will remain the major challenge to one-dimensional thinking. While these communities have real problems, they also have real assets—they have histories, rituals, and ways of conceptualizing reality that are already in place and which potentially stand in opposition to the dominant worldviews. Religion is likely to be the only game in town that addresses so many levels of human existence.

While I don't think that in order to engage in the struggle one must be part of a religious community, I do think there is within the established religious communities a set of intellectual and emotional and spiritual resources that could greatly strengthen any movement against Surplus Powerlessness. At the same time, the struggle against class domination and against those ideas that class society has managed to impose on the religious consciousness must be waged intensely. The metaphysical base of religion, and the questions it has the courage to raise, are important contributions to the movements for social change. But the insights of the social change movements must be infused into the religious communities if we are ever to construct a world based on real community, real wholeness, real justice, real love.

Anger and Compassion

One of the most compelling aspects of biblical religion is the way that it weaves together the themes of anger and compassion. The God of the Prophets is always shown to be deeply involved in both emotions. I think that such a portrayal has deep symbolic relevance to the needs of any movement to overcome Surplus Powerlessness.

The God of the Bible is striking to us because He is not some emotionless unmoved mover. God is a passionate being—deeply caring, deeply involved, and deeply in need of human beings. What does He need of human beings? That they become what they fully are. And what are they? They are created in the image of God. But what does that mean—what is God like?

When Moses approaches the burning bush, he asks God a difficult question. The Israelites and Egyptians will certainly demand to know which among their panoply of gods does Moses represent. What can Moses tell them about who it is who has sent him? God's answer: "I will be whom I shall be." (Exodus 3:14) This is a God who is not some static reality, but a God who is in process, and whose essence is freedom. To be like God is to be a creature who is in the process of creating himself. And precisely the problem with class-dominated societies is that they make it extremely difficult for us to define ourselves and become who we need to become. When Moses asks God to reveal Himself to Moses, the Bible records the following utterance (it is unclear whether it is said by God or by Moses): "The Lord, The Lord, a merciful and gracious God, long-suffering, and full of compassion and truth, keeping mercy to the thousandth generation, forgiving iniquity and sin and acquitting." (Exodus 34:6) So to be like God is also to be compassionate and forgiving.

But how then are we to understand the image of God as an angry God? Even Jesus in the New Testament is portrayed as angry at times. Isn't this inconsistent with a God of love and compassion?

Absolutely not. I believe that the Bible has an accurate and correct balance between anger and compassion. The kind of anger that the Bible sanctions is righteous indignation. Human beings might do well to imitate God in this respect. We need to be burning with a flame of indignation at the perpetuation of evil in the world.

No wonder the Bible is, when taken seriously, still a scandal. Our culture emphasizes keeping control, being on top of things, not "losing it."

We are taught to "be cool" while God is portrayed as being on fire, a burning bush, in response to the slavery of His people. We could well benefit from learning from God how to get back into our righteous indignation. God is portrayed as furious at the prevalence of evil, uncompromising in His desire to root it out, fierce in His command to us to pursue justice and destroy the forces of oppression.

But the actual basis for our righteous indignation is our ability to feel compassion. We need to understand what has been done to us, and done to each other, that keeps us from being all that we could be. The distortions that we see in ourselves and each other do not represent our essence, but are distortions that are products of the monumental pain that we all have experienced in childhood and which we are re-experiencing everyday in the economic and social world. Moreover, these distortions cannot simply be overcome by acts of will, because they are daily reinforced by the ways that everyone acts towards each other. Compassion involves having an understanding of why it is so very difficult for people to change, and how important it is for each of us to be directly involved in supporting each other to make these changes, allowing that mistakes will be made in this process. As we showed in the first part of this book, it is only when we have this kind of compassion for ourselves that we can really allow ourselves to feel the anger at the oppression we have experienced and in which we continue to live our lives. So compassion and righteous indignation are dialectically related to each other—and if the Bible taught us nothing else, this would be sufficient.

Compassion does not mean pity. It does not mean looking at other people simply as victims. Human beings who have been oppressed also have the capacity to be God-like, self-defining, free and transcendent. This potential can never be fully extinguished by the dominant ideology and the dominant emotional conditioning. It is this aspect of our God-like natures that continually reasserts itself, that makes it impossible for us to ever be fully accommodated to a world of oppression.

Once we allow ourselves to have full compassion for ourselves, our parents, our friends, our co-workers, we simultaneously begin to feel angry at the system of oppression. We may even have compassion for some of those who benefit most from the system. We may wish that they would voluntarily join us in the effort to democratize the society and reconstruct it on the basis of love and mutual respect. But, in spite of our compassion, we can be un-mitigatedly angry at the way things are set up, and express that anger with a thunder of righteous indignation. I do not believe it is possible to have real compassion for each other and a real understanding of the daily assaults on our dignity, intelligence, and ability to love, without experiencing strong and sustained anger at the economic and political order that fosters our weakness and undermines our beauty and strength.

This is the biblical message: to have real compassion is simultaneously to be outraged at evil. To the extent that the religious community keeps that message alive, it stands as a beacon of hope that our best selves can ultimately receive a fuller expression than is possible in the daily life of this society.

Why Are People Religious?

Many liberals and progressives tend to dismiss religious people. They see them as driven by fear, superstition, a desire to return to simplicity because of their inability to master complexity, or a desire to avoid the problems of politics and the social world. This is certainly true for many religious people, particularly those who cling to religious traditions that have not yet con-fronted, assimilated and attempted to transcend the truths of science and empiricism. But, this is also true of many people who join political movements, and even many who become liberals and progressives. Neither religion nor progressive politics are necessarily invalidated because some who participate in them do so for these reasons.

My experience leads me to believe that large numbers of people today are attracted to religion precisely because of the features of religion articulated in this chapter. Lacking any exposure to alternative analyses of powerlessness, they may be unable to articulate in our language what they don't like about the way the world is organized. But they sense that something is very screwed up. Religion plays the role of being one of the very few societal practices that keeps alive some of the hopes for a different way of being in the world. Our Human Essence finds expression in the religious world, even though sometimes in distorted forms. It is not my contention that all religions really do give full vent to the fulfillment of our Human Essence—but, rather, that religion is an expression of that Human Essence, and, within the framework of a bureaucratized and rationalized order of oppression, one can see traces of the Human Essence more clearly in many religious practices than else-where. So, even though there are many ways in which the fullest visions of who we could be are not fully articulated in the religious sphere, they are more articulated there than in most other places in the society. Moreover, religion is the only place where we can find any attention to the parts of our Human Essence that lead us to relate to the world not simply from the standpoint of manipulation and control, but also from the standpoint of awe, radical amazement and wonder. It is for these very good reasons that many people are drawn to the religious world. These reasons must be respected, and the people who are drawn in this way must be understood to be affirming parts of themselves that are otherwise under assault in a society based on domination.

There is no greater evidence of the desire of progressives to be isolated and to remain in the position of "losers" than their continual proclivity to dismiss religion and to make religious people feel uncomfortable and on the defensive in progressive political movements. The religious community has many people who could be deeply moved by an understanding of the social nature of oppression. But, equally important, progressives could learn much about overcoming Surplus Powerlessness if they were to open themselves to the teachings and ways of constituting communities that some religious traditions provide.

At the same time, religious leaders have much to learn from an understanding of Surplus Powerlessness. I have previously noted that some people get into religion in frenetic ways in order to avoid their feelings of self-blame. A religious community built on people who are using religion solely as a way of avoiding the pain of daily life will be fundamentally distorted. The kind of community this produces is one based on the "false group"—each person excitedly grasping onto a false "we-ness" and avoiding any real contact with other people, thereby escaping the anxiety they might otherwise feel at being recognized as free and creative beings. The most humanly alive and whole people quickly get turned off to that kind of community, and abandon religion to the more psychologically scarred. This tendency means that many of the most creative and spiritually sensitive people can be turned away from religious communities too deeply shaped by Surplus Powerlessness. So it is in the deepest interest of religious leaders to learn about and then fight against the dynamics of Surplus Powerlessness that otherwise play an inevitably distorting role.

Moreover, I believe that from the religious standpoint, the deepest connection with God is only possible for people who are deeply in touch with their Human Essence. To the extent that we live in a world in which that Human Essence is more deeply buried, we become people less likely to be able to acquire meaningful religious experiences. I believe that the forces of oppression and repression, and the complex dynamics of real and Surplus Powerlessness have denied most of us one of the richest and most important aspects of human experience: our relatedness to the divine. Is is, therefore, a supreme religious imperative to transform the world so that these impediments are eliminated.

Tendencies Towards Transcendence

In exploring the ways that politics and religion can potentially work as forces towards transcendence of Surplus Powerlessness, I have attempted to highlight the fact that the very way our Human Essence is suppressed simultaneously creates a pressure for the elimination of that suppression. Throughout this book I have attempted to show that no matter how sophisticated are the processes of socialization into our powerlessness, there are fundamental contradictions which cannot be resolved. In Part I, I showed that when our Human Essence is repressed there are real costs both on the physical and psychological levels—and that these show up most immediately in our personal lives, in the inability of most people to find the "personal satisfaction" that is promised to them as an alternative to fulfillment in the social sphere. In Part II, I showed that Surplus Powerlessness is built on a series of ideas that require a fundamental narrowing of our conceptions of reality. In Part III, I have argued that there are already existing spheres of human activity, politics and religion, that, in some of their manifestations, generate experiences that run counter to the domination of existing social arrangements. While both politics and religion are typically practiced in ways that try to keep these contradictions under the table, and attempt to accommodate us to social domination, there are, nevertheless, within both of these social practices real tendencies towards emancipation. In both politics and religion we have available sets of experiences that run counter to the dominant mode of seeing the world. It is no surprise, for this very reason, that ruling classes have always viewed these arenas with some suspicion and have put much energy into controlling and limiting the experiences in these arenas that would be available to most people. Politics and religion are spheres within which the Human Essence pushes towards articulation of our collective need for a different kind of world in which our mutuality, creativity, and love can be more fully expressed. In this sense, they will always remain potentially subversive.

• Part IV •

The Mass Psychology
of Compassion

Introduction

MOST INDIVIDUALS RECOGNIZE AT SOME TIME IN THEIR lives that things are very screwed up. Many people wonder, "Am I seeing things right—or am I crazy?" Others think, "I know I'm seeing things right, but I'd better not talk about it, because other people will think I'm crazy." They retreat from these moments of insight and sometimes even repress their memories of them because they experience them in lonely fear. Or they keep the insights alive by joining religious communities that recognize that there is a problem with the world, but channel that awareness in "safe" ways without engaging in real world struggles to change things.

The only way that people would feel safe enough to stay in touch with those moments of illumination and build lives based on them is if they could find many other people who would join with them. Yet, there is a continuing tendency among people to move back into fear, to doubt that they could ever be safe with others, and then to act as if that were a fixed fact—thereby making it more true. As desperately as we need to have a mass movement, we are continually acting in ways that subvert its possibility. And, as we saw in the chapters on politics, this same dynamic operates for people who have joined such movements—they still are constantly moving back into fear, and then acting in destructive ways towards each other, thereby confirming for each other their own worst fears that nothing can ever change.

For this reason, anyone hoping to accomplish any kind of significant changes must pay attention to the struggle against Surplus Powerlessness.

If you are a theologian committed to creating a society of love, if you are a health advocate hoping to eliminate the ways that people contribute to their own health problems, if you are an anti-nuclear activist, an anti-war activist, an environmentalist, a union activist, a feminist, a civil rights advocate, a therapist—you must first pay attention to the struggle against Surplus Powerlessness.

And that struggle is possible.

One part of the task is to challenge every idea that reinforces powerlessness. Whenever we hear those ideas restated in daily life, we must respond to them with the same emotional charge we now give against racist and sexist ideas. Ideas are not just "intellectual masturbation"—they are critical to sustaining our powerlessness.

Another part of the task is to create a social reality within which our feelings of self-blame, our repression of anger, our fears of each other can all be worked through and transformed. This is what I mean by a mass psychology.

The first task of such a mass psychology is to generate compassion. Compassion can be the key element, the framework within which all of our activities can be understood and our sense of self changed.

COMPASSION for ourselves as inheritors of a world that has diminished us and allowed us fewer opportunities to experience the deep loving connections we so badly need;

COMPASSION for our parents who themselves were badly damaged in their own childhoods, and whose adult life experiences reinforced their feelings of self-blame;

COMPASSION for our spouses, friends, lovers, children, co-workers, neighbors and people in our communities who have been similarly frustrated in their needs for love, have blamed themselves, have similarly given up on love and trust and mutual caring, and who have also acted out of their fears rather than their hopes.

With such compassion, we can alter our expectations about what we will experience in the process of making the world different. Our compassion must enable us to understand that, even as we take important steps to change ourselves, we are going to continue to make mistakes. The goals of our compassion must be to encompass that knowledge, and to fight against discouragement, and to accept the limitations on our transcendence without abandoning the efforts to overcome them.

Compassion will not last long if it is based only on an abstract love of humanity or a theoretical belief that people can be fundamentally improved, or even on a religious belief that everyone was born to be sinners. Such ideas usually don't have the power to help us deal with the daily realities of our frustrated hopes and disappointments. If we are to have a compassion that leads us to act to change things, then we must base it on a concrete forgiveness of the people around us. We need to know and understand the details of each others' life experiences, and possess a detailed understanding of how the social, economic and political world shaped those experiences. We can forgive each other and ourselves most deeply and truly, not by acts of magnanimity and grace but by acts of truly understanding why we all deserve to be forgiven, if we have this very concrete and specific knowledge of the particular realities that make us all be less than we want to be.

Deep compassion must begin with a full understanding of the current economic and political realities. We need to see how our shared powerlessness is not just "surplus," but also real. This is critical—because otherwise we will quickly fall into the trap of believing that all people really need to do is to change their heads and then everything will be OK. This then quickly leads to new levels of mutual blaming and self-blaming and to a sense that our problems are simply based on the defects of people who are not able to change fast enough.

Distortions are possible even here. We can even begin to put others down for not being compassionate enough—recreating a lack of compassion in the name of compassion.

To sustain our compassion, to make it more than a moment of enlightenment followed by a growing disillusionment that people are not changing fast enough, we must continually keep in our attention the specific ways that people are still pushed back into fear and mutual mistrust:

—the daily dynamics in the world of work;

—the mutually mistrusting feelings, reinforced by daily experiences in the competition of the economic marketplace;

—the fears generated by economic insecurity;

—the isolation that is reinforced by the way that family life is structured;

—the continuing legacy of unconscious forces that make us frame our current experiences in terms of dynamics that happened to us over and over again in the years that we were growing up;

—the many times in the past that people tried to let go of their fears only to find themselves betrayed and abandoned once again;

—the frustrations and defeats that people have encountered in their past when they tried to struggle for some kind of change in their world;

—the continuing real power of ruling elites—which gives a rational basis for people's ongoing fears that nothing much could be different.

When we look at each other and understand exactly how these elements play in each other's reality, we can begin to develop real compassion.

There are two elements to developing such compassion:

(1.) People must have an analysis of the dynamics of Surplus Powerlessness. We need to teach each other the ways that the economy works; the dynamics of the world of work; the interaction among work, personal life, and childhood; the ideas that make people feel powerless; the history of struggles to change things, and what worked and what didn't work; and the ways that people lose faith in themselves, and abandon all hope in the future. There is no substitute for this kind of abstract analysis; to develop real compassion, people must have a theoretical understanding, but the categories to develop that understanding are generally not available. A social movement that is interested in changing things on a mass scale must be involved in this kind of teaching.

(2.) People must listen to each other's stories. We must learn in detail how we all have come to be who we are. We need to learn the specific ways that each of us frames our experience—and the details of our childhoods, our work experiences, and our personal lives. It is through hearing each other's stories that we can come to deeply trust each other—because, in this very process, we recognize our common humanity, learn that we have very much in common despite our superficial differences, and see that which is beautiful and powerful in people whom we might ordinarily not even fully recognize as sharing our hopes and fears.

But how do we get people to engage in that kind of dialogue with each other? Who will talk? Isn't it almost always impossible to get people to open up? These are important questions. In the sections ahead, I will try to discuss some of the specific strategies that might be engaged to develop a mass psychology of compassion.

I believe that we are at the point in history where this is possible. Whereas I think it somewhat utopian to imagine a mass movement of tens of millions of workers moving towards fundamental social change as the next step, I think it quite possible that we could have such a mass psychological development that created the necessary precondition for the possibility of a successful political movement, a mass movement for compassion.

I have no doubts about the possibility of ten-year movements like the New Left re-emerging as flashes-in-the-pans. I am talking about a movement that could sustain itself until victory—not just achieve momentary prominence in a particular decade like the '30s or the '60s, or the anticipated radical 1990s.

What would such a movement look like? In the next few chapters I will outline a series of possible approaches, any one of which could make a serious contribution to the development of a mass psychology of compassion. I will start by discussing the limits of existing approaches to psychotherapy, and then outline a potentially liberatory therapy. I will outline what a mass movement for compassion might look like, and talk about my own experience in developing two experiments that can serve as models for activity. Finally, I will discuss what individuals can do in their own life circumstances to begin the process of developing a compassion process.

Just as feminism emerged in the late '60s and in twenty years has effected a profound transformation in societal thinking about women, a mass movement for compassion could, in a very short period, create a powerful transformation in how most people think about themselves.

Chapter 16

Psychotherapy: Repressive and Liberatory

T HE ACTUAL PRACTICE OF PSYCHOTHERAPY TYPICALLY HAS
contradictory results. On the one hand, many people learn to deal with
problems that they are facing in their personal lives—and they get real
handles on them. On the other hand, the very process by which they are
empowered tends to reinforce the set of underlying feelings and beliefs that
ultimately contribute to making them even more powerless.

Lacking a sense of social causality, most therapists interpret the frustrations
of family and personal life as individual failings. Instead of bringing their
clients to an understanding of the larger social forces that shape their individual experiences, therapists implicitly suggest that the problems are individual in scope, and can be adequately solved by changes in individual psyches
or through changes in their family systems.

Yet, as we have seen, it is this very perception of oneself at fault that is a
central part of the dynamic of Surplus Powerlessness. How ironic, but understandable, that at the very moment in which our personal lives feel out of
control or in too much pain to handle by ourselves, we turn to someone to
help us who will reconfirm that it is really true that the problems lie in our
own heads. Because most people interpret the frustrations and disappointments in their lives as further confirmation of their unworthiness, they are
likely to believe that the real problems lie in some deep levels of their own
psyches and that what they really need to do is to change themselves. This
creates the possibility of a whole new industry: The Transformers. Spiritual

gurus, religious leaders, "growth groups," and weekend trainings—all find new and sophisticated ways to market themselves as they promise that they will help individuals change the ways that they think about themselves or the world, and thereby overcome the frustrations and pain in their lives.

The most widely used form of treatment continues to be individual or group psychotherapy. There are many specific good results that can be obtained from psychotherapy, ranging from cures for specific phobias to better abilities for dealing with complicated life problems. There is no question that a good therapist can provide an opportunity for people to explore their problems and clarify the issues, rather than to impose "correct" answers.

The problem is that psychotherapy is most typically based on the assumption that the problems being faced in individual lives are primarily personal or individual problems. Clients typically come into therapy with this assumption: they are responsible for the failure of their personal lives and they must change themselves. Therapists confirm this analysis, by focussing attention on those aspects of their lives which have no social framework and that are not obviously related to issues of work, sexism, isolation, the breakdown of communities or the pressures of a competitive marketplace. If clients try to raise these issues they will be accused of seeking to avoid personal responsibility.

Most psychotherapists have very little familiarity with the class structure of this society, and even less with the psychodynamics of the world of work. They share the belief that this society is a true Meritocracy. Typically they believe that if workers are facing stressful work situations, they must be doing something to contribute to the problem, and that the therapist's task is to help workers focus on that which they are personally contributing to the problem. Many therapists simply do not believe workers when they describe the conditions they face in their work, because, for example, they do not understand how it could be to the benefit of management to make others feel powerless.

Therapists typically will try to focus clients away from stories about work (an area which makes therapists feel uncomfortable, in part because they know so little about it) and into the so-called "real" areas—personal life and childhood. Clients, learning what is expected, soon focus all their attention on these areas. Therapists show interest in these stories, make comments, suggest connections—and the clients quickly learn that it is here that the therapists will reward them with concern and involvement. The therapists' emphasis reconfirms the clients' pre-existing analyses that the real areas of concern are their own personal inadequacies—and the larger social context quickly drops from sight.

Although some therapists escape this trap, everything in their training and their social background tends to press in this direction. Therapists are rarely trained with any social perspective. Social psychology courses are typically accumulations of facts about how people actually do behave in the present society, rather than an attempt to analyze how the structure of the society shapes individual psychology. The personal experiences of most therapists tend to reconfirm the dominant assumptions of the society. Since they are "making it" by virtue of their own smarts, they feel that their own personal experiences tend to validate the prevailing ideology that rewards are based on merit.

Moreover, the enterprise of therapy as a "legitimate" and "scientific" enterprise went through a long struggle to achieve recognition. In that struggle, therapists had to represent therapy as fundamentally different from religious, political, and other ethically based pursuits. So they developed an ideology of "neutrality"—therapists must, above all else, avoid imposing their own views on clients. While this is fundamentally impossible—every interpretation, every intervention, flows from a theory that is ultimately based on a normative account of what is healthy behavior and what is not—it provides therapists with a good cover to avoid examining the ways in which they are in fact reinforcing the dominant world view. At the same time, it provides them with a standard answer to why they don't challenge the social categories within which clients have organized their own experiences. "To do that would be to violate scientific objectivity and ethical neutrality." Moreover, they would have difficulty doing this—since the therapists most typically share the same categories and think of them as "common sense."

Here is one place where the Social Unconscious is unrecognized by both therapists and clients. Both apprehend the totality as fixed and immutable and this judgment permeates every specific perception of situations and their possibilities. So, while therapists may be experts at uncovering new possibilities within that frame, they are simultaneously strengthening the hold of the frame itself and reinforcing the Social Unconscious.

This is truly a case of the blind leading the blind. Most therapists don't understand the social conditions which lead to so much pain in personal life, so they are unlikely to be able to uncover meaningful ways for individuals to deal with those social conditions. What they can do is to help people accommodate better to a reality which therapists accept as fixed and inevitable in its major dimensions.

The results of this will differ depending on the nature of the problem being dealt with, and, more importantly, with the class position of the clients. To the extent that an individual client comes from that sector of the economy where there is considerable freedom to change jobs and experiment with new social relationships, the kinds of changes encouraged in therapy can, if taken seriously, actually lead to dramatic improvements in the quality of life of the client. The client can change his or her work, break out of a repressive relationship, experiment with new ways of being in the world. The results can be dramatic and gratifying, both to the therapist and the client.

But, to the extent that an individual comes from those sectors of the economic and social structure where there is much less latitude for this kind of mobility and experimentation, therapy will miss the point altogether. The results are often destructive. Clients feel that they have "failed" in therapy, just as they have failed in every other aspect of their lives. This intensifies the self-blaming that was part of the problem in the first place. They have failed to create less oppressive realities, they have failed to feel satisfied in the lives that they have, they have failed to overcome feelings of anger and frustration and upset on a daily basis.

Blaming the Therapist

Ironically, this same set of results is misunderstood by most therapists, who end up blaming themselves for their failures to create wholly healed clients, not realizing the deeper source of the problem. Because the therapists do not understand the constraints and impact of the social world, they can only blame themselves for not having produced the desired transformations in the lives of their clients. This is part of the reason that so many therapists tend to be reluctant to discuss their cases in any detail with other therapists. They feel that they would be revealing their own inadequacies and failures if they were to honestly expose what they have tried and what results have been achieved. It is truly amazing how few journals there are in which therapists actually discuss in detail the moves they tried in their particular cases, and how few therapists participate in case conferences with fellow therapists in which they discuss cases in progress and share ideas and insights. The feeling of vulnerability is covered by elaborate rationales, but the underlying fear is that each therapist would be seen to be less competent and insightful than his or her colleagues. This problem would be considerably lessened if therapists understood how often the forces working against the success of therapy are rooted in social realities that a therapy can do little to change.

The feelings of shame and hiding by therapists are accentuated by another reality: the more highly paid therapists tend to have clients whose lives more easily admit to change, and they can then go around crowing about their successes, which, in turn, seem to justify their high prices, instead of recognizing that it is their high prices that tend to make it likely they will get clients who are most likely to succeed in the social world once they get their personal lives together. These successes make other therapists feel all the worse about their failures because they have no social analysis of the external factors in the world undermining even the most clever interventions. Many therapists who have middle-range incomes from their practices nurture the fear that the reason for their lack of success is that they just aren't that good. In reality, the class structure among therapists gets reinforced by the class structure in the society: the psychiatrists typically get the higher-paying clients with far more flexibility in their real world situations; the psychologists tend to get those with slightly less flexibility; the social workers and marriage and family counselors tend to get working class or poor clients with even less flexibility. The results of their interventions, in turn, reflect the differential realities that their clients tend to face in their real lives. But while social workers or family counselors will complain in public about the unfairness of the relative powerlessness and lack of respect that their professions get, I have found that in private many of these people secretly blame themselves and feel badly—believing that they lack the special skills that they fantasize others have—a thought that leads them to attend trainings and conferences, hoping to learn some magical new technique that will make them more successful.

To avoid responsibility for their own supposed failures, many therapists blame their clients, claiming that they weren't serious about therapy, weren't

really willing to take responsibility for their own lives, or were too dysfunc-
tional to benefit from therapy. Many of the diagnostic categories that have
been developed, e.g., "schizophrenic," "psychotic," and most recently, "bor-
derline personality," function to label clients in ways that help to reassure
therapists that there really is nothing that can be done, and therefore, that
they don't have to feel bad.

Forms of Delivery

We should not underestimate the importance of the very form of delivering
therapy in reinforcing the notion that it is the individual who creates his or
her own world. No matter how socially conscious the therapist, there is
something in the form of a one-to-one exchange in a closed-off room that
often helps to reinforce the notion that the problem really is the person who
is seeking help.

The development of family systems therapy was an important advance
because it insisted that emotional or behavioral problems could not be identified with a particular person but should be seen in terms of the entire
family system. The task, then, was to change the family system. This approach
was a strong step away from individual self-blaming. However, it was too
limited a step. It is correct to see problems in system terms, but incorrect to
identify the system as "the family." The family is itself primarily shaped by
a set of social forces that are rooted in the world of work, the structures of
sexism, the breakdown of communities of meaning, and the various social
patterns and structures that have been set up to help us avoid the anger and
frustration that we bring home with us from public life.

Most systems therapists totally ignore these realities in theory and in practice. The larger social structures are taken as given, and the only task for
the family is to find the most effective ways to function within those realities.
The problems are identified as existing in the personal sphere, although
here the personal sphere is seen to include one's entire family. The implicit
message remains: if only you could get your family system working, everything would be basically OK. And what it would take to do this is to make
some specific and limited behavioral changes on the part of these particular
family members. The inevitable conclusion is implicit in the premise: If
something is not working right in your family, it's because you or some group
in your family are not doing something right, and that can be fixed by some
adjustments within your family system. And if therapy doesn't work, it's
because the family has refused to change.

A therapist might protest here: "What's the alternative? Don't we have to
work with what we can work with, which is the individual or family that
actually comes into our office?" But, although this sounds realistic and hard-
nosed, it actually isn't a very sensible response. I think we could understand
the problem more clearly if we were talking about racism or sexism. It is
today generally understood that many of the bad feelings that women and
Blacks had about themselves in past decades were an inappropriate internalization of an external reality. So, suppose, as a therapist, you began seeing

a long line of Blacks, or women, who told you that they were unhappy because they were not succeeding in the economic marketplace, and suppose further that their explanations for their failures were totally in terms of their own personal inadequacies. Wouldn't it make sense to demand that you introduce into the discussion categories that were not available to your clients—social categories like sexism or racism? Indeed, wouldn't the most effective form of therapy be the creation of a civil rights movement or a women's movement?

In this context, any therapist who continued to interpret the problems primarily in individual terms might actually be working counter to the real health needs of the people involved. And, to the extent that therapists reinforce this individual interpretation of a social problem, we would say that they are more than just "missing the boat"—their interpretations may very well be helping to reconstitute the very set of problems that were a root cause of the pain from which their clients had come seeking relief.

Very often clients seeking to deal with "personal problems" are stuck in a social reality of which they have no understanding and for which they are deeply engaged in self-blaming. Does this mean that all "personal problems" are nothing but social problems? Assuredly not. The social realities that we have been talking about that undermine family life are lived through as one's personal life. We begin to form patterns of behavior and ways of feeling about ourselves that take on lives of their own, independent of the social realities that generated them. Any attempt to reduce the psychological to a mere reflex of the social is mistaken—the whole point of Surplus Powerlessness is that there is a set of emotional and ideological realities generated by and sustained by real powerlessness that must be dealt with and transformed.

"Aha!" responds the traditional individual or family therapist, "That is exactly what we are doing. We don't object to your social analysis—we are neutral about what our clients should do after they have been cured of their basic emotional problems that are currently crippling them. But you should be thankful to us, because we create the groundwork that is necessary so that people can feel good enough about themselves that they can, if they so choose, work more effectively in social change activities."

Unfortunately, this becomes much more problematic when the mechanism for self-empowerment involves reinforcing the dominant worldview. The very problems that keep people powerless and in pain are the ways that they have come to understand and interpret their powerlessness. The problem with most forms of psychotherapy is not that they are a distraction from social change, but that therapy all too often reinforces a way of understanding oneself and one's world that generates Surplus Powerlessness. The underlying ideology gets reinforced even at the very moment and through the very acts of seemingly empowering individual clients to somehow "make it" in the world as constituted.

Real Benefits, Real Limits

"But if this is true," our therapy advocate might respond, "How do you account for all the positive experiences people report from their therapy?"

It is obviously true that many people do get benefits from therapy. These benefits mostly fit into the category of "learning to cope with an oppressive reality." To return to our analogy with racism or sexism, we could easily understand that women or minority members might benefit from therapy situations. They could come in reporting that they are acting in self-destructive ways and want to stop doing so. Therapists might be able to teach them ways of understanding their situations that would allow them to keep calm when faced with affronts to their dignity, to simply "not let it get to them." Or they could learn how to accept those affronts as inevitable, and stop feeling anything about them. Or they could learn how to sublimate the anger or to redirect that anger into sports or competitive behavior in the economic market place. In short, they could learn to function in less self-destructive ways in the face of an oppressive reality. As people learn to do that, they will report therapy experiences as real successes, because their lives will really feel better. So the accommodation to an oppressive reality can feel better, and make one happier in one's life.

This can be viewed as the first step of an ongoing process. People can free themselves from self-defeating behavior, reduce their pain, and free up energy that had gone into maintaining self-destructive or self-limiting patterns of behavior.

While it is normally going to be true that this freed-up energy won't be used in ways that will deal with more fundamental social problems, and, while it is true that in the course of doing this people learn ways of understanding themselves that may limit their abilities to deal with the basic problems, we must still acknowledge that there are some real benefits in going through therapy.

So, even if the benefits are limited, they are real. Until the world is transformed, don't people deserve this kind of relief?

Yes, they do. I believe that therapy has positive value, and I believe that many therapists are making important contributions to the health and happiness of those whom they serve.

But there are some important limitations here that need to be kept in the forefront of the minds of those who are seeking therapy and those who are providing that service. Consider the following:

(1.) It doesn't work for most people. It's fine to tell people that, if they can create better coping mechanisms they can function more efficiently in the "real world." But what this advice ignores (usually because the advisors never knew it in the first place) is that the "real world" is class-structured in such a way that most people will have very little opportunity to shape the major objective dimensions of their lives, no matter how good they get at "coping." The oppressive structures of the world of work, the de-skilling, the competitive nature of the economy, and the unequal and unfair distribution of wealth and power will not change in any significant way, and many people will end up on the short end. Those few who succeed in improving their positions will testify to how very much they learned from therapy. But they will be only a tiny percentage of the total population. The rest will have failed—because a society with a hierarchical economic and political structure allows some people to succeed only on the condition that others stay in the same position of relative powerlessness and relative economic deprivation

(2.) While individuals learn techniques for coping or functioning within the world of oppression that work for a while after therapy is finished, ultimately the contradictions and tensions between the way the world is structured and their own inner needs reappear. But now, having been through therapy, what they have been taught is how to suppress these feelings, and how to misidentify them as being "a personal problem." So when they creep up again, people who have been in therapy get all the more upset with themselves; all the more fearful that they have really not quite "gotten it;" all the more convinced that they either need more therapy or, worse, that they are the kinds of people who can't benefit from therapy because their pathologies are too deep, despite all the best efforts of nice and sincere therapists. The struggles continue as they try their best to keep these feelings under control, feeling all the more crazy and isolated when they can't succeed. At this point, many people resort to medication, hypnosis, more therapy, alcohol, drugs, or other escapes to once again reassert their control over feelings that have not and cannot be adequately tamed—precisely because our Human Essence can never be fully extinguished, and, hence, makes us uncomfortable with our attempted accommodations to an oppressive reality.

(3.) Therapy keeps the world from being transformed. The categories and analyses of the problems that therapists popularize help people remain chained to the world that enslaves them.

What Should Therapists Do?

To have a different impact than that described here, therapists would have to start with a very different understanding of the world, one that would incorporate a full analysis of Surplus Powerlessness and how it operates in every judgment and every perception that clients have. Therapists would seek to unpack the set of assumptions that clients hold about the social world, and reveal the subtle operations of the Social Unconscious, and teach their clients about the ways that the class structure has shaped judgments about childhood, parents, and family life. Therapists would help relieve the deep levels of self-blaming and reverse the processes by which clients have seen themselves as having been responsible for creating their present realities. Therapists would help liberate repressed anger, and help clients find ways to channel it towards changing the conditions that generate it.

The process of a liberatory therapy would not simply involve "teaching," or "political education," or "learning to express one's anger at one's boss." The levels of self-blaming go very deep, and take on lives of their own. A meaningful therapy would have to involve a re-understanding of one's whole life, and a re-experiencing and reworking of one's childhood. In this process, there would need to be a gradual unlayering of unconscious feelings and meanings that have become the patterns for a client's understanding of the world. There is no simple miracle cure here—the process is complicated and deep. I believe that it would benefit greatly from the techniques and insights of psychodynamic psychotherapy, even as it would question some of its categories. In the intricate and subtle process of unlayering and disentangling the complex web of self-blaming, I have found that my training in psychodynamic psychotherapy has been most useful in providing an arsenal of techniques and insights that can be adapted to this task.

Two important caveats to the discussion so far:

(1). In rejecting the notion that individuals should take responsibility for having created their own realities, we must resist any tendency to see people as victims who can do nothing to change their conditions. The key here is whether clients come to think, "I can change my world" or whether they come to think, "We can change our world." Yes, individuals have responsibility, but it is a responsibility to get together with other people and collectively engage in activities to change things. In that process, they must be aware of all the forces that will work to undermine the possibility of people working together smoothly. Each person will enter the social change activity with pains and upsets—and will inevitably make mistakes, push others away out of fear, and have a tendency to give up too quickly. A therapy that assists clients to think of their situations in these terms, and helps them take responsibility for creating the conditions in which a real "we" can emerge and sustain itself, that prepares clients to understand the ways in which there will be inevitable setbacks and betrayals, and moments of weakness and despair, can give the term "taking responsibility" a new and important meaning quite different from that actually held by most therapists.

(2.) It would be unfair to expect that psychotherapists alone could transform the society, or that the burden or responsibility for failure should be placed on their shoulders. Even if all therapists were to incorporate a sophisticated understanding of the nature of social reality and help clients to understand that reality, oppression would still continue to function. Therapists who incorporated this perspective would face a substantial barrage of attack from the people who control the society. These progressive therapists would be criticized for not maintaining the alleged "neutrality" that "professionals" in health care should maintain. In short, going the route of talking honestly would involve taking real risks.

On the other hand, these are precisely the risks that everyone in every sphere needs to take in order for anything to change. Wherever you are situated in this society, you can make substantially the same argument: No one else is taking these risks, so why should I? After all, how much of a difference will it make if I act differently, given that no one else is living their lives at risk? It is literally millions of decisions like this, made on a daily basis by people who really wish that things would be different, but don't want to take unreasonable personal risk, that keeps everything in place. Since the process must begin somewhere, why not with those who make their livings through preaching individual responsibility!!

Ingredients of a Liberatory Therapy

I have seen many different approaches to how to do therapy, and I am convinced that there is no one right way. The same basic material can be gotten at using a wide variety of different techniques. Each technique has its own virtues and defects. But while I won't discuss techniques, I do believe that there are certain elements in a successful liberatory therapy which must be included:

(1.) Clients must dis-identify with their present selves, in order to see that they are not simply the sum of their current behaviors and lifestyles, and that these can be changed.

(2.) Clients must be helped to retrieve the emotional experiences that led them to form their Adult Personalities. They must come to understand that these false personalities are not who they really are, but are, rather, functions of their best attempts to cope with their circumstances.

(3.) Clients must side with the scared little children that still exist inside themselves. They must be helped to see how those scared little children were emotionally abused by their parents and the larger social order. They must then allow those little children within themselves to fully and unrestrainedly experience and express the anger that they were never allowed to express or feel as children. The expressions of that anger must be clearly directed at the parents internalized in themselves, not at their aging parents, but at their parents as they were when the clients were children. It is these scary and rejecting parents that they must confront and re-experience from the standpoint of children who are being fully supported in the expression and feeling of all their anger. Simultaneously, the little children must be nurtured and allowed to feel the justice of their rage. When they can feel their anger, they will also begin to rediscover many repressed childhood memories in which they were right to be angry—and these memories will help clients come to more compassionate views of who they really were as children.

In order for this to work, the anger must be safe. Any therapy process must ensure that the anger does not in fact lead to any "acting out" against the clients' current real-life parents. Moreover, the therapy must provide a context in which the anger goes very deep, so that the clients experience unconstrained and uncontrolled rage. These experiences are critical because until the clients can get to this place, they will never know that they can get beyond it. Clients must realize that the anger can be let out in massive amounts, and, yet, they will not go crazy, nor hurt anybody, and that the therapists can handle it. Once the clients realize that their uncontrolled rage and anger is not going to end the world, they can begin to reclaim their anger as part of their adult experiences and let it out in ways that are safe and yet still emotionally real.

Some people call this step "prosecution of parents." It is important that the prosecution not be undermined by a premature defense. The full energy of defense at that stage must go to the child—who must be deeply felt to have been a victim—though, of course, a victim that collaborated and made choices. Any residual feelings of self-blame must be seen as inappropriate.

(4.) This same little child, after having fully and unrestrainedly experienced anger and rage, and after having learned that it was not to blame for what happened to it, must now learn something else. The child must learn that the parents were not, in fact, responding to them, but were principally living out a set of patterns and ways of being that they had learned in their own childhoods and that had been strengthened and shaped through their experiences of the adult world. That is, the child must come to see that its parents were also once children, and that the same things that happened to them when they were children happened also to their parents.

This process, a defense of parents, can only be completed when the child inside comes to a full and deep forgiving of its parents. Just as clients had to have real compassion for the child buried in themselves, now the child must develop a deep compassion for its parents as they were when they were children, and see how this shaped how they were when they became parents. This step in the process usually requires an ability to emotionally re-experience the lives of those parents when they were children, and the feelings that those parents must have had as adults. Of course, this is not meant to provide an excuse for how the parents acted when they treated the client in destructive and hurtful ways. They were guilty, but they were not to blame. They made autonomous choices, but within a context that so severely constricted them that the client would be unfeeling to not forgive them.

(5.) Corresponding to the compassion for parents, and an indispensible part of it, is a new level of anger that clients can now feel at the social world for what it did to our parents and to ourselves. To some extent this anger may be directed at previous generations. But, to a much greater extent, it must be directed at the organization of the society. This is one place where the degree to which therapists understand economic and political forces becomes critical. It is only when the clients can understand specifically how the world of work, the organization of the economy, the legacy of sexism and racism, the ideology of Meritocracy and the dynamics of self-blaming all have shaped their parents' experiences of themselves that they can fully forgive their parents. Since it cannot be expected that most clients have this information at their disposal, the successful therapy process must, to some extent, be a teaching process.

Once this anger at social institutions has been fully experienced, it must be integrated into one's new adult being. The client must learn that anger is not necessarily destructive, but can, in fact, be healing, to the extent that it leads to constructive action to change the world.

(6.) Clients can proceed from this point to reclaim all that is positive in their own developed selves. They must once again rework their pasts, but this time with a much stronger sense of their own positive strengths. To some extent, this involves validating the incredible beauty and strength they showed in making choices in the face of an oppressive reality. To some extent, it also involves validating what was strong and beautiful in their parents, and in other people whom they came to know through their lives.

The point here is that reconstruction of ourselves does not involve simply relying on the undeveloped parts of one's essence. The task is not to reclaim our lost selves, to rediscover hidden beautiful selves as if therapy were some kind of archaeological dig. Rather, the task is to construct healthier selves—a task that can only begin once clients have re-integrated into themselves the split-off parts and fragments, and have truly accepted all that has happened to them. This process is aided by the energy for transcendence that is always potentially available from our Human Essence. But no re-integration can happen before they have been able to go through the painful processes described in the steps above.

(7.) The reconstruction of a new self is a long and difficult process. It is not a matter of an "instant conversion" or a "cathartic experience," but, rather, of a painful working through of each aspect of one's life, experimenting with new ways to understand one's self and new ways to be with others. There is a tremendous pull towards getting scared, retreating back into ways of thinking about one's self and others that feel "more comfortable," ways of being and thinking that we learned as we grew up that embody our deep fears about our own inadequacies and inevitable isolation.

The process of therapy must allow clients to test out time and again and continually find that it is OK to be more full, whole and trusting. To the extent that therapists can be fully present, they can help in the process. This does not mean overwhelming the client with how wonderful or "giving" the therapist is—because sometimes it is precisely these kinds of presentations of self by the other that will call forth neurotic responses as the individual seeks to fulfill their projections of the others' expectations. Sometimes interpreting how clients are transferring to the therapist feelings that fit some childhood situation but are inappropriate as a grownup, sometimes manifesting a lot of quietness when clients are geared up for noisiness, sometimes interpreting a dream, sometimes helping the client to see connections between different parts of their lives—any and all of these can work to allow the unconscious to feel safe, and to communicate a fundamental respect for the other person. Eventually, clients begin to feel strong enough to try out their own new ways in the rest of their lives. The inevitable problems that occur can then be discussed and worked through in therapy situations.

What is key here is the genuine encounter with another human being who is allowing us to be our fullest selves, and who is recognizing us as being capable of integrating our childhood needs and desires into our adult being. It is these moments of recognition, including the recognition of the therapist as a fellow being involved in the similar process of becoming more fully human, that is critical.

It is my contention that this kind of experience can only happen between two people who are being fully alive and real with each other. No matter how much a "neutral" and "passive" therapist can help to deepen the understanding of the client, in the end this will make the client feel that s/he is really alone in the world, and that there is an inevitability to that aloneness. I believe that the therapist may use passivity and neutrality at some moments as a technique, but that, ultimately, the therapist must allow him- or herself to be fully in the room, as another human being who is also part of the process of self-transcendence and who is not on a "higher plane" than that of the client.

Timing here is critical—because at the earlier stages in a therapy the clients often need to feel therapists' expertise and professionalism in order to believe that they are in safe enough hands to begin to explore issues that are otherwise quite terrifying. For that reason, the approach of some "radical therapies" of eliminating this "hierarchical relationship" at the beginning of therapy is sometimes misguided. But, ultimately, the therapist must become another person in the world, who has a need for the client just as much as the client needs the therapist. Nor is this some fantasy because if the therapist truly understands the social world then s/he understands that his or her own fulfillment requires a major social transformation, and that transformation requires that this client and millions more like him or her be strong enough to participate as equals. So, what happens in the therapy or group ultimately refers back to the world as constituted, a world that needs to be changed.

(8.) But the world as constituted still exists. The same pressures that formed us in particular ways will remain, no matter how deep and thorough our psychotherapy. As long as people exist in these deforming circumstances, there will inevitably be great difficulty in remaining whole.

A therapist needs to know enough about the details of the client's world to be able to correctly judge how much transcendence of old patterns is possible—and to encourage clients to maintain compassion for themselves when they are thrown back into old patterns.

Still, any individual process is going to be severely limited unless it connects with a much larger social transformation. And such a movement is always going to be problematic, because it is built on people who are not yet "whole" or "non-neurotic." The scars of experience remain in them, and, in fact, will be regenerated, as long as they still live in a society that functions in the ways described in the beginning of this book. We cannot expect to find a larger social movement that is already the embodiment of the full actualization of the human spirit. Rather, these movements will necessarily reflect in thousands of ways the limited and scared natures of all of us who will create it.

But there are grounds for hope. Once we deeply understand that we have all been through the same kinds of distorting experiences in childhood and daily life as adults, we can build a social movement that consciously acknowledges each other's pains, and makes it OK for people to not be perfect or truly healed yet. A movement that instantiates this kind of compassion has a fighting chance.

Because individual therapy is fundamentally and inherently limited in the ways I have described above, there is an urgent need for a larger process at a community level. Ideally, we need a movement dedicated to whole-scale social change. Yet such a movement is unlikely, or unlikely to be sustained for more than a few years, without the groundwork of a mass psychology of compassion.

A mass therapy process is necessary. A mass therapy process differs from individual therapy precisely in being able to acknowledge that there are certain root problems that everyone faces, and that must be addressed. Self-blaming, and the way that it is shaped in the world of work, carried home, and transmitted to the next generation, is a central enemy for such a mass therapy process.

Some people will find it "simplistic" or "reductionistic" to emphasize these issues. "Aren't people too complex to be reduced to these kinds of issues, however important they may be?" My answer here is a categorical "No." However different people are, they do face common problems in this society that have common psychological consequences. One part of the core problem is that people form a sense of themselves as unique and different from everyone else. This, in itself, becomes a basis of mutual estrangement and resistance to recognition of sharing in the same problems as everyone else. Individual therapy, done in isolation from a larger social movement, may actually intensify this problem, no matter how much it consciously insists on a social analysis, because the form may convey the message of specialness and uniqueness that undermines any social content being taught, and reinforces resistance to seeing what the individual has in common with everyone else.

A mass therapy process would be one which included all the elements outlined above for liberatory therapy. While it would necessarily provide space for people to explore all that was unique and special in the specific ways that they had lived through the socialization into their families and schools and workplaces, it would also help us understand the deep levels of common experience and common needs. If millions of people were going through this kind of therapy process at the same time, and then were involved in ongoing mutual support groups, they would quickly learn that their failures and "personal" flaws were really shared by many others. They could also see that their most precious part, their Human Essence, is something they have in common with others, and something that makes them potentially able to experience the world in terms of the same needs and desires as everyone else.

A whole new group of therapists is necessary—"Public Interest Psychotherapists"—who see themselves as the agents of developing a mass therapy process. Committed to mass empowerment and understanding the complexity of Surplus Powerlessness, dedicated to fostering compassion at all levels in the society, a Public Interest Psychotherapist could play a critical role in the development of a truly liberatory therapy.

The existence of a mass movement for compassion, instantiated in part through the development of mass therapy approaches, may be necessary to create the atmosphere of safety that will allow working people to seek services. If such a climate could be created so that they no longer identified themselves as "crazy" or "having personal problems" when they sought therapy, then we might see the possibility of tens of millions of Americans beginning to re-look at their lives in much different and deeper and more compassionate ways. This step might be a central part of the process by which we succeeded in undermining Surplus Powerlessness.

Chapter 17

Communities of Compassion

IT IS HARD TO KNOW HOW MUCH WE SHARE IN COMMON with others until we hear their stories. In our normal interactions with friends and co-workers we tend to keep at a relatively superficial level of self-disclosure. It is not unusual for people who work in the same office or plant to know very little about the pains and joys that constitute the "personal lives" of their co-workers. And even when people do talk about their problems, they often do so in ways that keep their real vulnerabilities hidden.

I am aware of the danger in discussion that seems to suggest that people don't have a right to keep their personal lives to themselves. We are rightfully frightened of any power that the state might have to invade personal life, because it is likely to do this for purposes that we do not share and which might be very destructive. And I have been part of religious and political movements which tried to force everyone to self-disclose so that they might be examined for political or religious "correctness." In the face of these realities, it is not unreasonable for people to want to build strong legal guarantees that protect them from unasked-for invasion and from attempts to undermine their right to privacy in personal life.

Yet, for reasons that we have already noted, the fierce privatization of "personal life" is too often a defense of our patterns of self-blaming. We will never realistically know ourselves until we know how much of what we perceive as unique and personal to ourselves is actually the shared experience of all those around us. It will always be impossible to fully love ourselves until we can see how others make the same unfair and irrational self-accusations that we do, and, through seeing that about them, begin to see how we are doing it to ourselves. Nor will we ever be able to build a movement for social change until we can hear the pain of others, can come to understand how that pain shapes their self-understanding, and can use this insight to help us cope with the ways that people in these movements will be less than we want them to be.

In short, compassion for ourselves and for others depends on us knowing others at a very deep level. For that reason, I believe that the first step towards building a mass psychology of compassion can best take place in a context in which people come together to tell each other their stories. While the frame of those groups may differ in terms of the initial reason why they come together, their shared purpose must be to create public spaces within which we listen attentively and caringly to others and let them hear us. Groups that do this can play a critical role as a first step for many people—a step that is both safe and that has a great attraction for people living in a society that has enforced isolation and loneliness on many familes. But how do we create a reality in which the majority of the population, already heavy into self-blame, is willing to participate in such groups?

A Picture of Groups

Imagine a psychological/political movement that organized the following program:

In each city there would be thousands of small groups of people who would meet together on a weekly or bi-weekly basis to explore the specific ways that they share common problems. The groups would focus on ways that people were inappropriately blaming themselves in relationship to these problem areas. They would encourage their members to externalize their anger appropriately and safely and help them to participate in social change activities. They would help people to learn to trust each other and provide a network of support through which people could deal with the developments in their "personal lives."

I emphasize thousands of such small groups to highlight two important features that would distinguish them from those groups that already do exist, either as therapy groups led by individual therapists or as self-help groups. The key to the success of the movement I am describing would be its size and economy of scale. When a city of 500,000 has 5,000 people in support groups, it is much more likely that the people in those groups will see themselves as "particularly needy" or "in trouble." But when that same city has 100,000 people participating in these groups, the understanding of what it means to be in any group is totally transformed. One is no longer identifying oneself as a problem case by joining the group; but, rather, one is participating in a social movement, a cause, a common project, a newly emerging community. The meaning of the experience is totally different.

This is critical, because the most immediate problem to be faced is "Who will join a compassion group?" If the definition of these groups is that they are for everyone, that the whole community is joining, that there is no "stigma" connected to joining, then there might also be the sense that people are fulfilling their civic responsibility and showing that they care for others by joining a group. In this way, precisely the people who most need the groups can feel safe in joining them. Moreover, the groups will work more effectively when they are promoted in this way—because then, when people hear each other's stories, they don't discount them by saying, "Well, sure these other people have some problems just like mine, but all that shows me is that I'm not the only nut case in the world, there a few others just like me, and we are all screwed up." Instead, knowing that this same process is going on with hundreds of thousands of others makes it possible for people to understand that what is happening in their own lives is really shared precisely because everyone is living within the same social reality that so dramatically shapes our individual experience.

Compassion groups must be part of an intentional movement, not just something that is in fact happening to lots of people. It is critical to their success that people in each group come to understand that they are part of something that is happening all around them, because other people have collectively decided to overcome their own powerlessness and become agents of their own lives. The fact of people taking this step intentionally, creating a mass movement to combat Surplus Powerlessness, provides a basis for optimism about the possibility of making social change. If so many people are willing to take the same step together, then perhaps it really might be possible for people to take the next steps together as well, and this perception then changes what can happen in the groups.

You might think, "Many therapy clients are willing to do this today without a social movement." But usually this is because these people are part of a social millieu in which there is real possibility that the results of their individual therapies could be translated into changes in their lives, given the mobility that is actually available to them. For much of the rest of the population, the very absence of this economic and social mobility becomes an important reason why it doesn't make sense for them to take the risks. But if hundreds of thousands of people were participating in these groups and talking about what they were learning about themselves, that fact would make people believe that something could be different in the rest of their lives—and that would make serious introspection much more possible. Moreover, mass participation creates a real basis for trust; since others are taking the same step in exploring personal issues, there is a real basis for counting on them in other respects as well, e.g., in social change activity.

Compassion Groups would be organized around a variety of different issues that face people in their lives, so that participation would flow from and relate to the events of daily life. Specific forms of Compassion groups include:

(1.) Occupational Stress Groups, based on the experiences of people at work. (I shall describe my own experience in creating a network of Occupational Stress Groups in the San Francisco Bay Area in the next chapter.)

(2.) Family Support Groups that would begin with a focus on family life and help group members see how their family lives have been shaped and undermined by the impact of the world of work, sexism, isolation of families, and the competitive marketplace. I shall discuss these in more detail below.

There would also be:

(3.) Children's Support Groups and children's clubs which would aim at providing places where children can talk about their emotional lives at home, and learn about the lives of other children. They would also aim at developing an understanding of the world which could help make greater sense of their parents' behavior.

(4.) Senior Citizen Groups would allow people to sum up their life experiences and contribute to the ongoing life of the emerging society. They would also focus on sharing their experiences with the young in Children's Support Groups, childcare centers and after-school programs.

(5.) Women's and Men's Groups would focus on the ways that traditional roles have been oppressive. They would aim at giving special support to struggles both within relationships and within the economy that aim to undermine sexism. These groups would also help create pressure towards ensuring that family support is not won by a new subordination of women.

(6.) Teenage Support Groups could share the experiences and frustrations of creating autonomous identities. At the same time, these groups would teach teens about the class structure, the struggles of working people, and the psychodynamics of work. They could also develop ideas about how to restructure the world more humanely.

7. There could also be special life situation groups, composed of people newly single, or new parents, or people facing unemployment, or people facing severe health problems, or disabled people, or minority groups with special problems, or children facing divorce, or children in newly blended families.

"Wait a second," you might object. "What's so special about all this? We already have these kinds of support groups, self-help groups, and special problems groups in almost every city, and they are certainly good—but they don't really make very much difference to the political climate of the country."

Yes, we do have some of these forms, and some of this existing work can be built upon. But the content of the groups and the meaning of the groups would be completely different if they were organized by a larger social movement as part of a self-conscious strategy to build a mass psychology of compassion. While existing groups often serve useful support functions, they are usually led by people who buy the ideology of the Meritocracy and have the goal of teaching individuals to "take responsibility" for making the best of their societal situations, situations which are conceived of as rather fixed and unlikely to change. Moreover, because the groups are based on the assumption that the members within them "have problems," they are unlikely to be the basis of people developing a new sense of solidarity with the people in the rest of the society who seem to be facing different circumstances. It would be quite different if these groups were aimed at teaching a new and uniquely liberating analysis of the situation facing people, an analysis that incorporated an understanding of real and Surplus Powerlessness. And, as part of an intentional movement, participation in these groups would take on a quite different significance, because the participants would see themselves as part of a movement and not just on a quest for individual personal happiness.

Psychotherapists, teachers, health professionals and other group leaders who today would tend to lead these groups in ways that reinforce the dominant ideology could be training to lead Compassion groups by coming to re-think their understanding of the relationship between individual problems and social reality. Using the skills of these professionals, however, could be useful in helping groups to delve deeply into the lives of their members. The goal of these groups would be to help people to re-understand all parts of their lives, and ultimately to forgive themselves. They would reject the self-blaming they had been engaged in since childhood, externalize the self-directed anger they had been carrying, and develop solidarity and trust with others so that they could then begin to work with others to try to change the world. This is quite a different agenda from that ordinarily held by "support groups." It is an agenda that makes the groups more than self-contained and "for their own sake"—because the groups would explicitly be sponsored within a framework that aims at larger social change.

Groups like these do not emerge spontaneously out of the experiences of people. They need leadership. People, after all, do not enter the groups straight from the "state of nature," as if untouched by civilization. Rather, they enter as people who have been formed and shaped by an isolating and alienating process of "normal socialization." We already have many such natural support groupings, and typically they tend simply to recreate the patterns of isolation, domination, mutual exploitation, disappointment and distrust, sexism, racism, and self-blaming that are so prevalent within the society. Whether it be the local "fraternal organizations," sports clubs, or family circles, it is an illusion to hope that these "naturally existing" social support mechanisms will eventually be sufficient to undermine the carefully constructed alienation of this society. If anything is going to change, it will happen only when people in these and other support systems have leadership and assistance in learning about the subtle psychological processes at work that bind us together in ways that reinforce our mutual distrust and powerlessness. This kind of education requires a time for people to consciously re-think their lives, unpack the elements of self-blaming, repressed anger, and reclaim their impulses towards transcendence and self-actualization.

The talents of therapists can be particularly useful in the process—helping to detect resistance and helping to create safe environments in which that resistance can be overcome. Therapists can help people make connections between present behaviors and underlying structures, whether those structures be rooted in the unconscious or in the social dynamics of family communication patterns. The skills can be central in helping the groups move to deeper levels of emotional reality.

The systematic unlayering that needs to happen in Compassion groups requires a special sensitivity to nuance, and to the needs of individuals. The groups cannot operate like bulldozers, plowing away every level of resistance and pounding in new truths. These are not "indoctrination" groups, and they must not have the flavor that religious or political organizations sometimes take on, of being the only place where salvation and truth can be achieved. Nor can they have the tone of self-righteousness that often afflicts those who are engaged in some therapy or growth process.

People move at different paces, and any attempt to force them to levels of emotional openness that they are not prepared to handle will either provoke massive resistance and slow everything down, or will be acceded to in ways that are destructive and hurtful. The processes of these groups are almost as important as their content. Since this is the first step that many people will be making towards trusting others, it is critical that they not find themselves scared by the way that the groups are run.

One important corrective in Compassion groups towards any tendency to group coercion is to focus on that very issue as a major problem in the society. We are all aware of the pressures to conform—to be like others. The pressure comes from internal sources as well: our fear that the only way we can get real love and validation is to appeal to other people, to meet their expectations, to show them that we can anticipate how they want us to be and then be that way. In the process, we often run away from ourselves. But we rarely establish good contact with others this way.

Each person is in the group seeking real connection and emotional honesty—but typically each will abandon her or his own reality in the fretful search to be "part of the whole." So, what we actually encounter in the group ends up being everybody else's false self—as everyone desperately gives up their real selves in order to identify with the false group. Ultimately, such groups are very unfulfilling, and people fall back into isolated personal lives, all the more despairing. If our project is to succeed, this very dynamic must be discussed at all times, and people must constantly be encouraged to check out the degrees to which they may be falsifying their real feelings in order to identify with a phony "We" that is inauthentic precisely because it is not based on a genuine coming together of real "I"s. The skills of the group leaders can do much to create the real safety and the avoidance of phony group solidarity that are necessary for a mass psychology to work.

An important contribution is also made by the theoretical framework that the Compassion groups endeavor to teach to their members. This framework emphasizes that we all have common pains rooted in our experiences of growing up in a society that encourages self-blaming as a substitute for righteous indignation against oppression. Every one of us, including the therapists or group leaders, has been nurtured on the same kinds of doubts and self-put-downs, even though there are millions of different ways that we then incorporated those feelings into our behavior and understanding of the world. At the most basic levels, we have common fundamental needs for the actualization of ourselves and others. We have years and years of learning how to deny those needs based on the assumption that a recognition of who we are by others was completely impossible and that our need for such a recognition was impermissible. We all had parents who had similar structures in their lives, and who have passed on their fears and doubts to their children. Most of us have experienced a society and an economic world which squashes the opportunity for our best parts to flourish. Moreover, we are all afraid to trust others because we feel sure that others will disappoint us. We still hold onto the belief that we are not fully deserving of recognition and love that we so desperately desire. Hence, we assume that people who are giving us respect and caring don't really know us. And all these feelings are very hard to overcome precisely because we live in a society that so massively invalidates us through the oppressive structure of the world of work, the impact of the competitive economy, and the dominant motif to put personal gain over love and community. We cannot expect massive changes in human beings without a simultaneous change in these social and economic structures, replacing them with a society and economy based on cooperation, trust, and taking care of each person.

This kind of framework, when understood by group participants, helps to create a context within which it is possible to explore repressed material. The ethos of a Compassion group is to understand that the ways that the real world is currently structured undermines our efforts at solidarity. It is through the understanding of the incredible power of the structures of real powerlessness, operating through our daily experiences in the world of work and manifesting in the resultant experience of family life and childhood, that we can forgive ourselves for not having been so wonderful, and then can come to forgive our parents and each other for all the failings that have pained us. And it is this same understanding of how the existing structures continually act to throw us back into self-destructive patterns that provides us with a basis for making these groups incorporate real compassion for all of their members—rather than an intolerant attitude of, "Now that you've heard the truth—get it all together and change." Sensitive group leaders will have as one of their central goals to avoid this dynamic of group coercion that ultimately undermines trust. They must seek to promote humor, spontaneity, rebelliousness against any authority that they get from being "experts," and a general feeling of aliveness to challenge all the self-imposed dogmas of "the right way" for a group to be.

The Compassion groups undermine the fantasy that problems are one's own, and that all one need do is find personal solutions. Ironically, it is through this very process that people are empowered—because they can then make realistic assessments of what they can do on their own, and what they need to do with others to change things.

It is here that individual responsibility asserts itself. Not as an implied injunction to make one's world perfect by oneself, but in the focus on creating a new community, a new "we" of people who have learned to trust and to have optimism about the possibility of changing larger social structures. So the groups do not teach that people are simply trapped victims. We have been victimized as individuals, but by creating a new WE, we can change things together.

"But what could someone do who started to feel empowered? Maybe these groups would give people a nice warm feeling, but when they actually tried to transform the larger social world, they would experience the massive powerlessness you know exists."

There is much that is true in the objection. These groups are necessary— but they are not sufficient. Ultimately, there needs to be a political organization, quite separate from these groups, that can lead people in concrete political struggles. A political party or a series of political movements around specific political and economic changes would be much more likely to succeed if their memberships were composed of people who have been through, or are currently participating in, these support groups.

An immediate step could be taken if the Democratic Party, the labor movement, the women's movement, the environmental movement, the anti-nuclear and pro-disarmament movement, the civil rights movement, and the various movements for a progressive foreign policy were to form a joint project whose goal was to create and promote a mass movement for compassion by generating Compassion groups throughout the society. And should there be a party or a revived left movement in the society, it too should have as a priority the creation of a movement for compassion.

Politics and Compassion Groups

It is important that the autonomy of the Compassion groups be preserved. A separate organizational structure that services and generates Compassion groups, and that trains group leaders, must be protected from any political pressures from the very movement-oriented groups that support it. Political parties and movements must see the Compassion groups as a parallel support process which they need, but which they cannot control. Most people in the society will rightfully be reluctant to explore emotional depths and painful childhood experiences inside a framework of a Compassion group that is thought to be subordinate to a political organization. People don't want their most basic fears and concerns to be manipulated in accord with the needs of someone's immediate political strategy—and that is precisely how the enemies of this process, the current elites of wealth and power, will try to represent this whole enterprise in any event. So, it is particularly important that people within the Compassion groups and within the organization coordinating the groups and training group leaders be able to report in full honesty that no such manipulation actually exists.

Yet it is very much in the interest of the various progressive political movements to support the development of a process that could lead to tens of millions of people participating in these groups. As people begin to be empowered, they will assert their new sense of themselves in every area of life. From the workplace to the ballot box to personal life—we will see a massive cultural and personal revolution that will be the fertile soil on which a wide variety of liberal and progressive political organizations can grow. The more people begin to see their personal lives in social terms, and the more they become optimistic about the possibility of changing larger social structures, the more they will provide support and encouragement for those

who do choose to be active politically. Moreover, because they are trained
to spot Surplus Powerlessness, they will be more likely to direct their political
movements towards larger and more significant social change, e.g., by challenging the right of capital to threaten capital strikes, as we discussed in our
chapter on politics above.

The parallel structure of Compassion groups and the political organizations would work something like this: People who were part of unions,
women's organizations, anti-nuclear groups, Democratic Party groups,
environmental groups, etc., would be urged by these political organizations
to join a Compassion group as part of their involvement in politics. They
would inform them of the wide variety of local Compassion groups, and
would periodically re-raise the issue to people on personal bases. But they
would not have any direct access to the content of what was happening in
the Compassion groups, except what their members decided to raise in the
meetings of the political organizations directly. The Compassion groups, on
the other hand, would feel free to provide space for people to problem-solve
together on ideas or activities that they might want to see happen within the
political organizations—but, they would then encourage group members to
go back into the political arena to try their strategies, rather than trying to
make the Compassion group itself into a new political vehicle. This kind of
autonomy should be the final goal—but in the process of building a movement for compassion, the various political movements may have to be more
directly involved in funding and supporting societal wide consciousness raising activities, such as the Friends of Family project described in Chapter 19.

Not everyone who participates in the Compassion groups will automatically
become active in politics. In this respect, the strategy is similar to that of the
first decade of re-emergence of the mass Women's Movement in the late
1960's and early 1970's. While there were some important political victories
that were won, the most important development was a mass change of consciousness, as literally millions of women changed their sense of themselves,
their rights, and the way that they would expect to be treated. This revolution
in consciousness has had lasting effects that have entered into every personal
relationship and every societal institution. A mass movement for compassion
would most likely work in that way—producing changes that would reach
into the very sinews of daily life in ways that cannot be fully predicted. Its
effects would be felt most dramatically by those engaged in social change
movements and by the Democratic Party and other liberal or progressive
parties that might be formed, but it would also cause changes to be felt in
the daily life experiences of most people in the society. While I have been
insistent that this change in consciousness would not be sustainable if we did
not simultaneously achieve success in important political struggles to change
the real power situations in the economic and political spheres, I also believe
that these struggles would be much more winnable if people were involved
in an ongoing process to diminish their Surplus Powerlessness. The Compassion groups would be an important element in such a process.

Yet all this would only really work if we could get millions of people involved in these groups. And that is a tremendous task. But it is not an impossible task—and not even as hard a task as that of getting millions of people involved in a political party that was dedicated to progressive politics. But it is hard.

We need a cadre of people who see themselves as dedicated to creating these groups. This cadre will experiment with formats and intervention styles, and then discuss with each other their techniques, their methods of presentation of ideas, their methods of recruitment, their strategies for termination, etc. To start with, we will need several thousand people who see this as the way they want to make their contribution to their fellow human beings. And we will need money to pay the organizers, national journals, conferences, and training centers. This is a big order. But it is do-able, and it is absolutely necessary if the movements for social change are not to find themselves permanently placed in the position of those with good ideas who always lose.

Originally, these groups should be led by therapists and other trained leaders who are paid for this work. Eventually, however, the movement for compassion must grow much larger than could be handled by professional therapists, particularly since we can only draw upon therapists who have been retrained with a social perspective. So, the participants in these groups during the first decade of building the movement for compassion will themselves have to be trained to be group leaders. Depending on their relative levels of skills and enthusiasm, this process may take months of evening meetings, or even years. Training leaders must be done carefully—and involve professional supervision, videotaping of trainees, and careful screening. There can be no assumption that everyone who wants to do it is automatically prepared to do so. Along with learning a sophisticated analysis of how Surplus Powerlessness works, the subtle skills of creating safety to allow people to overcome the dynamics of the "false group" and become real with each other must also be mastered. People who go through this training and are successfully graduated should then be paid for their services as group leaders. I mention this issue of pay, because a real movement cannot be based on good intentions alone—it must also provide a way for its activists to live, and must not see their participation as endless personal sacrifice. It must avoid making people feel ashamed if they want and need an adequate living—we are not looking for martyrs to run this movement, but regular human beings who, precisely because they are like everyone else, have the ability to show others that we all have common problems that underlie our individual differences.

While the compassion groups are a central part of the mass psychology that can defeat Surplus Powerlessness, we may also expect that some people will supplement their participation in these groups with individual therapy. Therapists who share the commitment to the Compassion groups, and who understand the issues and perspective raised in this book, could play an important role in supplementing the total liberatory process. In fact, it is likely that the total number of people seeking therapy would be dramatically increased, because many of the people who today would not dream of identifying themselves as "in need" of therapy will, in the social context created by a mass movement for compassion, feel perfectly safe about therapy, understanding that the issues they want to explore are not reflections of personal failure. It is ironic that in the present economic climate, many therapists feel that their field is over-crowded and wish to limit the number of new therapists, either through restrictive entrance exams or through limiting the number of accredited training programs. But the truth is that there are tens of millions of people who need help, but who will never seek it, given the current set of meanings attached to "therapy." This could be dramatically transformed if there were a therapy approach that understood the real needs and pains of working class life, and that created a climate within which stigmatization was significantly decreased. The creation of a mass psychology of compassion would simultaneously open up many millions of people who would be ready to explore their personal lives and change. But I have no expectation that most therapists would understand this or be able to participate in the creation of Compassion groups—because of their current ideological commitment to theories of the Meritocracy and "individual responsibility." But those who would join in creating this kind of movement would soon find that they could make real contributions to bringing empowerment to large sectors of the population that are today completely inaccessible to both traditional and "humanistic" psychotherapies. The building blocks for creating a movement for compassion are already in place. In the next two chapters I will discuss two projects that I developed that provide models for how to build the Compassion groups. But don't be literalists—you may find even better ways to generate the process of a mass movement for compassion than these—I offer them only as proof that it is possible, but not as a new ideological straightjacket that would constrain your own imagination and creativity.

Chapter 18

Occupational Stress Groups

FOR THE PAST SEVEN YEARS I HAVE BEEN INVOLVED IN LEADing Occupational Stress Groups for the Labor Movement. These groups are explicitly "preventive" in nature. They are aimed at working people who are coping with normal stresses of daily life at work. Though they are initially scheduled for only twelve weeks, partly to reassure people who have never been in a group before that they need not make a lifelong commitment, they often end up being ongoing. A stress group usually meets once a week on a weekday evening for two hours, though sometimes participants stay around talking for several more hours once the formal group meetings have ended.

The Stress Groups recruit participants from unions, and they tend to attract people who are not active in the unions. In fact, many participants tell us that they have never been to a union meeting, or have gone to such meetings only during contract negotiations. On the average, the stress group participant is between thirty- and fifty-years old, and has never participated in any kind of "group" or "therapy" or "growth process" before.

These groups usually attract machinists, telephone operators, machinists, telephone sales representatives, utility company white-collar employees, electronic technicians, auto assembly plant workers, nurses, clerical workers, secretaries, lab technicians, truck drivers, transit workers, bus drivers, electrical workers, firefighters, hospital and nursing home employees, teachers, department store sales people, waiters, longshoremen, government workers,

311

warehouse workers, airplane technicians, or construction workers. Some of
these groups are based on one workplace or one union, but most involve
participants from several unions or different workplaces within the same
unions.

The Stress Groups start out with fixed formats, and then gradually evolve
into a freer and more self-directed form. In the first twelve weeks they follow
a Stress Manual that we have developed, which includes didactic material
and homework assignments. The group meetings have three components:
an educational presentation by the group leader about some of the dynamics
of how stress operates and relaxation exercises including breathing, guided
visualization, meditation, and some instruction about diet and exercise, group
discussion of how these ideas apply to each person's particular experience,
with the group leader offering reflections or questions that help deepen
each person's self-understanding, and "check-ins," in which group members
discuss current realities in their work and personal lives.

The didactic material is presented to the group and repeated in the manual
in a very condensed and easy-to-understand format. We begin with a discussion of the psychology of stress, what actually happens to our bodies when
people are in a state of heightened alert. We proceed to a discussion of the
stress factors at work, and documented studies that show the high correlation
between certain physical problems and work conditions that combine high
performance demand with low level of control over work conditions. We
then teach participants ways to identify stress at the workplace. From there,
we discuss how work got to be organized in the way it is, the strategies
management has adopted for control, and the way that management divides
workers against each other. Next, we discuss the ideology of self-blaming,
and why people have been taught to fear their own anger. This discussion
leads us to the ways that stress is brought home into family life and into
child-rearing. Finally, we discuss how workplaces could be reorganized, and
what working people could do to accomplish this goal. Each presentation
usually lasts for about twenty minutes, and is sometimes supplemented by
a videotape or short movie. It is then followed by a group discussion away
from a general theoretical level, asking people to talk about the concrete
details of their own lives.

Homework assignments always include practicing a relaxation exercise.
But they also include some written questions which participants don't "hand
in." Participants themselves decide how much of the homework they are
actually going to do. An early assignment is to list reasons why they think
they got their jobs. What did they originally want to do when they were
children? When they were teenagers? What happened to change their minds
or their circumstances? How much do they blame themselves for having the
jobs they have?

By the middle of the process we are asking people to do assignments like,
"Ask your co-workers at the workplace to describe to you what things are
most stressful for them at work. List what they say. Then ask them to suggest
two or three changes that they would like to see, and how they envision them
being implemented." Or, "Describe three incidents that happened this week

at work that helped reinforce the divisions between workers, rather than encouraging their solidarily. Describe what role your supervisor or manager played in the process."

Towards the end of the twelve weeks the homework assignments include visualization exercises, such as, "Go to a place where you can yell at the top of your voice and not disturb anyone. Tell your family that you need twenty minutes alone in your bedroom and not to be surprised at the loud noises you are going to make. Envision yourself in a field with one big tree, and on the tree you have tied up and gagged your supervisor, boss, or a member of the corporate elite of this society. That person is securely tied and can't get out, but his or her ears are open and s/he is finally forced to listen to you. Now yell at him or her, tell him or her how you've been feeling all these years about your workplace, or about the competitive marketplace, or about how powerless you've felt, or about the abuse your parents had to take, or about the specific ways that s/he has oppressed you. Let out your anger, and then after twenty minutes of doing this, write down what you were feeling, or what resistances you had to really letting yourself get into the anger." Or another visualization, "Imagine that you could completely restructure your workplace and your union. What would they look like? Take twenty minutes writing about what you see, and what specific steps you might be able to take towards achieving these goals in the next five years."

Participants in these groups have not usually been part of a culture of therapy, and the first few weeks it's often quite difficult to get people to talk very deeply about their experiences. But invariably, by the fourth week someone opens up and really begins to reveal feelings of self-blame; tells other group members about what a mess they have made of their lives, and usually defends the various structures of their oppression. Group members participate in showing each other that there are other ways to understand their experiences, and in the process, they begin to re-understand themselves.

This is not a linear process at all. Sometimes in a group several people will get overtly "angry" at their supervisors or bosses. They will spend much time "bitching" about the situations. But the anger has a hollow quality, and I often find that this anger is merely a defense against really experiencing their own situations. In these cases, it is important to help group members uncover the underlying sadness and hurt even though superficially what that involves is going beyond the anger that the group member at first presents. Ultimately, this can lead to the participant getting to much deeper and truer underlying anger.

Getting to this level of reality is not always easy or always quick. Sometimes group members will experience instant conversions or flights into health, presenting themselves as having totally "gotten" the new framework and becoming "good" Stress Group members. These participants want my approval as group leader, or the approval of fellow group members, in order to feel secure and cared for. The reaching out to others in this way is not pathological—it actually represents in part a genuine expression of an underlying need to actualize their human potentialities. But, too often these are also simply repeats of the patterns they have learned in childhood, when they acted in accord with the norms of groups or situations in the hopes of receiving love, which they still believe they don't really deserve. They are still denying their own inner selves in order to get love, but they never really feel loved because the parts of them that are being affirmed aren't felt to be their true selves. This can happen in these groups in the early weeks as group members give up their own world views and their own senses of what is true about themselves in order to produce "acceptable" behaviors to fellow group members. Only careful attention and awareness can work to ensure them that they do not have to recreate the phony group life and that there is no substitute for real connection and deep recognition.

The goal of the group leader in this process is to both affirm what is legitimate and hopeful in the steps group members take towards each other and the group, and to interpret the phony solidarily and superficial conversions. The group leader must at once be an advocate for a position, and also an advocate for each individual's right not to become identified with any group consensus until it feels deeply and fully right for that individual.

Here we get to the critical importance of how resistance is treated. If people are made to feel that they have no right to their defenses and no right to their own interpretations of what has happened to them, then they will feel coerced into group norms. Such coercion is self-defeating. The group will be more of an entertainment for them than a true growth experience and once the group is over, the group's effects will quickly disappear. So, people in the group are given every encouragement to express their resistances and to honor their defenses. Simultaneously, they are lovingly and gently exposed to a whole different way to understand themselves and their world.

The impact is often very dramatic. After the false conversion and superficial levels of presenting behavior to please the group leader or fellow group members, something much deeper begins to emerge by the ninth or tenth week. Group members begin to have dreams about their childhood, recalling previously repressed material. In group they begin to listen to each other with a degree of comprehension and caring that is felt by everyone as real. When one member starts to tell a story about the way a supervisor has acted unfairly, other members feel genuine anger, and that then allows them to start to feel genuine anger about their own oppressive situations. The caring begins to extend outside the group; group members begin to support each other in pursuing grievances, in demanding more attention to their needs from their unions, and in dealing with daily life situations like childcare, medical problems or family hassles.

As the level deepens, people begin to talk about their relationships with their parents, spouses, children, and lovers in ways that reveal the details of their pain. As more people hear about each other's pain, they begin to feel less embarrassed at their own pains, and to feel more trusting about talking about them. And the deeper they go, the more they begin to realize that what they had previously experienced as merely their own personal hangups are actually shared and collective problems.

The support that people experience when they see their personal pains are widely shared by others, who initially appeared to them to be more "together," lets people move to a next level. Group members begin to feel the anger that they had worked much of their life to repress. At first, these experiences are quite scary, and group members report fears about going crazy or hurting somebody with their anger. Other group members report difficulties in going to work because they are seeing with fresh eyes how oppressive their workplaces are.

In supporting this phase, we have to balance two different considerations. On the one hand, we do not want people to act out their anger in any individual fashion. We know that they could lose their jobs and that life as an unemployed person is significantly worse than life in most oppressive jobs. Nor do we want people to quit their jobs —so we recognize that the defenses that they have built up in order to stay at work are often necessary and should not be totally discarded. On the other hand, we do not want to give the same messages to them that they have received throughout their lives: that their anger is objectively frightening and that it must be suppressed, otherwise they will be in deep trouble. We need to encourage the anger and also be sure that it is channeled in safe and non-destructive ways.

Luckily, there is an already existing form for this: the Labor Movement. The Stress Groups encourage people to take their anger into their union activity, where it can be directed towards constructive and important goals. The difference between individuals acting on their anger, something that often leads to disastrous and self-defeating consequences, and the working class acting in concert on this anger is quite profound. Some of the most important advances won by working people in this century have come from precisely this kind of focused anger. Nothing would regenerate the Labor Movement more effectively than if it validated this anger and provided a place for it.

The Stress Groups do not themselves attempt to become action groups in the unions, except to support their members in whatever activities they are engaged in. The Stress Groups have one substantive goal besides supporting their own members: to encourage other people to join Stress Groups, or in other ways participate in those kinds of discussion of the details of their life at work and in family life, so that they too can begin to discover the ways that they have been inappropriately blaming themselves and repressing their anger.

As this process continues, participants reach new levels of Compassion for themselves, their parents, their co-workers. It is often particularly striking to see a worker who initially complained that his or her co-workers were lazy or uncooperative reporting two months later that s/he has reached a new level of communication with co-workers, based in part on the ability to understand their life experiences and to imagine their pain.

Compassion manifests itself in many different ways. For some workers, it will be exhibited in a different attitude towards past lovers or towards parents that had been previously shunned. For other workers, it takes the form of honoring their own bodily needs, and thinking that they deserve their own health. For others, it takes the form of overcoming racist or sexist attitudes that they had towards co-workers which they were too embarrassed to express before but which nevertheless influenced their political behavior. It can be as "trivial" as a different attitude towards others workers when they are striking, recognizing that they are probably sharing similar problems, and wishing them well. It can be as "subtle" as recognizing that when the postal clerk or telephone information operator or billing clerk talks to you with an unfriendly tone, it's probably because they've been having a stressful work life every bit as exasperating as your own—so you then respond by making some comment about how stressful their work must be, and how much you wish that all work could be changed and made more humanly fulfilling. It can be as "overt" as being deeply moved by the pain of friends and family whose problems had previously elicited a shrug of your shoulder that seemed to imply, "Handle your own problems and don't expect me to worry about that—I've got my own issues to deal with."

The Stress Groups are one important way of reaching Compassion, and eventually helping people see the powerful interrelationships between their own personal subjective experience and the destructive ways that society, relationships, and childhood have been structured in response to the dynamics of powerlessness.

One of the reasons that Stress Groups can be so effective is that there is a general understanding in the society that "stress" is something that many people face. The political education that can happen when organizing Stress Groups can be valuable in helping people to deepen their understanding of where this stress comes from. For example, when we publicized the Occupational Stress Groups in California, we coordinated our outreach with a billboard campaign. The billboards proclaimed: "Powerlessness at work is bad for your health" and then went on to tell about how to contact us for Occupational Stress Groups. The feedback we got from many people who called for more information led us to believe that many people who would never dream of participating in anything that smacked of "therapy" are open to groups that focus on occupational stress. Of course, for this same reason, many opportunistic therapists have suddenly proclaimed themselves stress experts, or have otherwise sold themselves to corporate interests and may eventually make working people so suspicious of stress groups that they could take on the connotation of "adjustment to rotten working conditions" groups. But, in the meantime, the openness to dealing with occupational stress provides us with an important opening to begin the process of developing compassion on a mass scale. In doing mass psychology work, it is precisely the ability to find such openings that allows us to take a theoretical understanding of the need for compassion and transform that into a practical reality. All the flowery sermons and editorials and speeches about compassion are irrelevant if they do not help create this kind of direct experiential moment in which millions of people can begin to reunderstand the details of their lives and have compassion for themselves and each other.

Chapter 19

Friends of Families

IN JULY OF 1982 I WAS INVITED TO A NATIONAL CONVENTION co-sponsored by the Moral Majority and the New Right's think tank, The Committee for a Free Congress. I was the only non-New Right presenter, and I was invited to debate the Moral Majority about family life. They chose me because I had been speaking on tv and radio call-ins around the country about the family, arguing that it was the progressive forces, not the New Right, which actually offered the best hope for getting people what they really want in families—namely, long-term committed loving relationships. This was hitting the New Right at their most vulnerable place. Precisely what has enabled the Right to emerge from years of isolation has been its ability to portray itself as the only real champion of family life.

The New Right was speaking to important issues. Most people experience pain and frustration in their personal lives. They interpret this pain as a sign of their own failings. The quiet desperation can lead to isolation, drinking, drugs, family violence, endless quarrels and tensions between family members, and sometimes divorce. What the New Right did was to acknowledge that there was a mass problem and then present a program based on a false analysis of the problem. The analysis itself was quite mistaken—it blamed gays for breaking down family ties, it accused women of wanting liberation as a substitute for loving commitments, and it attempted to impose an ideal of family life from the past that had little relevance to the experience of most contemporary Americans.

317

But, however misguided its analysis and program, the New Right gained a strong following precisely because it helped to relieve people of painful responsibility for their own personal shortcomings. By presenting a social analysis of the problem, it gave people new hope that family life could be saved. It thus had a potentially empowering impact, and this empowerment was a part of the reason why people joining that movement had an experience of community.

I was drawn into thinking about these issues in the year before the 1980 elections, when I began to notice that many people whose objective economic interests should have led them to support the Democrats, were beginning to waffle. These were not "intellectuals" or "professional liberals" who were swayed by complex arguments from the Republicans or Reaganites. Rather, they were working people, Teamsters, longshoremen, secretaries, nurses, auto workers, machinists, retail clerks and even some unemployed people. I was puzzled. At first I thought that these people were just ignorant of the Republican program, or that they did not understand what the negative impact of Reaganomics might be. Perhaps they were moved by the argument that fighting inflation would be in the best interest of everyone, and would eventually even help create new jobs for the unemployed. But as I began to interview hundreds of these people in the ensuing years, I learned something quite different. True, some bought the lure of Reaganomics, coupled with a covert sense that too many of their tax dollars were being spent for the poor, particularly since none of the programs seemed to work, and nothing seemed to be curing poverty anyway. But most thought that there was no significant difference between the parties on economic matters, and that both parties were primarily interested in benefitting the large corporations, only disagreeing on what was the best strategy to do so. They were attracted to the Right because it was articulating their fears about their own daily·lives and suggesting a solution.

To many of these people, the collapse of the family was not an abstraction or political slogan. They were terrified about the problems in their own families. They had frustrations with their children, lack of fulfillment with their spouses, and feelings of isolation and betrayal within their family lives. They did not know what was wrong, but they knew that something was wrong. The New Right made it appear as if someone out there cared.

Some of the people I interviewed were single parents—mostly women—who were members of trade unions, and I thought that they certainly must have understood the reactionary implications of the New Right. In questioning them about their hopes, many of them articulated clearly that they would never agin enter into relationships in which they faced unequal power. These were not women who could buy the chauvinism implicit in the New Right's fantasy. But, nevertheless, many of them were drawn to what the New Right was saying. They felt that the Right was the only force around that even appeared to care about the problems in families.

Most of these people didn't vote for Reagan. but instead of voting for the Democratic candidate, many of them didn't vote at all. And those who did vote for Reagan told me that they told their friends they had voted for the

Democrats—because they knew that was what they were supposed to be doing as loyal labor union members. The conflict was intense: they knew Reagan was a friend of the rich, but they also heard him and those around him talking about the issue that they cared most about.

This could have been turned around if the progressive forces had been able to articulate a clear pro-family perspective that helped people understand the real forces that were undermining family life, including the structure of the world of work, the impact of the competitiveness in the society, the legacy of sexism, the isolation of families, the breakdown of communities of meaning, the marketplace in relationships, the way that capitalism benefits from our lack of solidarity and trust, the way that advertisers sell their products by appealing to our increased emotional neediness, and so forth. If only the progressive movements would have claimed the title of being the real supporters of families.

I was careful to insist that such a movement should not only support the traditional nuclear family. Single-parent families, gay families, alternative families, all had the same right to support that the traditional families did— and we had to be careful to avoid legislating one "correct" form of family life. It was also important to insist that a family support organization avoid creating a reality in which singles would feel pressured into coupledom, or in which women would be encouraged to stay in oppressive relationships after they had unsuccessfully struggled to transform them.

In the ensuing two years I contacted leaders of the women's movement, AFL-CIO, the liberal leaders of the Democratic Party, the opinion makers in the large community organizations and "progressive" foundations. I talked to them about what I had been learning in my research, and how these ideas might be looked at from their standpoint. I encountered tremendous resistance.

The liberal wing of the Democratic Party and the labor movement thought that getting into psychological issues around family would be too messy—and unnecessary. "Unnecessary," I was told, because we would win the elections strictly on the failure of Reaganomics. On this view, the high level of unemployment and the obvious tilt towards the interests of the rich had been sufficient to expose Reagan, and to re-mobilize workers whose support had dropped away previously. They were proven wrong in the 1982 and 1984 elections. But even if you are reading this book years hence, when liberals have won more electoral victories and the Right is out of power, you will find that the liberals in power are always acting very restrained in what electoral programs they push, fearful that the Right may quickly regain its strength. You may find yourself frustrated with these liberals—yet their fear is not unfounded. As long as the Right has cornered the market on the issues articulated as "family support," it will have a decisive advantage over liberals and will always be able to appeal to constituencies which, on economic and political grounds, "should be" with the liberals or even progressives. They may vote Democratic one year, but liberals correctly perceive that they are always on thin ice (but wrongly think that the way to protect themselves is to moderate their programs). Their only real chance of changing the ever-shifting pendulum is to become progressive champions of family life.

But the liberals and progressives continually dismiss these issues. If the people are attracted to the Right, liberals and progressives label this as some form of mass craziness, lack of information, brain-washing, or simply racism and sexism. What they rarely ask is, "What part of the Right's message makes sense and touches real needs that we have been ignoring?" Instead, the liberals and progressives tend to dismiss whole sections of the population who are moved by the Right—they are seen as either stupid or evil. Alternatively, the Right's victories are attributed to more money and access to mass media and direct mail and other technological superiorities—again, thinking that the population is just endlessly manipulable and that what they, the liberals, really need is a more efficient technology of manipulation. This kind of attitude, of course, gets communicated to the people, who are rightly resentful of the implied elitism in this kind of analysis. If, instead, the liberals and progressives were to re-think the issue of family, they would see that this very issue raises an important point of entree to the whole set of issues we have discussed in the first part of this book. It is precisely in the name of building support for families that we can demand a humane and democratic work environment, and that we can challenge the competitive values of a capitalist economy.

In fact, in the name of creating a society that is safe for love and intimacy, we can build a society that enhances, rather than represses, the Human Essence. While this switch of focus will be hard for many liberals and progressives who are settled into their traditional approaches to politics, they could eventually see that much of what they want is better argued for precisely because it promotes a loving society. The parts that can't be so articulated may also need to be re-evaluated.

Some feminists attacked the whole idea of creating a progressive pro-family analysis as automatically re-legitimating the patriarchal family. The only reason that people would be attracted to a pro-family movement, they argued, is because they wished for a revival of patriarchy and repression. Barbara Ehrenreich, attacking the idea of a progressive pro-family movement in an article in *The Nation* magazine in 1982, argued that "most of the impulses" that attracted people to the Right's pro-family stance "are nasty ones: misogyny, racism, sexual repressiveness and a punitive attitude towards young people." This analysis is misguided and contemptuous of the actual experience of most working people. My own research convinces me that most people who respond to the language of "family" and who want to strengthen family life have nothing in common with the misogynists that Ehrenreich dreams about. For most people, "family" is a code word that expresses their hopes for long-term loving and committed relationships. It is this that people yearn for, and this yearning represents a positive and hopeful fact. And if the Right is the only force that seems deeply committed to building a healthy and strong family life, people who are attracted to it cannot automatically be labeled in the elitist language that some women's movement activists employ.

It is certainly true that the way family life is constituted today, much of what people yearn for will not be available to them in their family life. A progressive pro-family movement would necessarily push for societal changes that would make it possible for families to be more loving and supportive. This would require a substantial reorganization of the world of work, a reconstruction of the economy, a vigorous fight against sexist practices both in family life and in the economic marketplace, and a reconstruction of communities to break families out of their isolation and into connection with each other on deep and personal levels. For all their sputtering, the Right can't deliver this. Their message is attractive only because the entire area has been abandoned by liberals, progressives and many feminists.

Feminists should have understood that an important part of the reason that they failed to gain adequate support for ERA in the early 1980s was that their opponents succeeded in convincing many people that ERA was anti-family. The fact is that most women in the women's movement understand the importance of families. In fact, the analysis of sexism and the struggle for equality is an important contribution that will make long-term loving relationships more, not less, possible. Most of the feminists I encountered who were close to the labor movement understood this point, and they were enthusiastic supporters of the idea of creating a "Friends of Families" organization that was explicitly feminist. The popular press is at fault in characterizing the women's movement as anti-family, and focusing on those women in the movement who are most outrageous in their male-hating, creating a false but enduring impression that feminism is counterposed to family life. But this is the impression that persists—and it will be up to the women's movement to counter that distorted image by creating a new image of feminists who are pro-family. Nor is this just a matter of image: there have been some strong anti-family elements in the women's movement that must be dealt with—just as strongly as feminists demanded that sexism be dealt with in the anti-war movements.

For example, within the women's movement there has been a tendency to question the feminist credentials of women who choose to make their role as mother and housewife a primary focus of their life activities. While recognizing the dangers that these choices might entail in a sexist society, a women's movement must come to grips with the reality that people really do want these kinds of relationships and will opt for them even if that means leaving the women's movement itself.

Ironically, the women's movement looks at times as if it believed that its primary enemy was women themselves. There is an underlying assumption that too many women have made the "wrong" choices. If the women's movement wants to be a continuing viable force it must speak to the needs of women who are opting for families and motherhood, and see these choices as potentially fulfilling and valuable. And, if it can, it must strongly and forcefully recast the struggle against sexism as a struggle for the possibility of loving relationships. Under that banner, not under the banner of ERA or abstract rights, it will win back many who have left in despair, and many who were never attracted in the first place.

Although many of us strongly believe in the right to full equality, and think that others should fight equally strongly for this right, we must understand that notions of abstract rights have never fully mobilized people to struggle. People will struggle for the abstract rights only when they see they are directly necessary to achieve their goals. In the current period, many people have come to believe that the rights in question actually make it harder to achieve their goals of loving relationships. We must help people to understand that what they really do want—love, commitment, solidarity— can only be achieved through the creation of full equality. But, to make that case, we must first insist that what we are most basically about is the fight for love, not the fight for equality. It is in the name of that love that we fight for equality, because equality is the best way to achieve the fullest development of people in loving relationships. Sexism is a major obstacle to loving relationships. What the majority of the population needs to hear is that we care about those relationships, not just about abstract rights.

Many people in progressive communities like to frame their issues around concerns of justice and fairness. Civil rights for blacks, equal rights for women, fair treatment for the poor or the unemployed, equal opportunities for everyone. These are goals that have tended to unify the largest constituencies in the liberal political world. Yet, there is a deeper value that ought to be the basis of progressive politics. That value could best be summarized in the following slogan: "We want a world that is safe for loving relationships." This is why putting forward a strategy around a Friends of Families project is so crucial.

This is a very different basis for a critique of capitalism than that of unfairness. It suggests a different kind of world view, namely that human beings should live in free, loving, and creative connection with each other, and that our social order systematically and deeply discourages this. The energy for our critique comes from our own experience of misrecognition, the frustration thereby engendered, and the pain of living lives in which we are systematically prevented from being all that we could be. The liberation of our Human Essence—understood as a collective project that requires new forms of human solidarity and affirmation of our We-ness—can form a more powerful basis for politics than any abstract commitment to individual rights.

The support for families goes directly to the experience of most people in this society. Its potential impact is precisely in that it does not address someone else's problem, "those poor suffering ———— (fill in the blank)." Rather, it gets to the heart of a problem that we all share, and opens up the need for us to discuss with each other our personal lives.

This may be one reason why some progressives don't want to deal with family support issues. Because of their own Surplus Powerlessness, many progressives feel comfortable only when they can isolate themselves from everyone else, (a fate they share with almost everyone who is socialized into a society that creates so many lonely individuals who are afraid to make deep contact with others). They accomplish this by adopting an elitist pose with regard to the masses: "*We* know the answers, but the rest of you boobs are too stupid to know them too. Moreover, we are sure that you won't listen to us if we try to tell you what we know, so we will phrase our ideas in language that is so strange and esoteric that no one else will possibly understand what we mean. But that's all right, because no one would have listened anyway." I do not want to be too harsh on these progressives. They are suffering from the same pains and fears as everyone else; and, naturally, they will adopt political strategies that reflect their own self-doubts, their own fears of the very masses they hope to organize, their own deep convictions that no one would really like them if people got to know them well.

The comfortable elitism is undermined when we start to talk about family life. Everyone faces problems in family life, and nearly everyone continues to blame themselves inappropriately for many of these problems. The "leftist" feels just as uncomfortable as anyone else when these issues are broached, and, moreover, fears that his or her previously adopted stance of protection of being above everyone else ("I have the 'right' ideology") will seem irrelevant.

Some of the progressive movements, particularly those that are most explicitly socialist, tend to be dominated by people in their twenties and early thirties. Many of these people have only recently struggled their way out of oppressive family relationships. They have not yet had the chance to fully experience their anger, and, hence, have not been able to move beyond that anger to compassion for their parents. To many of these, the word "family" conjures up a set of distasteful memories that they have only recently broken away from. They have not yet understood the way that their families were themselves trapped by the larger society, and instead think that "the family" itself was the problem. Until they develop real compassion for their parents and for themselves, they will stay stuck in positions that alienate everyone else.

We are all aware of how easy it is for the rhetoric of "family" to be misused and manipulated. In the name of "family" and "love," people are emotionally coerced into relationships in which they are required to give up much of their freedom and autonomy. The endless guilt trips by which one partner in a relationship batters the other, the mutual protection pacts in which partners agree not to discuss their real feelings for fear of hurting and getting hurt, the subtle expressions of anger masquerading as expressions of love, the endless struggles to dominate each other, the terrible disappointments that we inflict on each other when we cannot be available for our partner's emotional needs—all these have been justified or covered over in the name of "family."

But the problem here isn't "family life," but the kinds of relationships that are available in capitalist society. It is nothing short of foolishness to attribute these problems to "the family," when they are, in fact, problems that occur not only in the family, but every relationship. People who have created alternative forms—be they communes, gay relationships, open marriages, non-monogamous marriages, singles lifestyles, etc., all report the same problems. The ways that human beings are taught to relate to each other by the competitive marketplace and in the world of work, are reproduced in our most intimate places.

Supporting families does not mean supporting families to lie about themselves. On the contrary, we need to create a wide societal understanding of the pains in families so that individuals can then feel safe to explore their own experience and not feel "crazy" when they begin to uncover their own messes. A Friends of Families movement that created this kind of compassion would have dramatic political consequences.

Here are three areas that churches, unions, liberal democrats, civil and women's rights organizations could work on together to build a Friends of Families movement:

—*Family Support Groups and Classes.* A nationwide network of family support groups should be established. These groups would meet weekly and would have two foci: discussion of the kinds of political changes in each community that would be necessary to get real family support, and the establishment of a structured place for people to explore the problems in their own families, and to learn from each others' experiences. The latter function is central, and should be modeled on the Occupational Stress Groups discussed earlier. Therapists or other trained leaders could play an important role in making these groups safe for deep exploration of the pains that everyone experiences in family life.

At first, these groups would retreat into the safety of discussing the "objective" political issues like childcare, health care, support for the elderly, etc. But it would be part of their explicit constitution that people discuss problems in family life. And they would have a manual of topics, readings, and guides for group leaders of ways to get them to address the central family issues. In order to succeed, they must be part of a mass phenomenon, and they must work explicitly at transforming the powerlessness and self-blaming that cripple us.

Size is particularly important. It is only when this project is adopted nationwide and by millions of people that it will feel safe to those who are in the groups. Until such a critical mass is assembled, people who select to be in these groups will tend to feel that they are identifying themselves as having special problems. The very dynamics of self-blaming will prevent many people who badly need these groups from participating. When many millions of people are in these groups, the movement will suddenly become "legitimate"—and then it can increase geometrically to many tens of millions, and make a significant change in the consciousness of the society.

Intention is equally important. Many people today belong to family support groups that do not share the analysis of family problems put forward in this book. Their leaders do not usually have an analysis of how real powerlessness constrains the possibilities of individual and family change. They do little to help people understand why their very desire for long-term committed loving relationships necessarily requires that they be part of a larger struggle to humanize and democratize the society. Without this larger analysis, the value of these groups diminishes, and they may even degenerate into self-blaming ("Why haven't you been able to take the good ideas presented here and easily apply them to your life and get your family life together?").

The key to success is elimination of any stigma connected with participation in these groups. That can be done by promoting the notion that participants are showing their civic consciousness by helping others, not just dealing with their own personal problems. The groups must be peopled by everyone, including the leaders of progressive movements—who will be able to show, by their weekly participation in a group, that they really believe that these groups are for everyone, not just for people who are "in trouble." If church, civic, community, labor, feminist, environmental and anti-war leaders are all in these weekly groups, talking honestly about their own experiences in family life, it will be much easier to preach convincingly of the importance of these groups for everyone else.

—*Family Day and Family Support Activities.* Under the unified auspices of all progressive forces (unions, churches, women's organizations, civil rights organizations, peace groups, ecology organizations, anti-nuclear organizations) a National Family Day should be established. Unlike Mothers' and Fathers' Days, which are essentially private events, this celebration should be a convocation of families in a community celebration. The focus of this celebration should be to popularize an understanding of why people face problems in their families, and provide participants with problem-solving techniques, through workshops and speeches. A second focus should be honoring people for what they have accomplished in their family lives—and acknowledging that keeeping families working today is no easy task. Held on one day throughout the country, these events would turn out thousands of people in every city who would be exposed to the analysis we are presenting here for the first time. The very act of collectively creating a new national holiday would be empowering—as long as people insisted on the community focus, and on their right to participate in the planning of the community events.

Friends of Families would also sponsor ongoing family support activites. Included would be classes on child development, family dynamics, and communication skills. Summer camps for children and teens would encourage the early development of an understanding of the social sources of family problems, and facilitate learning skills for talking about those problems. Cooperative nurseries and daycare centers would mix professional staffs with volunteers from the senior citizen population who welcome opportunities to use their skills. Seniors would also play an important role in creating and leading support groups for grammar school students after school, and in teaching them some of their accumulated wisdom. Food and skills sharing, childcare swaps, and other self-help cooperative arrangements would be stimulated, and an extensive arrangement of support activities would be made available for families of the unemployed and families of striking workers.

My friend Peter tells me he won't go to these groups for the same reason he wouldn't send his children to camp; because he's afraid the summer camp and group could take on an authoritarian flavor. His concern is valid. We don't want some new Walter Mondale- or George Bush-type person to run our summer camps and make them joyless—and there's never any final guarantee that that won't happen. It is important to say that these activities should be available, but people shouldn't be pressured into using them. The libertarian impulse needs to be respected as one hedge against the tendency to create reified institutions.

—A Bill of Rights for Families. Friends of Families would develop a national and local legislative agenda that could be fought for both through legislation and through ballot initiatives. These programs would create the minimum support that families need: childcare services, family support allowances (e.g., tax deductions or direct payments to families that are caring for their aging parents in their home, or families that are paying for college tuition, or families that are spending monies to receive family therapy), free and community-controlled medical services, beautification of neighborhoods, subsidies for home mortgages for new families, and guaranteed maternity and paternity leaves of six months per child.

On a local basis, city governments can support the creation of family support networks. For example, the City of Oakland recently petitioned the California Legislature for funds to create a city-wide family support program based on the training of family support counselors. These counselors would be community activists, housewives, shop stewards, and leaders in churches and community groups who would attend a training for four hours a week for one year, learning the key tactics to leading family support groups. Supervised by licensed therapists, they would then lead family support groups. It was calculated that, with the expenditure of $4 million per year, over 40,000 people in the city would attend some set of trainings on family issues within a five-year period. Here, too, the key element is size. Precisely what ensures participation by the population you hope to recruit is that it is done on a city-wide scale, with churches, schools, city government and unions all combining their energies to urge people to participate in the groups. Friends of Families would push for the creation of these kinds of programs embodying our underlying philosophy.

The key advance made possible by a Friends of Families strategy is the popularization of the notion that we all share problems in family life, that we need to share our stories about what is happening in our families, and that we need to be aware of the ways that the economic and political order plays a major role in shaping the fate of our "personal life" experience. To create this kind of consciousness is to make a major step towards a mass psychology of compassion.

Of course, in this strategy there would also be the possibility that other interpretations would win out. Any mass strategy will face the challenge that those who control the media and shape public consciousness will do their best to take the edge out of the program, and to reduce it to the already established categories of mass psychological domination. We will hear many attempts to translate the message as "Get your own family life together," and "You have nobody to blame but yourself if you don't do your best to make your family life work after all that we are giving you now—like family support programs." The media will try to make Family Day a private event— "Be with your family, not with the community—and send people cards, buy them presents, etc.," as their alternative to our message to get together with other families and begin honest dialogue. The struggle will not end. It will take sustained and careful planning to ensure that the venture is not co-opted into a more sophisticated form of self-blaming. But the structure of such a movement opens up a very different possibility—that our ideas could be listened to and heard by tens of millions of people whose lives would be immeasurably improved to the extent that they began to unravel the chains of self-blaming.

The process set in motion by this effort would have many other ramifications. As people began to open up more about their lives to others, many would uncover issues that needed more sustained attention than could be provided in the family support groups. These people would be encouraged to seek other places to explore their issues, preferably with the guidance of trained and licensed therapists, who could offer the kind of therapy process described in the chapter on psychotherapy. These Public Interest Psychotherapists would not see their work with individuals as counterposed to political action, but adjunctive.

The creation of Friends of Families as an organization, and as specific nationally coordinated projects, could begin immediately. If coupled with the creation of Occupational Stress Groups, possibly under the same sponsorship, this project would make an immediate and substantial contribution towards the development of a mass movement for compassion. The objective conditions—the incredible pain and self-blaming that people experience in their personal lives and at work—creates this possibility. Whether people are too crippled by exisitng Surplus Powerlessness to act on this possibility will be known only as the next few decades are lived through.

We should also restate the underlying political philosophy here: If people are attracted to reactionary causes, don't first assume that they are crazy or evil. Instead, seek the rational component in their actions—what legitimate underlying needs are not being addressed in the current reality and how those needs are being addressed by the reactionaries. Then ask, "How can we dramatize to people how those same needs would be fulfilled in a deeper way, were they to support progressive social change?" In following this path around the issue of Family, I discovered that our underlying commitment to creating loving human relationships, far from being some "corny" concern, should be brought out of the closet and made the guiding principle of progressive politics.

Chapter 20

Compassionate Unions

NOTHING WOULD DO MORE TO RECREDIT THE UNIONS IN the eyes of their members than if the unions began to show that they cared about the effects of work on the workers' personal lives. So, while the unions should help in the creation of a national Friends of Families movement, it should also begin immediately to create its own internal Friends of Families inside each union local.

Family support programs inside unions would focus on the impact of stress on family life. Unions would create two kinds of groups: Occupational Stress Groups and Family Support Groups. Both would deal with the same kind of material, seeking to help people explore the relationship between their work world and the rest of their lives, but each would use a different point of entry into the discussion. I have found that union members are grateful to their unions for creating Occupational Stress Groups, and that they often find this to be the first activity their union has engaged in which relates to their own felt needs. The focus here is the opposite of what unions tradition-ally have done. Unions like to win concrete material benefits for workers. They often act as though workers can only understand money or other objective material accomplishments. They are unaware of the emotional and spiritual needs of their members—needs that get spoken to when workers participate in Occupational Stress or Family Support Groups.

Imagine the power of a union that had a majority of its members involved in Occupational Stress Groups. These groups would encourage participation in the other activites of the union, because people would quickly learn that their personal life problems could not be solved without significant changes in the workplace itself. The Stress Groups would also make people feel more willing to engage in struggles under the leadership of their union because a basis for trust and risk-taking would grow out of their intimate experiences with their fellow workers. Moreover, to the extent that the Occupational Stress Groups encouraged the expression of righteous anger against oppressive work conditions, they would feed directly into the ability of the union to mobilize support for contract demands. As a growing number of union members began to understand stress as a central issue, there would be a growing base of support for workers to demand more control over the entire productive process.

In the early part of the 20th Century the labor movement derived much of its strength from its ability to address the full range of needs of its members. Increasingly, unions put problems of family and personal life aside, seeing them as the province of social welfare agencies and Democratic Party politics, or as individual problems that had nothing to do with the unions. With that division came an increasing lack of involvement by members in their unions.

Occupational Stress Groups would help to show union members that their lives were really important to the union. Equally important would be the revitalization of a Friends of Families-type program within the union itself. Also, the union could sponsor clubs for children of members, and perhaps other children who thought they might eventually want to be members of that union. These clubs would teach labor history, labor songs, show labor movies, and would sponsor sports, camping and social activities as well. Unions in the same city would band together and buy a summer camp at which these activities could be carried on—preferably with weekend programs for the whole family as well.

Union staff would be hired whose primary function was leading Stress Groups and providing family support. This staff would help to create family support. Family support groups would be supplemented by "buying clubs," in which cheaper food deals could be made, exchanges of baby-sitting, child-care, children's clothes, and toys, could be arranged, and swapping of skills and services among union members would become a regular activity. The staff would also play a role in organizing groups of co-workers to visit sick or ailing union members, to send gifts or cards to family members of union members on their birthdays, anniversaries, and births of their children, and even to attend funerals and weddings of family members. The union would see itself as sharing the life experiences of its members—and of providing a vehicle by which people could more easily say to each other, "We really care about each other."

It may seem like a simple thing, but even a phone call from a union staff person to a union member or family member who is sick, expressing the care that fellow members had, could be an important step toward making people feel cared for. So much can be expressed in the seemingly little gestures of caring—so many deep ties can be built. Of course, these expressions of caring have to be genuine for them to be meaningful. The union must make it a priority to create forms within the union in which members can show mutual caring. Having the forms is very important, because they make it less awkward for people to begin to take the first steps towards each other in loving ways. These gestures may seem artificial or phony at first—but as people begin to feel that this activity is legitimate, they will feel freer to be emotionally real and caring without being corny.

Showing care for members can be done in other ways as well. For example, union officers should regularly invite members and their families to dinner. Fun-filled family picnics should be arranged on a regular basis. Union membership meetings should always have a simultaneously scheduled activity for children, so that parents can bring their children and feel that their children are having a good time.

Union meetings should also be structured to show a new attention to the concerns of members. The first half hour should be devoted to small group discussions in which members get to share with each other what's been happening at their workplace, what kinds of stress they have been experiencing, and what they think about what's been happening in the union. Meetings should also be structured to include some singing, and possibly some good humorist to share some "laugh therapy" with the members. Whatever these additions might cost to union leaders who first pioneered them (in terms of credibility with the conservatives who "always" ran meetings a certain way), they would very soon lead to a much greater connection between the union and its members, and a much greater sense of power on the part of members who felt that their union was actually caring about them.

Union meetings should be alternated with a bi-monthly political discussion on topics related to the union's industry, economic problems of the society as a whole, American politics, or labor psychology. They should also include topics like, "Demystifying Science," "Are Ethics Objective?" and "Are People Naturally Aggressive or Selfish?" The discussions should be structured as debates, so that people are encouraged to think about alternative perspectives, and encouraged to make up their own minds. Real protagonists of alternative viewpoints should be invited, so that the debate doesn't take on a show quality, or replicate the dull quality of many union newspapers in which only one view is ever fully aired.

Out of these meetings should emerge another activity for the empowerment of members: the door-to-door political education program. Unions should create programs in which particular issues are brought up and discussed. Then union members should do mass education around the issues in their community. Members of these political education committees would meet to discuss the issue of the month, and role play with each other how they would handle difficult arguments or situations. Each member would take twenty to thirty families that s/he was going to educate. They could be neighborhood-based, or they could be non-union friends. In a given month each of these families would be approached, handed literature the union published about the issue, and the union member would then attempt to create a conversation that would educate this neighbor or friend about the union's position on the question.

Feedback from these discussions would be brought back to the union, so that union literature could more accurately reflect the needs of those whom they were attempting to reach. At first only a few members would participate in these education committees, but as they became more exciting, other members would join in. Unlike the normal COPE projects, in which union members simply call people to urge them to vote for the Democrats who promise to support labor, this kind of political education would more directly involve union members, and would be carried on throughout the year.

Because this project could not run without the ideas and input of members, unions would have to be more responsive to union members' input. Moreover, the opportunity and encouragement to engage in this kind of activity would give many workers their first opportunities to be taken seriously. No one takes them seriously at work. It would undoubtedly have a very empowering impact on participants. It would also make union members feel more willing to talk at deeper levels and, hence, to participate in the Occupational Stress and Family Support groups that would deepen the empowering process even more.

One first step towards empowering working people and legitimating their right to talk with others about their personal experiences is for the union to create a yearly conference around occupational stress. At the Occupational Stress Conferences that the Institute for Labor and Mental Health organized for the Northern California labor movement, we used the following format. A large group of public officials was asked to sit on panels to take testimony from workers. These congresspeople, state legislators, mayors, city councilmembers, judges, tv and news reporters, church leaders, and health officials listened to a wide variety of rank-and-file workers describing the stress conditions that they faced at work. This experience was enlightening to the panel members, most of whom did not have the foggiest notion about the details of the work experience of most Americans. It was also empowering to the testifiers, many of whom had never spoken before in public and never felt that their stories had wider importance. It was most electrifying to the hundreds of workers sitting in the audience listening to the testimony. As one story followed another, they began to recognize how similar were the stresses they all faced. Such an event on a Saturday afternoon does more to cement solidarity among different unions than hundreds of pep talks at union meetings. People who have been through this experience are often very open to Occupational Stress Groups, family support groups, and classes in labor history.

Another program I developed is a yearly Honor Labor ceremony. This is a large public event to which thousands of union members and their families are invited. Along with entertainment, music, labor films and workshops on labor history and current problems facing the labor movement, there is a large assembly of people at which different occupations are honored. A speaker describes to the assembled group the actual work of a secretary, or a bus driver, or a machinist, or a telephone operator, or a teacher, or a social worker, or a government employee, or a health worker. The descriptions are not flowery romanticizations, but concrete descriptions of the stress, the assaults on one's dignity, the ways that workers get beat down. Then the speaker describes how workers have managed to survive these conditions, and the real contributions that they have made, despite the unhealthful conditions created by a profit- and control-oriented management. All the workers doing that kind of work are asked to rise, and other people in the assembly applaud. Special awards are given to shop stewards in these unions. This event has a tremendous emotional impact on all who participate. Unlike awards events held within unions, this is cross-union, so different kinds of workers can listen to each other's stories and develop a deeper sense of connection. Moreover, it is not the leaders or the most active union members alone who are being honored—it is the rank and file members. What a difference in ambience and feeling from the normal Labor Day picnics and parades, at which leaders, often not even directly elected by the membership, give speeches to the faithful and turn Labor Day into just another paid vacation, rather than an opportunity to truly acknowledge the dignity and the pain of work.

Union staffs may argue that they don't have the resources to run these kinds of programs—and certainly at first the membership will be reluctant to spend monies on Stress Groups, family support, and political education. Given their previous experience with their unions, it is not surprisng that their first response will be skepticism and a feeling that the union should spend as little money as possible and just keep to its already constituted task of pursuing grievances and negotiating contracts. Yet, in this single-minded path of loyalty and dedication to struggle, unions will find themselves largely unable to even maintain what they have won in the past in the face of the growing internationalization of corporate strength. Their only hope is to develop a membership that recaptures the union spirit of the 1930s.

But what has changed since the 1930s has been the degree of penetration of capitalist ideology into the minds of working people. Leftists have mistaken this penetration as an attachment to personal property, as though the main problem is that workers "have it too good because they now can afford a house and a car and a summer vacation." There is nothing wrong with workers wanting a level of material comfort that makes life a little easier. Nor is there any reason to believe that having material goods necessarily leads to accommodation to an oppressive system. The protest movements of the '60s and the anti-nuclear and pro-disarmament and anti-apartheid movements of the '80s were populated by many people whose level of material comfort considerably exceeded that obtained by the allegedly co-opted work-ers. This is not the kind of penetration that has weakened the labor move-ment. When union leaders tell you that their membership is too satisfied with their paychecks to take any other kind of risks they are misunderstanding the real issue and simultaneously helping to translate all issues into material terms. The actual problem of a culture of self-blame is much deeper and more destructive. It reaches into the workers' psyches, tells them that they are their own worst enemies, and convinces them that the lack of fulfillment they have in their lives is appropriate, and undermines their sense that they have a right to anything different. Precisely because this dynamic leads workers to distance from their unions, it is the struggle against Surplus Powerlessness which must have the highest priority if the unions are to ever become an important force for social transformation.

The importance of focussing on occupational stress and personal life becomes clearest when asking, "What would enable the unions to organize the unorganized?" As the economy becomes increasingly dependent on service sector work, and as production becomes increasingly dependent on computer technology, a new kind of worker emerges who has little tradition of experience with the labor movement. To these workers of the late 1980s and 1990s, it will not seem imperative to join unions. The anti-union ideology of the society, fostered by the media and schools, and reinforced by the absence of any serious education in the history of the labor movement in our schools, will go far to undermine support for unions. It is unbelievable how little most of us know about the history of labor struggles or even about what happened in our own industries and workplaces.

Most workers have no experience of being part of a "We," or their experiences have always been to be part of a "We" that was phony and required a suspension of what was their own deepest and most precious part. With such isolation and distrust comes an abiding fear that to be part of a union means to open oneself up to manipulation by yet another group of bureaucrats. If this is true, why not just use one's own personal energy to make the best deal one can with the bureaucrats who are running the work place?

The only way that this sentiment can be changed is by the union itself becoming something quite different from another faceless bureaucracy. I used to think, when I got to this point in the discussion, that it would be sufficient if the union appeared to be alive as a political community—and that would be enough to revitalize the unions. But I now believe that even the appearance of a genuine political life is inadequate when people are fundamentally unknown and unrecognized. I have had too many union activists and union leaders in therapy with me or in Occupational Stress Groups to pretend that participation in politics is sufficient. As long as political activity does not address the problem of self-blaming, as long as it does not confront the deep levels of isolation and separateness and aloneness that so many people continue to experience even when they are involved in political work, we will continue a fundamental estrangement that makes many union activists suddenly drop out, feeling "burned out" in one way or another by the experience of their union work.

From the standpoint of recruiting new members, the only way the unions can possibly hope to break through is by addressing the fundamental psychological issues head on. It is precisely by sponsoring Stress Groups and family support groups, not just as an add-on to an elaborate benefit package, but as a central focus of what the union is about, that they can challenge what it means to be part of a larger community in the workplace. Nor can this be done in some value-neutral way. The smarter corporations are already developing their own "stress groups" and "family counseling programs."

The unions will have to be explicit about what is different in their approach—which means promoting a deep understanding of the issues of self-blame, the formation of Surplus Powerlessness by the competitive economy, the implicit disrespect and lack of opportunity for self-actualization provided by the workplace, and the way that the corporate economy shapes our experience of personal life and childhood. These issues are not just interesting side concerns. Either they are made front-burner issues for the labor movement, or the labor movement will become increasingly peripheral, even to the lives of its members.*

There are many hopeful signs, however. An increasing number of labor leaders at local, regional and even international unions really care about their members and about the labor movement as a whole. Some were products of the movements of the '60s, some are creative and sophisticated feminists, others have emerged from rank-and-file struggles inside their own locals. To the extent that they can overcome their own Surplus Powerlessness, they will begin to strategize new ways to create a unified and powerful labor movement. If they have the courage to deal with issues that concern their own sense of self, and to develop an understanding of the many ways which even they, the people who have "made it" to some extent, are nevertheless still simultaneously dealing with conscious and unconscious processes and belief systems that make them feel more powerless than they have to be, they will be able to bring their understanding to bear in the construction of a winning strategy for the union movment.

Even without the union movement, and in places where the unions have had no organizing successs, people dedicated to social transformation can begin Occupational Stress Groups, family support programs, Honor Labor ceremonies, occupational stress conferences—all can be tools for those outside labor who are interested in empowering working people.

It may seem strange that I have given so much attention to unions when they represent less than twenty percent of the workforce. But the impact of unions is far wider. It is because unions have been strong in the past that management throughout the economy has been forced to grant workers basic safeties and wages—partially to prevent their own workforces from unionizing. A re-invigoration of the labor movement would have far-reaching consequences beyond the ranks of the already organized. Moreover, a union movement that appeared to care for its members in the kind of personal way suggested here would be much more successful in organizing new constituencies—particularly the kinds of workers that will be required in the high technology industries that are becoming an increasingly important part of the society's productive apparatus.

If unions are re-constructed to foster compassion and mutual caring, if

---

* Union leaders who reduce the call for a focus on family to putting forward a new demand for childcare or some other family-oriented benefit are really missing the point. While these benefits should be fought for, unless the unions begin to deal with emotional life, self-blaming, Surplus Powerlessness and the pains in family life, they will become increasingly irrelevant.

they begin to seriously focus on the quality of workers' experience both at work and in family life, this development will have an incredible spillover effect throughout the society. The empowerment experienced in the unions would then lead people to demand more fulfilling lives in other spheres as well. And if mutual caring were legitimated as part of the culture of unions, a new spirit of cooperation and love would permeate many other areas as these workers became living testimony to the possibility that community can replace selfishness, and trust replace isolation.

Chapter 21

Compassion in Daily Life

THERE IS ALMOST NO PERSON IN THIS SOCIETY WHO COULD not participate in the strategy to create a mass psychology of compassion. No matter what your work, no matter what your life situation, once you have come to understand how Surplus Powerlessness works, you can become part of the struggle to undermine it.

There are three easy first steps:

1. Challenge every idea that you hear expressed that reinforces Surplus Powerlessness. Whenever you hear theories about human nature as evil, theories about the inevitability of someone else having power, theories that make science the criterion of reality, or other theories that make it seem that any struggle for change is always going to be useless—stop the people who are saying that and tell them you don't agree, and talk to them about what function you see those theories playing.

2. Talk about the pains in your life with others, and share the details of your feelings, without pretending that it's all really OK. And put that conversation in the context of your own social analysis of the sources of these pains. Encourage others to feel safe in doing the same with you. Do it in a lunchroom at work, do it in your social club, do it at a union meeting. Let people know that its OK to talk to you about things that are really hard to talk about—and tell them why you think it's important to talk about these things. Set an example that people don't have to stay superficial with you, or pretend that their lives are free of pain.

3. Get friends, neighbors, or co-workers together to engage in systematic discussions of the details of their lives, analyzing the social context that shapes psychological reality, and fantasizing about how they would change things if they had real power to do so. Only one rule: Disallow all moves in the conversation that say: "They won't allow us to do . . ." [some change that you'd like to see]." Instead, reframe those moves into statements of the form, "This is how we have to move to get others to agree with us that we should do . . ." Eventually, you may want to share your copy of this book with them so that they will have the same theoretical background that you have on this issue. Or use the book as a basis to form a "study group" that can then move into discussions of personal life.

You can do this in any town or city, in any workplace, even without the existence of a larger social movement. And the social movement may well arise from the efforts of thousands of individuals who have participated in this kind of informal group. It is they who will go on to create the organizational context for a mass movement for compassion. In the meantime, you can insist that union leaders, Democratic Party activists, teachers, and therapists begin to discuss the ideas raised in this book. You personally can spread these ideas.

If you are especially fortunate, you may also have some kind of work that allows you to do even more to advance mutual compassion and undermine ideas that create Surplus Powerlessness. Here are some suggestions for a few specific occupations, and you can probably figure out other examples and ways to do this in your own line of work or activity:

Teachers and College Professors

Teachers can build an analysis of Surplus Powerlessness into their courses. They can present materials in ways that will enable students to learn that the way that people view reality and feel about themselves is an historical product, and, hence, potentially changeable. They can teach students that it is legitimate to challenge authority, starting with their authority as teacher.

There are some risky steps that can also be tried. Teachers can encourage students to talk about the details of their emotional lives, and their family lives. They can insist upon this to school administrators as a valid part of the curriculum. They can fight for the right to include this in their teaching, just as unions struggled for improved salary and wage conditions. Teachers can use after-school time as volunteers and urge the parents of their students to meet with them in bi-monthly family support groups. Using schools as legitimators of the need for families to come together to discuss shared problems can be a powerful ice-breaker and entree into constituencies that might otherwise be hard to reach.

Teachers can play an important role in communicating to students a basic sense of respect for the dignity of labor and the need to struggle to make the society more humane. Moreover, teachers can also help to undermine competitiveness and individual isolation by helping children of every age to understand the ways by which they are made to feel separate from each other. In this way, they can validate the yearnings of children for solidarity and mutual love. At first, these may seem like isolated acts of individual teachers—but they can help to eventually create a beachhead for further empowering actions which can happen later in the lives of children.

Teachers need to get together and create support groups in which they can share their various attempts at empowerment, and describe their attempts to help children acknowledge their pains and frustrations. These teachers' support groups are essential in helping to prevent teachers from getting burned out and despairing about their efforts, and in providing places for them to learn what has worked and what has not when others tried teaching techniques of empowerment. The support groups are critical for another reason: to counter the tendency of some teachers to despair when they don't see immediate results, and then to conclude that all that can really be accomplished is to teach "basics." Teachers, like all the rest of us, need to be constantly reminded that they are up against a massive social structure that reinforces powerlessness, and that the success of their teaching will only be complete when those structures are changed. That they can only go part of the way towards making a difference is not a reflection either on their skills or on the worthwhileness of the task, but only on the power of entrenched systems. To keep this in mind, and to still engage in active attempts to find new and creative ways to undermine the structure of powerlessness—these are the tasks that can make teaching a really exciting profession, and one that can attract the idealism that once played a major part in making people want to be teachers.

News Reporters, TV Dramatists, Movie Producers

In the next twenty years, some of these people will be articulating part of the analysis of Surplus Powerlessness in their media. Imagine the power of the news when a reporter or anchor person, after reporting on demonstrations or a strike, instead of ending the report with a cynical comment or grimace, or instead of reporting it as if it were a natural disaster like a flood or hurricane, concluded by saying, "Judging from past history, if thousands of these kinds of demonstrations continue, the government is likely to modify its policies," or "Whoever wins this one, those strikers sure were demonstrating the kinds of freedoms we have and can all use when we need to," or, "Whatever you think about their cause, this is historically the way Americans have won basic changes—and it's a tradition that is being carried on here in our own community today by ordinary people just like you."

Unfortunately, such comments tend to continue the tendency to try to put reality into some neat little package—like too much of the media already does. But, if it has to be put in a package, it's still a step to put it in a package of optimism and support for change.

We hope to soon see the day when newscasters will be willing to ask the tougher questions, and to challenge the fundamental assumption that the only "responsible" forces in the society are those who support the present distribution of wealth and power. Most of all, we hope to see a move of newscasters who renounce the phony neutrality and "above the battle" attitude, and acknowledge that they and their stations or newspapers have points of view that have influenced how they report and what they see. It would be an important move towards demystification if newscasters were to talk honestly about their impressions and biases, acting as if they were real human beings rather than "objective observers" with divine knowledge.

Creative tv dramatists and movie producers can begin to delve more deeply into the truth about the way most people work—and how that work affects their daily lives. They can begin to tell the many stories of little victories that people have won through struggle and thereby undermine the myth of worker passivity and impotence. Instead of exploitative films that focus on corrupt union leaders, there can be stories that depict the real struggles that workers engage in, the real victories that have been won, and the real defeats that have been sustained. What powerful films could be made about the UAW sitdowns in Flint, the 1934 longshore struggle that led to a general strike in San Francisco, the organizing drive of the farm workers, the early civil rights movement, the campus confrontations of the 60's, the organizing of the mass anti-war movement, the emergence of the women's movement, the trials against anti-war leaders, the mass plant closures of the early 1980's, the anti-nuclear movement. I don't mean movies that glorify these struggles and create new fantasy figures ("the strike leader," "the courageous feminist" or "the fearless organizer"), but rather stories that tell the truth, including all the moments of weakness and uncertainty, balanced by the focus on the extraordinary deeds of ordinary people. Most likely such stories will at first be rejected by big money interests, but there are some principled people with money who can back these productions. Through creative use of video, films for tv and movie formats, these kinds of productions will eventually attract mass audiences.

The closer to the truth the better. People love tv shows that provide an opportunity for people to talk about their lives with emotional depth—so shows that allow this, if they are true to the actual details of stress at work, the real frustrations in daily life, the pains of family life, will find important audiences. People love feature stories in newspapers for just this reason. They are hungry for real information about how other people live. The format of a therapist interviewing people, or the Edward R. Murrow-style visit to ordinary people's homes, infused with a social perspective that helps people each week make the connections between the interviewees' experiences and their social contexts, could provide tv with gripping, realistic and popular shows—if they were done with adequate humor, optimism, and sensitivity.

Even though media workers are still not yet able to use their medium directly to tell the truth or to develop compassion, they can play another important role. They can make contributions to the creation of neighborhood and workplace-based media truth squads whose goal would be to help the public see through the social myths that imprison them. Such a squad could organize block parties to watch a tv show, and then follow it with discussions of how the show falsifies reality. Each such gathering, led by a current media worker, would play its part in undermining the media-generated fantasy that everyone else's life is working well. A news reporter could agree to meet with neighborhood groups once a month and help them to learn how to read the newspaper critically. Similar groups could be organized to see a movie together, and then return to a neighbor's home to critique it together. Needless to say, activities like this can and should be organized by anyone reading this book. They get special power when the experts themselves help to demystify the various kinds of manipulation done by the media, but they are still valuable and effective if you just start doing it within your own circumstances.

Health Workers

The health establishment is one of the greatest reinforcers of Surplus Powerlessness. Nothing makes us more certain of our fundamental alienation than the experience of discovering, as we do over and over again, that the whole health system is primarily based on profit and not on human caring. How can one trust others if, even at the moment one may be sick or dying, the issue of money determines the quality of care that one receives. The anger that one feels, but cannot express for fear of alienating the doctors whose care we still need, only intensifies the way that anger is already eating away at the body's defense systems.

Health workers are often trapped within this system. Many doctors, nurses, lab technicians and other hospital staff understand the screwed up priorities—but they feel they have no immediate way of changing them. These health professionals and workers could sponsor legislation, initiatives, and public education that would work to change the system. Simultaneously, they have a more immediate obligation: to talk honestly to their clients or patients about what they see that is screwed up in the system, and to share their upsets about these issues with the public.

"Isn't this unprofessional?" Why should it be? The health of the client is not dependent on health professionals believing that the health system is a good one.

"But won't it undermine the clients' belief that they are in good hands, which may contribute to their own psychological resolve to engage in a process of inner healing?"

No. The issues are quite separable. In fact, health professionals can increase the resolve of patients to be involved in their own healing process to the extent that the issue of health is demystified, and patients come to understand the central role that their own spiritual and emotional resolves must play. Nothing can empower people more than honest, forthright discussion by people who normally only play more detached roles. The very process of breaking through the image of the health professional as "having it all under control" can contribute to the patient's ability to break through the role of passive recipient of health care from supposedly all-knowing professionals who know just what to do.

Health professionals may need to take initiatives in contacting people outside the normal channels. For example, a weekly meeting of the families of hospitalized patients could be called to discuss the health care system, and health professionals could discuss with them the problems and possible remedies.

It's no excuse for health professionals to say that they are too busy and exhausted from work to engage in political activity outside of work. Everyone is exhausted from work—and if things are going to change, everyone is going to have to make their contribution to the struggle to undermine Surplus Powerlessness.

But there is something else that they can do directly at the workplace. We have already explained how stress at work is destructive to one's health, and also often causes accidents both at work and in travel to and from work. Many of the patients the health professional sees are products of this situation. If the implicit attitude of the health professional to the situation is, "Well, let's get you well so you can jump right back into your healthy and wonderful life," then the patients cannot deeply trust them. The patient may not only not want to go back to work, or to a stressful family situation, but also may not want to admit that to him- or herself. So, unconsciously, s/he may be resisting the cure, while consciously "doing his or her best." A good health practitioner can only mobilize the patient's healing energies when s/he has helped the client to overcome some of these resistances. And the most direct way to begin this process is for the health worker to acknowledge how "most people" have this kind of resistance, and explain why the resistance is quite rational, given the way the worlds of work and family life are actually structured. Ultimately, every health issue may be linked in some way to these kinds of psychodynamic issues. In some cases, of course, the best way for this to be handled is through a private therapist. But, in many cases, a nurse or hospital attendant or doctor can begin the process of education by sharing their own understanding of what makes people feel defeated in this society. The key here is not to introduce a new kind of self-blaming ("You are causing your own health problems and it's up to you to get better"), but to undermine the self-blaming, and help to externalize anger, and thereby free up the client's creative energies for the healing process.

Groups of patients, both in-patients and out-patients, should be important adjuncts to any health practice. These groups should attempt to deal with the same kind of material that we discussed in Occupational Stress Groups and family support groups from the standpoint of health. If health practitioners, both in their individual dealings with clients and in the creation of these kinds of support groups, made it possible for people to discuss the emotional realities of their lives with others, the general health of the society would improve, and the costs of medical care could be dramatically reduced.

I can understand the temptations that lead people to find the single key to health in some specific area inadequately emphasized by the medical profession, such as nutrition and diet, correct exercise, jogging, massage, biofeedback, or in "internal emotional health." These are important parts of any health program. They are particularly important as adjuncts to Stress Groups, family support groups, other groups, or other activities that help us to develop compassion for ourselves, for our parents, and for each other. But they must be linked to a program that addresses the deeper issues raised in this book. There is no question in my mind that anything that undermines Surplus Powerlessness will automatically have a beneficial and measurable impact on the health of people in this society.

But, alas, I cannot rest the story here. The truth is that re-empowering people is only a necessary but not sufficient step. A true program for health care must directly address the re-ordering of society and the need to create a social reality in which human beings can be more fully creative, intelligent and mutually supporting, a society which will enable people to have real control and foster within them their innate desire for the full realization of each other's human potentials. As long as the Human Essence is repressed, people will be more unhealthy than they need to be, and the physical consequences in terms of heart disease, cancer, and emotional disorders will continue to plague us.

Public Sector Employees

When conservatives wish to disempower workers, an effective strategy is to get them to fight against each other. Public sector employees are often a good target.

Corporations and the wealthy have consistently used their political power to ensure that the tax burden falls most heavily on working people. Yet, apart from social security, government programs seem to have little relevance to the needs and problems that most people face. So, what are they getting for their money?

Most media attention for the past thirty years has highlighted social programs directed at the poor, so that most people have little understanding of how many of their tax dollars go directly to subsidize the projects of the large corporations. But these programs for the poor, always underfunded in the first place, and never aimed at doing more than alleviating the worst suffering generated by the economic system, appear to most people to be a waste of money because they don't solve the problems they address. Instead, they seem to be a bottomless pit in which middle-income families have their incomes redistributed to poorer families. People who might even be willing to pay higher taxes if they saw social problems disappear eventually become more conservative and against government spending when they see the problems persisting while taxes remain a burden.

Moreover, the "public" often feels abused by government offices and agencies. Their needs are frequently obstructed by bureaucratic red tape and by government workers who, themselves frustrated with the endless regulations and restrictions on their own creativity, sometimes act disrespecfully to those seeking government services. Why should their tax dollars go to people who do little that is perceived as competent, and who simultaneously make people feel bad?

These considerations make it possible for the elites of power to manipulate working people to oppose adequate pay raises for government workers, and to support conservative candidates who call for decreases in government spending. The whole labor movement should combat this problem. But public sector employees need to take the lead.

Government workers need to dis-identify with programs they administer but which they do not fully believe in. Through ads in the paper, on tv, and through leaflets and billboards, the government employees must communicate the following message: "Don't blame us when government programs don't work. We didn't design them, we think that they are distorted to fit the needs and concerns of the corporations either by being conceived too narrowly or by being underfinanced so that they will look bad, giving renewed credibility to the claim that the competitive marketplace will work better than programs designed more democratically. We will try to do the best we can to serve you within these programs—but please don't blame us if•they don't work. In fact, here's our idea of what would work . . . [and then suggest some alternatives]."

Government workers need to create a space for the people in their communities to think about what government would look like if it were in fact democratically controlled. Public sector unions should create public events where people from their communities can come to talk about how they would like particular kinds of public facilities to operate (e.g., the post office, the Department of Agriculture, the public health service, the welfare office). Public employees would sponsor these meetings and encourage people to define programs that really fit their needs, and then join with those people in political struggles to achieve those goals. The idea of government employees being there to listen and help would challenge the image that conservatives try to foster. Ideally, this should be paid time. But it won't be—and public-sector employees need to do this as part of their political work. It can be an important contribution to empowering people because, when they see that their ideas are being carefully listened to, it will help to counter the idea fostered by their own workplaces that they are unimportant and probably wrong. Fostering respect in one aspect of experience always has good results: people come to feel they have a right to respect in other aspects of their lives as well.

Government workers need to reclaim the idealism and positive energy that led them to their jobs in the first place. Most public sector workers entered this work out of a sincere desire to help other people. But they soon learned how frustrating the work would be in programs that were both too limited and underfunded. Not being able to use all their talents and creativity generated the same stress other workers faced—and that stress often generated anger.

But without a clear political focus to express the anger, and often rejecting larger social change as utopian, the public sector workers begin to let out some of the anger on the very public that is supposed to be served. The public, in turn, reacts with hostility—hoping to get the deference from public sector workers that they won't get in the rest of their lives. This hostility generates a new level of frustration and anger from public sector workers, many of whom are working their hardest to serve what they increasingly perceive as an ungrateful public. This dynamic will only be broken by government workers taking the first step. And the best way for this to happen is for the workers to be involved in Stress Groups in which their frustrations can be explored and seen in the larger social context. A next step is for these workers to discuss this problem openly with the public—both in the kind of public events that have already been described, and in tv and newspaper ads that can explain why it is hard to keep idealism and a sense of public service high when administering programs that workers know will not solve the basic problems, and which are underfunded and constructed to fail.

Lawyers

The legal system is an obvious source of real powerlessness. In the name of impartiality and representing the general interest, it protects and expands the power of the wealthy and the owners of capital, those who have enriched themselves by taking the collective resources of the Earth and appropriating them for their own personal profits, and who have had the capital to employ others whose labor was then used to create more wealth for the owners, those who have learned how to manipulate others to buy their products—these are the people whose property is protected. Under the guise of law, these people elect their representatives who then quite legally tax away the meager holdings of middle-income and poor people and redistribute it to the wealthy. Each power grab is sanctified by law, and those who challenge it are subject to fines or prison.

But the legal system is also a source of Surplus Powerlessness. The clients are passified by the legal system. They are encouraged to wait for experts who "know the law." Lawyers typically help this mystification along, telling clients that the technical issues are "too complicated" for others to understand.

Clients are asked to be spectators. They can watch the magnificent impartiality of the law as it is enacted out before them. Naturally they are impressed by the robes of the judge, by the height at which s/he sits, the awesome respect which s/he commands when s/he enters the room. They watch in hushed tones as "juries of peers" are selected. They may wonder why there is no place for serious discussion between opposing parties, and why crucial evidence is not admitted because it fails to meet the laws of evidence. But who are they to question?

Lawyers who are committed to empowering people can explain everything to their clients. They can explain to as many people as possible what is going on, and why the participants in the legal drama think that their rules are rational. They can help us see that what is really happening is simply a group of people sitting in a room, acting as though they had a special right to make decisions, with everyone else passively allowing them to proceed. Lawyers must help us understand that we can talk to the participants in this drama, address their real humanity, and eventually break through to them. The key to this is the jury itself: the one ray of hope in the entire legal drama is the fact that the jurors have not yet fully become "jurors": there is still hope that they can be reached as people. It was precisely for this reason that previous revolutionaries insisted on trial by peers, and why the system tries so hard to convince jurors to act "in their roles" rather than as regular human beings. Moments of truth happen when the clients in cases act like human beings and make contact on a human level with jurors.

Lawyers can do some of this demystifying in their own cases. But they could also make real contributions by leading public seminars and giving talks at churches and social clubs and unions to explore the truths of the legal system. Probably we need classes for jurors in which people would be taught, long before they were called to be jurors, how to not get trapped into thinking of themselves as "agents of the court," and how to keep alive their fundamental humanity. If this knowledge were diffused through the society, people would feel empowered to act as real humans in this sphere as well.

Creating a New "We"

You can go on from here to fill in a whole variety of ways that people you know could be engaged on a daily basis in the struggle against Surplus Powerlessness. People are endlessly inventive. I am sure that once the humanizing activity becomes a mass phenomenon, there will be levels of the struggle that no one has yet imagined, and that new forms will be created that fit our emerging needs. As people begin to create a mass practice of telling their stories to each other with sufficient detail so that others really can understand, and as we begin to liberate our anger and help each other undermine our self-blaming, we will see the development of a hitherto unknown level of mutual compassion. This compassion, in turn, will spark a level of activity and creativity that was only vaguely suggested in the 1960's because we were so unconscious of the need for compassion, and so deeply self-doubting.

The way this works is through mutual reinforcement. As I live in Oakland and hear the stories of what people have done to fight Surplus Powerlessness in Des Moines and El Paso, and Buffalo and Jacksonville and Tacoma and Charlottesville and Hartford, I begin to understand that my own efforts are part of a larger movement. The sense of myself and my actions as isolated decreases. Instead of asking "What difference does it make that I'm getting these thirty people in Oakland to think differently and to feel differently?" I start to see my own efforts as building on that of others. People engaged in the groups and activities begin to feel that they are not just "pissing in the wind," but, rather, are part of something bigger, something that matters. In experiencing ourselves as part of a larger "We," we begin to feel capable of taking greater risks without the fear of being singled out and isolated. That's why a mass movement for compassion will grow slowly at first—and then, when it reaches a certain critical mass of participation—say about two million people—it could suddenly grow exponentially, with tens of millions of people beginning to feel that they can be safe in this kind of activity.

Don't expect any help from mainstream institutions in supporting people to develop a sense of this "We." I remember all too clearly how hard the anti-war and anti-nuclear movements had to struggle to get any mention in the mass media, even when they had mass popular support. Very often the only coverage they got was when they engaged in confrontation demonstrations—and then the only thing covered was the fact of the confrontation. So, don't expect a mass movement building compassion and fighting Surplus Powerlessness to be presented effectively through the media. On the contrary—expect that every concrete effort in this regard will either be ignored or ridiculed.

For that reason, it will be critical to develop our own means of communication. People need a national newspaper that tells the stories of these groups and what is happening in them. We need videotapes and movies, radio shows and slide shows, books and pamphlets—all of which tell us the stories that are being shared in different places around the country. Imagine, for example, how powerful a glossy and attractive weekly magazine could be if it were focused on talking honestly about our daily lives, telling the real stories, and if ten million of them were distributed free each week at workplaces, schools, supermarkets, hospitals, post offices, and shopping centers.

Eventually, we need an organization that can sum up the experiences of all these various activities. Such an organization could play a formative role in creating new experiments, raising money to fund organizers and therapists who would play some role in creating groups, publish a national newspaper, create schools at which people could learn techniques of empowerment, and make assessments of what strategies will be most effective when people from different sectors of this movement pool their energies for a national unified effort. I say "eventually" because I am aware of the danger that within such a movement there will immediately be a reassertion of Surplus Powerlessness, and that people will become discouraged and disillusioned before it gets off the ground. So it is important to build the base—by creating thousands of small groups and projects like Friends of Families, activities within the Democratic Party, Stress Groups within the labor movement, and the other specific forms suggested here. Because base building will always be impeded by the absence of any sense of being part of such a larger national development, national organization should be the not-too-distant goal, and, in the meantime, there should be a newspaper, journals, and magazines that are self-consciously engaged in helping make the rest of us aware of what others are doing.

Here, too, the process of building something larger must be suffused with compassion. We must not be too harsh on ourselves for not getting this together immediately or without any hassles and problems. On the other hand, we must not use compassion for our own inadequacies as a new cover for Surplus Powerlessness, so that we don't begin the imaginative steps that would be involved in going from the mere vision presented here to a flesh and blood reality.

In the end, the process of creating a "We" will come out of tens of thousands of little acts in which each of us is engaged. For some, that will be creating stress groups. For others, it will be starting to talk about their pain and their fear with people in their neighborhoods or churches. For some, it will be inviting people over once a week to discuss a tv show or the news. For some, it will be getting people together in their union to create a Stress Committee that lobbies for more control over the workplace. For some, it will be developing sophisticated critiques of ideologies that foster powerlessness. For some, it will be taking these concerns into any political organization that they already belong to. For some, it will be creating national networks of information exchange amongst those engaged in the struggles against Surplus Powerlessness. For some it will be engaging in critiques of where this book is weak—and how it can be strengthened and refined. For some, it will be getting friends to read this book—and then talking to them about it. For some, it will be writing the music and songs that raise the key issues. For some, it will be creating national or regional organizations. For some, it will be creating colleges and graduate schools that focus on these issues. For some, it will be writing articles in local newspapers and magazines about these ideas. For some, it will be conscious acts of talking to other people in ways that break through the phoniness and mutual distancing. For some, it will be engaging in conscious rethinking of their own lives and re-experiencing parts of their childhoods that they had suppressed as children. For some, it will be new levels of compassionate acts towards others. For some, it will be new levels of self-acceptance.

Done as single acts, they do not create a "We." But done as part of the conscious intent to create a new reality of compassion, done with the understanding that the actions are part of something larger, these acts begin to add up. Moreover, each act has a different meaning when done with this kind of intention; they become acts of creation, giving birth to the kind of community that we ultimately want to be part of. Action is within our grasp, even given the current levels of real and Surplus Powerlessness.

The creation of communities of compassion and the forging of a new "We" will generate an historical subject capable of engaging in the struggle for a world based on love and mutual caring. Under the banner of compassion, with the demand that every social institution must participate in the fostering of our human capacities, a movement can be built which will have the sense of its own entitlement to build a healthier world. As we argued in Part III, such a movement will be empowered in part through its participation in politics, and in part through its ability to draw on the insights and rituals of the Prophetic religious tradition. While it will take considerable wisdom to build such a movement, the fundamental need structure of human beings will lead us in this direction. And the very process of attempting to create this reality will itself be empowering for the individuals who participate, creating a basis for compassion for self and others that can only deepen our human ties and satisfactions, while simultaneously helping us view with some humility our particular limitations within the frame of human history.

Index